A Social History of Soviet Trade

A SOCIAL HISTORY OF SOVIET TRADE

TRADE POLICY, RETAIL PRACTICES,
AND CONSUMPTION, 1917–1953

Julie Hessler

PRINCETON UNIVERSITY PRESS

PRINCETON AND OXFORD

Library of Congress Cataloging-in-Publication Data

Hessler, Julie, 1966–
    A social history of Soviet trade : trade policy,
  retail practices, and consumption, 1917–1953 / Julie Hessler.
      p.   cm.
    Includes bibliographical references and index.
    ISBN 0-691-11492-7 (alk. paper)
     1. Retail trade—Soviet Union—History. 2. Consumption (Economics)—Soviet
Union—History. 3. Soviet Union—Commercial policy. I. Title.

HF5429.6.S63H47 2004
381'.1'094709041—dc21   2003048612

British Library Cataloging-in-Publication Data is available

For Alex

Contents

List of Illustrations   ix

List of Tables   xi

Preface   xiii

Introduction   1

   Two Modes of Soviet Socialism   4
   Buyers, Sellers, and the Social History of Trade   9

Crisis: Revolution

CHAPTER ONE
Trade and Consumption in Revolutionary Russia   19

   Russian Retailing and Its Unraveling   20
   Effects of the Anti-trade Policy   27
   The Crisis Mode of Consumption   38
   Conclusion   48

CHAPTER TWO
The Invention of Socialism   51

   The Emergence of a Socialist Distribution Network, 1918–1921   53
   Rationing, "Commodity Exchange," and Price Controls   61
   The Antibureaucratic Backlash and Socialist Economic Culture   79
   Public-Sector Shops in the Transition to the NEP   87
   Conclusion   97

CHAPTER THREE
Shopkeepers and the State   101

   Poverty, Capital, and the Commercial Revival   103
   The Logic of Utilization and the Regulatory Context   113
   Shopkeepers' Stories: The NEP from Below   119
   Conclusion   130

Crisis: Restructuring

CHAPTER FOUR
War Communism Redux   135

   The NEP from Above: Trade Policy in the Shadow of the Goods Famine   137

Bureaucratism Ascendant: The Effects of Food Shortage on the
   Distribution System   154
Corporatism in the Service of the Plan   173
Crisis, Consumption, and the Market   184
Conclusion   193

CHAPTER FIVE
Toward a New Model   197

Socialist Modernization: "Cultured Soviet Trade"   198
Bureaucratism Restrained   215
Stalinism and the Consumer, I: Urban Attitudes and Trends   222
Stalinism and the Consumer, II: The Peasant Challenge to Cultured Trade   230
Conclusion   243

Crisis: War

CHAPTER SIX
The Persistent Private Sector   251

Stalin-era Bazaars   252
Travel, Bagging, and the Survivalist Consensus   273
The Revitalization of the Private Sector   279
Private Trade as a Social Formation: Continuity and Change   289
Conclusion   293

CHAPTER SEVEN
Postwar Normalization and Its Limits   296

From Wartime "Abnormalities" to the Paradox of Growth   298
Cadres Policy in Postwar Trade   310
Postwar "Cultured Trade": A Balance Sheet   316
Conclusion   325

Conclusion   329

Bibliography   337

Index   355

Illustrations

1. Curbside sales at Sukharevka   30
2. Small-town vodka queue, early 1930s   165
3. Sale of bread by coupons, Moscow, 1929   166
4. Bread distribution at the Trekhgornaia factory   179
5. The Eliseev "food department store" in Moscow, 1935   203
6. A typical Gastronom, 1935   206
7. Peasant bazaar in Bashkiria, 1932   254
8. Market day in the Central Agricultural Region, 1933   260
9. Artisanal trade in Arzamas, 1930s   275
10. German army photograph of a peasant market, 1941   278
11. Shoppers at a flea market under the German occupation   280
12. Queue for cloth and shoes in the Leningrad suburbs, 1947   308
13. The lace department at TsUM, 1948   320

Tables

3.1 Trade Licenses by Class, 1912 and 1926   106
4.1 Private vs. Socialist-Sector Retail Trade, 1924–1930   150
4.2 Private, Cooperative, and State Trade as a Source of Goods
for Urban Workers, 1923–1929   152
4.3 The Private Sector as a Source of Selected Foods and
Consumer Goods in Workers' Annual Per Capita
Consumption, 1932   187
4.4 Sales of Foods and Goods as a Percentage of Working-Class
Household Incomes   188
5.1 Average Annual Wages in Trade and Public Catering as
against Other Sectors   211
5.2 Workers' Annual Per Capita Food Consumption   227
5.3 Workers' Annual Per Capita Cloth, Clothing, and
Shoe Consumption   228
5.4 Working-Class Budgets: A Breakdown of Expenditures   229
7.1 Urban Per Capita Cloth and Shoe Consumption,
1934 vs. 1952   309

Preface

DOES anything provide a more devastating indictment of the communist economic system than the gaping shelves of Soviet shops? In the later years of perestroika, when this project first germinated in its author's mind, you would see groceries, piled high with just two kinds of canned fish and perhaps some dusty bulk spaghetti; drugstores, in which aspirin and toilet paper made occasional guest appearances, while tampons were the stuff of dreams; electronics stores, devoid of literally all the consumer appliances that had so altered daily life in the world's wealthy consumer societies and graced instead by a row of hideous lamps and an irregular supply of lightbulbs, half of which did not work. As a foreigner, you could not help but be struck by the organization of retailing: the extreme specialization of food shops and departments, so that no matter what, you had to queue up separately for milk, bread, and lentils; the oversized empty halls, with goods only along the wall behind a sales counter or perhaps in an unappealing glass case; the three queues, first to select the article, then to pay for it, and finally to pick it up; the surly sales assistants; the lunch breaks and monthly "sanitary" or accounting closures; the perennial shortage of change at the cash register; the cashier's categorical refusal to keep the change; the lack of packaging and shopping bags. It seemed no less peculiar when you realized that in Odessa, home of a major umbrella factory, there were no umbrellas to be had in the retail system; or when you watched as your fellow researchers, one by one, disappeared from the reading room to return with a frozen chicken from the archive buffet, which now lay thawing alongside one-of-a-kind documents on every other desk; or when, in the early 1990s, an acquaintance with a secretarial job at a newly privatized construction firm had to cope with the delivery of two tons of onions, a vestige of the long-standing relationship between this enterprise and a state farm. When the onions were dumped in the main vestibule of the firm's business office; when they began to rot; when the acquaintance had to find a way of disposing of this stinking mess, wasn't this practically a metaphor for the fate of the Soviet *smychka*, that organic bond between peasants and proletarians that supposedly underpinned the communist state?

Then again there were the hawkers: in the early 1990s, you could scarcely take a step in downtown Moscow without wending your way through two rows of hawkers, on both sides of the sidewalk. They didn't exactly accost you—hawking, in this period, was usually silent—but they did hold out one or two seemingly random items for your inspection: an elderly peasant woman might proffer a dozen eggs; someone else might be holding a bottle of vodka, or two hard salamis; some woolen shawls, a few bras, fingernail polish, a pair of boots. You wanted to try on the boots? The vendor would whisk out a battered piece of corrugated cardboard and lay it down in the slush. You tried to take off your shoes on this makeshift mat without dropping your parcels or losing your balance; tried to decide whether a boot two sizes too large was really intolerable; tried to figure out how much you could haggle; and then tried to pay up and leave before your fingers froze. All this—and I haven't even mentioned the markets or the foreigners-only "Beriozka" shops, about which tales could also be told—was extremely arresting to a young American researcher; and when friends informed you for the thirtieth or fortieth time that "before, we had everything," you shook your head in disbelief.

The present book is about the way retailing developed "before"—not exactly the "before" that my friends had in mind, when things *did* function better, but rather the origins and evolution of the Soviet trade system from 1917 to 1953. Out of curiosity, I would have liked to take the story up to the 1980s, but I was in over my head with this project as it was. My doctoral dissertation, completed in 1996, left me more depressed than satisfied. Since then, I have been able to do a great deal of additional research, and I certainly know much more. Thus, while the basic themes of this book (the invention and development of socialist retail trade; the ups and downs of private trade, especially in the guise of petty vending; the evolution of consumption habits and trends) were also the subjects of my dissertation, the treatment of these topics here is largely new.

Debts—personal, intellectual, and material—have accumulated in the interim. My initial doctoral research was funded in 1991–92 by the University of Chicago, which had an exchange with the Russian State Humanities University, and, in 1992–93, by a Fulbright-Hays fellowship in conjunction with the International Research and Exchanges Board (IREX). Dissertation fellowships from the Mellon Foundation (which had previously supported my graduate coursework) and the Social Sciences Research Council financed two years of write-up. Later, after my move to the University of Oregon, I spent an academic quarter researching and writing at the Kennan Institute for Advanced Russian Studies and another under the auspices of the Oregon Humanities Center. A junior faculty development grant financed a summer research trip to Russia, and IREX has supported two further trips. Last but not least, yet another Mellon Fellowship enabled me to spend an idyllic and productive academic year, in 1999–2000, at the Institute for Advanced Study in Princeton, New Jersey. I would like to express my warm thanks to Sheila Fitzpatrick, Bob Davies, Lewis Siegelbaum, and Joan Neuberger for recommending me to the Institute; to Jack Matlock for his encouragement there; and to Vera Tolz and Yoram Gorlizki for their companionship and for reading chapter drafts.

Intellectually and professionally my greatest debt is to my doctoral adviser, Sheila Fitzpatrick. Sheila's approach to graduate training set an inimitable standard: she immersed her students in Soviet sources, provided stimulation through the weekly Russian history workshop, responded immediately (overnight!) with detailed critiques of papers and dissertation chapters, and was unstinting in professional assistance and advice. The intellectual freedom that she cultivated is particularly worth underscoring. Sheila created a community at Chicago without founding a "Fitzpatrick school." Today, at a distance of seven years, I cannot help idealizing that formula. I am not sure whether I learned more then or afterward, but the feeling of discovery was certainly headier in those years, in part because of events in the former Soviet Union but largely because it was shared. My fellow students Golfo Alexopoulos, Matt Payne, Matt Lenoe, Jon Bone, John McCannon, Molly Pyle, Chris Burton, James Harris, Josh Sanborn, and Julie Gilmour were a vital part of my education. In addition, two powerful influences on my intellectual development also came out of the Chicago milieu. One is Terry Martin, whose work on nationalities policy has fundamentally shaped my understanding of the Soviet polity, and who has been a friend, confidant, and valued reader of my work; the other is my husband, Alex Dracobly, whose critical acumen and wide-ranging historical knowledge have continually sharpened and enriched my own.

This book is leaner than I would have liked. I was obliged to cut my manuscript drastically for publication, and many details, quotations, side arguments, and examples were jettisoned in the process. Footnotes suffered particularly. For the truly dedicated reader, I have reconstituted some of the expunged explanatory matter and data in a series of online appendixes at the Internet address http://darkwing.uoregon.edu/~hessler. The topics include: (a) cooperatives: literature review and source critique; (b) the Kredit-biuro: the database and its creation; (c) vodka production and sales; (d) household budget data and consumption trends; and (e) court cases and the market.

In closing, I would like to express my gratitude to a few other individuals and institutions: to Sofia Viktorovna Somonova and her assistants (Tanya, Nastya, and Inna) at the State Archive of the Russian Federation, as well as Galina Kuznetsova, for many happy lunch breaks and invaluable help; to Jim Mohr, Quintard Taylor, and Daniel Pope, the successive chairs of my department, for their encouragement and willingness to give me time off; to Matt Lenoe, for commenting on the introduction; to Don Filtzer, for sharing data and ideas on chapter 7, which chapter then appeared in the journal *Europe-Asia Studies* and I am grateful for their permission to reprint it here with slight modification; and to Brigitta van Rheinberg, who believed in the manuscript and saw it through to publication. The book is dedicated to Alex; I only hope that the next one will be less of a torment.

Eugene, September 2002

A Social History of Soviet Trade

Introduction

It is easy to forget that as recently as the 1940s the Soviet economy was widely admired. The USSR's extraordinary rates of growth in the extraction and heavy manufacturing industries during the worldwide depression, followed by its spectacular wartime mobilization, made communism seem a viable economic alternative to the crisis-ridden capitalism of Western Europe and the United States. Economists as deeply opposed to Soviet-style "collectivism" as Friedrich von Hayek and Joseph Schumpeter saw in it the wave of the future. In the years following the war, Western Europe's socialist parties nationalized key industries and communications, widened social security, and mooted ideas for an extraordinary tax on wealth. "Planning" was endorsed in many capitals as a solution not just to the immediate problems of postwar reconstruction but to long-term economic development as well. If a "command economy" patterned directly on the Soviet model was repudiated outside the Soviet bloc, the "administered economy" reigned supreme: with national variations, a new political consensus coalesced around the Keynesian ideas of counter-cyclical investment, demand management, modernization, full employment, and state-controlled growth.

How distant that era seems today! Between then and now lies a chasm: the *trente glorieuse*, *Wirtschaftswunder*, *miracolo economico*, call it what you will, that great economic boom that transformed North America, Japan, and Western Europe in the 1950s and 1960s. From an age of coal and steel, the economies of these regions entered into an age of consumer goods, electronics, the tertiary sector, and information technology. Contrary to popular misconceptions, the prosperity of the postwar period did not bypass Eastern Europe or the Soviet Union. There, too, living standards rose in connection with global agriculture's "green revolution" and with an initial burst of industrial growth. Nonetheless, the expansion was attenuated in comparison with that of the West. Industrial productivity soon stagnated, technology was applied mainly to the military-industrial sector, and a new "consumerist" paradigm is difficult to discern.[1] Soviet society may have progressed beyond "austerity," like its counterparts in

---

[1] For an up-to-date overview, see Ivan T. Berend, *Central and Eastern Europe, 1944–1993* (Cambridge, 1996).

the West, but "affluence" remained elusive. Some historians have gone so far as to argue that frustrated consumer desires brought down the regime.

Serious research in the 1950s and 1960s overturned the positive assessment of the Stalinist economy prevalent in the early postwar years. In the United States much of this research was sponsored by the federal government, which had an interest in exposing the weaknesses of its Cold War rival.[2] At the same time, in its emphasis on such questions as real national income, real wages, and the "human costs" of Stalinist industrialization, the scholarship of this period dovetailed with the concerns of an emergent consumer society. Now the success of an economic system was to be judged not on the basis of its coal and steel output but on its ability to provide consumers with an ever-increasing complement of goods. Amid the cacophony of scholarly controversy over methods of calculation and the accuracy of Soviet statistics, one verdict was unanimous: far from an unprecedented success, the Soviet economic system in general, and especially the period of forced industrialization, were deemed a debacle.

The American scholarship of the 1950s and 1960s greatly advanced our knowledge of Soviet economic development, as did some of the Soviet scholarship from the same era.[3] Not surprisingly, however, these works bear the imprint of the time and place of their production, whether in Soviet scholars' insistence on the inexorable progression from "capitalism" through "the building of socialism" to "developed socialism" and then "communism," or in American scholars' elaborate extrapolations from a narrow statistical base. Either way, it is striking that we continue to embrace, with very few modifications, an interpretation of Soviet economic development devised at the height of the Cold War. This is partly an effect of the natural migration of economists, who authored all the early American studies, to more contemporary issues: the Brezhnev-era military-industrial complex, the informal sector, the sources of stagnation, and so on. Meanwhile, American historians of the Soviet Union became embroiled in a rancorous debate over the validity of social

[2] RAND Corporation, a think tank connected to the U.S. Air Force, sponsored a number of important works on the Soviet economy; see, especially, Abram Bergson, *The Real National Income of Soviet Russia since 1928* (Santa Monica, 1961); and Janet G. Chapman, *Real Wages in Soviet Russia since 1928* (Cambridge, Mass., 1961).

[3] Soviet works that shaped my understanding of Soviet economic development include Z. V. Atlas, *Sotsialisticheskaia denezhnaia sistema* (Moscow, 1969); Sh. Ia. Turetskii, *Ocherki planovogo tsenoobrazovaniia v SSSR* (Moscow, 1959); A. N. Malafeev, *Istoriia tsenoobrazovaniia v SSSR (1917–1963)* (Moscow, 1964); and diverse studies by S. G. Strumilin.

history in a "totalitarian" setting, leaving economic issues largely to the side.

In Great Britain the situation was different. Historians often invoke a tradition of "Western" historiography, as against the Soviet scholarship, but that tradition was not, in fact, unified. In Britain, as in the USSR itself, economic history remained a vital area of historical research throughout the 1970s and 1980s.[4] In particular, many important monographs were produced under the auspices of the Soviet Industrialization Project at the University of Birmingham's Centre for Russian and East European Studies. Compared to their counterparts at Harvard and RAND, the Birmingham authors have tended to write "soft" economic history: they take quantitative data seriously, and put an effort into locating and evaluating Soviet statistics, but they typically use economic analysis as an entrée into social, institutional, or political history, not as an end in itself. As R. W. Davies has recently noted with respect to himself, the Birmingham investigations were often motivated by a socialist political agenda. While their hallmark is meticulous empiricism, a Marxist conceptual framework is often discernible, and hovering in the background are some essentially personal political questions. Can anything from the Soviet experience be salvaged for contemporary socialism? What, precisely, were the Soviet Union's achievements, and where did it go wrong?[5]

The present work is written from a decidedly non-Marxist perspective, but it resembles the Birmingham studies in both subject matter and interpretations. It echoes Moshe Lewin's arguments about the role of crises in the complex dynamics of historical change.[6] It echoes Vladimir Andrle's insistence on the centrality of cash incomes to living standards,

[4] Given the strength of the British and Russian traditions of economic history, it is not surprising that British and Russian scholars have authored most of the recent works on the Soviet economy as well. Important examples include R. W. Davies, Mark Harrison, and S. G. Wheatcroft, eds., *The Economic Transformation of the Soviet Union, 1913–1945* (Cambridge, 1994); Mark Harrison, *Accounting for War: Soviet Production, Employment, and the Defence Burden, 1940–1945* (Cambridge, 1996); V. F. Zima, *Golod v SSSR 1946–1947 godov: proiskhozhdenie i posledstviia* (Moscow, 1996); V. A. Shishkin, *Vlast'. Politika. Ekonomika. Poslerevoliutsionnaia Rossiia (1917–1928)* (St. Petersburg, 1997); V. P. Popov, *Ekonomicheskaia politika sovetskogo gosudarstva, 1946–1953 gg.* (Tambov, 2000). For studies specifically relevant to trade, see below.

[5] R. W. Davies, "The Archives and the Stalinist Economy," unpublished paper for the European University Institute's conference, "Reappraising the Stalin Era," Florence, Italy, October 30–31, 2002. Davies is the author of several studies that have influenced this book: *Crisis and Progress in the Soviet Economy, 1931–1933* (London, 1996); *The Soviet Economy in Turmoil, 1929–1930* (Cambridge, Mass., 1989); and, with E. H. Carr, *Foundations of a Planned Economy, 1926–1929* (London, 1969).

[6] See, especially, the essays in Moshe Lewin, *The Making of the Soviet System* (New York, 1985). Lewin was at Birmingham from 1968 to 1978.

as against the commonly cited view that perquisites and access were everything.[7] Stretching further back, it echoes Stanislaw Swianiewicz's analysis of Soviet demand management, in which anti-peasant discrimination and repression played fundamental structuring roles.[8] These and other interpretive affinities, of which I was scarcely cognizant at the time of writing, place this book squarely in the Birmingham tradition. It applies the questions, methods, and archival orientation of social and political history to a cluster of economic topics—retail trade, distribution, and popular consumption—and it uses these subjects to reexamine how the Soviet economy took shape. Proximate causes, including such disparate factors as power struggles and political decisions at one or another juncture, social psychology, and short-term economic conditions feature as prominently in my story as any "deep systemic logic." Readers will not find evidence here for János Kornai's proposition that once a Communist Party achieves "undivided power . . . this historical configuration bears the 'genetic program' that transmits the main characteristics of the system to every cell within it."[9] Instead—though of course this is no more than the historian's creed—they will find evidence that if policy makers and even ordinary citizens had made different choices at various moments, things could have turned out differently.

What is gained from a new social and political history of the consumer economy? Much of my information concerns points of detail. Nonetheless, this study offers new interpretations of central aspects of Soviet economic development: the relationship between the New Economic Policy (NEP) and the economic structures that preceded and followed it; the significance of what is sometimes called the "Great Break"; the role of the market in both practice and principle at various moments; the social dimension of Soviet trade policy; and the approach of policy makers to pricing, among other issues. I will briefly review a few of these arguments here.

Two Modes of Soviet Socialism

With respect to trade, it is misleading to speak of "Stalinism." The consumer economy operated not in one but in two modes during Stalin's dictatorship and, as these two modes also describe Soviet socialism in the

[7] Vladimir Andrle, *Workers in Stalin's Russia* (New York, 1988).

[8] S. Swianiewicz, *Forced Labour and Economic Development: An Enquiry into the Experience of Soviet Industrialization* (London, 1965).

[9] János Kornai, *The Socialist System: The Political Economy of Communism* (Princeton, 1992), 368.

civil war and NEP periods, I will generally eschew the term. True, the two modes shared common elements, which united the thirty-five years from the Bolshevik Revolution to Stalin's death into a single, coherent era. The government's reliance on repression as a routine instrument of economic management was one of those unifying factors; it was characteristic of both modes of Soviet socialism in its formative decades, and placed Lenin and Stalin on the other side of a divide from Stalin's successors. Other points of commonality included the large though never exclusive role of the state in producing, distributing, and marketing foods and consumer goods; the state monopoly of the railroads, river transport, and foreign trade; the existence of both state and cooperative socialist-sector retailers and of outdoor markets for private sales; and the country's meager material base. None of these characteristics was distinctive to either mode of Soviet socialism, much less to war communism, NEP, or any one part of the Stalin period, but rather typified the era as a whole.

What differentiated the two modes of socialism was, at root, the condition of the economy. Although the archival record suggests that food crises afflicted one or another part of the Soviet territory in all but a few years of our period, the major famines of 1921–22, 1932–33, and 1946–47 stand out in relief. Each was the culmination of a multiyear economic and political crisis involving, among other things, the militarization of food procurement and of the distribution of "primary necessities." For our purposes, then, a crisis mode governed the supply and distribution of foods and consumer goods, and also consumers' behavioral patterns, in 1917–22, 1928–33, and 1939–47, and in the vicinity of each localized famine in the intervening years, whereas a recovery or normalization mode was in place the rest of the time. Until the 1950s normalization never actually led to normalcy; instead, internal and external factors conspired to swing the pendulum back to another crisis phase.

Crisis socialism, as a matter of policy, featured the state's efforts to monopolize commodity flows. Each time, the impetus came from local officials, who had to confront the effects of intensifying shortages on public order. Urban authorities tended to start with limits on purchases but to proceed quickly to rationing, issuing coupons to different classes of consumers in accordance with a system developed during the civil war. Each time, the Kremlin eventually generalized these measures to urban areas throughout the USSR, and added additional perquisites for the most important urban consumers through a network of workplace shops and canteens. A corollary to rationing was open discrimination against rural consumers, whose access to scarce goods in the urban stores was blocked, while rural shops obtained shipments almost exclusively in connection to the increasingly militarized "procurement campaigns"—that is, purchases of agricultural products by state and cooperative agencies at a submarket price. Yet another corollary was the war on the market: while private sales of nonessential foods and of used, homemade, or abundantly available consumer goods were never declared illegal, crisis socialism brought sharply increased rates of repression against private vendors and an attempt to eliminate the market from the distribution of essential foods and goods. Crisis socialism's closest analogues were the economies of war-torn Central Europe during and immediately after the two world wars.[10] This is not surprising: two of the three Soviet crises grew out of these same conflicts, and the third coincided with the Great Depression abroad.

Again from the perspective of policy, most striking about crisis socialism is that it was always jettisoned before the crisis had peaked. In 1921, 1931–32, and 1946–47, famine was still intensifying while the centralized distribution system was pruned back. Normalization as a policy predated the normalization of economic conditions and consumer behaviors. The government's program for recovery in each instance included the decentralization of supplies and decision making; the stabilization of the currency; the reestablishment of money as the primary unit of value and determinant of consumer access; the reduction and eventual elimination of guaranteed rations; and the liberalization of official policy toward the market. The desperate state of the economy that each time formed the backdrop to these reforms has led many Western and post-Soviet Russian historians to portray them as a "strategic retreat."[11] Soviet scholars, by contrast, stressed the extent to which the reforms were consistent with Lenin's, Stalin's, and, indeed, socialism's long-term goals of modernization and economic growth.[12] With qualifications, my judgment is closer to the Soviet view than to that of the previous Western scholarship. No

---

[10] Cf. Michael Wildt, *Der Traum vom Sattwerden: Hunger und Protest, Schwarzmarkt und Selbsthilfe* (Hamburg, 1986); and Kazimierz Wyka, "The Excluded Economy," in *The Unplanned Society*, ed. Janine Wedel (New York, 1992), 23–61.

[11] This is less true of the specialized literature on 1921 than on the later reforms, though see E. G. Gimpel'son, *NEP i sovetskaia politicheskaia sistema. 20-e gody* (Moscow, 2000), 20–21. On 1931–32, see John T. Whitman, "The Kolkhoz Market," *Soviet Studies* 7, no. 4 (April 1956): 384–204; here, 387; Davies, *Crisis and Progress*, esp. 58–64, 94–97, 201–28. On 1946–47, see Donald Filtzer, "The Standard of Living of Soviet Industrial Workers in the Immediate Postwar Period, 1945–1948," *Europe-Asia Studies* 51, no. 6 (summer 1999): 1013–38; here, 1020–22; Zima, *Golod* 51–52; E. Iu. Zubkova, *Russia after the: Hopes, Illusions, and Disappointments, 1945–1957 War* (Armonk, N.Y., 1998), 40–50.

[12] On 1921, see V. P. Dmitrenko, *Sovetskaia ekonomicheskaia politika v pervye gody proletarskoi diktatury* (Moscow, 1986); G. A. Dikhtiar, *Sovetskaia torgovlia v period postroeniia sotsializma* (Moscow, 1963), 139–52; Atlas, *Sotsialisticheskaia denezhnaia sistema*, 173–91; on 1931–32, see 248–61.

less than the normalization policies, crisis socialism itself, after all, was introduced through a series of emergency measures. In the early years of Soviet rule it had vocal ideological advocates in the administration, but other leading Bolsheviks, including A. I. Rykov and probably also Lenin, saw the regimentation of distribution as a step backward and welcomed the NEP as an advance. This was clearly true of Stalin in subsequent decades: when he articulated his vision of socialism in the consumer economy, he firmly rejected crisis socialism in favor of an approach more akin to the NEP.

The NEP laid the foundation for the future development of the socialist economy by combining a massive state presence with market mechanisms and institutions. As is well known, many of these were dismantled during the second episode of crisis socialism, Stalin's "Great Break." Less well known is the extent to which market mechanisms were restored within the socialist economy during the subsequent normalization phase. In the supply sector, for example, the mercantile exchanges and fairs of the 1920s may have remained shut after their forcible closure in 1930–31, but the wholesale bases that eventually replaced them were intended to streamline the socialist market, not to suspend it. Moreover, as in the 1920s, formal wholesale institutions were supplemented by directly negotiated contracts between industrial marketing agencies, factories or farms, and the socialist trade networks. David Shearer has recently drawn attention to market practices in Soviet heavy industry, arguing that they undermined the regime's stated goal of constructing a planned economy. Their effect, Shearer maintains, was that "what emerged in the 1930s . . . was a command-administrative economy but not a planned one."[13] No doubt this is partly a difference between the two sectors, but, in trade, market practices were not considered incompatible with the construction of socialism. Although here, too, the employment of traveling buying agents (a particularly common method of circumventing overly rigid supply structures) was repeatedly castigated by would-be rationalizers, the point remains that in 1935–38 and 1948–53, as in 1921–28, state and cooperative supplies were organized both in practice and in principle on the basis of buying, selling, and the discretion of the manager, not simply planned allocations of a fixed quota of goods.

Policy makers did not want to relinquish their control of prices, by contrast; on this question, Soviet socialism diverged sharply from market-economy norms. Even during the NEP, if the first step toward normalization involved stabilizing the currency, and hence freeing prices,

[13] David Shearer, *Industry, State, and Society* in *Stalin's Russia, 1926–1934* (Ithaca, 1996), 236.

policy makers soon resumed their interventions into the prices of the "most important" categories of goods. These interventions fed into a vicious circle: the artificially depressed prices in the socialist sector created shortages, which, in turn, heightened demand for these goods in the private sector; private retailers responded by raising prices to equilibrate supply and demand. Goods were inevitably diverted from the regulated to the unregulated retailers, which only strengthened the Bolsheviks' hostility to the market and led them to try once again to lower prices by decree.[14] Their interventions became increasingly radical as shortages and dislocations intensified. The end point, crisis socialism, was neither a planned nor a desired outcome, yet economic officials followed a similar course of price regulation in the late 1930s, with a similar result, and they returned to it yet again in the postwar years.

So, to summarize, it is useful to think of the whole period from 1917 to 1953 in terms of a cyclical pattern of crisis and recovery, which was broken decisively only at the end of the period. This pattern provides the framework of this book, which uses the three protracted crises, sparked in turn by the revolution, Stalin's "restructuring of the national economy," and the war, and their aftermaths, to investigate the relationship between long-term agendas and short-term exigencies in the development of trade policy, and also between survival-threatening scarcity, shortages, and economic growth. With the exception of the revolutionary period, when their position had not fully coalesced, I argue that Soviet policy makers pursued their principled objectives in relation to supplies, wages and prices, trade cadres, and retail organization during the recovery phase of each economic cycle, and much less consistently during the crisis phase, when the perceived requirements of emergency management pushed less urgent priorities aside. In view of the contemporary expansion of chain stores, cooperatives, and department stores in the West, I also argue that several of the Soviet policies corresponded to modernizing trends in global retailing. They took advantage of economies of scale; in a market setting, with a different overall policy mix, they might even have laid the foundations for an effective system of socialist trade. That this did not occur by the end of Stalin's life I attribute to the weaknesses of Soviet price policy, to the circumscribed role granted to private enterprise and the market, and, above all, to the pull of crisis methods of economic management at the first sign of dislocations in the market for foods and consumer staples. Soviet trade policy was on a hair trigger; the policy preferences of Lenin, and especially Stalin, drew on economic ra-

[14] V. V. Novozhilov, "Nedostatok tovarov," *Vestnik finansov*, no. 2 (February 1926): 75–96, remains the best analysis of this problem.

tionality, but their political culture was steeped in the mentality, privations, and struggles of the civil war.

Buyers, Sellers, and the Social History of Trade

Thus far I have presented this book as a study of large-scale structural developments in the political economy of communism. It is also a book about people, whose economic activities both shaped and reflected the evolution of the economy as a whole. The cyclical pattern of crisis and recovery had a profound impact on the daily lives of Soviet citizens, as did the changing structures of Soviet trade. A key argument here is that citizens were affected not just as buyers but also as sellers. Peasants, still 46 percent of the population in 1939, marketed their produce throughout the period of this study. In times of crisis they were joined by virtually all urban residents, who sold off surplus possessions, bought and resold scarce commodities, or hawked handicrafts at the bazaar to help cover the escalating cost of food. Extensive studies of household budgets carried out by the Central Statistical Administration (TsSU, TsUNKhU) make it possible to quantify the role of occasional sales in working-class, clerical, and managerial or technical household incomes on a year-to-year basis; in the most acute phases of economic crisis, up to 30 percent of these incomes derived from unofficial trade. What this means for the social history of the first half of the Soviet epoch is that the outdoor bazaars, where the bulk of occasional sales took place, preserved a face-to-face culture of exchange that was not unidirectional. Urbanites, as well as peasants, experienced trade from the vantage point of both the buyer and the seller. That high market food prices compelled townspeople to resort to petty trade prevented them from identifying with peasant food vendors, but by no means were all peasants in a position to profit from dearth, and the sheer universality of market vending in these periods made it a kind of cultural glue.

Participation in trade ebbed and flowed with the tide of economic crisis; as each crisis receded, wage earners and salary earners withdrew from the market, leaving in their wake a thinner stratum of artisanal vendors, hawkers, and professional traders. The New Economic Policy was, of course, distinctive in legalizing this last group, which, accordingly, remained much larger and more diverse in the 1920s than in the later two recovery phases. NEP-era traders also left traces in different parts of the Soviet archives: I was able to reconstruct NEP-era business histories from credit records for chapter 3, whereas the criminal justice system yielded most of my information on individual traders after 1930.[15] This is a fundamental difference between the NEP and the later period, and, in stressing continuities across the "Great Break," I do not mean to minimize it. It is the continuities, however, that have not been properly appreciated in the historiography, and these existed even in that least likely of areas, professional private trade. An exploration of the ingredients of commercial success in the NEP context highlights many of the same kinds of businesses that persisted, admittedly in an altered, reduced, and often criminal guise, in subsequent decades. This is still more true of the ingredients of commercial failure: particularly in the Soviet Union's provincial backwaters, impoverished NEP-era traders eked out a living in precisely the same economic niches and by dint of the same methods as impoverished informal traders would later use.

Poverty emerges rather sharply from this study as an important category of social analysis.[16] I initially conceptualized the consumption side of the project through what I called a culture of shortages, the constellation of behavioral responses to shortages that acquired, or so I imagined, a degree of autonomy vis-à-vis the material conditions at their root.[17] Although shortages did indeed dog the consumer economy throughout this thirty-five-year period, I now treat them as a historical problem rather than an explanatory mechanism. Shortages were the product of the planned disequilibrium between wages and prices, a nearly constant feature of the state's economic policy, and also of the rhythms and incentives inherent in bureaucratized production.[18] This raises interesting questions about Soviet economic priorities and policy formation, but it also underscores the extent to which poverty limited consumers' options. Most households had an extremely narrow margin of discretionary income at their disposal. As a result, it was usually the lowest-grade, least-expensive goods that were in short supply, while more expensive goods languished on the shelf. Shortages exacerbated the distance between the better-off and the

[15] An exception was 1945–48, when financial organs and inspectorates of trade and manufacturing cooperatives reported on private shops and cafes. See my article, "A Postwar Perestroika? Toward a History of Private Enterprise in the USSR," *Slavic Review* 57, no. 3 (fall 1998): 516–42.

[16] A study of poverty in the Brezhnev period by Mervyn Matthews, *Poverty in the Soviet Union* (Cambridge, 1986), is the only book-length treatment of this topic, though it figures in various social histories and sociologies as a minor theme. This is clearly a topic worth investigating further.

[17] This was the theme of my doctoral dissertation, "Culture of Shortages: A Social History of Soviet Trade" (University of Chicago, 1996).

[18] Kornai, in *Socialist System*, ascribes the greatest weight to bureaucratization in his explanation of shortages, though he also discusses them in connection with monetary policy as a measure of repressed inflation.

poor, since consumers with money could often simply pay a premium and avoid long hours in line.

As for culture, it is an aspect that is certainly difficult to discern in consumer behaviors during the crisis periods. Crisis modified patterns of consumption and consumers' methods of acquiring goods in a wholly predictable manner; Amartya Sen's description of crowd behaviors during one of India's periodic food crises could apply to any one of the Soviet crises, as could Pitirim Sorokin's observations about "hunger as a factor in human affairs."[19] Hoarding and panic buying typified the first period of a crisis, before supplies had disappeared altogether; theft from shops, warehouses, and transportation mounted; free-market prices rose sharply; citizens in possession of desirable goods traveled to near or distant villages to exchange them for food; and starving villagers flooded the cities in hopes of finding relief there. Consumption of both foods and manufactured goods deteriorated both quantitatively and qualitatively. Finally, and I am able to demonstrate this with greater precision than I have encountered in any existing work on food crises and consumption habits in any national setting, citizens spent increasing amounts of their income in the remnants of the private sector (sometimes termed the *black market*) and spent increasing amounts of time both buying and selling goods. These adaptations involved very little that can be identified specifically with Russian culture or socialism. They did, however, shape crisis socialism as a constellation of policies by justifying its dual emphases: repression and bureaucratic control.

During the recovery periods the increased availability of goods in the shops and the concomitant drop in market prices boosted citizens' buying power. Aggregate demand accordingly widened and encompassed more diverse interests, as personal tastes entered into the calculations of consumers who were further and further down the income scale. Of course, the destruction of wealth that was a by-product of class warfare during the first two major crises militated against the diversification of consumption, and the liquidation of private shops played a role here as well. These obstacles notwithstanding, the later 1920s, the later 1930s, and the period after 1948 supported a lively trade in luxury goods and specialty items in both the private and socialized sectors. This is not to say that Soviet society became a consumer society; the preoccupations with marking status and expressing individuality through consumption choices, identified by several commentators as essential components of modern consumerism, remained restricted to a small minority of the

---

[19] Cf. Amartya Sen, *Poverty and Famines* (Oxford, 1981), 55–57; Pitirim A. Sorokin, *Hunger as a Factor in Human Affairs*, trans. Elena P. Sorokin (Gainesville, 1975 [1922]).

buying public.[20] Still, in each of the recovery periods we can discern shifts in a consumerist direction. Perhaps most striking, the burden of shopping was lightened by newfound pleasures in shopping. Catering to the popular demand for recreation, outdoor markets offered a variety of amusements during the recovery periods; so, too, did the private shops, bars, and billiard rooms of 1921–30 and their less-familiar counterparts of 1945–48. Meanwhile, as of the early 1930s, the state tried to capture the luxury market by creating a pleasurable atmosphere in its new "premiere" shops and chains.

Rural consumers were left out of these developments, both for reasons of poverty and because of their limited access to goods. Each of the three crises caused a severe contraction of the retail infrastructure, and each time rural shops reopened last. The central government devoted attention to this problem in 1923, 1936–38, and 1949, but the recommendations and decrees that were issued in these years were backed neither by sufficient funding nor by a threat of enforcement. When push came to shove, rural interests were the first to be sacrificed in the drive for socialism. Even in the normalization periods, shops were fewer and more scantily stocked in rural areas than elsewhere, and their prices fixed at a substantially higher level. The trade networks exacerbated these problems by halting shipments to rural areas whenever goods became scarce. Disparities in access reinforced the effects of the state's low procurement prices for agricultural products; while my research challenges an old view of the Stalin era as a period of increasing disparities between working-class and managerial incomes, it confirms the notion of a widening urban-rural gap.[21]

It will be apparent from this discussion that my "social history of trade" is not primarily a history of shop assistants. They do figure in this study; state and cooperative shops relied on a burgeoning class of clerical employees, whose wages, demographics, and workplace ethics elicited frequent interventions from above. The prewar Stalin period was the turning point: between the late 1920s and the early 1940s a new sectoral

---

[20] Status has figured particularly prominently in the work of sociologists, from Thorsten Veblen to the post-structuralists Jean Baudrillard and Pierre Bourdieu. Historians have been more successful at linking shifts in consumption with the imagination; see, for example, Colin Campbell, *The Romantic Ethic and the Spirit of Modern Consumerism* (New York, 1987); Rosalind H. Williams, *Dream Worlds* (Berkeley, 1982); and William Leach, *Land of Desire* (New York, 1993).

[21] The old view, it should be noted, derived largely from qualitative description rather than quantitative analysis; cf. Leon Trotsky, *The Revolution Betrayed: What Is the Soviet Union and Where Is It Going?* (New York, 1937); and Vera S. Dunham, *In Stalin's Time: Middle-class Values in Soviet Literature* (Durham, N.C., 1990), esp. 3–24.

hierarchy was consolidated, in which retailing and public catering came to anchor the bottom end of the wage scale. Demographically this coincided with the feminization of retail work, a shift actively encouraged by the productivist state.[22] These are significant developments, whose ramifications for capitalist society have been explored by historians and sociologists of Western Europe and the United States.[23] The present work briefly discusses them in relation to the Soviet case, but I spend more time on the crystallization of a socialist retail culture from such contradictory pressures as communist moralism, the struggle against bureaucratism, material hardship among retail employees, and the endemic shortages of consumer goods. Ultimately the story of the feminization of the sales staff, a variation on a global theme, seemed to me less compelling than other stories more distinctive to the Soviet setting. For social history, these included citizens' changing relationship to the market as buyers and sellers, and the role of money (or poverty) as against access (or discrimination) in the social distribution of goods.

The last comprehensive histories of Soviet trade appeared in Russia in the 1960s; these were books written by trained economists G. L. Rubinshtein and G. A. Dikhtiar.[24] Dikhtiar's three-volume history exemplifies the best side of Soviet scholarship; the product of a life's work, it is exhaustively researched in both published and archival sources (Western scholars sometimes forget that access to the archives is new for us but not for the whole field), and Dikhtiar also strove to preserve a relatively objective tone. Even so, he remained tied to the Whiggish underpinnings of Soviet historiography, and his books are much richer in data than in historical interpretation. The present volume is intended to supersede his in some respects, notably by fleshing out the political and social aspects of trade; by integrating the private sector, particularly in its pre- and post-NEP, informal guise, into a global picture of the consumer economy; by exposing unflattering new consumption data; and by presenting

[22] Amy E. Randall has studied the recruitment of women into the retail sector, adopted as policy in 1931; see her unpublished paper, "Women Workers and the Gendering of Soviet Trade," presented at the annual conference of the American Association for the Advancement of Slavic Studies in Denver, 2000. My decision not to emphasize shopclerks in this book was influenced by my awareness of Randall's research on this subject.

[23] For discussions of the feminization of retailing in, respectively, the United States, Britain, and Western Europe, see Susan Porter Benson, *Counter Cultures* (Urbana, 1986); Bill Lancaster, *The Department Store* (London, 1995), 171–94; James B. Jefferys and Derek Knee, *Retailing in Europe* (London, 1962), 19–21.

[24] G. L. Rubinshtein, *Razvitie vnutrennei torgovli v SSSR* (Leningrad, 1964); G. A. Dikhtiar, *Vnutrenniaia torgovlia v dorevoliutsionnoi Rossii, Sovetskaia torgovlia v period postroeniia sotsializma*, and *Sovetskaia torgovlia v period sotsializma i razvernutogo stroitel'stva kommunizma* (henceforth, *Torgovlia* I–III) (Moscow, 1960–65).

the economic establishment in a less sympathetic light. The idea of comprehensive coverage exerted a strong influence on my research and presentation of the subject, so that readers looking for answers to particular questions about trade policy, retail venues, or consumption at one or another moment might use this book as a reference. For more narrowly economic topics, such as trade finances or wholesale institutions, researchers will nonetheless still need to turn to Dikhtiar; yet other topics, such as the specificities of trade in particular republics, must await their own historian, as they figure no more than haphazardly in this or any other existing work.

Several authors have written on particular aspects of the consumer economy in recent years, but none has done more to bring it to the attention of the scholarly community than Elena Osokina, the author of two books and several articles on trade, distribution, and daily life in the period between 1927 and 1941.[25] The thrust of her interpretation is to emphasize what the Stalin regime (usually, in her most recent book, identified as the Politburo) *did* to society: it *created* food shortage through its disastrous agricultural policies and then *used* its monopoly on food supplies to *starve* peasants and to *control* everyone else. For Osokina, the centralized rationing system of the early 1930s epitomized Stalinism. Through it, the regime prioritized groups of consumers whose survival was most important to key industrial goals; it inscribed the population in a rigid hierarchy of consumption rights; and, finally, it policed those rights through extralegal repression. All these points are both important and relevant to the present study; in chapters 4 and 5, which treat the prewar Stalin period, readers will find many echoes of her ideas. In the end, though, I argue that Stalin's oft-stated preference for nonrationed "cultured Soviet trade" needs to be taken seriously. In terms of high-level trade policy, I thus portray the Stalin regime as much more concerned with modernization and economic growth than it appears to be in Osokina's writings. In addition, since my research covers a broader period, this study identifies longer-term changes and continuities between the epoch of the five-year plans and its successors and predecessors, including both war communism and the NEP.

[25] Elena A. Osokina's recent synthesis, *Za fasadom "stalinskogo izobiliia." O zhizni liudei v usloviiakh stalinskogo snabzheniia.* (Moscow, 1998), incorporates most of her previous findings. It is now available in English as *Our Daily Bread: Socialist Distribution and the Art of Survival in Stalin's Russia*, trans. Kate Transchel and Greta Bucher (Armonk, N.Y., 2000). Osokina's earlier works included *Ierarkhiia potrebleniia. Raspredelenie i rynok v snabzhenii naseleniia v gody industrializatsii, 1927–1941.* (Moscow, 1993); "Za zerkal'noi dver'iu Torgsina," *Otechestvennaia istoriia*, no. 2 (April 1995): 86–104; "Liudi i vlast' v usloviiakh krizisa snabzheniia 1939–1941 gody," *Otechestvennaia istoriia*, no. 3 (May–June 1995): 16–32.

A final author who merits specific mention is the late V. P. Dmitrenko, the preeminent specialist on early Soviet trade. Dmitrenko's many works, published over a period of two decades, have influenced chapters 1 through 3 of this volume with their detailed reconstruction of policy formation.[26] Dmitrenko was a scholar of a certain generation; he insisted on a degree of ideological coherence in Lenin's policies that most contemporary historians would find implausible, overemphasized the "leading role of the Communist Party," and predictably downplayed the role of coercion in the revolutionary regime. But he was also a shrewd and extremely knowledgeable interpreter of Bolshevik politics, society, and economic development, and his work deserves to be more widely read.

The Bolsheviks' desire to construct an alternative to "bourgeois trade" and to market mechanisms led them into uncharted waters in global economic and social history. This book traces their course across three and a half decades with reference to three major themes. One is the invention and development of a socialist retail system, the subject of chapters 2, 4, 5, and 7. A second is the progressive constriction of private trade to bazaar and black market forms, treated in chapters 1, 3, and 6. The third theme, the evolution of consumer habits in connection with the structural transformation of trade, figures in parts of chapters throughout the book.

[26] V. P. Dmitrenko, "Nekotorye itogi obobshchestvleniia tovarooborota v 1917–1920 gg.," *Istoricheskie zapiski* 79 (1966): 225–42; idem, "Bor'ba Sovetskogo gosudarstva protiv chastnoi torgovli," in S. S. Khesin, ed., *Bor'ba za pobedu i ukreplenie sovetskoi vlasti, 1917–1918* (Moscow, 1966); idem, *Sovetskaia ekonomicheskaia politika*; idem, *Torgovaia politika sovetskogo gosudarstva posle perekhoda k NEPu, 1921–1924 gg.* (Moscow, 1971); V. P. Dmitrenko, L. F. Morozov, and V. I. Pogudin, *Partiia i kooperatsiia* (Moscow, 1978).

Crisis: Revolution

As if in a gigantic centrifuge, two layers settled out of the vortex
of the revolution: on top, the visible, official, proletarian-natural
economy, and underneath it, the hidden, underground, commodity and commodity-capitalist economy. With each step in the
evolution of the official economy came a corresponding expansion
of its inalienable shadow. With the successive annihilation of the
regular, legal market, came a parallel development of the demonetized economy of the proletariat, on the one hand, and the
illegal economy, which was born during the imperialist war of
1914–1917 as a supplement to the regular market, but subsequently became the only market.
   —L. N. Kritsman, *The Heroic Period of the Great Russian Revolution*

CHAPTER ONE

Trade and Consumption in Revolutionary Russia

THE ECONOMIC CRISIS of 1916–22 was the crucible of Soviet socialism as an economic system. Produced originally by the Great War, the economic crisis helped to create the possibility of a socialist revolution and conditioned the policies of the revolutionary regime. Crisis led the Bolsheviks to intervene increasingly radically into the economy, until the state controlled transportation, industry, and all vital supplies. Later, the unabated crisis caused these same measures to be moderated or abandoned.

This chapter is not primarily concerned with the evolution of the crisis or even of Bolshevik policy but with the short-term impact of the crisis on consumption and trade. The adjustments and initiatives of diverse economic actors during the revolutionary period set important precedents for later years. With respect to trade, one major precedent was the transformation of the small, uncoordinated network of consumer cooperatives into a vast, centralized distribution system. Along with other elements of war communism (the crisis model of socialism that coalesced in 1918–21), a consideration of this development will be postponed until chapter 2. The precedent to be discussed here was the decomposition of the existing private trade network in connection with the Bolsheviks' war on the market and the reconstitution of private trade on an informal and smaller-scale basis. How that happened—when, how, and why "bagging" and outdoor bazaars replaced the mercantile houses and shops of prerevolutionary Russia, and how they changed over time—is the principal theme of this chapter.

For social history, this development, which the Socialist Revolutionary economist N. D. Kondrat'ev called the "degradation of trade," raises a series of related questions. For example, what happened to the prerevolutionary traders? Can we draw any conclusions as to who adapted best to the altered economic and political environment, and determine which factors contributed to their relative success? When and how were consumers drawn into the informal economy, and how did their consumption habits change under its influence? Finally, to what extent did consumers share or internalize the Bolsheviks' view of private trade as "speculation," when they were forced both to shop at the market and to sell things in order to survive? After a brief synopsis of prerevolutionary trade, the chapter will describe the Bolsheviks' anti-trade policy and explore some of these social and economic effects.

RUSSIAN RETAILING AND ITS UNRAVELING

On the eve of the world war, Russia's retail system consisted of five types of venues. In first place were the large metropolitan shops, called *magaziny* after the French *magasin*. Representing the modern end of the retail spectrum, these shops had proliferated since the 1870s and now garnered just under half the country's retail sales. They were widely outnumbered by *lavki*, small shops of a traditional complexion. In 1912 *lavki* accounted for four-fifths of all retail licenses, though the modest turnover of these establishments, on the average of some ten rubles a day, meant that they did much less business as a group (30 percent) than their numerical preponderance might suggest. "Treasury shops," or franchises connected to the state liquor monopoly, formed the third, highly profitable category, with 12 percent of recorded sales receipts. Virtually all other retail sales went through some form of outdoor trade—fairs, markets, or street vending—which remained important components of the retail system in Russia long after their decline in Western Europe and the United States. Finally, the shops of the fledgling cooperative movement brought a novel, civic-oriented ethos to the trade system, though their economic role remained negligible until the outbreak of the war.[1]

Each of these venues embodied a characteristic exchange culture, and to some extent they served distinct clienteles. The traditional forms of petty retailing—the *lavki*, market stalls, hawkers, and traveling pedlars— were socially and physically interactive. Vendors typically chatted with patrons, who pinched and scrutinized the merchandise and then haggled over the price. To educated Russians, these attributes evoked disorderliness and "medievalism"; accordingly, for at least fifty years, they predicted that the flea markets and hawkers would disappear. Yet, as one student of late imperial trade has suggested, "the population of Moscow in the nineteenth century was largely of country origin and felt more comfortable in the informal atmosphere of street and bazaar than in the colder and more impersonal shop, especially the more modern *magazin*."[2] This was surely still more true of provincial consumers, who were exposed to modern retailing methods only during visits to the big city.

---

[1] Dikhtiar, *Torgovlia* I, 68–92; Strumilin, *Statistiko-ekonomicheskie ocherki*, 672–87.

[2] Robert Gohstand, "The Internal Geography of Trade in Moscow from the Mid-nineteenth Century to the First World War" (Ph.D. diss., University of California, Berkeley, 1973), 37.

Magaziny catered mainly to prosperous metropolitan customers. Established, in many cases, by foreign capitalists and clustered in such elite shopping districts as Kuznetskii Most in Moscow and Nevskii Prospect in St. Petersburg, these stores projected an image of modernity and Europeanness as against customary modes of trade. They featured glass display cases, polite salesclerks, and nonnegotiable prices; they also were much more aggressive than their traditional counterparts in their retail strategies. The larger *magaziny* invested in advertisement and customer service, instituted mail-order or catalogue sales, and established branches in provincial towns. The Singer Company, with its flagship store on Nevskii Prospect (now Dom Knigi), affords a good example: to sell its sewing machines in an expanding Russian market, Singer opened four thousand stores around the country, employed more than twenty-seven thousand shopclerks and traveling salesmen, and advertised extensively via posters, murals, and the periodical press.[3] Another successful class of *magaziny* were the high-end emporia, such as the Eliseev delicatessans or Moscow's mammoth department store Muir and Merilees.

Even in the immediate prewar period, the density of Russian trade remained low. The construction of the railroads had facilitated the year-round circulation of commodities, making provincial trade somewhat more viable in the previous forty years; retailers could now keep smaller, more liquid stocks, and reduce their outlays on trips to the capitals and to the summer wholesale fairs.[4] Nonetheless, many areas had very few shops and stores; the national average was sixty-five trade establishments per ten thousand inhabitants (ten *magaziny*, thirty-five *lavki*, and twenty market stalls), and backward areas, such as the Central Agricultural Region or Belorussia, came nowhere close to this norm.[5] The thin distribution of trade outside the major cities reflected, and probably contributed to, the relatively weak integration of peasants into the cash economy. If

[3] Fred V. Carstenson, *American Enterprise in Foreign Markets: Studies of Singer and International Harvester in Imperial Russia* (Chapel Hill, 1984), 69. See also Christine Ruane, "Clothes Shopping in Imperial Russia: The Development of a Consumer Culture," *Journal of Social History* (summer 1995): 765–82; Sally West, "The Material Promised Land: Advertising's Modern Agenda in Late Imperial Russia," *Russian Review* 57, no. 3 (July 1998): 345–63.

[4] On these shifts, see Anne Lincoln Fitzpatrick, *The Great Russian Fair: Nizhnii Novgorod, 1840–1890* (London, 1990); and David Christian and R.E.F. Smith, *Bread and Salt* (Cambridge, 1984), 327–56.

[5] Dikhtiar, *Torgovlia* I, 92–94. For comparison, Saxony, a relatively industrialized region of Germany, had 637 retail establishments per ten thousand inhabitants as early as 1895. Cf. Dietrich Denecke and Gareth Shaw, "Traditional Retail Systems in Germany," in *The Evolution of Retail Systems, c. 1800–1914*, ed. John Benson and Gareth Shaw (Leicester, 1992), 83.

the average per capita expenditure in any part of the trade system was twelve kopecks a day, the trade network in underdeveloped regions averaged barely a third of that. The low purchasing power of peasants, combined with the still quite high cost of shipping to remote locations, made for a retail structure disproportionately weighted toward the major cities and especially the capitals, which alone accounted for one-third of all retail turnover.[6]

The war brought a number of changes to the trade system. Liquor outlets were abruptly closed in connection with the vodka prohibition, enacted in autumn 1914, in Moscow and other cities.[7] As discussed in chapter 2, the war also sparked a takeoff of consumer cooperatives, which grew exponentially to become the chief provisioners of urban working-class districts. The experience of private merchants and shopkeepers was much more checkered, depending on the locality and objects of their trade. By late 1916 most retailers were experiencing shortages of fuel and consumer goods, as military needs displaced manufacturing and transport for the civilian market. Prices accordingly rose and, contrary to what one would expect in a more stable period, inflation stimulated, rather than inhibiting, consumer demand. Queues, the commercial newspaper *Kommersant* announced, were "the law of our time."[8] Sudden price hikes on basic necessities elicited panic buying, as risk-averse consumers sought to lay in reserves. At the same time a stratum of risk takers made speculative purchases on the gamble that they could profitably resell the goods in the future. By early 1917 the objects of speculation spanned the entire spectrum of consumer goods, from such basic provisions as flour and tobacco to luxuries threatened by an impending import ban. Arrests of large-scale profiteers regularly made headlines in the weeks before the tsar's abdication.[9]

Other symptoms of the emerging economic crisis could be seen in the rash of shop closures in the winter of 1916–17, and in the fact that both retailers and consumers were traveling long distances for consumer goods. As in the early nineteenth century, retailers had to descend on manufacturing regions in person. Unable to afford the cost of travel, and forced to pay substantially more for their supplies than bigger firms, small pro-

[6] Dikhtiar, *Torgovlia* I, 92–94; Dmitrenko, "Bor'ba Sovetskogo gosudarstva," 308 f.

[7] See Sergei Romanov, *Istoriia russkoi vodki* (Moscow, 1998), 234–36.

[8] *Kommersant*, February 4, 1917. See also the newspaper's overview of the previous year's impact on the major commodity markets, published serially in January.

[9] Ibid., January 2, 3, 5, 13, and 14; and February 1, 8, and 13, 1917. Profiteering flourished throughout Europe alongside the regulated war economy; cf. Michel David, *Le marché noir* (Paris, 1945), 8–9; and Edward Smithies, *The Black Economy in England since 1914* (Dublin, 1984), 19–37.

vincial merchants were disproportionately affected by these dislocations. By early 1917 shops stood empty around the country; whole districts were left without retail outlets, as small and medium-sized businesses shut down for lack of goods.[10] Sellers who survived these difficulties tried to boost profits by making the availability of "deficit" goods contingent on purchases of overstock items.[11] Provincial consumers were often faced with a choice of buying artisanal products or traveling to the capitals for factory-produced wares. Specifically, in January 1917, trains from Siberia were filled with people carting foods and local products to sell at Moscow or Petrograd markets so that they could buy manufactured goods unavailable at home.[12]

Retailers were also affected by governmental encroachments on the grain market. As early as 1915 many provinces instituted embargoes on shipments of grain across provincial lines, while the central government tried to counteract these ordinances and to regulate prices on grain sales. It soon mandated fixed prices on all grain transactions (September 1916) and introduced a centralized system of requisitioning that assigned specific delivery quotas to every farm (November 1916). While grain requisitioning served its immediate purpose by placing a regular supply of food in the hands of the government, it also contributed to the catastrophic decline in grain cultivation in subsequent years. Both the Provisional Government and the Bolsheviks thus inherited their approach to food problems; the institution of a grain monopoly by the Provisional Government (March 1917) and a "food dictatorship" by the Bolsheviks (May 1918) represented coercive elaborations of the tsar's policy. Within weeks of the collapse of the monarchy, all grain officially belonged to the state. Producers were required to register all their grain, from which they were allowed to keep a quota for their own sustenance. After October the Bolsheviks' main innovation in the area of grain policy was to militarize procurement by entrusting it to armed "food detachments."[13] All these interventions had ramifications for food retailers, whose ability to obtain bread and flour, as well as to profit from their sale, was predictably damaged.

[10] *Kommersant*, January 2, 4, 5, and 17; and February 1, 1917.

[11] Ibid., January 3, 1917.

[12] Ibid., February 1, 1917.

[13] See Lars T. Lih, *Bread and Authority in Russia, 1914–1921* (Berkeley, 1990); N. D. Kondrat'ev, *Rynok khlebov i ego regulirovanie vo vremia voiny i revoliutsii* (Moscow, 1991 [1922]); Silvana Malle, *The Economic Organization of War Communism, 1918–1921* (Cambridge, 1985), 322–95; and see also *Sistematicheskii sbornik dekretov i rasporiazhenii pravitel'stva po prodovol'stvennomu delu* (hereafter, *Sistematicheskii sbornik dekretov*, vol. 1 (Nizhnii Novgorod, 1919).

Alongside the dramatic political events of 1917–18, the deepening economic crisis formed the backdrop to these policies. Food shortages in Petrograd triggered the February Revolution, as is well known, but their severity would appear to have been exaggerated by popular anxieties. Even at the height of the demonstrations the city's reserves never fell below a twelve-day supply. Petrograd was, moreover, unusually vulnerable to disruptions in food deliveries by virtue of its size and location, so that shortages there should not be extrapolated to the country as a whole.[14] By mid-summer, however, the chaotic breakdown of the railway system had generalized what might have been a local problem to every region that ordinarily imported food.[15] A year later famine deaths were recorded in Petrograd, Turkestan, and other areas, and epidemic diseases—cholera, dysentery, typhoid, and the "famine fever," typhus—claimed growing numbers of victims as well.[16] The crisis also spilled over into the manufacturing sector, as workers became caught up in revolutionary politics and joined the Red Army, or abandoned the factory for the sake of land rights or food.

(Until the Bolshevik Revolution, retailers were a casualty of interventionary policies rather than their explicit target. While the Bolsheviks retained and indeed radicalized their predecessors' emphasis on controlling grain and other essential goods, they fundamentally altered the equation with their simultaneous "war on the market" and "expropriation of the bourgeoisie.") Within three days of their coup d'état, the Bolsheviks had issued a decree giving local commissars an unlimited mandate to regulate commerce and to "confiscate, requisition, and sequester for their own use all private buildings, foods, articles, equipment, instruments, means of transportation, warehouses, and so forth."[17] While this placed the initiative at the local level, retailers and merchants everywhere soon felt themselves under siege. Short of outright expropriation, business owners were presented with enormous tax bills, for which, in Nizhnii Novgorod and other cities, the entire commercial class was made

[14] George Katkov, *Russia 1917* (New York, 1967), 249–51; Kondrat'ev, *Rynok khlebov*, 142–43. For a more negative assessment of the food situation in February, cf. Z. Lozinskii, *Ekonomicheskaia politika vremennogo pravitel'stva* (Leningrad, 1929), 124; and Dmitrenko, *Sovetskaia ekonomicheskaia politika*, 16.

[15] See the interesting discussion in Roger Pethybridge, *The Spread of the Russian Revolution: Essays on 1917* (London, 1972), 1–56.

[16] See Stephen Wheatcroft, "Famine and Factors Affecting Mortality in the USSR: The Demographic Crises of 1914–22 and 1930–33," CREES Discussion Papers, Soviet Industrialization Project series nos. 20–21 (Birmingham, U.K., 1981–82); and, on Turkestan, *Pobeda oktiabr'skoi revoliutsii v Uzbekistane* (Tashkent, 1972), 71–280, passim.

[17] *Sobranie uzakonenii* (1917), 1:6.

collectively responsible; some were evicted from commercial premises or apartments; and many had run-ins with the new authorities over prices on essential goods.[18] For retailers, the Bolsheviks' punitive social policies compounded the economic difficulties stemming from the unavailability of supplies. As of the spring of 1918 some retailers were still trying to increase their insurance coverage against the heightened risks of the revolutionary period, but many others took down their shingles and closed shop.[19]

Soviet trade policy in 1917–18 comprised contradictory elements. On the one hand, local officials were encouraged to "crush the bourgeoisie" and to prevent traders from making a profit. On the other hand, Lenin insisted on using "bourgeois specialists" in the socialist economy, and although he rarely applied this term to private traders, it found expression in several edicts from the first part of 1918.[20] The idea was that private stores could be forced to adhere to submarket prices if placed under rigorous supervision. "Utilization" was, at this point, a practical necessity. Even in the capitals, the network of government stores coalesced gradually; one year after the Bolshevik seizure of power, Petrograd's 426 municipal shops could service only 40 percent of the population, and if cooperatives now handled much of the remainder of rationed bread distribution, private shops remained the primary distributors of specialty goods and foods.[21]

Between May and November 1918, however, Soviet policy swung sharply away from utilization toward the purposive elimination of private trade. The symbolic beginning of this shift was the May 13 announcement of the "food dictatorship," which was accompanied by shrill rhetoric against "speculation," the establishment of commissions to enforce price limits, and a general increase in bureaucratic intervention.[22] The climax came in November, with the promulgation of the decrees "On the organization of provisionment" (November 21) and "On the state monopoly over trade in certain foods and items" (November 26). Articulating for the first time the ultimate goal of "the replacement of the private trade apparatus" with cooperatives and Soviet institutions, the November

[18] See, for example, GARF, f. 393, op. 4, d. 23, ll. 21–22; d. 24, ll. 155, 177; d. 25, l. 34; d. 34, l. 13; RGASPI, f. 5, op. 1, d. 2615, ll. 4–20.
[19] GARF, f. 130, op. 1, d. 44, ll. 44–47.
[20] Lenin, *Polnoe sobranie sochinenii*, 5th ed. (Moscow, 1958–1965) (henceforth, *PSS*), 34: 310–11, 36: 137–42; *Sobranie uzakonenii* (1918), 23:326. See also Dmitrenko, "Bor'ba Sovetskogo gosudarstva," 293, 321, passim.
[21] Dmitrenko, "Bor'ba Sovetskogo gosudarstva," 294.
[22] The crucial edict was VTsIK's "O chrezvychainykh polnomochiiakh, predostavlennykh Narodnomu Komissaru po Prodovol'stviiu," *Sistematicheskii sbornik dekretov*, 33–34.

21 decree was the closest the regime ever came to a general ban on the "free market" or "free sales" (*volnyi rynok; volnaia prodazha*).[23] It represented a political victory for the leftist lobby, centered in the food-supply commissariat (Komprod), over the moderates grouped around Supreme Economic Council (VSNKh) chairman Aleksei Rykov.[24] The decree authorized Komprod to "nationalize" wholesale commercial establishments, while local food committees (*prodkomy*) were to "municipalize" retail stores.[25] First in line were sellers of goods subject to the state monopoly, which now included nearly all basic consumer necessities: grain, paper, salt, kerosene, matches, iron, sewing thread, galoshes, tea, coffee, cocoa, agricultural implements, imports of all kinds, and most categories of factory-produced consumer goods.[26]

Although the November 21 decree anticipated the eventual elimination of private trade, the tensions in Soviet policy were not immediately resolved. Not only did it not actually prohibit trade, it put forward neither a definite timetable for municipalization nor a solution to the problem of supplies. As with most laws of this period, local officials could implement the decree at their own discretion. An immediate takeover was not on the horizon, the head of Petrograd's *prodkom* insisted in a newspaper interview on December 7: "We have no intention of closing all shops right away." Rather, municipalization would occur gradually: first, shopkeepers would provide the city with exact inventories and report their intakes and outlays (a measure designed to deter "speculative" pricing); then small shops would gradually be closed, and large ones would be taken over for state trade. The expropriated shopkeepers would be invited to enter into state service, as had happened with tobacco sellers when the tobacco trade was municipalized a short while before.[27] The only available data indicate that the tempo of municipalization and nationalization ranged widely: at one extreme, Moscow, Riazan', Simbirsk, and Tula *gubernii* reported at the end of 1918 that municipalization and nationalization were being carried out "fully and in accordance with a plan," whereas Arkangel'sk, Penza, and Chernigov *gubernii* admitted to having taken no steps at all in this direction. The remainder of the twenty-five provinces surveyed fell somewhere in between: they had

[23] Ibid., 35–39.

[24] On Rykov's advocacy of utilizing private trade, see M. Feigel'son, "Meshochnichestvo i bor'ba s nim proletarskogo gosudarstva," *Istorik Marksist* 85, no. 9 (September 1940): 71; Dmitrenko, "Bor'ba Sovetskogo gosudarstva," 304–5, 311f.; GARF f. 130, op. 2, d. 2, ll. 304, 312–14.

[25] *Sistematicheskii sbornik dekretov*, 35–39.

[26] Ibid., 202.

[27] *Krasnaia gazeta*, December 7, 1918.

taken over some branches of retail trade, in no particular order, and had put most private wholesalers out of business.[28] No matter what the local conditions, nearly all surviving merchants took the November decrees as a signal to liquidate their shops. As V. M. Ustinov, a NEP-era historian, observed, even without an outright ban "it was not difficult to draw the conclusion that the economic system in place by the end of 1918 left no room for trade."[29]

EFFECTS OF THE ANTI-TRADE POLICY

The Bolsheviks' actions against shopkeepers and merchants set into motion a train of unintended social consequences. Particularly in the ethnically mixed border regions of the Russian Empire, occupations in trade, which the Bolsheviks treated exclusively in terms of class divisions, tended to represent specific ethnic groups. Throughout Eastern Europe and southwestern Asia, Jews, Armenians, and Greeks were known as trading peoples; as such, they were bound to suffer disproportionately from the Bolsheviks' persecution of traders and the forcible closing of their shops. With regard to the Jews, two reports from Belorussia confirm this development, which would recur at the end of the NEP. The first, a letter that found its way from a small town near Mogilev to the central government in January 1919, is worth quoting:

> Here there are neither workers nor Communists, nor yet anti-Communists; there is only the man in the street, the indistinct ordinary person. Such people are divided into categories not only according to their occupation but also by nationality. The villages are inhabited by the Russian peasant; the small towns primarily by the Jewish tradesman or shopkeeper. One could not describe these groups as friendly, yet they coexisted without especial animosity.... But now you have declared war against speculation and marauding. And in the Mogilev area, that was understood as a war against Jews—against each and every one of the Jewish population, who were all declared to be speculators and marauders.[30]

The letter-writer went on to relate a series of anti-Semitic incidents, which left the area's Jews, "paupers and near-paupers, petty vendors and tradesmen," feeling apprehensive and aggrieved. Jews were body-searched when they appeared in nearby villages, and peasants refused to sell to them for fear of unpleasant consequences. In an incident the au-

[28] Dmitrenko, "Bor'ba Sovetskogo gosudarstva," 309–10.
[29] V. M. Ustinov, *Evoliutsiia vnutrennei torgovli v Rossii, 1913–1924* (Moscow, 1925), 36.
[30] GARF, f. 130, op. 3, d. 129b, ll. 8–11.

thor portrayed as typical, the manager of the municipal shop in Rodno announced to a crowd of Jews and peasants, "Russians, remain in the line; the Jews can get what's left over. They're speculators." Traveling through Belorussia a year later, the American correspondent Marguerite Harrison observed much the same thing: a relatively satisfied peasant population, and a mass of impoverished, discontented Jews, whose small shops had been closed and who could not even draw rations unless they could find work with a passing regiment. As a result, she reported, "many of them existed on secreted supplies or devious and dangerous contraband trade with Poland."[31]

An irony of the anti-trade policy was that the poorest and least resourceful traders tended to suffer most. Class war notwithstanding, the richer members of Russia's commercial class often found niches in the Soviet economic administration. "Kulak" merchants in a rural county in Kursk *guberniia*, the subject of a 1922 investigation, typified this tendency: nearly all made the transition to the socialist sector under war communism, then successfully returned to private trade after the announcement of the NEP. D. A. D'iakov, the wealthiest of the group, can serve as our example. D'iakov's steam-powered mill, general store, and cereal mill were transferred to the local cooperative in 1918, along with his family's seven houses and barns. In compensation, the cooperative named him chairman. Before the civil war ended, D'iakov had served in four different supply agencies, gaining valuable connections for his return to the private sector in 1922.[32] His case was by no means exceptional. Complaints about *kulaks* (a term often applied to rural traders) dominating soviets and cooperatives were common in 1918–21, and expropriated urban merchants frequently found jobs in the administration of supplies. As in the case of industrialists retained as factory managers, state agencies needed the services of "trade specialists" to make the distribution system work.

If prosperous merchants moved into the bureaucracy during the civil war period, many smaller shopkeepers simply moved outdoors. Private trade did not disappear as a result of Bolshevik policies; rather, in the words of a pro-nationalization pamphlet, "Trade has scattered, and from the big warehouses and stores, trade has moved out onto the street. Go into any store, and you will almost always receive a negative response to your demands. At the same time all urban public squares are overflowing with every kind of trader, bearing the widest variety of goods in their

[31] Marguerite Harrison, *Marooned in Moscow* (New York, 1921), 29–30.
[32] Ia. Iakovlev, *Derevnia kak ona est.' Ocherk Nikol'skoi volosti* (Moscow, 1923), 44–7.

own hands."[33] Makeshift bazaars proliferated at all the traditional venues for outdoor trade: railway stations, docks, and urban and rural market squares. In light of the regime's stated policies, many consumers undoubtedly shared the confusion of a woman from Sumy (Ukraine), who sent in the following query in March 1920: "Respected Comrade Lenin! I bow humbly before your mind and deeds of genius. I'm just a little person; could you explain something to me? What does it mean to ban free trade when bazaars exist?" In Sumy, the letter writer explained, there was nothing available in the local food department, whereas at the bazaar, "the traders use the ban on free trade to charge whatever they want."[34] Throughout the country, bazaars were a refuge for private traders who had lost their shops.

Sumy fell under Bolshevik rule in late 1919, but in the center these conditions prevailed from 1918 on. Even before the November municipalization decree, the regular trade network had dwindled to the point where a bazaar, rather than a store, symbolized capitalism and commerce for Soviet officials. Bolshevik spokesmen represented the unofficial and official antipodes of the civil war economy by means of two Moscow landmarks: Sukharevka, the capital's most famous bazaar, and Red Square, home of the Soviet food-supply administration.[35] Numerous descriptions of Sukharevka, which historian and diarist Iu. V. Got'e called "one of the two great manifestations of the Russian revolution" (along with Lenin!), have come down to us from contemporary observers.[36] Every day, but especially on weekends, men and women crowded into the streets and alleys around Sukharev Square with their bags, purses, and, in wintertime, sleds. Sitting on curbs and hovering around the entrances to the market, once-prosperous townspeople proffered used clothes to shoppers or held out sugar cubes with silver tongs (figure 1). Inside, the market was laid out in rows of stalls, from which the larger and better-organized vendors sold produce, household wares, cloth, and books; between these, crammed into every available space, petty traders

[33] S. Vasil'ev, *Natsionalizatsiia vnutrennei torgovli* (Moscow, 1918), 5.

[34] *Golos naroda* (Moscow, 1998), 56–57.

[35] Cf. P. Fedorov, "Sukharevka—Krasnaia ploshchad'," *Izvestiia Narodnogo Komissariata po Prodovol'stviiu*, no. 8 (July 1918): 23–27; N. Orlov, *Deviat' mesiatsev prodovol'stvennoi raboty sovetskoi vlasti* (Moscow, 1918), 353–55 (essentially plagiarized from Fedorov); Nikolai Bukharin and E. Preobrazhenskii, *The ABC of Communism* (Ann Arbor, 1966 [1919]), 323; *Ekonomicheskaia zhizn'*, February 18, 1920.

[36] Iu. V. Got'e, *Time of Troubles* (Princeton, 1988), 312; Harrison, *Marooned in Moscow*, 150–57; William J. Chase, *Workers, Society, and the Soviet State: Labor and Life in Moscow* (Urbana, 1987), 26–27; Mauricio Borrero, *Hungry Moscow: Scarcity and Urban Society in the Russian Civil War, 1917–1921* (New York, 2003), 171–75.

Figure 1. Curbside sales at Sukharevka. *Courtesy of the Russian State Archive for Cinematic and Photographic Documents (RGAKFD).*

parked pushcarts, old women stood with baskets of cabbages, and others simply spread out their wares on the ground. One section featured cafes selling various kinds of fast food. Sukharevka accounted for as much as half of all market trade in Moscow in the spring of 1919. As a contemporary commentator noted, it was the one place in the capital where goods were sold "from kiosks and stalls, with weights, wrapping paper, and all the attributes of normal commerce."[37]

The legal status of the bazaars was ambiguous. There was never a blanket prohibition against bazaars any more than there was a blanket prohibition against private trade. Local officials did occasionally clamp down on them; police and Cheka units in many cities periodically swept through and made arrests. Writing a few years later, Lev Kritsman vividly recalled police raids at Sukharevka:

[37] *Kooperatsiia*, June 14, 1919, p. 2, cited in Borrero, *Hungry Moscow*, 177; Dmitrenko, "Nekotorye itogi," 232.

The symbol of the ineradicability of the illegal commoditized economy was "Sukharevka," an enormous market square, perpetually black with thick crowds of people, in Moscow, the very center of the severe proletarian dictatorship. This was the site of an extraordinarily intensive trade in absolutely everything, and especially in foods supposedly under control of the state monopoly. It was an underground trade, with cautious, furtive glances, interrupted from time to time by noisy raids, which, though accompanied by shots in the air, shouts, and commotion, accomplished nothing more than the temporary relocation of the trade, most often no further than to another section of the same enormous Sukharev Square.[38]

Kritsman's recollection notwithstanding, for some vendors, the consequences of a raid could be unpleasant. A police roundup at the flea market in Nizhnii Novgorod, for example, took an approach that would become common during the Stalin years: four hundred hawkers were detained for questioning, after which anyone with an undesirable social profile (deserters, a group that figured particularly prominently in descriptions of civil war markets; "idlers," criminals, etc.) was arrested and sent to jail.[39] Such repression could backfire. When the risk of arbitrary police action became too great, peasants stopped marketing the foods that were still eligible for private sales, which in turn provoked central government organs to refute "nonsensical rumors" about an imminent ban on all trade, and to prohibit the closing of bazaars.[40] The response of central policy makers to overzealous policing indicated that, even in their eyes, the market remained a necessary component of distribution throughout the civil war period.

Complicating the question of the status of the markets was the universally acknowledged fact that "trade at the bazaars went far beyond the narrow boundaries of legal trade."[41] Non-monopolized foods, including such staples as potatoes, vegetable oil, dairy products, and fish, were certainly sold in large quantities, but so, too, were grain and other supposedly monopolized foods. Some bazaars sheltered traffic in ration coupons, organized either by food administrators or by private individuals who had managed to obtain extras.[42] Many, if not most, of the manufactured goods that were sold at the market were first stolen from state

[38] L. N. Kritsman, *Geroicheskii period velikoi russkoi revoliutsii* (Moscow, 1924), 137–38.

[39] GARF, f. 130, op. 3, d. 415, l. 95ob. On soldiers and market trade, cf. Mary McAuley, *Bread and Justice: State and Society in Petrograd, 1917–1922* (Oxford, 1991), 282.

[40] Ustinov, *Evoliutsiia vnutrennei torgovli*, 37–38; Dmitrenko, "Bor'ba sovetskogo gosudarstva," 320–21; Lenin, *PSS*, 37:422–3.

[41] Ustinov, *Evoliutsiia vnutrennei torgovli*, 38–39.

[42] GARF, f. 393, op. 4, d. 34, l. 30; *Biulleten' MPK*, July 26, 1918.

agencies. Reviewing the situation in Ukraine in October 1920, Cheka
agents reported that "nearly all goods sold on the free market originate
in Soviet institutions. Petty speculation, expressed in petty bazaar sales, is
fueled almost exclusively by theft from transport or the transportation
agencies; large-scale speculation occurs in an organized manner between
RSFSR and Ukrainian SSR institutions, made possible by speculation in
all of the agencies' resources."[43] This constant refrain of Soviet officialdom during the civil war years contained more than a grain of truth.
Market raids always yielded up "treasury property," and thefts of cargo
were epidemic, declining only after the inauguration of the NEP.[44] Allegations about theft should nonetheless be kept in perspective. Not only
were workers paid wages in kind, with the expectation that they would
sell off or barter away the excess, artisanal manufacturing had always
been the mainstay of the production of consumer goods. After the revolution its proportional role increased, so that, by 1920, artisans were producing all furniture, 84 percent of clothes, and the large majority of most
other consumer articles. Naturally they very often sold their wares at the
market, though some small artisanal shops were allowed to remain open
as well.[45]

Did the bazaars evolve in an identifiable way between 1917 and 1921?
In his encyclopedic study of the Russian revolution, E. H. Carr suggested
that illegal market trade accounted for "an increasing proportion of the
internal distribution of goods in Soviet Russia" as the civil war progressed.[46] I have not seen the evidence for this assertion; on the contrary,
statistical data seem to point the other way. In 1918 nearly half the nationalized industrial enterprises were still marketing their products on a
private contractual basis, whereas, by 1920, market methods were the
exception.[47] With respect to food supplies, we also know that the state

[43] RGASPI, f. 5, op. 1, d. 2618, ll. 32–34; see also Groman's comments in *Trudy I.
Vserossiiskago S"ezda Sovetov Narodnago Khoziaistva* (Moscow, 1918), 433–44; M. Vladimirov,
Meshechnichestvo i ego sotsial'no-ekonomicheskie otrazheniia (Khar'kov, 1920), 9–11, 21; Fedorov, "Sukharevka—Krasnaia ploshchad'"; Kritsman, *Geroicheskii period*, 137–8; and numerous reports in *Sovetskaia derevnia glazami VChK-OGPU-NKVD*, vol. 1 (Moscow, 1998).

[44] *Trudy TsSU* 8 (4): 155.

[45] There were evidently 18,000 registered private shops in Moscow in December 1919,
of which 13,000 sold artisanal products and services, and 5,000 sold nonrationed foods
(including stalls and cafes at the market). The war communist fervor of 1920 caused this
number to dwindle to 3,736 traders plus 44 family assistants by July 1920. Dmitrenko,
"Bor'ba Sovetskogo gosudarstva," 315; idem, *Sovetskaia ekonomicheskaia politika*, 166; *Trudy
TsSU* 8 (7): 32–3.

[46] E. H. Carr, *The Bolshevik Revolution, 1917–1923*, 3 vols. (London, 1952), 2:244.

[47] *Trudy TsSU* 8 (2): 354.

procured more than four times more grain in 1920–21 than in 1917–18 and three times more than in 1918–19.[48] Still more telling are statistical estimates of the changing role of markets in the distribution of grain products and other foods. According to Kritsman, the role of the markets declined in workers' food budgets from 59 percent in 1918 to only 25 percent in 1920, and although the vast majority of townspeople continued to buy bread on the black market, a growing minority did not.[49] On the other hand, consumers in rural areas continued to buy nearly all their food at the bazaar, when they were unable to produce enough themselves.[50]

The qualitative evidence on bazaar trade paints a messier picture of change over time. Statements by Soviet officials suggest that, in 1918, bazaars, along with private and cooperative shops, were a principal source of foods and consumer goods in all parts of the country. After that year, reports registered contradictory tendencies. In some towns and districts (mainly in the north) bazaar trade partially dried up in 1919–20; in many others it flourished. To some extent, what happened in each region reflected the degree of repression there.[51] Insofar as any generalization can be made, police reports from 1920 suggest that the acquisition of new territory—the Soviet conquest of Ukraine, Siberia, and the lower Volga from the Whites—fueled private market trade as well as increasing the availability of food for the Soviet administration. These regions had not been subjected to Soviet trade policies and supported active markets; as a result, they were immediately flooded by consumers, private purchasers, and food-supply agents from the rest of the federation in search of marketable goods.[52]

In the end, policy makers came to recognize that the eradication strategy had its limits. On this theme, the Moscow-based diarist Got'e made an acute observation: the Bolsheviks did not want trade, represented after

---

[48] Arup Banerji, *Merchants and Markets in Revolutionary Russia, 1917–30* (New York, 1997), 206; Feigel'son, "Meshochnichestvo," 84; Dmitrenko, "Nekotorye itogi," 228.

[49] Kritsman, *Geroicheskii period*, 133–35; see also *Trudy TsSU* 8 (1): 16–17, 24–25; and *Trudy TsSU* 30 (1): 34–35.

[50] Dmitrenko, "Nekotorye itogi," 230–31; Kritsman, *Geroicheskii period*, 133–35.

[51] This point was made by R. I. Vaisberg, *Den'gi i tseny (Podpol'nyi rynok v period "voennogo kommunizma").* (Moscow, 1925), 36; see also GARF, f. 130, op. 3, d. 414, ll. 39–40; RGASPI, f. 5, op. 1, d. 2618, ll. 8–10.

[52] For an example, see R. A. Khaziev, "Rol' svobodnoi torgovli v ekonomike Bashkirii perioda 'voennogo kommunizma' (1919–1921 gg.)," *Vestnik Leningradskogo Universiteta*, series 2, no. 2 (1989): 85–87. This was also registered in the Urals, Minsk, Khar'kov, and Baku; cf. RGASPI, f. 5, op. 1, d. 2618, ll. 8–10, 32–34; d. 2458.

1918 mainly by the open-air markets, but neither did they want a "Suk-harevka [to] spring up on every corner and crossing," the inevitable con-sequence of sealing off the bazaars.[53] The logic of utilization, accordingly, continued to influence Bolshevik policy toward the markets long after the November 1918 decrees. Sukharevka itself was closed for a few months as of December 1920, but historians have probably read too much into that. Marguerite Harrison viewed the closing of Sukharevka as part of a pattern of vacillation:

> One week it would be legal, for instance, to sell meat, two weeks afterwards there would be a decree forbidding the sale of meat and a raid would be made on all meat dealers. It was the same with butter and many other things. In the late spring, the market on Okhotny Riad was closed and the booths torn down, but the Soukharevka was allowed to go on undisturbed. Still later all the small stores were closed, then they were opened and the Soukharevka closed. Finally, in the early part of March, 1921, after the decree permitting free trade, markets, stores and street booths were reopened once more. The policy of the government with regard to the regulation of private trade was so vacillating that no one knew exactly what was legal and what was not.[54]

This same vacillation was evident in the directives and counterdirectives in the provinces over the legality of bazaar trade, as well as in the attitude of Soviet authorities toward small service-sector businesses and artisanal shops. From late 1918 on, these three primitive forms of private enter-prise (bazaar trade, small service shops, and artisanal trade) constituted a gray area in the socialist economy. As discussed in later chapters, both this gray area and its periodic constriction turned out to be enduring legacies of the civil war.

The social effects of the war on the market were thus fraught with contradictions. In its earliest form, the Bolsheviks' anti-trade policy was little more than a proxy for the class war against Russia's "bourgeoisie." Yet practice revealed that the most "bourgeois" among the prerevolu-tionary merchants were best positioned to withstand the Bolshevik as-sault. Two avenues proved most profitable: the relatively secure route of employment in the socialist economy or the riskier route of underground trade. The former, however, was open only to those who could pass themselves off as experts—which tended to mean a more prosperous group. Petty traders, from the Jewish pedlars and artisans of Belorussia to small shopkeepers everywhere—hardly "bourgeois" by economic cri-teria—had few choices besides the semi-legal and illegal trade at the

---

[53] Got'e, *Time of Troubles*, 304.
[54] Harrison, *Marooned in Moscow*, 154; and see also Borrero, *Hungry Moscow*, 185.

markets. Their plight was a common one; and ultimately it made the Bolsheviks' anti-trade policy no match for the bazaar.

The bazaars of the revolutionary period served the combined functions of farmers' markets, flea markets, and markets for stolen goods, but they were also the retail outlets for a rudimentary form of wholesale trade. The acquisition of new territory in 1919 threw the distinguishing feature of this commerce into relief. Not only were the newly Sovietized regions inundated with procurement agents and the gamut of unofficial buyers, each addition of territory opened up routes to a new hinterland for possible contraband ventures. Inhabitants of Tsaritsyn and Astrakhan provinces did a lively border trade with the Don and Kuban until those regions were subdued. Eastern Siberians traversed Russia's porous border with Manchuria. From the northwest, Russians streamed into the newly independent Baltic countries. Constantinople was a major entrepot for Russian trade throughout the civil war years, as was Tiflis, not conquered by the Bolsheviks until February 1921. Markets in the "near abroad" overflowed with sugar, glassware, textiles, shoes, electric lamps, medicines, technical instruments, and agricultural machinery for avid Russian buyers.[55]

Bazaars inside the Soviet federation became the terminus for a petty wholesale trade built on individual travels within and across the constantly changing Soviet borders. Termed "bagging" [*meshochnichestvo*], such travels linked regions with a surplus of a given commodity to regions where that commodity was scarce. They had their origins in the 1916–17 shortages of manufactured goods, which led provincial consumers to travel to Moscow and Petrograd to buy cloth. The deepening of the food crisis reversed the flow of travel between the center and the periphery. By mid-1917, despite the Provisional Government's best efforts,[56] bagging had surged to massive proportions. Nor did it decline under the Bolsheviks. Surveys from the winter of 1917–18 showed that 40 percent of the population of Kaluga *guberniia* and 80 percent of peasants in Kostroma had taken journeys to buy or sell grain, and approximately 30,000 residents of Petrograd made their living from bagging. At the receiving end, such grain-surplus provinces as Kursk, Tambov, Simbirsk, Saratov, Kazan', and Viatka were besieged by 100,000 or 150,000

[55] RGASPI, f. 5, op. 1, d. 2618, ll. 8–10, 32–34; d. 2368; Carl W. Ackerman, *Trailing the Bolsheviki* (New York, 1919), 46; A. Iu. Davydov, "Meshochnichestvo i sovetskaia prodovol'stvennaia diktatura, 1918–1922," *Voprosy istorii*, no. 3 (1994): 41–54; here, 45.

[56] See *The Russian Provisional Government, 1917: Documents* (Stanford, 1961), 2: 703; *Sistematicheskii sbornik dekretov*, 122–23.

baggers a month. These numbers may have leveled off as food supplies in the north improved, but as late as January 1921 a Voronezh newpaper reported that 20,000 baggers were transporting an average of eight *puds* (288 lbs) apiece along a 160-kilometer segment of track each day.[57]

The trade routes for the unofficial grain trade were determined by railway lines and the military situation. Before the summer of 1918, when the civil war cut off the granaries of Ukraine, Siberia, and the North Caucasus from Soviet Russia, baggers spread out from the industrial north in all directions. For example, from Kostroma *guberniia* in north-central Russia, according to an early 1918 study, nearly half the baggers had journeyed to Omsk, some twenty-three hundred kilometers to the east. Of the remainder, approximately half had traveled to the east-central grain provinces Viatka and Simbirsk; only one-fourth of the total number had ventured south.[58] After the front lines hardened, the grain trade operated mainly along a north-south axis, though Viatka and Simbirsk remained important destinations.

Bagging has ordinarily been discussed in reference to the unofficial grain trade, but grain was by no means its only object. Contraband runners dealt in everything under the sun. Within Soviet Russia, tsarist money, gold, and foreign currency were the object of innumerable profit-oriented trips.[59] Although it is impossible to reconstruct a commercial route for currency, which moved erratically with the flow of soldiers and refugees, at least two commodities did generate regular bagging circuits comparable to those of the grain trade. A specialized bagging trade developed around low-grade tobacco [*makhorka*], grown in certain districts of Riazan' and Tambov *gubernii* and in the Volga German *oblast'* and prepared by peasant artisans there. Like grain, tobacco could be transported in relative bulk in 150-pound sacks and resold in small quantities for a profit. Since tobacco was never as much of a regime priority as grain, measures to quell this trade were even less effective. Through 1919, police reports indicated that producers had no choice but to sell to the baggers, since the state had sent hardly any buyers of its own.[60]

Salt, also a bulk commodity, was another major item around which a separate bagging circuit coalesced. Its route followed the Volga; efforts to combat it began in August 1920, several months after the full length of

[57] Kritsman, *Geroicheskii period*, 135; Kondrat'ev, *Rynok khlebov*, 308; Feigel'son, "Meshochnichestvo," 78; Orlando Figes, *A People's Tragedy: A History of the Russian Revolution* (New York, 1996), 611; Banerji, *Merchants and Markets*, 27; Dmitrenko, "Nekotorye itogi," 236.

[58] Feigel'son, "Meshochnichestvo," 78.

[59] GARF, f. 130, op. 3, d. 414, ll. 150b; d. 415 l. 950b.; RGASPI, f. 5, op. 1, d. 2618, ll. 8–10, 32–34.

[60] GARF, f. 393, op. 1, d. 37, l. 34; RGASPI, f. 5, op. 1, d. 2615, ll. 4–20.

the river was reunified under Soviet rule. This trade was fabulously profitable. In December 1920 a *pud* (36 pounds) of salt, which sold for between eight hundred and nine hundred rubles in Astrakhan, fetched from thirty thousand to forty thousand rubles in Nizhnii Novgorod or Kazan'. With this incentive, salt running became the primary source of income for peasants as far as one hundred kilometers from the river. In Tsaritsyn a "significant percentage" of the urban population was also said to be involved. The extent of this commerce can be glimpsed from the results of a raid on the "Red Star" steamer: in one night nearly two tons of salt were confiscated from the ship's passengers. Not surprisingly the profits to be made upriver created shortages in Astrakhan, where fisheries relied on abundant cheap salt.[61]

What was the economic impact of bagging? The impact on the urban market, and on the grain-deficit regions more generally, was mixed. Without a doubt, bagging disrupted an already overburdened and dysfunctional transportation system. We have no reliable estimates of this impact, but it is obvious that a freight car filled with baggers and their bags could transport less food than a car filled exclusively with grain. At a time when the country was desperately short of rolling stock, such inefficiency in the use of transportation was costly.

The picture looks rather different, though, from the perspective of results. From the beginning of 1918 through the summer of 1919 baggers are estimated to have procured 25 percent more than the official food-supply apparatus, and they continued to play an enormous role as the civil war dragged on. As late as the winter of 1919–20 official agencies supplied less than 10 percent of the food sold in at least three northern provinces.[62] Under the circumstances, as Ustinov wrote in 1925,

> the population was compelled to resort to the "free market," without worrying about the fact that it was an illegal market and that by doing so they encouraged "bagging." It is true that the baggers significantly obstructed the work of the Commissariat of Food Supplies and made it less productive. The result was a vicious circle. Nonetheless, the population was pressed by famine; it could not simply wait passively until the state supply apparatus became effective enough to render the expensive and clumsy baggers unnecessary.[63]

When the Bolsheviks considered this problem, however, they viewed the baggers' success in terms of a zero-sum game. As they understood mat-

[61] *Krasnaia gazeta*, December 25, 1920. See also RGASPI, f. 5, op. 1, d. 2618, ll. 32–34; M. Alexander Schwartz, *The Voice of Russia* (New York, 1921), 127–28.

[62] Dikhtiar, *Torgovlia* II, 130; Feigel'son, "Meshochnichestvo," 79, 84; Dmitrenko, "Nekotorye itogi," 231.

[63] Ustinov, *Evoliutsiia vnutrennei torgovli*, 41.

ters, every ounce procured by unofficial means was one ounce less for the socialist economy. Economic theory would lead us to reject their interpretation; according to the classical model, the baggers should have been able to extract more grain (or salt or tobacco) than state purchasers could, as the higher prices that they offered would have occasioned a shift upward on the supply curve. This model, of course, omits coercion; the question remains whether, or to what extent, coercion counteracted the market forces inhibiting sales at the state price.

Bolshevik or not, virtually every commentator agreed with Kondrat'ev's assessment that the substitution of baggers for the capitalist wholesale system amounted to the "degradation of trade."[64] The war on the market did not elevate trade to a higher level of social and economic organization; rather, it replaced a modern system for the large-scale movement of goods with an archaic system based on individual movements of people. Kondrat'ev's negative appraisal was echoed in a number of publications from the NEP era. Kritsman focused on retailers, who became, he alleged, "less qualified" in the move from the shop to the bazaar.[65] Ustinov emphasized the moral blows to the trade sector: "Compelled to resort to all kinds of subterfuge, the trade apparatus became corrupted and depraved."[66] As a caveat, dishonesty was hardly alien to the traditions of Russian commerce; foreign travelers had commented on it for more than three hundred years.[67] What made the unscrupulous exchange culture of the civil war period so uniquely unsettling was its context: life-threatening scarcity, communist moral sensibilities and revolutionary policies, and the fact that "speculation" was no longer confined to the prerevolutionary merchant class.

THE CRISIS MODE OF CONSUMPTION

The dislocations that accompanied war and revolution fundamentally altered consumption habits. As early as February 1917 the panicked reaction of the Petrograd crowds to the bread and flour shortage showcased behaviors that would prove reflexive in subsequent years. Huge lines, mostly of women, gathered outside bakeries. Crowds shattered some windows and sacked a few bread shops when supplies ran out. Residents

---

[64] Kondrat'ev, *Rynok khlebov*, 307–10.

[65] Kritsman, *Geroicheskii period*, 142.

[66] Ustinov, *Evoliutsiia vnutrennei torgovli*, 21, 25,

[67] For a précis of travelers' accounts of Russian merchants from 1571 through the mid-nineteenth century, see J. Patouillet, *Ostrovski et son théatre de moeurs russes* (Paris, 1912), 99–100.

dried bread in their ovens to create private hoards in the form of hard rusks. One week before the tsar's abdication, bread queues, characterized by the security police as a breeding ground for revolution, stood over-night in subzero temperatures. In this setting, rumors both fed on and fueled mass hysteria. It is hard to imagine that Petrograd residents had not developed flour reserves for this kind of emergency; in Moscow an investigation of working-class life in the early 1920s revealed that vir-tually every household had amassed grain and flour for the previous eight years. That consumers chose to spend all night in queues in minus 30- to 40-degree temperatures instead of using their reserves testifies to their lack of faith in the ability of either the market or the government to regularize supplies. In part, the disruption of consumer behaviors was thus a by-product of the declining legitimacy of the tsarist establishment, though it certainly also reflected the reliance of lower-class consumers on access to affordable bread.[68]

Hoarding and queuing became universal activities as the economic crisis intensified. In Saratov, in the heart of the grain belt, diarist Alexis Babine recorded how shopping came to dominate everyday life. Within six weeks of the Bolshevik takeover Babine was arriving at his local bak-ery at 5:00 A.M., two hours before it opened, in order to purchase a loaf or two of white bread. Ten months later he recorded spending three to four hours each morning in line for black rye bread, the only kind avail-able.[69] Queues formed for other basic necessities as well:

October 15, 1918. A young woman felt jubilant yesterday because during the day she had obtained meat, jam, and salt by having stood all day in three successive lines. My hosts are spending most of their time hunting for provi-sions, in bread, meat, and other provision lines, and cooking and washing dishes. Their work—teaching and hospital duties—is at present a mere side issue with them.

November 7, 1918. The system of bread, produce, and other lines is firmly established. The nation unproductively wastes an immense amount of time in obtaining the supplies that have been removed from the market to please the despotic rulers' socialist fancies. No butter, cheese, bacon, sausage, sugar, honey, meat, eggs are to be had in the face of a great abundance of these items in the country. People still have to get up at 3 A.M. in order to get near enough

[68] See E. N. Burdzhalov, *Russia's Second Revolution: The February 1917 Uprising in Pet-rograd,* trans. and ed. Donald J. Raleigh (Bloomington, 1987), 103–4; George Katkov, *Russia 1917* (New York, 1967), 249–50; Tsuyoshi Hasegawa, *The February Revolution* (Seat-tle, 1981), 198–202; Figes, *A People's Tragedy,* 307. On grain hoards, see E. O. Kabo, *Ocherki rabochego byta. Opyt monograficheskogo issledovaniia* (Moscow, 1928), 149–56.
[69] Alexis Babine, *A Russian Civil War Diary* (Durham, N.C., 1988), 32–34, 112.

to the head of lines for kerosene, meat, linseed oil, and other items, and frequently go home empty handed.[70]

Queues generally formed before daybreak, though occasionally unsatisfied customers took numbers at the end of the day. They were the diarist's main source of news, not all of it reliable, about the course of the civil war, conditions in other parts of the country, and impending shipments of goods. Queues could also be a site of disputes over places in line or the size or cut of meat.[71] Although they certainly fostered grumbling, queues do not appear to have been the breeding ground for rebellion in civil war Saratov, as the Okhrana had feared of the Petrograd queues back in February 1917.

If Babine's experience in Saratov led him to paint a fairly uniform picture of queues, correspondent Bessie Beatty observed that the demographics and sociability of queues varied according to their object. In Petrograd, where she lived in 1917–18, queues for bread and kerosene were made up of "working-women, servants, a few students, and schoolchildren," who occupied the long waits with homework, crocheting, and complaints about the high cost of living. Queues for tobacco, dominated by soldiers, were more jocular, an attribute Beatty ascribed to the soldiers' expectation of profitable resale. Students and scalpers formed the main contingents in the theater ticket lines, the liveliest queues of the revolutionary period; here, "the students chatted gaily of the soprano Z., or the feet of the ballerina X.," while the scalpers remained silent. Queues for chocolate attracted men and women of the bourgeoisie, who bemoaned the current situation in Russia; and, finally, queues for streetcars—the most aggressive lines that Beatty observed—consisted of teachers, clerks, businessmen, students, and low-ranking officials, all anxious to push their way into a car. Beatty also noted a change over time in queue etiquette: in early 1917 mothers with babies were allowed to go to the head of the line without waiting, but this privilege became untenable as women began hiring children to shorten the wait.[72]

Even in small towns in provincial Russia, queues played an important role in provisionment. Emma Ponafidine, an American who married into the Russian provincial gentry in 1896 and spent the revolutionary years on or near the family estate, recorded long waits at the local cooperative for matches, kerosene, salt, and soap. By the end of 1917 this was all that could be purchased at a regular store in the nearest market town, and although additional goods were available through irregular traders, many

[70] Ibid., 112, 119.
[71] Ibid., 34, 36, 46, 68, 116.
[72] Bessie Beatty, *The Red Heart of Russia* (New York, 1918), 316–19.

articles, including pens, buttons, and medicines, could not be obtained at all.[73] Like other memoirists of the period, Ponafidine listened in on conversations in queues as a way of gauging public opinion. In the backwoods of Tver' *guberniia*, these conversations gave her the impression that everyone was completely preoccupied with the economic crisis. As she wrote in a letter dated December 1, 1917, "One never hears talk of the war or politics, only bread, bread, bread!" Five months later she recorded an overheard discussion in which peasants expressed some regret, in light of the food crisis, over having broken up her family's productive dairy farm.[74] The tendency of Ponafidine, and other foreigners, to gauge public sentiment by the temper of the queues was shared by Russian security organs from the First World War through at least the 1960s; in the absence of more reliable indicators of public opinion, queues, and bread queues in particular, would remain a key source of information for the Soviet regime.

It is impossible to evaluate their conclusions regarding the effects of consumer difficulties on popular opinion with anything resembling accuracy. Two issues have divided historians: the extent to which Soviet society internalized an "entitlement" mentality and the attitudes of citizens toward baggers and petty trade. With respect to the latter, my reading of the evidence supports the view of Davydov and Feigel'son, as against McAuley and Lih, that ordinary Russians [*obyvateli*] repudiated the war on the market. Public sympathy for the baggers appears in several speeches and publications from the period. One Komprod spokesman wrote in 1920 that peasants resented the harassment of baggers, since so many seemed to be driven by hunger and desperation. Another reported that workers openly identified with the baggers, on the grounds that bagging was the only way to make ends meet. Lenin himself expressed frustration over intellectuals' defense of petty traders: "More and more frequently we have to listen to [this criticism] from the intelligentsia: 'but the baggers are rendering us a service, they are the ones feeding everyone.'"[75]

[73] Emma Cochran Ponafidine, *Russia—My Home* (Indianapolis, 1931), 102, 148–49, 150, 154.

[74] Ibid., 140, 148–49. Other memoirs citing public opinion as heard in the queue include Beatty, *Red Heart of Russia*, 316–20; Sir Paul Dukes, *Red Dusk and the Morrow* (Garden City, 1922), 45.

[75] See Feigel'son, "Meshochnichestvo," 73–75; Davydov, "Meshochnichestvo," 49–50; Lih, *Bread and Authority*, 169–71; McAuley, *Bread and Justice*, 299–304; Daniel R. Brower, "'The City in Danger': The Civil War and the Russian Urban Population," in Diane Koenker, William G. Rosenberg, and Ronald Grigor Suny, eds., *Party, State, and Society in the Russian Civil War* (Bloomington, 1989), 58–80; here, 77; see also Vladimirov, *Mes-*

Public solidarity with the baggers can also be discerned in the archives
of the Commissariat of Internal Affairs. According to this agency's infor-
mants, the paramilitary groups charged with policing the baggers [*za-
graditel'nye otriady*, or railroad chekas] had chronic problems with morale.
In Tula *guberniia*, for example, a review of bagging identified police re-
calcitrance as the principal reason why illegal trafficking continued to
grow. The provincial capital's 250-person railway detachment fled in the
summer of 1918, "because it didn't want to take measures to fight bagging," while, at another station, a railroad brigade informed its commissar that "our job is not to requisition grain, but to guard bridges and
stations, and to protect employees." Similar reports came in from Orel
guberniia, where one 200-man squad actually took to drinking with the
incoming baggers, preventing both railway workers and other police
units from harassing them.[76] This is only one side of the coin—the Commissariat also reported numerous clashes between baggers and the railway guards, in which confiscations had "the quality of armed robbery,"
and recourse to a "bacchanalia of shooting" or "unorganized, unnecessary terror" was practically routine.[77] Still, the incidence of reported resistance to the anti-bagging measures suggests that solidarity with the baggers did hamper enforcement on the ground.

Without an adequate number of subjective accounts, it is similarly
difficult to judge whether, as some historians have suggested, war communism inculcated a psychology of dependency vis-à-vis material needs.[78]
Diarists Babine and Got'e did not evince this attitude; although both
men accepted such perquisites as the state's system of allocations apportioned them, both viewed fixed-price food rations as a shameful symbol
of their own, and the country's, impoverishment, and also of a regime
they despised. They were, however, middle-aged anticommunist intellectuals, whose experiences differed from those of other social groups.
D. Kh. Ibragimova, who has studied letters to the peasant newspaper
Krest'ianskaia gazeta in 1923–24, has concluded that a sizable group of
peasants did exhibit an entitlement mentality, but an equally large number of correspondents appeared self-reliant and oriented toward the market.[79] A study of children's attitudes, undertaken over the decade following the revolution, is also revealing. Asked to describe their favorite
activities, the children of the civil war era tended to come up with such

bechnichestvo, 12; Vasil'ev, *Natsionalizatsiia vnutrennei torgovli*, 7–8; Lenin, *PSS*, 36:407; Orlov, *Deviat' mesiatsev*, 68–69; idem, *Sistema prodovol'stvennoi zagotovki* (Tambov, 1920).
[76] GARF, f. 393 op. 1, d. 55, ll. 4–6, 31; d. 56, l. 1.
[77] Ibid., l. 5; d. 63, l. 21; d. 83, ll. 4–11.
[78] McAuley, *Bread and Justice*, 304.
[79] D. Kh. Ibragimova, *NEP i perestroika* (Moscow, 1997).

answers as "eat, and drink tea with sugar" and "stand in line when the women are cursing"—but also "speculate" and "sell things at the market."[80]

The one conclusion we can draw with certainty is that a psychology of dependency did not constrain citizens' actions. For all the importance of queues to popular consumption during the revolutionary period, scarcity did not induce passivity; rather, it forced citizens to exercise initiative in their own provisionment through unauthorized self-help. Not only did citizens buy food, fuel, and other necessities from baggers on the illegal market, they also took direct measures to supply themselves with essential consumer goods. Russian villagers and, to a lesser degree, townspeople responded to galloping inflation and the shortages of manufactured goods by expanding their home production: they grew vegetables in kitchen gardens, wove cloth on handlooms, and fashioned harnesses, furniture, and agricultural implements in rough workshops at home.[81] They also participated in the rampant theft, which, along with artisanal production and trips to the countryside, was a basic technique of self-help employed by the urban population. In Khar'kov *guberniia*, for example, a survey of economic trends indicated that theft rates had reached 40 percent of output in the textile industry and 50 percent in food processing in 1920. The introduction of bonuses in kind in April 1921 brought these rates down, but, until then, neither propaganda nor punishment had any discernible effect. As the report noted, "under the circumstances, when 99 percent of workers were engaged in theft, the pronouncements of the Disciplinary Courts did not make a big moral impression."[82]

The fuel crisis, which extended across the revolutionary period, gave rise to particularly vivid manifestations of "self-provisionment" [*samosnabzhenie*]. Rather surprisingly, heating materials were omitted from the state monopoly when other necessities were nationalized in the summer and autumn of 1918. Until February 1920 municipal fuel committees concluded contracts directly with suppliers and distributed the fuel—usually firewood—to institutional and individual consumers on their own authority.[83] Institutions had priority; but throughout the civil

[80] S. A. Zolotarev, *Chetyre smeny molodezhi (1905–1925)* (Leningrad, 1926), 82. Children and youths played an active role in the black market, to judge from the number of juvenile arrests for speculation, pickpocketing, and ration-card crimes. Cf. *Trudy TsSU* 8 (2): 95.

[81] See Figes, *People's Tragedy*, 608–9; Brower, "'City in Danger'"; Dikhtiar, *Torgovlia* II, 131.

[82] *Otchet Khar'kovskogo gubernskogo ekonomicheskogo soveshchaniia za 1. ianvaria–1 oktiabria 1921 g.* (Khar'kov, 1921), 91.

[83] *Sistematicheskii sbornik dekretov*, 202; Orlov, *Deviat' mesiatsev*, 213–21; Malle, *Economic Organization*, 221–22.

war era official supplies could barely maintain a "hunger ration" for each class of consumer.[84] Diarist Got'e spent an inordinate amount of his time securing firewood for Moscow's Rumiantsev Museum, which he directed. Even on those rare occasions when an official shipment arrived at the railway station, delivery remained stalled until the museum coughed up "a certain rather small quantity of tobacco, salt, matches, and cigarettes" to the haulers or, in another instance, until museum employees themselves unloaded the wood. A notable fuel source for the museum was a speculator who doubled as a member of the railroad cheka.[85]

Particularly in the capitals, private citizens found it nearly impossible to keep their apartments heated. Small woodburning stoves known as "bourgeois ladies" [*boorzhuiki*] became standard equipment in every household in the northern cities, which had previously relied on coal and gas, but there was still the problem of obtaining wood. As Got'e wrote in November 1919, "The problem of food supplies overshadows everything else except the problem of heating." During the worst cold snaps, such as November 1919 or February 1920, temperatures dropped below zero both at work and at home.[86] Marguerite Harrison, the American correspondent, described how a private person would go about obtaining fuel through official channels in Moscow in 1920, after the formal nationalization of supplies:

> To procure the wood was a matter of time and endless formalities. First it was necessary to have a Trudovaia Knizhka, or workers' book, showing where the applicant for wood was employed. . . . [I]t was also necessary, in order to secure wood, to have an order from your place of employment which was to be presented at the regional office of the Moscow Fuel Committee and exchanged for an order signed by the committee, after which you had to wait until there was a distribution of fuel in your region, then go to the appointed place, stand in line and wait your turn for fuel. Sometimes, if you were not early, the supply gave out and you were obliged to come back another day.[87]

The friend who made Harrison privy to this process had to haul the wood home, for which urbanites typically used a sled; chop it into the desired lengths in his courtyard; and lug it up four flights of stairs. The official allocation was sufficient to heat one stove for just three months; putative nationalization notwithstanding, the majority of this man's firewood came from private sources, purchased through agreements with peasants or with private wood agents in town. Having arrived in Moscow

[84] Cf. *Krasnaia gazeta*, May 15, 1920.
[85] Got'e, *Time of Troubles*, 313, 317, 375–76.
[86] Ibid., 316–17, 337–39.
[87] Harrison, *Marooned in Moscow*, 95–96.

after the February 1920 nationalization of firewood, Harrison did not observe open wood sales at Moscow's markets. Before this time memoirists reported that each market in the capitals had a fuel section with huge piles of wood.[88]

In addition to commercial sources, citizens obtained fuel by denuding the landscape. In the countryside the seizure of woodlots was among the peasants' first revolutionary actions against the gentry estates. Given Russia's huge expanses of forests, however, the fuel shortage, like the food crisis, mainly affected residents of the big cities. Petrograd and Moscow became as barren as no-man's land in 1919–20; in Ukraine the port city Nikolaev lost the trees along its central boulevards in just two days. An even more characteristic practice was the dismantling of streets (paved with wooden paving blocks) and wooden houses for use as firewood; some three thousand such houses (just over four a day) were torn down in 1919–20 in Petrograd alone.[89] The fuel shortages also gave rise to black humor: one routine by Moscow's favorite clown of the period, Bim Bum, featured difficulties in obtaining wood.[90]

The replacement of capitalist trade with smaller-scale, more participatory forms elicited the most common forms of self-help. As A. A. Goldenveizer quipped, "The nationalization of trade means that the whole nation trades."[91] At open-air markets former merchants were joined not just by peasants and baggers but by soldiers trading uniforms for loaves of bread, aristocrats selling off silk dresses, gramophones, and gilt clocks, and even workers, who, according to 1918–20 budget investigations, earned 25 to 30 percent of their income through occasional sales. Workers and other urban *survivors*, to adopt Daniel Brower's term, sold off used clothes and household goods, articles produced or stolen for the purpose of barter, and wildfowl and furs that they had illegally trapped.[92] Railway workers were exceptionally active in this trade by virtue of their access to transportation, as were textile workers by virtue of their access to cloth. In Kiev and Khar'kov these two cohorts were earning fully two-

[88] Ibid., 46–47; 82; 95–96; Vladimir Koudrey, *Once a Commissar* (New Haven, 1937), 53.

[89] Figes, *People's Tragedy*, 604; Got'e, *Time of Troubles*, 280; H. G. Wells, *Russia in the Shadows* (New York, 1921), frontispiece.

[90] Harrison, *Marooned in Moscow*, 166–67.

[91] Cited in Brower, "'City in Danger,'" 69.

[92] S. G. Strumilin, *Zarabotnaia plata i proizvoditel'nost' truda v russkoi promyshlennosti za 1913–1922 g.* (Moscow, 1923), 29; *Biudzhety rabochikh i sluzhashchikh*, vol. 1: *Biudzhety rabochei sem'i za 1922–27 gg.* (Moscow, 1929), 22. In terms of cash income, the role of market sales would have been much higher, especially in 1920. Total income figures included the value of foods and other goods received in kind.

thirds of their income from trade in 1920.[93] The near-total demonetization of wages also played a role in that year. If nationalization advocate S. Vasil'ev was already concerned about the social-psychological effects of the mass exposure to petty marketing in 1918, by 1920 Lenin publicly fretted that "in the soul and actions of every petty proprietor" (a Bolshevik synonym for "peasant") was a "little Sukharevka."[94]

Both men exaggerated the novelty of this experience. Rural or urban, nearly all workers and artisans, and many peasants, had occasionally purchased used clothes in the prerevolutionary period. In the lower-income brackets, used clothes were the norm, while individuals in the lowest bracket of all were caught up in a cycle of selling their shoes to purchase a more ragged pair but also a pair of trousers, or selling trousers to buy a shirt. Sales of clothes and miscellaneous household items did not add a tremendous amount to the family income in 1908–13—between 1 and 4 percent in the average budget, as against 25 percent or more during the civil war—but both selling used possessions at the bazaar and shopping for them were familiar enough activities to urban Russians of the lower classes.[95] In this respect the dislocation of trade after the revolution must have been much less shocking to these groups—the overwhelming majority of urban consumers—than to their social superiors.

Budget studies offer some quantitative evidence on changes in consumption over the revolutionary period. In Moscow the average working-class household spent 71 percent of its outlays on food in 1918, as against 45 to 60 percent before the war. Other expenditures went to clothes and shoes (8%, down from 14 to 15%), now almost invariably used; lodging and fuel (6%, though they had increased to 15% by 1921); books and newspapers (2%); hygiene (3%); and packages and monetary gifts to relatives (4%); a mere 7 percent went to everything else.[96] These structural changes were accompanied by a striking deterioration in the quality of the two main items, foods and clothing, from a degree of variety and plenty to a starvation diet and worn-out clothes.[97] The report of a

[93] Dmitrenko, "Nekotorye itogi," 241; and on railwaymen, see also Robert Argenbright, "Bolsheviks, Baggers, and Railroaders: *Political Power and Social Space, 1917–1921" Russian Review* 52 (October, 1993): 506–27; I. S. Kondurushkin, *Chastnyi kapital pered sovetskim sudom* (Moscow, 1927), 9; GARF f. 130, op. 3, d. 415, 46–47; RGASPI, f. 5, op. 1, d. 2618, ll. 8–10; ll. 32–4.

[94] Vasil'ev, *Natsionalizatsiia vnutrennei torgovli*, 7–8; Lenin, *PSS*, 42:158.

[95] N. K. Druzhin, A. D. Bok, and E. G. Diukova, *Usloviia byta rabochikh v dorevoliutsionnoi Rossii* (Moscow, 1958), 29, 50–51, 122–23.

[96] *Statistika truda* nos. 1–4 (January/February 1919): 1–5.

[97] See E. O. Kabo, *Pitanie russkogo rabochego do i posle voiny (po statisticheskim materialam 1908–1924 gg.* (Moscow, 1926); and Druzhin, Bok, and Diukova, *Usloviia byta.*

provincial correspondent on labor statistics in Mtsensk *uezd* (Orel *guber-niia*), described this consumption cycle with pathos: expenditures greatly exceeded incomes, with the sole exception of well-paid bachelors; workers covered the deficit by trading with peasants and curtailing expenditures beyond survival needs. Food consisted of little more than rye bread and cabbage soup; new clothes were a pipe dream; nonfood expenditures were limited to absolutely unavoidable expenses like shoe repair or—in an extreme case—the purchase of a pair of secondhand shoes. "The everyday life of today's worker," the correspondent concluded, "is enough to make one weep."[98]

The Bolsheviks were nonetheless quite proud of certain changes in urban household budgets in 1918–19, notably the near-complete elimination of vodka from lower-class expenditures; the decline in payment of church tithes; and a small increase in purchases of newspapers and books. Even as sober a sociologist as S. G. Strumilin saw in these changes evidence of the revolution's salutary effect on working-class "culture," though, in the case of vodka, the drop in consumption dated to the tsar's wartime prohibition.[99] These were not the only structural changes on which the Bolsheviks could put a positive spin. For example, metropolitan workers' reduced expenditures on public transportation were attributed rhetorically to the lower cost of a streetcar ticket, when, in fact, workers spent less mainly because they could get a streetcar only half as often as before the war.[100] Rents, which had consumed 12 to 16 percent of prewar budgets, were more justifiably the subject of Bolshevik propaganda. When they municipalized urban buildings, Soviet officials did bring about an amelioration for lower-income families by sharply reducing the real cost of rent. Was the increased proportion of expenditures devoted to food, then, merely a reflection of the disappearance of rent and vodka, the second and fourth major items of prewar urban budgets? Unfortunately the answer is no, as lighting and especially heating materials—mainly wood and kerosene—functionally replaced lodging in the budget as the civil war progressed.[101]

It is important to note, however, that the economic crisis created winners as well as losers. Until the 1921 famine bagging was a bonanza for

[98] *Statistika truda*, nos. 5–7 (March 1–April 15, 1919): 40; see also Strumilin, *Zarabotnaia plata*, 31.

[99] Strumilin, *Zarabotnaia plata*, 26–27. As a caveat, the increased expenditures on "culture" (newspapers and books) was observed in 1918 budget studies of Moscow and Petrograd, which one would expect to have become more politicized during the revolution than provincial towns.

[100] Ibid., 25–26.

[101] Ibid., 24–25; see also *Biudzhety rabochikh*, 1:27.

the more fertile regions of the country. Baggers not only inflated the market price of grain and other foodstuffs, they provided agricultural producers with coveted manufactured goods. Without coercion at their disposal, the baggers could extract grain from the peasantry only by offering something attractive in exchange. Through the middle of 1918 calico cloth often substituted for cash.[102] As the terms of trade shifted further in favor of food over manufactured goods, barter equivalents became more valuable and elaborate. According to a 1919 study of what Kostroma baggers offered in exchange for grain, salt, and cotton cloth, the first equivalents, soon gave way to soap, kerosene, tobacco, and used clothes. By mid-1918 tea, coffee, sugar, and hard candies; expensive cloth; jackets, trousers, and shawls; and pocketwatches were the items of choice. Six months later the baggers had graduated to offering beds, sewing machines, gramophones, riding equipment, and samovars.[103] The collapse of agricultural and industrial production thus affected the population unevenly, occasioning a sharp decline in the material well-being of urban consumers of all classes vis-à-vis peasants and of residents of the less fertile north and northwest relative to residents of the more fertile south and east.

CONCLUSION

The Bolsheviks adopted their antimarket policies in the context of the civil war, which they had effectively begun with their October 1917 coup d'état. Remarkably, in this situation, Bolshevik leaders did not train their attention narrowly on winning the civil war but tried to bring about a social revolution at the same time. Trade policy was one prong of their revolutionary social strategy. The near-total elimination of private stores after November 1918 reflected the Bolsheviks' propensity for radical social action: what better time than when the economy was in shambles to strike a mortal blow against the bourgeoisie? Given the weakness of the socialist sector in late 1918, the decision to proceed from utilizing private trade to eradicating it conflicted with the Bolsheviks' responsibilities for civilian provisionment. Having inherited, and greatly expanded, a rationing system for basic consumer necessities, the Bolsheviks had become the custodians of a rudimentary welfare state. Protestations aside, the forcible closure of private stores when the socialist economy was incapable of

---

[102] *Biulleten' Moskovskogo Prodovol'stvennogo Komiteta*, July 16, 1918; Fedorov, "Sukharevka–Krasnaia ploshchad'," 23; Feigel'son, "Meshochnichestvo," 77.

[103] Feigel'son, "Meshochnichestvo," 77.

replacing them) showed that the Bolsheviks' social program of class warfare preempted other economic and social considerations.

The war on the market was prosecuted vigorously, but it proved unenforceable in both the short and long run. The closure of private stores was largely accomplished, but private commerce flourished in petty, primitive forms. Bazaar and street-corner hawking, foraging-*cum*-barter trips, low-grade artisanal manufactures and sales, and the peddling of services proliferated during this period as citizens sought a sustainable income against the escalating prices of basic goods. In 1920, in the flush of victory, Soviet officials in many northern and central localities tried to eradicate these last vestiges of the market economy. Their experiment failed, as did the initial stages of the war on the market in the newly reconquered peripheral parts of the empire. Soviet citizens proved capable of subsisting on minimum levels of consumption during the civil war years, but consumption was not so elastic that repression—itself haphazardly applied—could prevent them from looking after their needs via informal exchange. By the spring of 1921, Lenin, at least, had concluded that a strict anti-trade policy was unworkable. His declaration on the subject is worth quoting: "in this respect, we committed many errors [*ochen' mnogo pogreshili*] by going too far: we went too far in the direction of nationalizing trade and industry and in the direction of shutting down local sales. Was this a mistake? Without a doubt."[104]

The civil war period and its immediate aftermath constituted the first of three catastrophic economic crises in the first three decades of Soviet power. The second, from 1928 to 1933, was likewise precipitated by Soviet leaders' rash attempt to impose a revolution on Russian society; the third, by the entrance of the Soviet Union into the Second World War. The transformation of trade and consumption during the revolutionary epoch set a precedent for these later periods, as well as for the numerous localized famines and crises of the next thirty years. At the first sign of an emergency, Soviet citizens switched into a crisis mode of consumption, in which purchases of nonnecessities were eliminated and scruples about law-breaking set aside. With each crisis came a reprise of the "degradation" of the consumer economy that had begun in 1916–17 and reached its nadir in subsequent years: a deluge of acquisitive travels, mass profiteering or "speculation," abrupt reversals in the relative value of foods versus manufactured goods, extreme shortages of everything, and a nearly universal deterioration of consumption, at least in urban areas. With each crisis, too, came an attempt on the part of the Soviet government to

[104] Lenin, *PSS*, 43:63; Dikhtiar, *Torgovlia* II, 139; Dmitrenko, *Sovetskaia ekonomicheskaia politika*, 162.

constrict still further the gray area of private enterprise—bazaar hawking, artisanal trade, and the informal provision of services—as these
practices proliferated against the breakdown of normal supplies. By crystallizing a constellation of emergency exchange practices, the revolutionary period inaugurated seven decades of contestation over the role and
acceptable boundaries of the market.

CHAPTER TWO

The Invention of Socialism

CHAPTER ONE IDENTIFIED some of the ways in which early Soviet conditions and policies derived from the experience of the First World War. It bears repeating that neither wartime desolation nor an interventionary economic strategy was unique to Russia; throughout Europe the "Great War" was perceived as "total" not least for the extent to which social and economic forces were marshaled for military ends. The war led states to intervene in the market in unprecedented ways: Britain and Germany, which traveled the farthest along this route, drafted civilian labor, planned production, and rationed everything from foods to electrical power. European states also followed a common inflationary course during the war, and more than one currency collapsed in its wake. Likewise, Russia had no monopoly on abandoned shops. Marguerite Harrison, who was posted in Vienna before being sent to cover the Russo-Polish war, was one of relatively few observers of revolutionary Russia with this perspective; as she noted, Moscow's "boarded shops, deserted streets, houses with paint peeling off their mouldy facades, snow-blocked pavements, long lines of patient citizens waiting outside government shops for rations" differed little from the daily scenes she had witnessed in Vienna, Warsaw, Vilno, and Minsk.[1] This broader perspective—wars bring social and economic turmoil, and the longer and more brutal the war, the worse the dislocations—should be kept in mind when we consider the Soviet economy of the revolutionary epoch. Russians (and Ukrainians, Belorussians, etc.) fought wars on their own territory for nearly seven years; to a certain extent, conditions were bound to be bleak.

Nonetheless, Russia's revolutionary economy was distinct in several ways. It was unique in the duration of wartime desolation, and, above all, it was novel in the relationship between wartime conditions and a revolutionary social and economic policy. With respect to trade, the war on the market accelerated and universalized the abandonment of stores, and made it extremely difficult for others to open in their stead. As I argued in chapter 1, the anti-trade policy was instituted on social rather than economic grounds. Drawing an absolute dividing line between the "proletariat" and its "bourgeois" enemies, and assigning the entire spectrum

---

[1] Harrison, *Marooned in Moscow*, 40, 46–7.

of traders to the bourgeois camp, the Bolsheviks targeted shopkeepers, "kulaks," and other "marauders of trade" for assault under the slogans "rob the robbers" and "expropriate the expropriators."[2] While "class war" did not necessarily prevent expropriated businessmen from being hired into Soviet agencies, it did limit their employment opportunities and sharply restricted their access to rationed foods and goods.

If the Bolsheviks' class antagonism toward traders—seemingly visceral as well as ideological at base—made the elimination of private shops attractive, it is also true that the expropriation of shopkeepers corresponded to an embryonic conception of how the "socialist" economy should work. Fleshed out in the months and years after the decision to municipalize private shops, this conception was radically anti-trade—and particularly striking is the fact that anti-trade sentiment was not limited to private trade but was attached to public-sector buying and selling as well. In one meeting after another, and in innumerable pamphlets, articles, and public speeches, Bolshevik economists and policy makers opined that trade as such had no place in the new order; their fondest hope was that both trade and its correlate, money, would soon exit from the historical stage. By March 1919 the Soviet economy was geared "unwaveringly" toward the policy of "replacing trade with the planned distribution of goods, organized at the state level."[3] Within this framework the margins of dissent were narrow. Some Bolsheviks wanted to nationalize consumer cooperatives along with private stores, while others felt that cooperatives should continue to exist as separate entities but should be subjected to Party and state control. Some wanted to eliminate all street and market vending, while others thought that citizens could legitimately sell such items as mushrooms, berries, and used clothes. Some thought that money should be replaced by a labor unit of value, while others felt that goods should be distributed strictly according to need. Whatever the shading of opinion, war communism reflected a shared assumption about the historicity of trade. "Bourgeois" economists might equate distribution with trade, irrespective of time or place, but Bolshevik theorists viewed trade and the market as the forms of distribution distinctive to capitalism; they would necessarily be replaced by a higher, "socialist" form of distribution under a "proletarian" state.[4]

In keeping with this assumption, the distribution policy of war communism had two thrusts. The destructive side of the policy comprised

---

[2] On "speculation" and "kulak" as key concepts in Bolshevik civil-war rhetoric, see Lih, *Bread and Authority*, chap. 6; and McAuley, *Bread and Justice*, 282.

[3] Lenin, *PSS* 38:100; *KPSS v rezoliutsiiakh*, 1:427.

[4] See, especially, Lenin, *PSS*, 36:74.

the various measures, described in chapter 1, to limit and combat trade. The constructive side—the invention of socialist distribution—is the focus of this chapter. By the end of the civil war period the Soviet regime had not succeeded in eradicating the market, but it had established an alternative system for the distribution of goods. The chief characteristic of this system was its replacement of economic mechanisms with bureaucratic procedures. At least in principle, prices were determined by a decision of state, not by supply and demand. Goods were assigned to "distribution points" through a bureaucratized supply system, which directed shipments to particular regions and distribution networks. Within a given locality, governmental agencies apportioned all basic necessities among consumers through ration coupons, in urban Russia, and through a system of allocations misleadingly called "commodity exchange" [*tovaroobmen*] in rural areas.

A key question for this chapter is the extent to which the distribution system that emerged under war communism remained in place after 1921. While Western literature on the NEP has focused disproportionately on private trade, Russian scholars have devoted detailed research to the NEP-era socialist sector since at least the mid-1950s. The best of them were sensitive to historical ruptures and contingencies, but the standard line in this voluminous literature was to insist on the continuous unfolding of "Lenin's plan." I will argue that, even in the socialist sector, the New Economic Policy brought unforeseen changes connected with the legalization of the market. During the NEP era, distribution reverted to trade as economic relations were restored. However, war communism left a complex legacy of ideology, habits, and institutions that continued to shape state and cooperative trade. Many of these traits were captured by the epithet "bureaucratism," an all-purpose derogatory term for the behavioral side effects of a bureaucratic system. The NEP sought to eliminate inefficiencies connected with too much, and too rigid, centralized control over the economy, but neither at the executive level nor below were the tensions between a policy of liberalization and the habits of the revolutionary epoch effectively resolved.

The Emergence of a Socialist Distribution Network, 1918–1921

Prewar patterns of trade were disrupted not just by the disappearance of private shops, which occurred in many countries as a result of war and defeat, but also by the development of "socialist" channels of distribution. Petrokommuna, Petrograd's all-encompassing economic bureaucracy, is the model familiar from the English-language literature. At its height in 1920 Petrokommuna employed nearly 10 percent of Petrograd's adult population; managed some 250 large central canteens, 398 shops, and 3,948 stalls; and obtained and distributed supplies of all major foods and consumer goods.[5] Unparalleled in size, scope, and degree of integration, Petrokommuna was atypical of socialist institutions during the civil war. It did, however, embody the cherished Bolshevik goal of a fully centralized, bureaucratized, universalist, state-run economy, which exerted a strong influence on the evolution of socialist distribution everywhere. By the final stage of war communism—the second half of 1920 and early 1921—other municipalities had begun to imitate the northern capital's administration.

Until that time Petrokommuna defined one end of the spectrum of socialist institutions, while most "distribution points" were clustered near the other. Lacking the resources and staff to administer distribution directly, local governments—including, initially, Moscow—fell back onto consumer cooperatives, the major alternative to private trade in the prerevolutionary era.[6] Formed in the 1860s, Russia's consumer cooperative movement had expanded rapidly since 1914 to include some twenty thousand consumer societies with a combined membership of seven or eight million by the time of the Bolsheviks' coup d'état. The revolution accelerated the process: within two months cooperative membership had expanded by 45 to 60 percent, and, by the end of 1920, the cooperative press claimed thirty million members and a service reach (including members' families) of 70 percent of the population. This virtual explosion in membership was reflected in cooperative sales, which grew from a mere 1 percent of Russia's retail trade in 1912 to an estimated 28 to 35 percent of trade in foods and consumer goods by 1918–19, with private sellers at the market accounting for most of the rest. Notwithstanding the precipitous decline in Russia's total domestic trade, the volume of cooperative sales continued to rise through the entire revolutionary pe-

[5] McAuley, *Bread and Justice*, 280–86.

[6] A vast scholarly literature from the Soviet era traced the steps by which consumer cooperatives became the nucleus of socialist distribution in 1918–19. Though shaped by their ideological context, these studies worked through a prodigious quantity of primary source material and reached a consensus on many important points. I rely on V. V. Kabanov, *Oktiabr'skaia revoliutsiia i kooperatsiia (1917g.–mart 1919g.)* (Moscow, 1973); idem, *Kooperatsiia, revoliutsiia, sotsializm* (Moscow, 1996); L. E. Fain, *Otechestvennaia kooperatsiia: istoricheskii opyt* (Ivanovo, 1994); L. F. Morozov, *Ot kooperatsii burzhuaznoi k kooperatsii sotsialisticheskoi* (Moscow, 1969); Dmitrenko, Morozov, and Pogudin, *Partiia i kooperatsiia*; Henri Chambre, "La coopérative de consommation durant les premières années du pouvoir soviétique," in Henri Chambre, Henri Wronski, and Georges Lasserre, *Les coopératives de consommation en U.R.S.S.* (Paris, 1969).

riod.[7] They grew in part by default, as private retailers fled the market, but also through the involvement of cooperatives in the distribution of rationed foods. Their success depended on the special relationship of consumer cooperatives with Komprod and with provincial food committees [*prodkomy*] and economic soviets [*sovnarkhozy*], which supplied them with goods; on the efforts of their own agents, who, as noted in chapter 1, were not infrequently former "experts" from private commerce; and, finally, on the Central Union of Consumer Societies [Tsentrosoiuz], the cooperatives' central coordinating body.

During the early years of the revolution numerical preponderance ensured that cooperatives would define the exchange culture of the nascent socialist system. The hallmark of their heritage was a moralistic view of economic relations; it was this feature that identified them as an obvious candidate for collaboration with the new regime, notwithstanding their "bourgeois" demographic base. Vituperations against "private capitalist thieving trade," scarcely less violent than the Bolsheviks' own, had dominated the cooperative press for decades.[8] Moralism infused the cooperatives' commercial organization and gave activists a sense of mission: trade should satisfy needs, not manipulate desires or extract profits. Consumer associations accordingly focused on selling everyday goods and implements, and kept prices low. They chose the negligent approach to appearances characteristic of traditional retailers over attractive displays, advertising, and other modern techniques of arousing consumer demand, but broke with Russia's traditional exchange culture by making prices nonnegotiable, whether in money or in kind. In all these respects, the traditions of consumer associations dovetailed with the Bolsheviks' aspirations and set the tone for socialist trade.

Where cooperatives came into conflict with the Bolsheviks, and lost, was in the independent, democratic, and voluntary aspects of their heritage.[9] The Bolsheviks' radical impulse to centralize and bureaucratize the economy gradually transformed consumer societies from self-governing public organizations into the distribution apparatus of Komprod. This occurred over a series of stages but was conceived very early on. Lenin's December 1917 draft decree on "consumer communes" argued for the

[7] Cf. Kabanov, *Oktiabr'skaia revoliutsiia*, 210–11, 220, 256; Chambre, Wronski, and Lasserre, "Coopérative de consommation," 29.

[8] See, for example, *Kooperativnaia zhizn'*, vol. 1 (December 15, 1912): 6; *Soiuz potrebitelei*, 1904, 1:12–13, 2:53–6; 1908, 2:2, and 5:86; 1912, 2:51–4.

[9] Prerevolutionary cooperatives allowed anyone to join, subject to approval by the cooperative's general assembly. This body elected a board of directors each year and sent delegates to the provincial union of consumer societies (Chambre, Wronski, and Lasserre, "Coopérative de consommation," 14–16; Morozov, *Ot kooperatsii burzhuaznoi*, 6–12, 36–50).

unification of all existing cooperative shops, warehouses, stocks, and personnel in each region under the control of the regional governmental bureaucracy; the mandatory incorporation of all inhabitants into the new regional cooperative; and the elimination of membership fees and dues. Although the "bourgeois cooperators" were able to stave off these measures in 1917–18, the concessions they then obtained—the principle of voluntary membership; the retention of membership dues; and the right to assess special taxes and fees on nonmembers who availed themselves of their services—proved ephemeral.[10] Sovnarkom's March 16, 1919, decree, "On consumer communes," codified all the major principles of Lenin's 1917 proposal, demonstrating in the process the feasibility of utilizing cooperatives (as opposed to the private sector) on terms dictated by the state. Although profoundly anti-cooperative in the sense that cooperatives lost the last of their prerevolutionary rights, this decree fueled another expansion of cooperative trade by ejecting Komprod and its local branches from the retail sector. The capitals' elaborate municipal supply agencies were left undisturbed, but throughout the rest of the country the stores, shops, and warehouses of municipal food committees were officially transferred to the nearest cooperative, which became the sole authorized distributor of rationed foods and goods in each region.[11]

Centralization was the governing principle behind Soviet interventions. Successive decrees sought to unify and agglomerate existing cooperatives; as early as April 1918 no more than two consumer societies, one open to all citizens and one specifically for the working class, was supposed to exist in any locality or urban district.[12] If this provision represented a step toward the ideological goal of establishing "communes," it also reflected concrete economic and political motives. Unified cooperatives would streamline the work of state and municipal supply agencies, remove the possibility of multiple memberships,[13] and eliminate potential centers of resistance in the form of associations, such as teachers' or salesclerks' cooperatives, with a distinctive social base. Implementation lagged considerably behind governmental directives, but over the course

[10] "O potrebitel'skikh kooperativnykh organizatsiiakh," *Sistematicheskii sbornik dekretov*, 158–59. On Lenin's draft decree, see Kabanov, *Oktiabr'skaia revoliutsiia*, 139–42; and Dmitrenko, Morozov, and Pogudin, *Partiia i kooperatsiia*, 64–66.

[11] Tsentrosoiuz already handled the bulk of rationed distribution in the majority of provinces by the fall of 1918; cf. Dmitrenko, Morozov, and Pogudin, *Partitiia i kooperatsiia*, 84. For the March 16, 1919, decree, see *Sobranie uzakonenii* (1919), 17:191. It is the subject of an extensive discussion in every book listed above.

[12] *Sistematicheskii sbornik dekretov*, 158–59.

[13] A common practice; cf. N. M. Makerova, "Potrebitel'skaia kooperatsiia v SSSR," in *Kooperatsiia v SSSR za desiat' let* (Moscow, 1928), 103–26; here, 107f.

of the revolutionary period the number of self-standing cooperatives dwindled. By the autumn of 1920 even the workers' cooperatives had been forcibly merged into their region's "unified consumer society" (EPO), which began to resemble Petrokommuna in structure and scope.[14]

Centralization also effected the transformation of consumer societies from loosely associated public organizations—a movement—into subsidiaries of the state—an *apparat*. This trend began as early as May 1918, when provincial governments were instructed to subordinate cooperatives to a special department of the regional economic soviets, in which cooperatives would have minority representation.[15] The principle of "supervision" held true from bottom to top; by the end of the revolutionary period Tsentrosoiuz, the cooperatives' central union, had been purged of its prerevolutionary leadership in favor of a few delegates from workers' cooperatives and a greater number of representatives from the state economic agencies Komprod and VSNKh.[16] "Cooperative democracy" went the same way as administrative autonomy. Although elections to the cooperative boards of directors continued to take place during the revolutionary period, they were usually ordered from above and hemmed in by Soviet directives about who could, and could not, serve. Private traders and industrialists, priests, kulaks, former members of the tsarist gendarme, and other anti-Bolshevik groups were, in principle if not in practice, excluded, whereas working-class Communists were guaranteed a disproportionate number of slots.[17]

Third, centralization meant that the expanded role of consumer cooperatives' in the economy came at the expense of their economic independence, profitability, and even solvency. Before the revolution shares purchased by members—typically limited to ten rubles' worth per person, so as to prevent any individual from profiting excessively from the association or exerting undue influence over it—composed the operating capital of a cooperative. This capital was augmented by membership fees and dues, and, of course, by profits accruing from sales. At the end of each year the cooperative redistributed a percentage of its profits to shareholders at a fixed rate per share, and the remainder went to capital improvements and cash reserves.[18] After the revolution Soviet economic

[14] Dmitrenko, Morozov, and Pogudin, *Partiia i kooperatsiia*, 78–79, 105–8; *Trudy TsSU* 8 (2): 76; 8 (4): 129.

[15] *Sistematicheskii sbornik dekretov*, 159.

[16] See Miliutin's report on cooperatives in *Trudy I. s"ezda sovnarkhozov*, 436–37; Chambre Wronski, and Lassserre, "Coopérative de consommation," 19–28; Dmitrenko, Morozov, and Pogudin, *Partiia i kooperatsiia*, 83, 94–97, 107–8, 114–15.

[17] *Sistematicheskii sbornik dekretov*, 158, 163.

[18] Chambre, Wronski, and Lasserre, "La coopérative de consommation," 14–16.

policy limited cooperatives' monetary intake both in sales (through price controls on most basic goods) and in capital formation. The March 1919 decree that made cooperative membership mandatory simultaneously eliminated membership fees and dues, and suspended the obligation to purchase shares in the cooperative.[19] Exacerbated by inflation, which rendered previously accumulated capital worthless, these changes enfeebled cooperative finances to the point that the very existence of the cooperatives depended on the life support they received from the state. In 1919–21 central and provincial economic agencies issued goods to consumer cooperatives without even expecting compensation. Without capital, however, the cooperatives were unable to maintain their physical infrastructure and equipment, a problem that would plague them in later years.

By the final period of war communism the socialist distribution network was shaped more by centralization and bureaucratization than by the prerevolutionary cooperative milieu. Even in the cooperative sector, the differences between then and now were palpable. Take the case of store names: as of mid-1918 all state and cooperative shops in the capitals had to bear such inscriptions as "Eleventh Book Store of the Moscow Soviet," "Cloth Store Number One of Tsentrotekstil'," and "Petrokommuna's Public Eating House Number 42."[20] Ostensibly designed to rationalize distribution, this measure reflected the Bolsheviks' emphasis on standardization as a key element in the revolutionary transformation of the economy—and it was soon generalized to the rest of the country. This became a standard pattern: whether the question concerned trade practices, shop layouts, sanitary norms, or advertisement, rules first promulgated in Moscow or Petrograd were gradually extended to apply to "distribution points" everywhere. By 1920 the passion for centralization and uniformity had reached such a pitch that the central government tried to legislate identical hours of operation for all of the country's cooperative shops (9:00 A.M. to 6:00 P.M, with a lunch break between 2:00 and 3:00). The only nod to the diversity of local conditions in this directive was that stores could petition for alternative hours—12:00 noon to 7:00 P.M.[21] With such a ham-handed approach, no wonder many Bolsheviks eventually conceded that they needed to "learn how to trade."[22]

[19] *Sobranie uzakonenii* (1919), 17:191.

[20] *Biulleten' MPK*, July 24, 1918; see also Dukes, *Red Dusk and the Morrow*, 45; and Arthur Ransome, *Russia in 1919* (New York, 1919), 26.

[21] GARF, f. 1235, op. 56, d. 30, l. 8. It seems virtually certain that VTsIK, Komprod, and Tsentrosoiuz were deluged with petitions after this directive, but I have not actually seen them.

[22] *Pravda*, January 11, 1922; see also V. S. Aksel'rod, *Kak my uchilis' torgovat'* (Moscow, 1982); Lenin, *PSS*, 43:242–44.

During the civil war, however, this realization had not yet dawned. The Bolsheviks' refusal to countenance any degree of independence poisoned their relationship with cooperatives, even as they depended on them to distribute nationalized supplies. In the early stages of this collaboration, many Soviet officials took the view that since cooperatives were "bourgeois," they should be harassed or indiscriminately shut down along with the private shops. Since the Party line stressed the necessity of utilizing cooperatives—Lenin reportedly went so far as to say, in April 1918, "What is socialism, if not a cooperative?" [*Chto takoe sotsializm, kak ne kooperativ?*][23]—the central economic administration had to exhort local authorities to leave the cooperatives alone. At the First All-Russian Congress of Economic Soviets in May 1918, for example, V. P. Miliutin, the VSNKh deputy charged with explaining the regime's cooperative policy, urged delegates to be more patient with the consumer associations:

> MILIUTIN: . . . The reports that we received in December and January testified that as long as cooperatives remained outside the framework of correct mutual relations with Soviet organs, there was, naturally enough, a whole wave of violations against cooperatives in the localities.
>
> VOICE FROM THE HALL: Because they were speculating!
>
> MILIUTIN: It wasn't just a matter of speculation. Naturally enough, the new regime had to establish its own organs, and, of course, the colossal number—some twenty-three thousand consumer cooperatives and fifteen thousand credit cooperatives—couldn't immediately grasp the new way. . . . In the provinces there were separatist captures [*zakhvaty*] of individual cooperatives, and these separatist actions, horribly uncoordinated, often expressed haphazard conceptions and motives.[24]

Similar exchanges occurred at many Bolshevik gatherings, particularly whenever officials from the food-supply administration were present. Though the central government issued a series of injunctions against "nationalizations" and "separatist" closures of cooperative stores, they continued to take place throughout 1918. Meanwhile local soviets, economic soviets, and Committees of Poor Peasants [*kombedy*] interfered in cooperative management, disbanding cooperative boards or naming well-known Communists to them by fiat, assessing extraordinary taxes, requisitioning goods and cash assets, and establishing rules, again with no input from the membership, to prevent well-to-do citizens from purchasing goods.[25]

[23] *Trudy I. S"ezda sovnarkhozov*, 297 (cf. Lenin, *PSS*, 36:161).

[24] *Trudy I. S"ezda sovnarkhozov*, 438.

[25] Kabanov, *Oktiabr'skaia revoliutsiia*, 164, 173, 187–88; Dmitrenko, "Bor'ba sovetskogo gosudarstva," 297–98; Dmitrenko, Morozov, and Pogudin, *Partiia i kooperatsiia*, 78–81.

Despite all the changes the Bolsheviks imposed on cooperatives, their suspicions of them did not abate over the course of the civil war. Rather, as with the war on the market, the Red military victories of 1919 stimulated maximalist demands for the replacement of consumer cooperatives with nationalized "communes" that would not merely be "supervised" by state agencies but fully integrated into the state. These arguments surfaced at the Ninth Party Congress in March–April 1920, where the spectrum of expressed opinions toward cooperatives has been described as ranging from "hostile" to "nihilistic," and again at the exceptionally militant Second All-Russian Food-Supply Conference at the end of the following December.[26] Though the policy circle around Lenin rejected these demands at both forums, they clearly reflected a widespread sentiment on the part of the communist rank and file.

What fueled Communists' animosity toward cooperatives, now that the prerevolutionary leadership of the latter had been eliminated and they were successfully prosecuting the distribution of rationed goods? The literature on cooperatives points to several factors. First, the Bolsheviks construed Marxism to entail a utopian shift from an economy based on trade, discrete corporate actors, and the habits of the market to an economy based on all-embracing communes and distribution according to need. Second, Bolshevik suspicions of the cooperative movement became ingrained through the confrontations and compromise of 1917–18, and these suspicions were reinforced in the months and years after the virtual state takeover, since cooperative spokesmen continued to petition for price increases and other concessions to market economy norms. Third, although Tsentrosoiuz and the provincial cooperative unions were firmly in the hands of Communists by the beginning of 1921, primary cooperatives—actual shops—were staffed by prerevolutionary "cooperators" and even former kulaks and private traders up through the announcement of the NEP. Finally, consumer cooperatives probably suffered by association with agricultural and especially manufacturing cooperatives, which were left largely alone by war communism and which sheltered some capitalist manufacturers from nationalization by enabling them to reconfigure their factories as "artels."[27] As a result of these real and ascribed characteristics, nearly all Bolsheviks considered cooperatives significantly less reliable than state or municipal trade throughout the civil war.

[26] Dmitrenko, Morozov, and Pogudin, *Partiia i kooperatsiia*, 110–11; *Tri goda bor'by s golodom*, 13–14; Lenin, *PSS*, 38:164–65; Davydov, *Bor'ba za khleb*, 177–80.

[27] Dmitrenko, Morozov, and Pogudin, *Partiia i kooperatsiia*, 87, 125; Kabanov, *Oktiabr'skaia revoliutsiia*, 249.

The socialist distribution network did include other elements besides cooperatives during the revolutionary era: there were Petrokommuna and Moscow's food committee, of course, and a few other state agencies became involved in trade. Readers will recall from chapter 1 that the November 1918 decree, "On the organization of provisionment," specified that small shops would be "municipalized," whereas large businesses were to be "nationalized" or taken over by the centers, syndicates, and *glavki* [sectoral supply agencies] coordinating supplies of a particular product line. While most of these operated strictly on the supply side of the economy, providing goods to municipal distribution agencies and cooperatives, a few undertook to sell to the public directly. The organization of retail trade by *glavki* and nationalized factories preoccupied economic policy makers in 1919, to judge from the VSNKh presidium's recently published protocols from that year, but the very frequency of these discussions suggests that little direct marketing occurred.[28]

In the absence of a comprehensive network of state shops, consumer associations necessarily became the cornerstone of socialist distribution during the revolutionary epoch. This arrangement was advantageous to the new regime, which, in successive decrees, both expanded the purview of consumer cooperatives and bound them ever more tightly to the state. From the first directives on consumer cooperatives in the spring of 1918, Soviet policies progressively dismantled the financial, organizational, and commercial foundations of the cooperative movement, and reorganized them into a unified bureaucracy under state control. In this guise, cooperatives performed vital distribution functions for the incipient planned economy—a role they would retain through all the decades of Soviet power. In the eyes of many Bolsheviks, however, they simultaneously acquired a taint. Like markets and small service-sector businesses, if not quite to the same degree, cooperatives emerged as a gray area of the socialist economy during the revolutionary era; and this, too, would endure from the Soviet government's infancy until its declining years, when "cooperative" was the name given to newly legalized forms of private enterprise.

RATIONING, "COMMODITY EXCHANGE," AND PRICE CONTROLS

The Bolsheviks' reorganization of cooperatives was one manifestation of bureaucratization, the structuring principle of socialist distribution in its

---

[28] *Protokoly Presidiuma Vysshego Soveta Narodnogo Khoziaistva, 1919 god* (Moscow, 1993), 66, 69, 93.

formative years. Bolshevik theorists hoped that eventually this principle would cover all aspects of economic life: that the "anarchy" of the market would give way to a comprehensive, rational plan. Although the spectacular failure of war communism to demonstrate the superiority of bureaucratic over market methods of coordinating production precipitated a "strategic retreat" to market principles in 1921, it did not immediately lead to a reconsideration of long-term goals. Political economist L. N. Kritsman expressed a view widely held in Bolshevik circles when he wrote that the Achilles' heel of war communism had not been its bureaucratization but rather that bureaucratization was insufficiently supported by a plan. Supplies had become "anarchical," to the economy's detriment, he noted in his 1924 analysis, *The Heroic Period of the Great Russian Revolution*; but, in retail distribution, war communism had taken a step forward with its conscious appraisal of consumers' needs:

> Products were issued only after an explanation of why the consumer needed the item and whether he really needed it in the requested amount. Making every effort not to exceed the available resources (stocks of the product and anticipated deliveries), the decision as to whether it would be issued to the consumer depended on an evaluation of the importance of his stated aim.[29]

The ideal, especially among food administrators of the civil war period, was what one writer termed "Taylorism in consumption": the total rationalization of distribution according to "scientifically determined physiological needs." Analogous schemes were published rather frequently in the economic press during the civil war era.[30] Their characteristic feature was to subsume all demand under the concept of need—a conceivable approach to consumption in the survival-threatening circumstances of the day.

Although projects for the total rationalization of consumption were never accomplished, one of the main pillars of socialist distribution during the early Soviet period was indeed the bureaucratic determination of who could obtain what. In cities, this determination occurred in the context of a rationing system. Like other elements of socialist distribution, rations had been introduced during the wartime crisis of 1916–17, thus predating the Bolshevik seizure of power. The revolution did not alter the basic purpose of rationing, which was to secure food for the cities

---

[29] Kritsman, *Geroicheskii period*, 114–17 (quote, 117).

[30] See, for example, A. Gol'tsman, "Teilorizm v potreblenii," *Prodovol'stvennoe delo*, no. 35 (September 29, 1918): 4–6; Al'perovich, "Zamknutyi krug," *Ekonomicheskaia zhizn'*, February 15, 1919; N. O. [probably Orlov], "Voprosy raspredeleniia" and "Naturalizatsiia zarabotnoi platy," *Izvestiia Narodnogo komissariata po prodovol'stviiu* 1919, nos. 3–6 (February–March): 26–27, 27–28.

and for the army, but the Bolsheviks' rationing system modified the war-time regime in several respects. First, it was far more ambitious in scope: it covered a broader array of goods, from staple foods to clothing, agricultural implements, metal wares, and eventually fuel, and it was implemented in nearly every major city in addition to the capitals. Second, the Bolsheviks radically altered the context of rationing by forcibly closing private stores. Third, both the tsarist government and the Provisional government had taken an egalitarian approach to food rationing, whereas the Bolsheviks opted for a socially differentiated system. Finally, payment for rationed foods and goods was gradually suspended, until the New Economic Policy revived the use of money in socialist-sector transactions. In its scope, centralization, and eventual renunciation of cash accounting, the Bolsheviks' rationing system created a new global benchmark in wartime economic control.

In nearly all these respects, the turning point in the development of the rationing system occurred during the second half of 1918. As we have seen, the elimination of private stores accelerated dramatically after the decree "On the organization of provisionment," while the state simultaneously strengthened its claim on consumer goods supplies. Highly differentiated rations had been introduced in August, when Moscow and Petrograd reorganized food distribution around the so-called class ration, with differently colored ration cards for each class. This system formalized not only an enhanced ration for heavy manual laborers (up to 200% of the standard issue of all rationed foods) but also a reduced ration (50% of the norm) for "bourgeois" groups. Ration categories took account of both social policy and need: in addition to heavy laborers, pregnant women and nursing mothers were entitled to food supplements in the highest ration category, while the bourgeois list included the full range of pariah groups from investors and businessmen to priests. If supplies ran out, the four classes were to be served in order of priority. Similar systems were adopted in many other cities in imitation of the capitals until a uniform policy standardized the rules of rationing (again based on the class ration) at the end of 1919.[31]

Discrepancies between principle and practice emerged on the basis of two loopholes in the rationing policy. The first concerned the status of meals eaten at cafeterias and other public dining facilities, including, initially, private restaurants and cafés. Through most of 1918 ration coupons for meat and cereals were canceled for a full meal, but diners could take bread, sugar, and eggs without touching their rations. This in itself

[31] *Biulleten' MPK*, August 21, 1918; McAuley, *Bread and Justice*, 287; Carr, *Bolshevik Revolution*, 2:232; Dikhtiar, *Torgovlia* II, 124.

was enough to scuttle plans for the rationalization of food supplies. Both bread and eggs were extremely scarce in the Soviet retail system in 1918; while they were still being distributed without coupons at Petrograd eateries, egg rations were often withheld from ordinary purchasers, and children in hospitals had to do without.[32] The rules on prepared meals were only gradually tightened up as canteens became the primary conduit for food distribution in the capitals, especially in Petrograd. By the end of 1919 more than three-quarters of a million Petrograd residents took their rations at a public dining hall.[33]

Long after practices had changed in the regular distribution system, ambiguities persisted over the status of meals served in restricted-access canteens. These dining halls, located in factories and public institutions for the use of employees, were typically better provisioned than municipal canteens. The new, showcase dining hall at the Porokhov textile plant outside Petrograd was an extreme example, according to a December 1920 report:

> When you walk into the hall, you are suddenly unsure of where you are: in a café in some European capital city, or actually in a workers' cafeteria? Small tables, carefully arrayed in rows, are covered with sparkling plate glass; only the seated workers in their factory smocks put an end to your confusion. Here and there, a mirror gleams on the decorated walls, reflecting everything; between the mirrors, pictures have been hung. What strikes you about the enormous hall is its spaciousness, cleanliness, and brightness; the flowers and potted palms; the stage, on which an orchestra plays three times a week; the general cleanliness and order. Here there is not a speck of ash or a cigarette butt. A sign reads "No smoking," and no one smokes—the Porokhovniki know how to maintain discipline in word and deed. All this is no less comfortable than an old, bourgeois café; but it is somehow more spacious, and the public is different.[34]

Even if we adjust for exaggeration, this description highlights the difference between a "model" cafeteria, into which financial and organizational resources had been poured, and an ordinary public dining hall. In Petrograd's regular cafeterias, the same newspaper indicated two days later, the norm was poorly prepared meals, made of unpeeled potatoes and unwashed grain; ugly surroundings; and employees whose main energies were devoted to stealing food.[35] In the end, workers with strong factory

---

[32] M. Shmit, "Kommunizatsiia pitaniia," *Prodovol'stvennoe delo*, no. 24 (July 21, 1918): 2–3; no. 26 (August 4, 1918): 17; *Biulleten' MPK*, July 16, 1918.

[33] McAuley, *Bread and Justice*, 285; Dikhtiar, *Torgovlia* II, 128–29.

[34] *Krasnaia gazeta*, December 17, 1920, p. 3.

[35] Ibid., December 19, 1920, p. 3.

cafeterias were doubly privileged; not only were their meals quantitatively and qualititatively better than those served outside the factory gates, they had to surrender fewer coupons for them, since the food supplies rested on the efforts of factory foraging brigades, which were formed specifically to supplement workers' food. In mid-1920, some 15 percent of urban residents had access to a cafeteria at their place of employment, as against the 33 percent who patronized public dining halls.[36]

Perhaps the luckiest beneficiaries of the inconsistent approach to cafeteria meals were central government officials themselves. Officially entitled to rations of the second category (150% of the basic worker/employee norm), "responsible workers" in top-level state and Party positions enjoyed access to the Sovnarkom, VTsIK, and Comintern cafeterias in the Kremlin as well as to specially stocked commissaries for consumer goods. In 1920, when, admittedly, rations for ordinary Muscovites had improved somewhat, the Comintern cafeteria norms included a half ounce each of butter and caviar for breakfast, an ounce of cheese, a half ounce of sugar, and a half pound of bread; for the main meal, three-quarters of a pound of meat or poultry, or its caloric equivalent in starches, plus bread, cereals, and various condiments were provided. Not surprisingly, rumors of this bounty provoked "serious discontent," and a secret control commission recommended that it be scaled back.[37]

The second loophole in the rationing system emerged as a result of the procedure for determining ration levels. The administration of the "class ration" depended on accurate reporting from institutions and enterprises concerning their employees' "class." From the start, however, factory committees, state agencies, and occupational groups placed their own institutional interests above the Bolsheviks' overall agenda of rationalization. This can be seen in the tendency to hoard resources, a hallmark of socialist enterprise behavior that was already pronounced by the middle of the civil war. Rykov, the chairman of VSNKh, criticized this tendency in mid-1920 as a psychological vestige of capitalism:

> Besides organizational measures, the resolution of the supply problem requires that we overcome the proprietary [sobstvennicheskuiu] psychology, which officials in the present transition period have not yet been able to renounce and which affects the activity of every economic agency and every commissariat.
>
> This psychological trait is displayed in the fact that the administrators of factories, plants, glavki, provincial economic soviets, food-supply agencies, and

[36] *Trudy TsSU* 30 (1): 34. An additional 10 percent of urban residents were children who had access to a free breakfast at school.
[37] *Neizvestnaia Rossiia. XX. vek* (Moscow, 1992), 2:265–66. See also the reminiscences of Lidiia Shatunovskaia, *Zhizn' v Kremle* (New York, 1982), 39–42.

the organs of the Commissariat of Agriculture do not put an all-out effort into helping the economy stand on its feet but rather try to save, at whatever the cost, whichever little business the given comrade or economic organ happens to run. This is why instances are often observed when organizations and their managing organs, although staffed by unquestionably honest and loyal people, strive not to provide full information about their reserves and stocks but rather to conceal them, and moreover devote an all-out effort to supplying themselves for the longest possible time with materials for which they have no need not only in the immediate future but for a long time to come.

One can often observe instances like this: people from a particular city travel hundreds and thousands of *versts* for a small quantity of cement, while in the very same town some textile factory or other has thousands of *puds* of cement just lying around, which the factory might need in a couple of years, if then.[38]

In the area of food supplies, the same "proprietary psychology" (or "institutional egotism") led administrators and factory committees to try to maximize the amount of food allotted to their workforce by inflating, in one way or another, the ration rosters. The most striking expression of this tendency was the phenomenon of "dead souls," that is, the excess of registered "eaters" over enumerated residents or employees. Evident as early as June 1918, when one-third of Petrograd's rations was found to be redundant, the figure for the entire urban rationing system may have reached 40 percent by 1920, and for the railroad rationing system nearly 50 percent.[39] Enterprises and trade unions were particularly anxious to augment the food available to their workforce; while systematically failing to report truants, they lobbied heavily for employee foraging trips and for the enhancement of their workers' ration class.[40]

Petitions for improved classification often met with success, as it turned out; the general tendency in the evolution of Soviet rationing was the progressive expansion of the top ration list. By April 1920, during a second round of statewide standardization, workers and officials whose employment was deemed to have "especially important governmental significance" and "individuals practicing especially qualified types of mental work" were formally entitled to supplementary "special" rations alongside workers performing "especially heavy" physical labor.[41] Further elab-

[38] A. I. Rykov, "Voprosy snabzheniia i raspredeleniia," in *Izbrannye proizvedeniia* (Moscow, 1990), 136–37.

[39] Ibid., 135; Strumilin, *Zarabotnaia plata*, 29–30.

[40] Enterprises lobbied heavily for railroad cars for this purpose; many such authorizations exist in the VTsIK archives, for example, GARF, f. 1235, op. 94, d. 19, l. 112.

[41] GA Kursk. ob., f. R-367, op. 1, d. 9, l. 12.

orations followed. Members of the executive committees of provincial, district, or urban soviets; members of the collegium of central, all-Russian, and provincial agencies and their departments; and members of the central committees and administrations of all-Russian and provincial professional organizations were specifically identified as eligible for "special" rations. So, too, were schoolteachers, university professors, telephone operators, stenographers, Red Army soldiers on furlough, labor inspectors, and anyone working a night shift—a list so broad that it almost necessitated particularly special treatment for a smaller subgroup.[42] Additional guarantees could be obtained by lobbying to be placed on the military supply rolls, which, not surprisingly, offered better provisions than the civilian lists. Military rations differentiated between servicemen at the front and at the rear—an area for negotiation within the Red Army—and provided supplements for soldiers' families. Petitions from civilian enterprises and agencies for a military classification were again often granted. Alongside Komprod's "Commission for Worker Supplies," which approved petitions for "special" supplements, a "Commission for Transfers to Red Army Rations" was established in September 1919 to facilitate the registration of defense factories, Cheka personnel, the Red Guards, the arts establishment, political agitators, and a motley selection of other groups onto the military supply lists.[43]

If the original regulation of rationing reflected an attempt to balance physical needs against a punitive social agenda, these anomalies in the distribution of food were the product of pragmatic concerns. Soviet policy makers took an instrumental approach to food with regard to several high-priority objectives. The connection between hunger or satiety and political sentiment was a pervasive theme of intelligence reports during the civil war period, and military advisers occasionally suggested mobilizing food supplies as a tactical weapon in the civil war.[44] At the policy level it was almost certainly a factor in the urban bias of the "food dictatorship," which privileged supplies for workers in the northern industrial cities, the Bolsheviks' primary constituency and geographical base.

More relevant to the cafeteria meals and generous interpretations of ration categories, the regime used food rations to boost the productivity of its highest-priority workers. Better rations were effective, as Cheka agents reported from Petrograd in February 1920; wherever workers had

[42] Ibid., l. 18.
[43] Carr, *Bolshevik Revolution*, 2:232. See also GARF, f. 4737, the files of the SNK Commission for Aid to Scholars, est. 1921.
[44] For example, GARF, f. 393, op. 1, d. 37, l. 2. For a sampling of intelligence reports on the effect of food supplies on popular attitudes, see *Sovetskaia derevnia glazami VChK-OGPU-NKVD*, or the *svodki* in RGASPI, f. 5, op. 1, dd. 2615–18.

begun to receive Red Army rations, productivity rose.[45] With more food from official sources, people were less likely to skip work in favor of foraging trips or days at the bazaar and were better able to concentrate on their jobs. A similar logic applied to the most important workers of all, the policy-making elite. Special provisions for Kremlin officials were conceived neither as a perquisite, as in the case of the "bourgeois special-ists" in the Bolsheviks' employ, nor as the equivalent of a large salary, but simply as a way of ensuring that food-related difficulties did not distract their attention from the business of state.[46] Unable to supply all citizens or even all workers with adequate provisions, the Bolsheviks took it upon themselves to prioritize needs in relation to governmental objectives; for this purpose they gave food committees a degree of discretion in the disbursement of food. As long as scarcity made food rationing necessary, the loopholes in the urban rationing system facilitated the satisfaction of the "most significant" consumers' needs.

Interestingly, the priorities that emerged in 1918–20 continued to dominate centralized food distribution after economic conditions had changed. The Soviet government remained in the business of "planned" food distribution until 1924, though by August 1922 an internal memo could report that "provisionment by ration cards [*paikovoe snabzhenie*] has disappeared, except for the army and some of the social welfare contin-gent" (disabled veterans, etc.).[47] These were not, however, the only groups receiving centralized allocations. Monthly food packages for high-rank-ing officials remained ample: some fifty-five Party and state officials in each province received a standard allotment of 60 pounds of flour and 11.5 pounds of meat, as well as vegetable oil, salt, sugar, kerosene, coffee substitute, tobacco, soap, and matches; and although caviar had disap-peared from the Kremlin ration, the top echelon of the central bureau-cracy continued to receive large quantities of vegetables, eggs, meat, but-ter, and various other goods.[48] Furthermore, factory and transportation workers, who had enjoyed supplementary cafeteria meals under war com-munism, remained the beneficiaries of specially earmarked food funds.[49]

[45] GARF, f. 130, op. 3, d. 414, l. 1a.

[46] On perquisites for specialists, see Mervyn Matthews, *Privilege in the Soviet Union: A Study of Elite Life-Styles under Communism* (London, 1978), 61–67; and *Protokoly Presidiuma VSNKh*, 1919, 25, 29, 132, 154, 182, 193. The effort to make the lives of Party and state leaders unproblematic is perhaps most evident in discussions of medical care, for example, RGASPI, f. 17, op. 84, d. 317, l. 20.

[47] RGASPI, f. 17, op. 84, d. 295, l. 57.

[48] Inexplicably special food supplies for central bureaucrats differed substantially from one agency to the next (RGASPI, f. 17, op. 84, d. 317, ll. 10–12).

[49] RGASPI, f. 17, op. 84, d. 295, l. 57.

The difference, after 1920, was that the epicenter of hunger had shifted from the northern industrial cities to rural areas in the south and southeast, and, by and large, the Soviet food administration failed to adjust to this situation. A detailed account of centralized food distribution after 1921 can be found in Christopher Mizelle's dissertation on famine and food relief in the Tatar autonomous republic; what Mizelle found there was a strong bias toward urban areas in general and toward industrial workers and war invalids in particular. Peasants received some aid from the American Relief Agency, but if they got anything from the Soviet government, it was almost always seed grain.[50] As we will see in future chapters, here was another legacy of the civil war period: if the state was going to intervene in food distribution, it would act only on behalf of its favored urban class.

The distribution of manufactured goods followed a different trajectory from that of food in 1918–21 because of the shrinking stocks at the Bolsheviks' disposal and because of the acknowledged need to supply rural areas as well as towns. Whereas Komprod commanded three times as much grain in 1920–21 as in 1918–19, it had fewer and fewer manufactured consumer goods. Inevitably supplies were earmarked from the start for particular claimants and ends: for the Red Army, which, if more successful than others, still obtained only part of what it required; for workers at consumer goods factories, most often as bonuses [*naturpremirovanie*] designed to raise productivity; for the individuals whose "especially important governmental significance" conferred special food benefits; and for peasants, to whom some concessions were deemed necessary for the sake of extracting grain. The Bolsheviks sought to juggle competing consumer claims by linking manufactured goods provisionment to food rations, on the one hand, and by prioritizing "especially important" cities and regions, on the other. With respect to the former, special issues of cloth and clothing dated to the introduction of the class ration. Beneficiaries in the designated group were typically given a short list of stores where they could present their food card as proof of entitlement.[51]

Regional disparities in provisionment were likewise motivated by the effort to marshal resources for high-priority consumers. Cotton cloth, for example, was distributed among the provinces "on the basis of the

[50] P. Christopher Mizelle, "Battle with Famine: Regional Response to Crisis in the TASSR" (Ph.D. dissertation in progress, University of Virginia).
[51] *Biulleten' MPK*, July 24 and 27, 1918; Got'e, *Time of Troubles*, 403 (Got'e was on the "academic list" for food rations and unexpectedly received a clothing allocation in February 1921).

degree of importance of the given region or province for product exchange."[52] Concretely this meant that in April 1918 the country was divided into four agricultural zones, with cloth supplies allocated to the most fertile zone at a coefficient of approximately one meter per inhabitant per month, and to the least fertile zone at a quarter of that rate. Cities were to be supplied at the lowest level, but exceptions were made for especially important and politically sensitive cities (Moscow, Petrograd, Baku, and Astrakhan).[53] Applied not just to cloth but to all standard articles of peasant consumption, regional disparities were justified by the need to augment Soviet food supplies at any cost. By issuing consumer goods in exchange for food deliveries, the regime hoped to spur peasants in the chief agricultural regions to fulfill their delivery obligations to the state and to resist selling to baggers.

The term chosen for this approach to rural distribution, *tovaroobmen*, or *commodity exchange*, emphasized reciprocity and equivalence, but, in a time of famine, equivalence proved a chimera. Some Soviet officials came away from their first experiment in *commodity exchange* with the view that peasants had taken advantage of them. Orlov, writing for Komprod, asserted that the value of the manufactured goods that had been shipped to the villages in the first four months of organized "exchange" was far greater than that of the food the government had received in return.[54] Echoed by other officials at the time, Orlov's plaint became the standard position in Soviet-era historiography. By August, Soviet agencies claimed to have sent more than forty-two thousand freight car loads of "valuable manufactured goods," while state procurements of agricultural products during the same period amounted to thirty-nine thousand loads.[55] Orlov and later historians based their version of nonequivalence on a fixed relationship between the value of food and the value of manufactured goods—specifically, the price ratios prevalent before the First World War. Peasants, by contrast, understood value in market terms. To them, the value of grain was the quantity of money or goods that the grain could command on the open market at a given conjuncture; since this quantity had risen dramatically by the summer of 1918, they viewed the Bolsheviks' "equivalents" as flagrant underpayment for their crops.[56] The

---

[52] Orlov, *Deviat' mesiatsev*, 234.

[53] *Sistematicheskii sbornik dekretov*, 148–49, 351–56.

[54] Orlov, *Deviat' mesiatsev*, 350.

[55] *Trudy II. S"ezda Sovnarkhozov*, 97; Dikhtiar, *Torgovlia* II, 98–101; Dmitrenko, *Sovetskaia ekonomicheskaia politika*, 55–57.

[56] Peasant unwillingness to sell for fixed prices was axiomatic, but a remark by Komprod Tsiurupa in July 1918 should cast doubt on the claim that peasants were bilking the state: "From many incidents that have reached us, we have become convinced that that measure

result was that *tovaroobmen*, far from cementing an alliance between peasants and the Soviet economic administration, merely reinforced their mutual suspicions.

The Bolsheviks' response to this problem was to make commodity exchange obligatory, first for the provinces that constituted Soviet Russia's breadbasket and, in the summer of 1919, for rural Russia as a whole. At every territorial level, food agencies and cooperatives were to receive manufactured consumer goods in accordance with their total food procurement receipts. Per capita manufactured goods rations for that region (county, district, or village) would be determined by dividing the quantity of goods allocated to the region by the number of inhabitants. Consumers would be required to produce evidence of having met their delivery obligations before they would be issued manufactured goods, and shops would be held accountable if articles fell into the hands of the wrong peasants.[57]

This schema emphasized collective responsibility to the detriment of *tovaroobmen's* stated aims of equivalence and stimulation, since ration levels corresponded to the aggregate food deliveries by a village or *uezd*, while requisitioning levels differed from one household to the next. Collective responsibility was policy makers' way of reconciling the exchange principle with the politics of class. If commodity exchange had been carried out on an individualized basis, the recipients of state-supplied manufactured goods would have been prosperous peasants with surplus crops. For ideological and political reasons, the Bolsheviks were reluctant to see that happen. Like the *kombedy*, on which its implementation was to rest, *tovaroobmen* was shaped by the Bolsheviks' decision to seek social support not from a broad worker-peasant coalition but from a narrower alliance of workers and the poorest stratum of peasants. Poor peasants were accordingly exempted from requisitioning obligations but were permitted to benefit materially from a successful requisitioning campaign. The Bolsheviks thus routed incentives through an intermediary, the poor peasants, who were expected to use coercion to ensure that the incentives had the desired effect.[58]

Even so, with incentives for producers diluted by the indirect, collective structure of rewards, *tovaroobmen* might have worked had the food

---

on which we placed so many hopes—specifically, commodity exchange—could not prove very helpful. In our experience there have been many cases when peasants, seeing that there were no goods, announced, "Without the goods we won't give up [our grain]" (GARF, f. 1235, op. 4, d. 9, l. 54).

[57] *Sistematicheskii sbornik dekretov*, 351–56; Dikhtiar, *Torgovlia* II, 98–101.

[58] On the evolution of the concept of the "*smychka*," or alliance with the poor peasants, see Moshe Lewin, *Russian Peasants and Soviet Power* (London, 1968).

committees cornered an adequate supply of goods. Instead, their stocks were miniscule. In the first eight months of 1919—the high point of *tovaroobmen*—they were able to distribute not quite one pound of sugar per rural inhabitant, two to three meters of cloth, and one pair of shoes for every forty to fifty people. Given what could be obtained from baggers at the same time, this bounty hardly sufficed to woo peasants away from the free market.[59] By 1920 even "moderates" in the Soviet economic administration had concluded that *tovaroobmen* would remain futile "until workers manage to organize industry and get it working again, creating a commodity fund." In the meantime, "forced requisitions are the only correct route"—a view substantiated by the heightened effectiveness of the 1919–20 procurement campaigns.[60] The attempt to find even nominal equivalents of the requisitioned food dissipated as stocks of manufactured goods dwindled and grain deliveries increased. Dikhtiar has estimated that peasants were compensated for only 10 to 30 percent of the value of their grain deliveries after the 1919 harvest; if we adjust for the changes in relative values during the revolutionary era, this means that they received only a tiny fraction of the market price for their food.[61] Lenin, significantly, began to deemphasize equivalence in his public discussions of *tovaroobmen*, portraying it instead as an obligatory "loan" from peasants to the state, which the state would repay at some indefinite future date. Meanwhile, cloth, clothing, and other manufactured goods were redirected to the army and to urban consumers, who began to see an improvement in supplies.[62]

Commodity exchange, like food rations, survived into the 1920s but only barely, although it was restructured in light of the altered approach to the peasantry that the New Economic Policy prescribed. Soviet leaders portrayed the NEP as a means of revitalizing and expanding the *smychka*, the term used for the social goal of uniting workers and peasants behind the Soviet government. Whereas war communism had enlisted poor peasants to the revolutionary cause, the NEP broadened the Bolsheviks' appeal by offering concessions to the peasantry as a whole. The continuing dearth of manufactured goods notwithstanding, policy makers initially placed their hopes for an agricultural recovery on the revival of

---

[59] Dikhtiar, *Torgovlia* II, 100; Carr, *Bolshevik Revolution*, 2:233–34.

[60] Rykov, *Izbrannye proizvedeniia*, 124. Less surprisingly the Second All-Russian Food-Supply Conference (December 30, 1920–January 6, 1921) acknowledged the "fruitlessness of seeking an equivalent" and concluded that the "only possible method" for extracting grain was "coercion" (*Tri goda bor'by s golodom*, 13–14).

[61] Dikhtiar, *Torgovlia*, II: 101.

[62] Ibid., 133–34; Lenin, *PSS*, 39:123, 154; Dmitrenko, *Sovetskaia ekonomicheskaia politika*, 116–22.

tovaroobmen, albeit on a voluntary, individualized basis. A series of decrees in May 1921 spelled out the procedure whereby manufactured goods would be issued to peasants: henceforth, instead of making payment to any one peasant contingent on the entire village's fulfillment of its requisitioning or tax quota, cooperatives were instructed to pay individual households directly for foods and agricultural raw materials. Payment would take the form of manufactured goods of a "peasant assortment"—cloth, clothing, nails, scrap metal, agricultural implements, kerosene, sugar, and so on—according to a fixed schedule of exchange equivalents denominated in a new, fictitious unit of currency, the "commodity ruble." This was essentially an accounting device; besides *tovaroobmen*, it was used in interagency deals in which barter and other moneyless transactions continued to play a major, though declining, role throughout 1921–22.[63]

"Exchange" with the countryside was channeled through consumer cooperatives, based on the existing division of labor between cooperatives and the state. The language governing relations between the cooperative and governmental bureaucracies was new—on May 26 Tsentrosoiuz signed a *general contract* with Komprod, a term unthinkable six months before—but, in practice, cooperatives' functions continued to consist of handling *tovaroobmen* and distributing consignments of supplies from state agencies, while Komprod carried out agricultural procurement as well as the collection of the tax-in-kind. The tax-in-kind, which rested on the tried-and-true method of coercion, was not without success, but *tovaroobmen* was declared a failure even before Komprod had managed to transfer its supply of exchangeable goods to Tsentrosoiuz for distribution.[64] Local authorities plainly privileged tax collection over exchange operations, which they often banned for the duration of the tax drive. This could have "unhealthy" consequences, according to one widely disseminated report: "workers begin to take supplies into their own hands" for "anarchical trade at the bazaar."[65] Cooperatives, meanwhile, had the unenviable task of persuading peasants to turn in their produce for the sake of "equivalents" that were still well below the market price of food, while the cooperatives themselves received only minimal commissions for their efforts. Before long, they jettisoned the program. According

[63] B. Udintsev, "Kooperatsiia," in *Na novykh putiakh* (Moscow, 1923), 1:142–74, here 143, 158–59; Malafeev, *Istoriia tsenoobrazovaniia*, 29.

[64] Malafeev, *Istoriia tsenoobrazovaniia*, 29–30; Udintsev, "Kooperatsiia," 143; RGASPI f, 17, op. 84, d. 260, ll. 4–7; Dmitrenko, Morozov, and Pogudin, *Partiia i kooperatsiia*, 136–39; A. F. Chmyga, "Iz istorii organizatsii tovaroobmena v Sovetskoi Rossii v 1921 g.," *Istoricheskie nauki* (1958), 1:78; Atlas, *Sotsialisticheskaia denezhnaia sistema*, 166–91.

[65] GA Kursk. ob., f. R-367, d. 25, l. 14.

to Dmitrenko, it was a matter of weeks before cooperatives in Gomel', Kursk, Orel, and Briansk provinces diverted their *tovaroobmen* supplies to monetized sales. By the end of the summer nearly every cooperative in the country had followed suit.[66]

In 1921, as in 1918, the idea behind *tovaroobmen* was that socialism demanded a form of distribution distinct from trade. "Commodity exchange" seemed an appropriate alternative: through it, as Lenin later wrote, it seemed possible to effect "a transition *without* trade, a step toward truly socialist products exchange [*sotsialisticheskii produktoobmen*]."[67] When "direct" exchanges of the products of peasant agriculture for those of industry gave way to exchanges mediated by money, however, hopes for a fundamentally new form of distribution, and hence *smychka*, were dashed. Between August and October the Soviet leadership reluctantly sanctioned consumer cooperatives' unilateral reversion to trade. First, the use of money in rural transactions was legitimized; then individual cooperatives and their shops acquired the right to set prices according to local conditions; and, finally, cooperatives were set loose from their "contractual" relations with Komprod.[68] It is difficult to escape the conclusion that *tovaroobmen* failed because it served neither peasants' interests nor the interests of the cooperatives themselves. As in 1918–19, political ideals led the Bolsheviks to try to construct an economy based on social solidarity over economic interest. Although this is not, in itself, an impossible ideal—solidaristic policies have been enacted in twentieth-century economies in the form of welfare socialism—the popular consensus on which they have rested was not present in postrevolutionary Russia. It was also highly characteristic that the interests to be sacrificed, once again, were those of peasants rather than urban workers, specialists, or functionaries of the state.

Irrespective of the viability of the enterprise, the failure of *tovaroobmen* in 1921 also resulted from organizational and material deficiencies. Although procedures were revised under the New Economic Policy, the shortcomings of *tovaroobmen* were, for the most part, the same problems that had plagued it all along. As in the civil war period, nonmonetized exchange failed in part because of the rigidity of the equivalency schedule, which left cooperatives unable to compete with the burgeoning private sector; above all, it failed because of the dearth of desirable goods in

---

[66] Dmitrenko, *Torgovaia politika*, 61; Udintsev, "Kooperatsiia," 158–59; Atlas, *Denezhnaia sistema*, 180–81.

[67] *Leninskii sbornik*, 23:267; see also Dmitrenko, *Torgovaia politika*, 43–49.

[68] Dmitrenko, *Torgovaia politika*, 62–66; Chmyga, "Iz istorii"; Udintsev, "Kooperatsiia," 143.

the hands of the cooperatives. Tsiurupa's findings during the initial *tovaroobmen* campaign held as true as ever in 1921: without goods, peasants would not give up their crops.[69] This time, however, the leadership elected to supplement the stick with the carrot; coercion was retained for the purposes of tax collection, but, in addition, peasants were empowered to seek such compensation for their surplus as the market would bear. With the emancipation of the peasant market, socialist-sector "goods exchange points" had to reorient themselves to market pricing if they were to obtain any agricultural products at all.

The preceding discussion points up the third pillar of bureaucratized distribution during the revolutionary and early NEP years, namely, price controls. These, too, predated war communism, having been introduced by the tsarist government in response to wartime inflation—but, as in the case of food rations, the Bolsheviks greatly expanded their scope. The importance of price controls peaked during the first stages of the revolution, when pricing and food rations were the main levers used by the Provisional and Soviet governments to regulate distribution; it declined over the course of the civil war as a result of the progressive "naturalization," or demonetization, of the economy. Price controls were revived in 1921 along with *tovaroobmen* and the legalization of "local trade." Although they did not fare particularly well in the transition, they nonetheless remained a portal for state intervention into the economy in subsequent years. By the end of the 1920s bureaucratic pricing had emerged as a core value of the socialist economy, together with planning and the public ownership of the means of production. The institution of a stable and autonomous system of prices became a point of great pride for Soviet policy makers; after Stalin's death, economists and Party leaders extolled the Soviet Union's low, constant food prices as one of the chief accomplishments of the socialist system.

How did the Soviet price system develop? Since the overall tendency of pricing in the revolutionary epoch is well known—the radical undervaluation of agricultural products vis-à-vis going market rates—I will pause here on just a few specific issues.[70] Having embarked on a course of price regulation, Soviet planners had to devise a set of principles and techniques to resolve the practical issue of how to assign prices to goods. One avenue was that chosen by the tsarist government with respect to

[69] For one analysis, see *Otchet Khar'kovskogo gubekoso* (1921), 20.

[70] Overviews of civil war price policies can be found in Atlas, *Denezhnaia sistema*, 93–150; Malafeev, *Istoriia tsenoobrazovaniia*, 18–28; and *Denezhnoe obrashchenie i kreditnaia sistema Soiuza SSR za* 20 let (Moscow, 1939), 1–32.

grain prices, that is, to establish upper limits on prices for a specified duration, at the end of which time the limits would be revised. Price maxima were set somewhat higher than the prevailing market prices at the time of their introduction, which meant that they probably tended to draw market prices up to their level.[71] On the other hand, the wartime expansion of the money supply and the intensifying dearth of consumer goods made a degree of inflation inevitable. The tsarist government's approach to price regulation, which included price limits on many raw materials as well as foods, can thus be described as "managed inflation": prices were allowed to rise in response to market forces, but the state tried to channel inflation into a series of plateaus, on which it could, for a few months, obtain military and civilian supplies.

The Bolsheviks rejected this approach to price regulation, but they did not have a coherent program of their own to put in place. When the widening gap between market prices and the so-called hard prices led to shortfalls in the state's grain collections, they, too, found it necessary to make concessions to free-market price movements. In August 1918 grain procurement prices were tripled, though, as an early historian noted, "from the moment of their inception these prices lagged significantly behind those of the free market."[72] The premise behind further adjustments in the price structure was described a year later by S. A. Fal'kner, one of the Bolsheviks' leading theorists regarding financial affairs:

> The villages, which had utilized without reflection all the positive aspects (from their point of view) of the new revolutionary order, completely overreacted to all the aspects that they found inconvenient, and interpreted them as evidence of a conscious policy of unfairness toward the village. One such aspect was the disjuncture in the system of legal prices, which was in fact the result of the protracted, seasonal strengthening of agriculture against the background of constantly rising industrial prices. The solution thrust itself upon us: we had to resurrect prewar commodity equivalency ratios as the only ones that the village would understand, even at the expense of sacrificing a portion of the commodity stocks that the cities held, so as to achieve an improvement in food supplies for the cities.[73]

Fal'kner's description was, in fact, more detached than that given by the economic apparatus when the new price structure was adopted in 1918; V. P. Miliutin, for example, had characterized the restitution of prewar

[71] Dikhtiar, *Torgovlia* I, 181–93; Kondrat'ev, *Rynok khlebov*, 234–58; Lih, *Bread and Authority*, 19–22.

[72] Ustinov, *Evoliutsiia vnutrennei torgovli*, 34; Atlas, *Denezhnaia sistema*, 95.

[73] S. A. Fal'kner, "Printsipy postroeniia sistemy tverdykh tsen," *Narodnoe khoziaistvo*, no. 7 (1919): 15–21, here, 19.

price ratios in rosy terms on the grounds that they represented "more or less normal conditions of economic life."[74] Ironically, then, despite their deep-seated suspicions of the market, Soviet policy makers grudgingly found themselves according the prewar market price of goods the status of a "just price," as opposed to the "abnormal" market prices of the revolutionary era.[75]

This view of 1914 prices continued to influence Bolshevik policy well after the decision to sideline *tovaroobmen* in favor of coercion had emancipated planners from the need to provide "understandable" equivalents. In 1919 price policy was again thrown open, and this time leading economists hoped to build up a whole system of "just prices," in which money would serve merely as a convenient vehicle for expressing the real equivalence of things. An enormous bureaucratic effort went into pricing in the first half of 1919, when VSNKh's Price Committee reviewed and set prices on, among other items, 950 distinct products of the textile industry, some 550 articles in the leather industry, 4,250 metal goods, and 1,500 chemical products.[76]

Such frenetic activity notwithstanding, articles published by Miliutin and Fal'kner in July made clear that the committee was still operating largely in the dark. Each author proposed an approach to calculating hard prices, both of which took the prewar prices as a starting point. The technique favored by Miliutin could be described as "demand-side economics." All prices would be structured around the prices of consumer goods and ultimately of grain, which would in turn be based on the amount of money in circulation (for the establishment of price levels) and on an idealized picture of consumer demand (for the establishment of equivalency ratios). This picture was to be drawn from prerevolutionary worker budgets, with only a few correctives to reflect Russia's putative "cultural progress"; hence Miliutin's method of calculation was little more than a roundabout way of justifying the retention of the prewar price structure.[77] Fal'kner, the more sophisticated of the two, proposed what might be termed "supply-side pricing", in which both the money

[74] Miliutin, "Tovaroobmen i novye tverdye tseny," *Narodnoe khoziaistvo*, nos. 8–9 (September 1918): 1–6, here, 6; see also 34–39.

[75] Z. V. Atlas, an economist who advocated some reliance on market forces under normal circumstances, echoed this sentiment in his informative history of Soviet monetary policy: "Under the circumstances, the shift from voluntary to obligatory *tovaroobmen* was objectively necessary, since commodity exchange at the prices formed by the market was *not equivalent*." See Atlas, *Denezhnaia sistema*, 98.

[76] Miliutin, "Tverdye tseny i metody ikh ischisleniia," *Narodnoe khoziaistvo*, no. 7 (July 1919): 11–14, here, 12.

[77] For a critique of Miliutin, see Atlas, *Denezhnaia sistema*, 136f.

supply (its coefficient of expansion since 1914) and the commodity supply (its coefficient of contraction) would be taken into account. Since industrial production had declined more precipitously than agricultural production in the civil war era, Fal'kner maintained that Soviet price policy had artificially *raised* agricultural prices, and that a just price system would be skewed still more in favor of urban goods. Again, the base for his calculations was the "normal" prices of the first half of 1914.[78] What both proposals neglected to consider was that demands are not equally elastic; as we saw in chapter 1, famine and price shifts occasioned major changes in the structure of demand during the revolutionary years.[79]

In 1920 the search for a pricing system that would reflect "real values" was not abandoned, but demonetization lessened its urgency. By 1921, when the value of goods that workers received in kind was thirteen times greater than their cash wages, the demonetization of consumer goods distribution was virtually complete. Equivalency still played a role in interagency transactions, but in the interest of efficiency these deals were effected without cash transfers, through the manipulation of account balances at the nationalized banks.[80] As Atlas, the historian and one-time architect of Soviet monetary policy, has observed, "naturalization" resulted from "objective factors" connected to the manufacturing crisis and hyperinflation, but also from an important "subjective factor": the proclivity of Soviet policy makers to view money as the vestige of capitalist society and to assume that its disappearance, in the words of a December 1920 Finance Commissariat report, "will bring us closer to the bright beginning of the communist order."[81] Similar sentiments echoed throughout the revolutionary era; a sampling might include Price Committee member M. N. Smit-Fal'kner's report to the First Congress of Economic Soviets in May 1918, in which she imagined socialist distribution "not [as] an exchange, in which money is an independent factor in price formation, but an exchange of human labor for human labor"; Miliutin's July 1919 prophecy that "with the downfall of the capitalist system the monetary fetish—that god of the capitalist world—dies out, and the unit

---

[78] Fal'kner, "Printsipy postroeniia," 15–21.

[79] This fixation on "objective factors" in price formation appears to have been a lasting feature of Soviet economic thought. As Alec Nove once pointed out in reference to a 1957 article in *Planovoe khoziaistvo*, "Even original and critical thinkers, such as Strumilin, are sidetracked into recommending a criterion for price-fixing totally unconnected with changing patterns of demand" (Nove, "The Politics of Economic Rationality," in *Economic Rationality and Soviet Politics, or Was Stalin Really Necessary?* [New York, 1964], 60).

[80] L. Obolenskii, "Bezdenezhnye rasschety i ikh rol' v finansovom khoziaistve," *Narodnoe khoziaistvo*, nos. 1–2 (January 1920): 7–11.

[81] Atlas, *Denezhnaia sistema*, 139, 150–51.

of currency is inevitably transformed into a labor coupon for the receipt of the corresponding food or material portion"; and a June 1920 VTsIK resolution that promoted moneyless settlements as the first step toward "the total abolition of the monetary system."[82] The Bolshevik position on money was less categorical than these quotations might suggest—Iurii Larin's advocacy of the immediate, permanent elimination of money placed him on the Party's far left wing—but this "subjective factor" helped Communists to view the destruction of the Russian economy as a positive step.

Pricing without money proved an impossible task. In 1920–21 economists were told to devise a "labor unit of value" and a strictly "material," nonmonetary state budget, but these projects fizzled even before the announcement of the NEP.[83] The subsequent seachange in the regime's goals can be seen in the fate of G. Rokhovich, who, in 1921, sent Rykov, Lenin, and Molotov a series of letters denouncing those "leaders of our financial policy [who] in today's conditions speak out in favor of the annihilation of money and the transition to moneyless exchange." Such people, he argued, were "the most accursed enemies of Soviet power—all the more since they have already traveled along this false path toward the realization of their wild and harmful fantasies." Far from being rebuked for his pro-money stance, Rokhovich was invited to join the general planning commission of The Council of Labor and Defense (STO).[84] Until the end of the decade, when journalists once again heralded the dawn of a moneyless utopia, Soviet policy aimed at strengthening the currency and remonetizing economic relations. As we shall see, however, this agenda did not preclude the revival of price controls, the defects of which contributed considerably to the recurrent crises of the NEP years.

The Antibureaucratic Backlash and Socialist Economic Culture

Soviet policy makers consciously elected to construct a bureaucratized distribution system in the aftermath of the revolution. Sensitive to the plight of the urban poor, they aimed to divorce access to life's necessities

---

[82] *Trudy I. s"ezda sovnarkhozov*, 291; *KPSS v rezoliutsiiakh*, 1:427; Miliutin, "Tverdye tseny," 6; L. N. Iurovsky, *Currency Problems and Policy of the Soviet Union* (London, 1925), 33–4. Carr, *Bolshevik Revolution*, 2:260–68; and R. W. Davies, *Development of the Soviet Budgetary System* (Cambridge, 1958), 26–29, 38–45, both viewed antimoney rhetoric as a way of putting a positive spin on the economic debacle.

[83] Atlas, *Denezhnaia sistema*, 141–50; Davies, *Budgetary System*, 38–45.

[84] RGASPI f, 17, op. 84, d. 260, l. 9, for Rokhovich's June 27, 1921, letter; d. 233, for additional letters and career moves.

from citizens' ability to pay. The concentration of decision making in the hands of people who were both committed to the Bolshevik platform and, by virtue of their office, knowledgeable about the economy as a whole seemed the only way to ensure the rational, equitable utilization of resources. Fairly rapidly, however, this optimism was tempered by a dawning awareness of the distinctive disability of the bureaucratized economy. Bureaucratization tended to beget *bureaucratism*, a word that connoted rigidity, unwillingness to take decisions, and obsessive paper pushing on the part of Soviet functionaries on the ground. As early as December 1918 economic officials, from Larin on the ultra-Left to Dalin on the Menshevik Right, deplored the fact that bureaucratism had become a "characteristic feature of the socialist government" and called for measures to counteract it.[85] In the context of war communism, however, this was a lost cause. As long as the main line of Soviet policy was to accelerate bureaucratization and centralization, bureaucratism, too, would persist.

However hesitantly the Bolsheviks moved in the new direction in 1921, the New Economic Policy was, fundamentally, an antibureaucratic initiative. The legalization of "local trade" was soon followed by a series of decrees freeing low-level Soviet institutions to look after their own needs. Existing experiments in decentralization were expanded; factories were now ordered to create an "exchange fund" for trade with the villages, as many had quietly done on their own, by converting some of their workshops to the manufacture of consumer articles.[86] By late summer decentralization had progressed to the point where socialist-sector shops could set retail prices "in accordance with local conditions" on all but a fairly short list of basic goods. Bureaucratic methods thus reverted back to market mechanisms. The central government and the Communist Party encouraged this development, albeit often after the fact. At the "commanding heights" of the Soviet economy as well as at the bottom, however, the habits of bureaucratism proved hard to relinquish—and doing so became all the more difficult with each passing month, as the chief alternatives that presented themselves to bureaucratism were capitalism, corruption, and collapse.[87]

Two examples may illustrate the tensions between the economic culture of the Soviet establishment and the antibureaucratic strand of the

---

[85] *Trudy II. s"ezda sovnarkhozov*, 104–5, 134.

[86] Atlas, *Denezhnaia sistema*, 173.

[87] This tension has been discussed extensively in the literature. Good treatments include Daniel T. Orlovsky, "The Antibureaucratic Campaigns of the 1920s," in *Reform in Modern Russian History*, ed. Theodore Taranovski (Cambridge, 1995), 290–311; Gimpel'son, *NEP i sovetskaia politicheskaia sistema*, 373–92.

NEP. Pricing, which returned to the forefront of the regime's economic policy with the revival of monetary relations, is the first. Whether pricing received more publicity in the 1920s than any other policy issue, as Malafeev contended, it was indeed the subject of innumerable articles, reports, and bureaucratic debates from the beginning of the NEP until its effective abandonment.[88] New price regulations were announced in response to the failure of demonetized goods exchange. Absolutely essential consumer goods such as salt, sugar, kerosene, matches, tobacco, and cotton cloth would remain subject to "hard" retail prices, as established by the Finance Commissariat's Price Committee. Governmental regulation of all other goods was to occur at the wholesale level, through the imposition of hard prices for bulk sales by state enterprises, agencies, and trusts. In view of hyperinflation, which continued to accelerate in 1921–22 with the exponential expansion of the money supply, hard prices were to be revised monthly and to take into account price movements on the free market. Essentially the 1921 policy resurrected the tsarist government's wartime strategy of "managed inflation," albeit with respect to a much larger number of goods.

By the beginning of 1922 it was evident that the Soviet bureaucracy had wasted its efforts. Noncompliance with the hard prices was ubiquitous. Although two different Price Committees continued to publish price schedules for nationalized industry, these prices were acknowledged to be purely "orientational," that is, nonbinding.[89] This was, however, by no means the final word on the subject of prices in the early years of the NEP. Left to themselves, Soviet industrial managers acted on the basis of what Rykov had termed, in 1920, the *proprietary psychology*: that tendency to further "whichever little business the given comrade or economic organ happens to run," without considering ramifications for the economy as a whole. If this attitude had caused economic organs to hoard resources under war communism, the abrupt cessation of governmental supplies and funding in late 1921 led them to sell off their material assets, very often below cost, in order to finance current operations. By the middle of 1922 the universal depletion of stocks had made sharp price increases on manufactured goods appear imminent; once again, the government's published prices were declared binding on state enterprises and economic organs, at least with respect to essential consumer items.[90]

What next? Debates and zigzags in policy continued, while prices on manufactured goods soared. Declining sales threatened socialist-sector

[88] Malafeev, *Istoriia tsenoobrazovaniia*, 7–8.
[89] Ibid., 30–32.
[90] *Protokoly presidiuma Gosplana za 1921–1922 gody*, vol. 2, no. 2: 113–14.

industry and shops with mass bankruptcy. Perhaps price controls should be lifted, as G. L. Piatakov suggested in the fall of 1922?[91] Perhaps foreign trade should be opened to private merchants so that grain exports would raise peasants' purchasing power?[92] Perhaps cooperatives should be "forced" to "skim off less profit" on the principal items of rural demand?[93] In the end, the "marketing crisis" caused by the price scissors triggered a new round of regulation, which included the creation of more committees, forcible price cuts, and the transformation of STO's trade commission into a commissariat with full regulatory powers. Ustinov, author of a 1925 economic history, pointed to the crux of the problem from the point of view of planners when he identified the difficulty "from the organizational perspective, but also from the ideological, so to speak, and even psychological perspective" of avoiding "two extremes: excessive freedom of state trade, through which the latter would become indistinguishable in its methods and goals from private trade, and excessive dependence on administrative organs, through which it would [lose its character as trade and] become a system of distribution."[94] In short, having progressed fairly rapidly from hard prices to the concept of "orientational" prices in 1921–22, Soviet leaders were loath to revert back to a "system of distribution" in 1923–24; but if the only alternative was for state and cooperative trade to become more "capitalist," then "ideologically" and "psychologically," bureaucratism was a price that many were willing to pay.[95]

The second example of the political tensions inherent in the struggle against bureaucratism has to do with the means by which public-sector retailers obtained their wares. Even during the civil war period, cooperatives and state agencies had hired buyers to purchase auxiliary supplies

[91] Piatakov had this to say at the October 26 Gosplan meeting devoted to price policy: "Generally speaking, regulating prices in the way that we are going is impossible, and unnecessary, and harmful. We therefore did not need to establish a price commission and we should call off the one that we have" (ibid., 118, 124).

[92] Malafeev attributes this idea to Kondrat'ev; see *Istoriia tsenoobrazovaniia*, 36. For a resumé of several leading authorities' views on the price "scissors," see the synopses of debates in Komvnutorg's Price Commission in *Ekonomicheskaia zhizn'*, September 7 and 27, 1923, and the series of interviews under the heading, "Pochemu dorozhaiut promyshlennye izdeliia?" (September 12–25).

[93] Suggested by Tamarin, a member of SNK's ad hoc "scissors commission." GARF, f. 5446, op. 55, d. 309.

[94] Ustinov, *Evoliutsiia vnutrennei torgovli*, 96.

[95] For a similar conclusion, see Paul Gregory, *Before Command: An Economic History of Russia from Emancipation to the First Five-Year Plan* (Princeton, 1994), 94–97. For a detailed discussion of the scissors crisis, see E. H. Carr, *The Interregnum, 1923–1924* (New York, 1954), 3–154.

from peasants, factories, and other possessors of salable goods. The employment of purchasing agents was outlawed at the end of 1920 in the final, radicalized phase of war communism, but the ban was of such short duration that it scarcely constituted a break.[96]

Contracts annulled on January 1 were simply reinstated in March. Moreover, since the NEP reforms threatened to cut off Komprod deliveries, trade organizations tended to expand their network of agents, stationing some in major cities to scout for deals on consumer goods and employing others to travel around and buy up food in the countryside. By 1923 a Soviet official charged with prosecuting economic improprieties asserted that "not a single" public trade organization, trust, or syndicate was without its full complement of these "representatives."[97] Kurtorg, the governmental trade agency of Kursk Province, was probably typical in employing permanent representatives in four cities (Moscow, Leningrad, Khar'kov, and Orel) to supply its ten stores; larger public-sector commercial entities had literally hundreds on their payrolls. Buying agents could have a significant impact on the local economy of supply hubs; in Moscow more than fifty-five hundred representatives had offices in 1926.[98]

The retention of agents was an antibureaucratic approach to obtaining supplies, seemingly in accord with the guiding principles of the NEP. Employers valued the representatives' services; although the emergence of mercantile exchanges and contracts linking factories and syndicates with retail organizations gradually regularized the wholesale market for bulk commodities, the large number of representatives in the later 1920s indicates that personal contacts and initiative still lubricated many deals.[99] Why, then, did the Soviet government wage a virtually perpetual campaign against the employment of representatives, creating commissions to study and combat them, and repeatedly slashing the budgets of economic agencies in hopes of eliminating precisely these jobs? The two arguments against representatives, and the proposed alternatives, underscore the limits of Soviet antibureaucratism even during the NEP.

[96] Dmitrenko, *Sovetskaia ekonomicheskia politika*, 173–74.

[97] Kondurushkin, *Chastnyi kapital*, 30–32.

[98] GA Kursk. ob., f. R-192, op. 1, d. 55, l. 115; Fitzpatrick, "After NEP," 197; V. I. Dudukalov, *Razvitie sovetskoi torgovli v Sibiri v gody sotsialisticheskogo stroitel'stva (1921–1928gg.)* (Tomsk, 1978), 53–57. According to a feuilletonist in *Krasnaia gazeta* (January 14, 1924), Petrograd's financial department reported no fewer than forty thousand "agents and middlemen" in the northern capital in 1923!

[99] Mercantile exchanges appeared in most large cities in 1922; see Ustinov, *Evoliutsiia vnutrennei torgovli*, 71–78. On contracts between state industry and consumer cooperatives, see *Ekonomicheskaia zhizn'*, September 11, 1923.

The first was an argument from the standpoint of efficiency. Central government and party officials viewed representatives as another manifestation of the "proprietary psychology"; notably Rykov's illustration of this problem, which I have already cited, had in fact concerned purchasing agents: "people from a particular city travel hundreds and thousands of *versts* for a small quantity of cement." Although marketization might have seemed to justify a manager's focus on profits, and hence the employment of representatives, policy makers continued to brood about the replication of functions, high transaction costs, and transportation bottlenecks that they attributed to these agents. Worse, competition among the representatives of different state and cooperative organizations for the same goods surely contributed to inflation. When rationalizers attacked this problem, however, they either established a committee, notably STO's trade commission, Komvnutorg, which soon spawned trade commissions in every city and province; or, inevitably, they sought to reunify socialist-sector supplies.[100] Bureaucratization was thus promoted as the solution to "inefficiency."

The choice appeared still more stark with respect to the second, ideological and moral, argument against representatives. Purchasing agents, critics alleged, had introduced a "capitalist" element into state and cooperative institutions. Publicistic works on "private capital" and the Soviet economy could render their activities in lurid prose; in the following passage, for example, Andrei Fabrichnyi likened "privateer penetration" of cooperatives to a cancer,

> resulting in the total putrefaction of the cooperative organization and the corruption of any workers in the state apparatus with whom the infected cooperative comes into contact. Under these conditions, the criminality of the privateer sharply rises. From malicious speculation he proceeds to embezzlement, theft, bribes, and fraud.[101]

Rhetoric aside, several factors made such scaremongering plausible to a Bolshevik audience. Unlike ordinary employees, representatives worked on a commission basis, receiving a per diem for living expenses and a cut of any deal. In a very real sense, this arrangement, combined with the fact that they worked on their own schedules without governmental supervision, gave their activities a "private," even "capitalist," quality. Like private businessmen and especially contractors, their stake in fulfilling an assignment was a direct financial stake; moreover, the means by which

---

[100] *KPSS v rezoliutsiiakh*, 1:588; Malafeev, *Istoriia tsenoobrazovaniia*, 32; GARF, f. 5446, op. 55, d. 2228, ll. 116–21.

[101] Andrei Fabrichnyi, *Chastnyi kapital na poroge piatiletki. Klassovaia bor'ba v gorode i gosudarstvennyi apparat* (Moscow, 1930), 37.

they obtained supplies were entirely of their own choosing. They frequently combined their public-sector services with spinoff businesses of their own, which could mean that state commissions and contacts laid the foundations for a private business empire. The Leningrad millionaire Semen Pliatskii epitomized this danger: a wealthy merchant before the Revolution, Pliatskii had collaborated with the Bolsheviks during the civil war and had then made the transition to the NEP as a representative for the nationalized metal industry. He regained his fortune in 1922–23 by selling scrap metal and dross on the open market on the side. Pliatskii was said to have connections in more than thirty state agencies, and though he was brought to court eighteen times for suspected violations between 1922 and 1926, he was convicted only in 1927. Bolshevik commentators feared the potential cultural influence of people like Pliatskii even more than they resented "the emptying of the state's pocket into the pocket of the private contractor, without any kind of compensation."[102] Reliance on private contractors, and, above all, the presence of "capitalists" in the state and cooperative administrations, could render the regime vulnerable to subversion from within.

There can be no doubt that bribery was more than a figment of the Bolsheviks' imagination; it played a pivotal role in the commercial representatives' milieu. Kondurushkin, the public prosecutor for economic affairs, called "bribes and speculation . . . the fundamental methods of such agents, deputies, and representatives, who considered it their legal right to 'earn a bit on the side.'" Since representatives were often used as go-betweens between state agencies in the 1920s, "things could turn out rather strangely, with one state institution paying a bribe to another state institution." Kondurushkin was, of course, professionally predisposed to suspect wrongdoing and to view prosecution as the best way to deal with public-sector corruption.[103] Trade officials had different concerns. It transpired that prosecution, including the highly publicized show trials that Kondurushkin staged almost continually in the trade sector from 1922 through the end of the NEP, had negative side effects. Here is an excerpt from a 1923 petition by the head of the trade commission, A. M. Lezhava, asking that criminal proceedings against state trade employees be curtailed:

> Our trials do not expose, with blinding clarity, the darkest forms of embezzlement and bribery, which alone would justify the application of the highest punitive sanction. The general impression that remains from the recent trials

[102] Kondurushkin, *Chastnyi kapital*, 70; Iurii Larin, *Chastnyi kapital v SSSR* (Moscow, 1927), 21–22. On Pliatskii's conviction, see *Krasnaia gazeta*, January 12, 1927.

[103] Kondurushkin, *Chastnyi kapital*, 30.

is that we are instead using the death penalty to wage a struggle against a centuries-old, mundane fixture of Russian life.

From my everyday interactions with large numbers of our economic workers, both Party members and otherwise, I have taken away a definite conviction that, when we use a court sentence to obliterate individual criminals who stand out for their practical intelligence and energy, *we simultaneously kill the energy, creativity, and initiative of the honest and loyal cadres who remain among the living.* This is frightful, for of course a paralysis of the energy that we so desperately need is not limited to a short period of time but can become a deeply dislocating factor. Honest officials' will to work and to create is killed by these verdicts because the majority of the trials that conclude in death sentences do not really leave the mass of our workers with the conviction that such an extremely serious punishment is fairly applied *or that it is applied to a truly heinous crime.*

It is precisely this that explains the phenomenon that one meets everywhere today, when unquestionably true and valuable workers in positions of responsibility refuse to take independent decisions about one or another practical commercial deal, saying, "I don't want to be seated on the bench of the accused." This means that our repressions have gone beyond their goal, they are disrupting *us.* It is *terrible* that our best workers have responded to our courts and law with such feelings and stress [*perezhivaniikh*].[104]

Refusal to take decisions, lack of initiative, constant recourse to higher authorities: evidently the alternative to bribery was bureaucratism, the socialist economy's default mode.

What emerges from these dilemmas is that the socialist economy *had* a default mode, which, as Ustinov observed, was psychological as well as organizational and ideological, and which we can characterize as a distinctive economic "culture." Like the profiteering and survivalist mentalities fostered by the "underground" markets of the civil war era, the socialist economic culture coalesced out of the abnormal conditions of 1918–21. For socialist-sector functionaries, war communism had, above all, been an exercise in bureaucratization: obtaining supplies from the provincial economic soviet or from a branch of Komprod, calculating the size of each ration contingent, canceling coupons, and writing reports. The NEP slashed centralized supplies and loosened governmental control, but it did not correspondingly reduce the paperwork demanded by

---

[104] GARF, f. 5446, op. 55, d. 419, ll. 26–29. For reference, Gimpel'son asserts that a staggering 40 percent of all owners of private industrial enterprises had been arrested by 1923; cf. his *NEP i sovetskaia politicheskaia sistema,* 35–36. Lenin strongly endorsed the use of show trials and harsh punitive sanctions in the economic sphere; for quotations, see V. A. Shishkin, *Vlast'. Politika. Ekonomika* (St. Petersburg, 1997), 188–89.

Party and government offices. Not surprisingly, "bureaucratism" continued to be identified by commentators of the 1920s—especially from the Opposition—as the bane of state and cooperative trade.[105] The Politburo agreed; but, at the same time, the main expedient for public-sector personnel who wanted to cut through the red tape was to evade governmental oversight and to pay their suppliers bribes. Bureaucratism or capitalism? Bureaucratism or corruption? These Hobson's choices of Yeltsin's Russia defined the alternatives for Soviet trade in the NEP years.

PUBLIC-SECTOR SHOPS IN THE TRANSITION TO THE NEP

Up to 1921 the Soviet government's concerns in the trade sector boiled down to *controlling goods*—getting them in the first place and then distributing them according to plan. Trade, as such, was almost irrelevant to this process, and, for historians, one consequence is a dearth of information on the state and cooperative trade networks of 1918–21. Soviet policy makers were greatly interested in how many cooperative *associations* existed, and how many people were enrolled in them, as these questions had ramifications for the allocation of supplies. They did not particularly care about the number or location of functioning public-sector shops. This changed only after the announcement of the NEP, when the diminished role now assigned to allocation and the renewed importance of trade argued for expanding data collection. Accordingly, 1922–23 is the first year for which we have the kind of statistical data about stores and their retail turnover that was regularly collected before the First World War. A census of urban trade was taken at the start of 1923, and the cooperative press began reporting on stores at approximately the same time.[106] Using these and other figures, as well as descriptive information about state and cooperative trade in the first half of the 1920s, this section will consider how public-sector trade weathered the transition to the NEP and will assess related structural changes since 1912.

What happened first was a massive "bank run" on socialist trade. With respect to consumer cooperatives, although we do not know the number of shops in 1918–20, we can gauge the extent of the crisis from the 51,000 shops designated as "goods distribution points" during the abortive attempt to revive *tovaroobmen* in the summer of 1921. Six months

[105] Trotsky and Preobrazhenskii both wrote on this theme in 1923; see Leon Trotskii, *The New Course*, trans. Max Schachtman (Ann Arbor, 1965 [1923]), esp. 24, 45; E. A. Preobrazhenskii, *O morali i klassovykh normakh* (Moscow, 1923), 105–7.

[106] Cf. N. N. Riauzov and N. P. Titel'baum, *Statistika torgovli*, 5th ed. (Moscow, 1968), 346–47.

later only 19,600 were still functioning. The explanation for the collapse given by a NEP-era analyst was that "state agencies favored private trade over cooperatives on the ground that it was a more flexible, lower-cost apparatus."[107] A longer view might include the weakening of cooperative finances during the revolutionary period, which made the regime's new insistence on economic self-sufficiency unsustainable; the loss of credibility that the consumer cooperatives suffered in the eyes of peasants, who viewed them as having capitulated to the discriminatory policies of the state; and the depressed purchasing power of Soviet citizens, especially in the famine regions.[108] The data on cooperative sales strongly confirm the role of this last factor: in 1921–22 cooperatives sold only 1 r 09 k per capita in rural areas.[109]

Notwithstanding this initial crisis, consumer cooperatives soon resumed their role as the primary conduit for socialist-sector distribution. Early 1922 turned out to be the nadir; thereafter the number of shops and consumer associations climbed steadily, as did their sales volume. By 1926 consumer cooperatives boasted some sixty thousand to seventy thousand shops and 12.5 million dues-paying members.[110] While cooperative sales dipped in 1921–22 to 10 percent of domestic retail trade, consumer associations soon regained their civil war position (28–35%), and by 1926 the cooperative movement as a whole had captured nearly 50 percent of the retail market. When we consider that, in 1912, cooperatives had handled just 1 percent of the country's trade, these figures reveal the huge and lasting impact of the Revolution on prevailing commercial norms.[111]

Among working-class households, the role of cooperatives was still greater. *Worker cooperatives*—a term that now embraced factory canteens and commissaries as well as EPOs, the unified municipal cooperatives left over from war communism—comprised one-ninth of cooperative shops but generated more than half their sales.[112] Budget studies of industrial workers showed that cooperatives handled nearly 60 percent of this co-

---

[107] Makerova, "Potrebitel'skaia kooperatsiia," 110.

[108] On *khozraschet*, see Pethybridge, *One Step Backwards*, 29; Morozov, *Ot kooperatsii burzhuaznoi*, 177–78. On peasants' suspicions of consumer cooperatives from 1919 to 1921 see M. Frumkin, *Tovaroobmen, kooperatsiia, i torgovlia* (Moscow, 1921), 21.

[109] Makerova, "Potrebitel'skaia kooperatsiia," 113.

[110] Voluntary membership, with dues and shares, was reinstated in December 1923. For figures, see ibid., 110; *Trudy TsSU* 8 (5): 262–90; GARF, f. 5446, op. 55, d. 2228, ll. 85–87; *Sovetskaia torgovlia. Statisticheskii sbornik* (Moscow, 1956), 15.

[111] *Sovetskaia torgovlia. Statisticheskii sbornik*, 14; Makerova, "Potrebitel'skaia kooperatsiia," 114, 117.

[112] Makerova, "Potrebitel'skaia kooperatsiia," 118–19. Most EPOs were renamed TsRK after 1924.

hort's expenditures in the mid-1920s. Large factory and municipal associations were able to undercut the private-sector competition, since they not only enjoyed tax breaks and lower transportation charges but also kept operating costs low through economies of scale. In addition, subjective factors came into play: industrial trade unions put a major effort into promoting cooperative membership among factory workers, and any workers with a socialist orientation were likely to prefer to shop at the cooperative store.[113]

Although worker cooperatives were the most profitable part of the consumer cooperative system in the early 1920s, cooperatives were associated in the minds of Soviet leaders with their least profitable component, rural trade. Viewing the agrarian population more as a source of raw materials than as a pool of consumers, both state agencies and entrepreneurs concentrated their retailing energies on the more lucrative urban market. Only 10 to 20 percent of commercial licenses issued in 1921–22 were for rural trade, as against 47 percent of the much larger total number of businesses before the First World War.[114] This shift can be seen clearly in the density of trade, which nowhere came close to the prewar national average of sixty-five stores, shops, and stalls per ten thousand inhabitants. In 1923 not even urban areas reached that threshhold: at the high end the cities and towns of the Central Industrial region had thirty-seven permanent retail outlets (including stalls) per ten thousand inhabitants, as against thirteen in the towns of northeastern Russia, and between two and sixteen in rural regions. The rural retail network subsequently expanded, but as late as 1926 there were roughly four private shops, one consumer cooperative, and one agricultural cooperative or governmental shop for every ten villages.[115] This contributed in turn to the economic weakness of rural trade, which handled 18 percent of the country's sales volume in 1923–24 and sold only 4 to 5 percent as much per capita as urban outlets. Peasants, Dmitrenko has estimated, made 40 to 50 percent of their purchases in town, as against 20 percent at rural cooperatives and 30 to 40 percent from rural privateers. In proportional sales, however, a "return to normalcy" did occur: by 1925 rural businesses were doing 25 percent of all retail trade— just under the proportion that had been the norm, albeit with respect to a larger total volume, in 1910–13.[116]

[113] Ibid.; *Sovetskoe narodnoe khoziaistvo v 1921–1925 gg.* (Moscow, 1960), 458–59; Dmitrenko, *Torgovaia politika*, 193–98.

[114] This last percentage refers just to those parts of the prerevolutionary Russian Empire that were now under Soviet control (GARF, f. 5446, op. 55, d. 958, l. 182; d. 2228, l. 83).

[115] Dmitrenko, *Torgovaia politika*, 207 (for 1923); GARF, f. 5446, op. 55, d. 958, l. 182; and *Sovetskaia torgovlia. Statisticheskii sbornik*, 138–40 (for 1926).

[116] Dmitrenko, *Torgovaia politika*, 207f.; *Sovetskoe narodnoe khoziaistvo v 1921–1925 gg.*,

As Dmitrenko's estimate indicates, cooperatives were associated with the rural market not because of their preponderance—here, too, private traders outnumbered and outweighed them in the first half of the 1920s—but because they anchored rural public-sector trade. In contradistinction to the private and state sectors, the retail network of the cooperative sector was skewed toward the villages; some 70 percent of consumer societies' shops were located outside urban settlements.[117] The rural orientation of cooperatives acquired political importance during the scissors crisis of 1923, when the low purchasing power of peasants became the focus of an intense policy debate. The need to expand cooperative trade, as a lower-cost, virtually nonprofit marketing system, was one of the few solutions on which nearly everyone agreed.[118]

Unfortunately this conception corresponded more to wishes than to reality. Rural private traders typically did charge more, and took in more profits, but rural cooperatives had substantially higher costs. In the villages the smaller the retailer, the lower the overheads. Although rural cooperatives were not exactly large operations—in the Odessa region, for example, they employed an average of two salesclerks, one accountant, and one guard[119]—they were nonetheless bigger than the typical one-man private shop or still more typical itinerant peddler. The sluggish rate of rural sales could occasionally help cooperatives to flourish by scaring away the competition, as occurred in the rural hinterland of Riazan' Province, but it more often left the village co-op without sufficient capital to maintain even a basic selection—a situation only worsened by the narrow profit margins of cooperative trade. Many consumer associations fell into a cycle of indebtedness; unlike private traders, who purchased most supplies from manufacturers, syndicates, and urban stores in cash, cooperatives did almost everything on credit.[120] In addition, that some cooperatives continued to sell to peasants for grain in lieu of money added to their cash-flow problems, which remained chronic throughout the NEP.[121]

461; Dikhtiar, *Torgovlia* I, 82–83. See also A. Stetskii, "Osnovnye voprosy vnutrennei torgovli," *Bol'shevik*, nos. 3–4 (May 20, 1924): 45–59.

[117] Makerova, "Potrebitel'skaia kooperatsiia," 117.

[118] See, especially, *Ekonomicheskaia zhizn'*, September 11, 1923; October 10, 1923; and the series of articles commemorating "cooperative week" in early November 1923.

[119] GA Odes. ob., f. 1217, op. 1, d. 117, ll. 80–81 (1925).

[120] GARF, f. 5446, op. 55, d. 958, l. 182; d. 2709, l. 57; GA Riaz. ob., f. R-787, op. 1, d. 50, l. 54.

[121] In Nikol'skaia volost', 75 percent of cooperative sales involved grain payments, rather than cash, in early 1923, and dues were likewise denominated in grain (Iakovlev, *Derevnia*, 43–44, 53). Nationally Rabkrin's trade department estimated that 50 percent of rural trans-

All in all, notwithstanding the cooperatives' preferential rates of taxation and shipping, the difference in scale gave rural private traders a competitive edge through at least the mid-1920s. This can be seen particularly clearly in the area of supplies, where one might expect cooperatives to have enjoyed an advantage by virtue of their participation in a colossal buying consortium (Tsentrosoiuz). Tsentrosoiuz did indeed obtain goods for cheaper rates than virtually any rural privateers paid, and in the later 1920s this would tilt the market dramatically in favor of the cooperatives; but the reliance of rural cooperatives on the bureaucratic pipeline also tied up capital and imposed long delays while supplies traveled through as many as six intermediate way stations en route to the village store. This is why socialist trade organizations with sufficient resources preferred to hire purchasing agents on their own; it also explains the continued vitality of "bagging": a peddler, with no rent to pay and many opportunities to evade taxes, could quickly return to town whenever his stocks ran short. As an early student of rural private trade had to conclude, "Their assortment is significantly wider and richer than the cooperative movement's, and satisfies the demands of the local population better."[122]

By December 1923, when the last holdouts finally reverted to paying, voluntary membership, consumer cooperatives were no longer simply an *apparat*. Moscow bureaucrats could not command them into existence. While the large worker cooperatives (EPOs, TsRKs) remained highly bureaucratized entities throughout the NEP, other cooperatives, including the vast majority of village associations, drew on the old civic ethos. As in the first decades of the twentieth century, consumer cooperatives proliferated in Russian villages in the 1920s not because they received instructions from above and not even primarily because their organizers anticipated profits but because rural inhabitants needed goods. They formed when a quorum of citizens concluded that a cooperative would bring a wider selection of goods into the village and offer them at a reasonable price. The reversion to the prerevolutionary organizational structure did not, as we have seen, preclude the continuation of two wartime economic trends: the expansion of cooperatives' sales, in both absolute and relative terms, and the enfeeblement of cooperatives' finances.

In addition, consumer associations were saddled with a third legacy of

---

actions were moneyless through early 1924 (GARF, f. 374, op. 28, d, 2549, l. 5). On co-op finances, cf. RGASPI, f. 17, op. 84, d. 903, ll. 13, 29–33.

[122] Starikov, "Chastnyi kapital v derevenskom torgovle," 37. On delays in socialist distribution, see I. Ia. Trifonov, *Klassy i klassovaia bor'ba v SSSR v nachale NEPa (1921–1925)*, Part 2: *Podgotovka ekonomicheskogo nastupleniia na novuiu burzhuaziiu.* (Leningrad, 1969), 236.

war communism: the Bolsheviks' suspicions of them as "more capitalist than socialist" and "less proletarian than bourgeois." The long-term goal of Soviet policy makers was for cooperatives to squeeze out private-sector retailing, but they wanted this to happen on their own—that is, centrally planned and controlled—terms. Outside the worker cooperatives, such oversight was lacking: rural consumer associations stemmed from public initiative and rural communist officials were scarce. One does not have to accept Rabkrin's attribution of the defects of cooperative retailing to the "kulaks, former traders, and sometimes even priests," who had putatively seized control of rural co-op boards, to imagine that consumer societies occasionally served as a front for private trade. Iakovlev provided one illustration in his 1923 study of a rural district near Kursk. The district's sole cooperative shop, registered as part of a cooperative chain [mnogolavka], was, in fact, run by a local merchant's son; it had no members and imposed no fees. Iakovlev's description is the more credible in that he cites the success of the shop and the peasants' positive evaluation of its "chairman" as a "useful person for us."[123] While the use of cooperatives as tax shelters was identified more strongly with manufacturing artels, which had clearly played this role during the revolutionary period, than with consumer associations, other examples of what Iurii Larin termed *pseudo-cooperatives* are not difficult to find.[124] Still, no source gives any indication of their numbers or suggests that a significant percentage of consumer associations was fraudulent. The Bolsheviks' enduring distrust of them should be ascribed to a more fundamental motive: an antagonism toward public initiative scarcely less profound than their antagonism toward private, profit-oriented initiative.

With this attitude, the Bolsheviks had a difficult balancing act to maintain. The guiding principle of the NEP was to utilize spontaneous social forces and initiative to consolidate socialist Russia's economy. As we have already seen with respect to commercial representatives, however, this principle conflicted with the bureaucratizing impulse that defined "socialist" economic culture. Lenin's ideas on cooperatives, published in a late, important article in May 1923, both exposed these tensions and reified them, since the article became the starting point for every subsequent policy discussion. Even more clearly than in 1918 he identified

[123] Iakovlev, *Derevnia*, 54–55. For a summary of Rabkrin's report on rural cooperatives, see *Ekonomicheskaia zhizn'*, December 11, 1923, 3. The feeling that rural cooperatives were led by kulaks emerges from many documents from the 1920s, for example, RGASPI, f. 17, op. 84, d. 319, ll. 27–31.

[124] A 1927 visitor to Russia maintained that all it took to open a cooperative shop was "a cousin, a couple of brothers-in-law, and an uncle or two," but this author seemed unreliable (Harry James Greenwall, *Mirrors of Moscow* [London, 1929], 36). Larin, *Chastnyi kapital*, 113–22; GARF, f. 374, op. 28, d. 2521, ll. 91–93; Fabrichnyi, *Chastnyi kapital*, 38–40.

cooperatives with socialism and insisted that they retain their traditional character as independent public organizations, with voluntary membership, dues, elections, and an orientation toward the market. At the same time, however, he argued that the state should ensure that cooperatives advance the interests of the regime: cooperatives should be increasingly centralized, monitored, and forced to work within a plan.[125] Clearly cooperatives continued to occupy an in-between position in the socialist economy.

One result of these tensions, with lasting consequences for the Soviet economic system, was the emergence of techniques of control. The approaches adopted to ensure reliability in the trade sector in the early 1920s remained virtually unchanged for the next thirty years. As has already been discussed, they included publicized campaigns, replete with show trials and harsh penal sanctions, against misconduct in trade. They also included personnel restructuring. Lenin's article concluded that "elections" need not mean that the regime hand cooperatives over to the "bourgeois parties"—a concept which, not surprisingly, given the intensified repression against members of Russia's other socialist parties at the beginning of the NEP, now included Mensheviks and Socialist Revolutionaries (SRs). Purges of cooperatives, which had begun during war communism with the expulsion of the "bourgeois cooperators" from the Tsentrosoiuz administration, were carried out first in one place and then another.[126] Where possible, the expelled SRs, kulaks, and others were replaced from above with Communists who had gone through a series of newly organized courses on cooperative trade. The number of these graduates, however, fell far short of the cooperatives' staffing needs. As in the civil war era, the mobilization of Communists into cooperative management mainly affected central- and republic- or province-level cooperative unions, though, even in the villages, 15 to 20 percent of cooperative board members were Communists by 1924.[127]

The situation of consumer cooperatives in the NEP era was in some respects akin to that of December 1917. At that point they functioned within a modified market economy, but they were already very large or-

[125] Lenin, "O kooperatsii," *PSS*, 45:369–77. See also 43:226–7; Dmitrenko, Morozov, and Pogudin, *Partiia i kooperatsiia*, 188–89.

[126] Dmitrenko, Morozov, and Pogudin, *Partiia i kooperatsiia*, 167–68; Dudukalov, *Razvitie sovetskoi torgovli v Sibiri*, 94; Morozov, *Ot kooperatsii burzhuaznoi*, 184–86.

[127] Morozov, *Ot kooperatsii burzhuaznoi*, 187; Dmitrenko, Morozov, and Pogudin, *Partiia i kooperatsiia*, 167–78. Cooperative courses were a natural extension of the short courses offered by Komprod and VSNKh during the civil war (cf. *Tri goda bor'by s golodom*, 7). In the 1920s Sverdlov Communist University had a cooperative department, and both Tsentrosoiuz and the Central Committee offered training in cooperative management.

ganizations with strong ties to the governmental distribution system—and, as Lenin's draft decree on consumer communes forewarned, they had already become vulnerable to a state takeover. Between that time and the mid-1920s, of course, considerable water had passed under the bridge. Among other changes, "worker cooperatives" had emerged as a distinct, particularly docile, but also particularly successful, class of consumer associations; cooperative finances were in shambles; and Tsentrosoiuz had made the transition from a central coordinating body to the cooperatives' executive organ, and more recently to a national purchaser and distributor of consumer goods. The vulnerability remained. Although Soviet authors acknowledged that cooperatives, much more than state trade, were what supplanted the private sector at the end of the 1920s, the cooperatives would be pillaged by the state in the 1930s.

State trade, by contrast, came into its own in the early 1920s; in the aftermath of the civil war, it spawned many of the trade networks that would dominate Soviet cityscapes through 1991 and beyond. If cooperatives went through a period of collapse followed by retrenchment after the announcement of the NEP, the major trend in governmental trade was proliferation. The NEP reforms left every commissariat, sectoral agency, and central institution scrambling for cash, just like cooperatives; but as has already been observed, these agencies often had marketable assets, and their solution was to obtain a commercial license to sell them off. The Commissariat of Education, for example, came out of the civil war era with control over the state publishing house (Gosizdat), the movie industry, sound recordings, and school supplies; the Commissariat of Agriculture claimed jurisdiction over alcohol reserves and grain storage sites; Komprod organized flour milling and trade in all kinds of comestibles; and the Commissariat of Health operated a chain of drugstores. Even the state bank, Gosbank, traded extensively in consumer commodities through its sixty branch offices (a 1922 publication described it as "virtually the only centralized organization of a commercial type"). Moreover, the bank and other governmental bodies owned controlling shares of several quasi-state corporations, the most important of which was Khleboprodukt, Russia's largest grain merchant in 1922–23.[128]

Hemmed in by licenses that stressed such noneconomic goals as "regulating the market" and "selling as cheaply as possible," governmental agencies performed better in a wholesale capacity than in retail trade. For example, in Riazan', state agencies dominated the wholesale market,

---

[128] A. L. Burinov, with L. D. Borodulin, "Gosudarstvennaia torgovlia," in *Na novykh putiakh*, 1:107–41; quote at 119.

accounting for 88 percent of sales on the city's mercantile exchange. The major players were twelve syndicates and trusts representing the salt, sugar, alcohol, wine, fish, prepared food, matches, textile, clothing, sewing machine, and publishing industries, all of which had opened trading houses in the city in the first few years of the NEP. By contrast, with the exception of a single department store, said to be identical to that of the worker cooperative (TsRK), and one general store in a rural district that lacked a consumer association, governmental agencies had almost no direct involvement in the province's retail trade.[129] This division of labor was in line with the expectations of policy makers at this stage of the NEP; the Thirteenth Party Congress explicitly endorsed the idea of leaving socialist retailing to the consumer cooperatives and concentrating state agencies' commercial activities on larger-scale wholesale trade.[130]

This injunction notwithstanding, two characteristic types of state business emerged in retail trade in the early 1920s. The first was the retail counterpart of Khleboprodukt. Classified under the rubric of state trade, these businesses were actually commercial corporations [*paevye tovarishchestva*] in which state agencies held most or all of the shares. They were typically national or broadly regional in scope, and operated numerous retail outlets in a particular market niche. An example is the Ukrainian corporation Larek, which had divisions in each of the major Ukrainian cities by the end of 1922. As its name suggests (a *larek* is a stand or stall), Larek ran a chain of very small shops and kiosks, which, according to its charter, were to sell tobacco, matches, tea, coffee, groceries, and "other consumer goods for the mass market." By the end of 1924 Larek's Odessa division had 289 retail outlets and had cornered nearly one-quarter of the city's retail trade, including 62 percent of all state trade and a still more surprising 88 percent of "petty retailing," a category dominated in other cities by privateers. Larek's miscellaneous assortment included buttons, combs, neckties, and cosmetics, all traditional staples of petty trade, but also cloth and leather wares, and in 1925 Larek became the city's largest retailer of fruits and vegetables. This hugely successful enterprise gives the lie to the notion that state-run businesses are inherently inefficient and unprofitable. During the NEP state trade had to operate on a commercial basis; and if Larek was criticized for selling to private vendors or for the dubious condition of some of its fruit, it also proved very adept at

---

[129] GA Riaz. ob., f. R-787, op. 1, d. 42; d. 50, ll. 14–15, 43–47, 69; f. R-298, op. 4, d. 4852, ll. 6–8, 15–17, 59.

[130] *Direktivy KPSS po khoz. voprosam*, 1:472; *Sovetskoe narodnoe khoziaistvo v 1921–25 gg.*, 450.

capturing and expanding a market. Larek remained a major retailer at least through the 1930s.[131]

The second, and in most parts of the country, less successful variety of state retail trade was organized at the provincial level by the trade department [*torgotdel* or *torg-finotdel*] of provincial economic soviets [*gubsovnarkhozy*]. Here, the legacy of war communism was often debilitating; like cooperatives, provincial governmental trade went through a crisis in 1921–22 connected with the central government's withdrawal of subsidies and supplies. The major assets of the economic soviets, the commercial premises that had been "municipalized" or "nationalized" from 1918 to 1920, desperately needed renovations; moreover, the economic soviets had no experience in obtaining supplies contractually or in managing shops with an eye to the bottom line. Kurtorg, the commercial agency set up by the Kursk provincial economic soviet, is a good illustration. When the trade department started renting out municipalized and nationalized shop premises, it reserved seven of the best in downtown Kursk and one in each county seat for Kurtorg. A few of these were already occupied by trusts and syndicates, which had come in during the civil war era; in these cases, the trade department authorized Kurtorg simply to take them over and ordered the employees of the shops to remain at their posts. Thus civil war habits died hard; but Kurtorg also responded to the new economic climate, stationing representatives in four cities outside the province and offering sales agents in the small-town shops a cut of their proceeds.[132]

Such evidence of a commercial orientation notwithstanding, the province's business faltered. Kurtorg seemed to have a genius for acquiring articles that nobody would want, in part because local industries, with which it was simplest to conclude a supply contract, manufactured such shoddy goods. The worst blunder along these lines was the purchase of some two hundred pairs of shoes that disintegrated in two weeks because the soles were made of cardboard, leading to the dissemination of "the most undesirable rumors, which undermine prestige and—utterly undeservedly and contrary to reality—cast a shadow on the general activity of all state agencies and their chiefs." If rarely so absurd, supply shortcomings were routine. Kurtorg's hopelessly unprofitable rural shops came in for constant criticism at governmental meetings for stocking only expensive, inappropriate wares, while even the larger stores of the provincial

---

[131] GA Odes. ob., f. 1217, op. 1, d. 106, ll. 23–26. The success of Larek's Odessa division contributed to the unusual strength of the socialist sector there; cf. *Trudy TsSU* 8 (7): 282–83. For criticisms of Larek, see GARF, f. 374, op. 28s, d. 2523, ll. 48–50.

[132] GA Kursk. ob., f. R-192, op. 1, d. 57, ll. 1, 20; d. 68, ll. 7–8 (1922).

capital either stood empty or lacked some major segment of consumer goods such as cloth, women's clothing, or peasant linens or—more commonly still—offered a selection "of an accidental character," that is, whichever random articles Kurtorg had recently obtained.[133] The weakness of Kurtorg's shops contributed to the fact that the province's retail sales in 1923 remained 74 percent below the 1900 level.[134] As a rule, only in Moscow, Petrograd, and the resource-rich Siberian provinces did the new provincial commercial agencies [gubtorgi] prosper in 1922–23.[135] The gubtorgi and municipal gortorgi nonetheless had staying power; though they were bound more tightly to the central trade commissariat in the early 1930s, they did outlast the NEP.

Thrown back onto local resources and talents for their commercial recovery, provincial governments and cooperatives floundered from 1921 to 1923. All the same, the large socialist sector, no less than the distortions of the market after seven years of war, famine, and industrial collapse, prevented a simple return of prewar patterns of trade. War communism left its imprint not just on Russia's exchange culture (bureaucratic in the socialist sector, unscrupulous and survival-oriented in private trade) but also in the smorgasbord of agencies and organizations involved in goods distribution: the EPOs, TsRKs, torgotdely, and trusts. Moreover, the civil war turned out to be only the beginning of what a biologist might describe as a spurt of extraordinary evolutionary creativity. New forms and organizations of socialist trade continued to proliferate in the early 1920s, as government agencies at all levels had to come to terms with the economic landscape of the NEP. Interestingly, in light of these conditions later disappearing, the organizational forms generated in the early NEP period were very often "crown species"—not evolutionary dead ends but entities with a cluster of related "species," and with significant staying power. From the drugstores opened by the Commissariat of Health to the chains of stores run by the provincial gubtorgi, many state merchandisers of the NEP era were alive and well six decades later. This was not equally true of cooperatives, which were forced to evolve again during the Stalin years.

CONCLUSION

This chapter began with a metaphor drawn from mechanics—invention—and ended with one drawn from natural history—evolution. The

---

[133] Ibid., d. 68, ll. 3–8; d. 57, l. 17; d. 79, l. 23.
[134] Trudy TsSU 8 (4): 284.
[135] Dudukalov, Razvitie sovetskoi torgovli v Sibiri, 45–49.

shift in language was intended to highlight a major change that occurred in Soviet Russia as social revolution and civil war gave way to reconstruction and a modicum of social peace. War communism, the legal economy of the revolutionary era, had developed partly out of unavoidable deprivations, but it was primarily the product of conscious policy decisions. With the NEP, the socialist economy was set loose by its makers: spontaneous social forces could now respond to changing market conditions, as the Bolsheviks put it, *stikhiino*—in an "elemental" way. If the new forms of socialist distribution of the revolutionary epoch (EPOs, *prodkomy*, etc.) had been invented by Soviet policy makers at the very top, the new forms of the early NEP era drew on a much wider set of social, political, and economic actors. The socialist economy was no longer controlled by anything resembling a unified political will.

The interpretation of socialism as "invented" shares features with both the ideologically driven and reactive versions of Russian revolutionary politics. Clearly, when Lenin wrote his proposal on consumer communes in December 1917, he had a conception of how socialist distribution should be organized; but he cannot be said to have pursued this vision single-mindedly in the period that immediately followed. Rather, he and his associates responded to perceived short-term opportunities and constraints with partial compromises, reversals, and innovations, all the while retaining the original agenda for the medium to long term. So while the invention of socialism involved a fairly early identification of the main goals of a socialist economy, this did not preclude improvisation to find the forms and mechanisms that might bring them about. Such improvisation on the part of policy makers continued throughout the early Soviet period, whether in the experiment with moneyless distribution and accounting in 1920–21 or in the licensing of governmental corporations in 1921–22.

The guiding principle behind most economic policies of the civil war period was centralization. I have portrayed this tendency in two lights: first, as a rational effort to ensure that scarce resources were utilized according to the Bolsheviks' priorities and conception of needs; and, second, as a kind of personal commitment—a belief in the value of centralized decision making that went beyond, and was actually impervious to, evidence concerning its benefits and flaws. Following a couple of acute commentators from the 1920s, I have suggested that, when the pragmatic argument for centralization and bureaucratization was reconsidered, a psychological and ideological residue remained. High-level political actors, whose personal commitments had been sealed by participation in the revolutionary regime's victories, struggles, and crimes, were reluctant to relinquish the identification of socialism with bureaucratic control by the state. This bureaucratizing impulse was a source of friction in the NEP era, since official policy went the other way.

In the lower echelons of the Soviet power structure, pragmatic, ideological, and psychological commitments to the bureaucratized system were often tempered by the pressures and incentives of working within one. Crucially war communism's "command economy" did not take shape in a vacuum but within a context of extreme scarcity, on the one hand, and brutal state terror, on the other. The threat of repression led many functionaries to adopt a prudent stance: to defer to bureaucratic superiors even on trivial matters; to wait and see which supplies arrived of their own accord through the bureaucratic pipeline; and, generally, to eschew independent initiative in favor of filing reports. Identified and excoriated as a special pathology of socialism within months of the Bolshevik seizure of power, this behavorial and organizational syndrome could not be cured as long as war communism continued to nurture it. Even after 1921 the regime's continuing reliance on repression served to perpetuate bureaucratism, which in turn hindered the restructuring of socialist-sector trade.

Nor was bureaucratism the only behavioral adaptation to the Bolsheviks' invention. If bureaucratism became the hallmark of an emergent socialist economic and political culture, so, too, did the "proprietary psychology"—a syndrome diametrically opposed to a propensity for red tape. Many Bolshevik functionaries reacted to the bureaucratized economy not by waiting passively for directions from on high but by hoarding resources, petitioning superiors for special privileges, bribing suppliers, and taking risks. By dint of these methods, they could sometimes keep their particular nationalized enterprise running, albeit at the cost of diverting scarce resources from other, needier concerns. Like bureaucratism, "institutional egotism" proved a structural inefficiency of the socialist economy that the latter's architects had not foreseen. It was, of course, better suited to the post-1921 market setting than to war communism, but, even so, it inevitably clashed with the bureaucratic residue in the top echelons of the state.

Did the Bolsheviks "learn how to trade"? We will return to this question in future chapters, but for the so-called recovery [*vosstanovitel'nyi*] period, 1921 to 1925, the evidence is mixed. The socialist sector had some commercial success stories, such as Larek and Khleboprodukt, but the nature of these enterprises elicited ambivalent feelings in socialists of the old school. As A. Z. Gol'tsman wrote in the preface to one of innumerable analyses of the NEP-era private sector:

[State-run commercial enterprises] frequently merge with private capitalist forms. Thus, for example, the form of a joint-stock corporation is characteristic both of the way private capitalists raise capital in the USSR and of the mobilization of state capital; likewise, the hiring and firing of the labor force is, if purely from an external point of view, identical in private and state enterprises; the exchange of products between various state enterprises takes the form of buying and selling commodities; and so on. In form, the activities of socialist enterprises are still difficult to distinguish from private capitalist activities. In the twilight of the NEP, all cats are gray.[136]

In such a context of ambiguity, the Bolsheviks' suspicion of trading—a product of the prerevolutionary cooperative movement's ideology as well as that of the Marxist revolutionary movement, and also of the "speculative" markets of the civil war—became attached to their own economic institutions, state and cooperative trade. Punishments, purges, mobilizations of Communists, and political and occupational training became the standard techniques for counteracting the antisocialist tendencies inherent in commercial activity. Nonetheless, with this legacy of suspicion, it is not surprising that the utopian dream of socialism *without* trade would resurface in less than a decade after it was declared a fantasy and a mistake.

[136] A. Z. Gol'tsman, preface to I. S. Mingulin, *Puti razvitiia chastnogo kapitala* (Moscow, 1927), 11. Gol'tsman was on the Rabkrin collegium at the time.

CHAPTER THREE

Shopkeepers and the State

DURING THE NEP the various types of "socialist" enterprise were shaped by their coexistence with private trade. The relationship between social-ist and private commerce comprised contradictory strands: private traders competed with the socialist sector for supplies, customers, and credit, but they also complemented it, filling out the retail network in areas where cooperatives were ill-equipped to cope. This duality was reflected in the rubrics under which Soviet policy makers understood the public-private relationship. On the one hand, they continued to regard it as a mani-festation of class warfare, the private sector naturally representing "capi-tal" and the "bourgeoisie" as against the "proletarian" bureaucratized forms of trade. On the other hand, they imagined the relationship in terms of the socialist sector's "utilization" of private trade, a concept that kept the hostilities inherent in class warfare in check.

The utilization thesis dated to the NEP's inception, when the econ-omy's near-total collapse had persuaded Lenin that the strictures against private enterprise had to be relaxed. Hotly disputed at the time, mar-ketization was soon validated by glimmers of an economic recovery. By the middle of the decade Communist officials and economists generally agreed that private trade had, indeed, helped strengthen the Soviet re-public in 1921–22. Where Trotsky's Opposition split from the Politburo was not over the NEP's beginnings but over the continued utility of the private sector in a period of punctuated economic growth.[1] Through the mid-1920s most policy makers retained a healthy skepticism of Trotsky's calls for radical restructuring, in light of the experience of the recent past. "Private capital," socialism's enemy, obviously had to be regulated, but, with the proper oversight, the economic establishment expected it to continue to play a "useful" role. The functions assigned to private traders included rural retailing, particularly in remote regions where coopera-tives were not yet organized; the manufacture and sale of clothing, spe-cialty items, and other goods with an artisanal component; and establish-ments providing food, drink, and entertainment. More generally, private

[1] Leon Trotskii, *K sotsializmu ili k kapitalizmu?* (Moscow, 1925); see also Alexander Erlich, *The Soviet Industrialization Debate, 1924–1928* (Cambridge, Mass., 1967); Leonard Schapiro, *The Communist Party of the Soviet Union* (New York, 1959), 267–308.

traders were viewed as a reservoir of experience for the fledgling socialist sector, from which the latter could "learn how to trade."[2]

This chapter chronicles the development of private trade in the NEP interlude, both by reviewing trade policies and commercial trends in the aggregate, and by exploring the experiences of particular firms. While historians have long since identified the changing policies, market conjunctures, and rates of taxation that defined the overall contours of private enterprise in the 1920s,[3] the view from below is new and merits a word of introduction. A search for subjective materials eventually led to the NEP-era credit agency, Kredit-biuro, whose archive yielded a cache of brief business histories in the form of credit reports. This source has its defects, the most serious being the invisibility of the impoverished peddlers and petty vendors who were ineligible for formal credit. It does, however, make it possible to trace the fortunes of private wholesalers and small and large retail shops, and to reconstruct their business world. I have thus developed a database of 304 private traders from northwestern Russia, Ukraine, and Central Asia—regions selected not for principled reasons but because their records are still extant and in Moscow (others are held in an archival repository in the Urals).[4] Their stories have not redressed the dearth of subjective, first-person accounts of entrepreneurs' experiences, but they do provide individual information of a kind missing from previous studies of NEP-era trade.

Using the credit reports and other sources, the chapter is organized as much as possible around the experience of trade from below. The first section describes the reprofessionalization of trade from 1921 to 1925 against a backdrop of poverty and capital exhaustion. Then we turn to the political context, highlighting the tensions between the logic of utilization, class warfare, and constitutional rights. The chapter's third and final section discusses the ingredients of commercial success in those areas where private trade was deemed "useful." The fate of merchants

[2] A. M. Kaktyn', *O podkhode k chastnomu kapitalu* (Moscow, 1924), 16; R. Arskii, *Kak borot'sia s chastnym kapitalom* (Moscow, 1927), 28–34; Larin, *Chastnyi kapital*, 190–91; L. B. Zalkind, ed., *Chastnaia torgovlia SSSR*, e.g., 37, 66, 69, 143–45, 157–58; Mingulin, *Puti razvitiia chastnogo kapitala*, 43–47; Ia. M. Gol'bert, introduction to Ts. M. Kron, *Chastnaia torgovlia v SSSR. Po materialam Soveta S"ezdov Birzhevoi Torgovli.* (Moscow, 1926), 5.

[3] Alan M. Ball, *Russia's Last Capitalists: The Nepmen, 1921–1929* (Berkeley, 1987) is the best single volume in English. See also Carr, *Bolshevik Revolution*, 2:331–44; idem, *The Interregnum, 1923–1924* (New York, 1954), 3–152 passim; idem, *Socialism in One Country*, 3 vols., *1924–1926* (New York, 1958–64), 1:420–41; Banerji, *Merchants and Markets*; Dmitrenko, *Torgovaia politika*, 131–90; Strumilin, *Statistiko-ekonomicheskie ocherki*, 687–722; Dikhtiar, *Torgovlia* II, 141–253.

[4] See on-line appendix "Kredit-biuro and the NEP database" for details on how I constructed the database from unnumbered case files in RGAE, f. 7624.

and shopkeepers in the core socialized sectors of the economy, and the erosion of the conviction, virtually unanimous in the first part of the 1920s, that the war on the market had been a disastrous mistake, will be postponed until chapter 4, which traces the resurrection of war communism in Soviet trade policy.

POVERTY, CAPITAL, AND THE COMMERCIAL REVIVAL

The first year and a half after the Bolsheviks' landmark decision to legalize "local trade . . . through cooperative organizations but also at markets and bazaars" was very much a transition period.[5] Omnipresent hunger and poverty perpetuated the survival-oriented exchange practices of the previous few years. Indeed, when Soviet authorities formally extended the right to buy and sell a range of goods to all citizens in late May, petty trade was more than ever a universal pursuit. Along with factory workers, whose new "bonuses-in-kind" came with an explicit authorization to sell the goods at the market, the refugees from the famine who streamed into the cities resorted to hawking to make ends meet.[6] The experience of textile worker R., who later participated in Elena Kabo's sociological study of Moscow working-class life, is representative of a whole class of hawkers. In 1921 R.'s wife and daughter died of hunger at their home in Samara *guberniia*. Selling his house for fifty pounds of flour, R. moved to Moscow with his younger son and took up street vending from a tray until he obtained work at the Trekhgornaia textile plant.[7] With or without the famine, unemployment motivated many petty vendors in 1921–22; the simultaneous downsizing of every public-sector institution in connection with the elimination of centralized subsidies left laid-off workers and employees with few alternatives besides the market. Lacking capital, they purchased or crafted small quantities of goods to resell and hawked them on street corners or at railroad stations or bazaars.

The pathetically small scale of this trade, and the large number of participants, figured in every early analysis of the NEP. A summary of the third-quarter reports from the provinces noted, in December 1921, that

[5] *Direktivy KPSS i Sovetskogo pravitel'sva po khoziaistvennym voprosam*, 1917–1957 (Moscow, 1957), 1:225–27.

[6] Bagging surged in the spring and summer of 1921, an increase which several commentators ascribed to the "starving regions." Cf. Ts. M. Kron, "Chastnaia torgovlia," in V. P. Miliutin et al., ed., *Na novykh putiakh: Itogi novoi ekonomicheskoi politiki, 1921–1922.* Vol. 1: *Torgovlia* (Moscow, 1923), 1:175–6; *Derevnia glazami VChK-OGPU-NKVD*, I: 412–14, 416, 444, 453, 463, 470, 473; RGASPI, f. 5, op. 1, d. 2620, l. 3.

[7] Kabo, *Ocherki rabochego byta*, 55.

"everyone trades, if only a little: socialist employees, workers, invalids, former shopkeepers, etc. . . . the inundation of the market with innumerable petty traders, trading from their bare hands, from trays, and only in the very best case, from some small enclosed structure, is the universal fact of contemporary private trade."[8] Fourth-quarter reports indicated a decline in the number of people trading but no change in the character of their business: "people trade from their hands, from trays, from carts, and from the ground; they sell either exclusively foods, as in Petergof, or in addition tobacco products, petty haberdashery, and the like."[9] From the first quarter of 1922 came similar news from every corner: "Private trade is noticeably developing; in the main, it has a *market* character" (Kursk *guberniia*); "Petty bazaar trade, both hawking from the hands, and trade from stalls or kiosks, is developing" (Kaluga *guberniia*); "Private trade in the new economic conditions is very intensely developing; it primarily has a petty speculative character, and bazaar trade is also widespread" (Samara *guberniia*).[10]

From this starting point, private trade gradually acquired a more "normal" profile. Workers, at least, were able to extricate themselves from petty trade in connection with the remonetization of wage payments. This occurred somewhat fitfully; while the monetary portion of wages rose steadily after 1920, when it dipped to 6 percent, both the quantity and variety of goods issued in kind peaked in the second half of 1922. Some 185 articles were distributed to workers, from rye and oats to poppyseeds, caviar, and cranberries; from birch-bark boots and long underwear to "ladies' outfits"; and from thread and cloth to bricks and iron castings.[11] In certain sectors, enough goods were sold off by recipients to distort the market; cooperatives had difficulty competing with unlicensed vendors of tobacco and sugar, for example, until those factories finally stopped paying wages in kind in early 1923.[12] A survey of working-class budget trends identified a similar pattern among textile workers:

In the first period of the New Economic Policy, before the [1924] currency reform, the significance of nonmonetary elements of wages was so great that working-class households in the textile regions were transformed by the sheer weight of goods into little shops for the sale of cloth that was either unnecessary for their personal consumption, or, more often, unaffordable.[13]

[8] *Ekonomicheskaia zhizn'*, December 21, 1921.
[9] Ibid., April 27, 1922.
[10] Quoted in Kron, "Chastnaia torgovlia," 175.
[11] Strumilin, *Zarabotnaia plata*, 19–43, esp. 39.
[12] *Krasnaia gazeta*, January 23, 1923, 3; Malafeev, *Istoriia tsenoobrazovaniia*, 37–38.
[13] *Biudzhety rabochikh i sluzhashchikh*, Vol. 1: *Biudzhety rabochei sem'i* (Moscow, 1929), 1:22.

Certainly, in poorly paid households, wages in kind were more likely to be traded for food than consumed during the transition period. The household of depot worker B., another participant in the Moscow study, was probably typical of this group: despite receiving significant quantities of cloth from their employers in 1921–22, family members had almost no new clothes between 1917 and 1923; payments in kind were bartered at the market for flour and potatoes.[14]

The decline in market hawking as a component of working-class household budgets, first registered by successive studies from Voronezh in the first half of 1922, accelerated as wages shifted over to cash. By December 1922 the first of several large, national surveys showed that the percentage of workers' incomes attributable to sales of possessions had dropped to 7.4 percent (a further 1.8 percent came from sales of homegrown food) from the civil war norm of 24–30 percent; one year later those components each contributed 3.5 percent to the household budget. By 1927 occasional sales of possessions had fallen to a mere 0.6 percent of the average household intake—less than the average in the period from 1908 to 1913.[15] The effective disappearance of sales as a significant source of workers' income reflected more than mere monetization; more important, it was a sign that workers' well-being had rebounded from the radical impoverishment of 1917 to 1922. As several students of 1920s working-class budgets observed, a high proportional role of market sales tended to signify poverty. Across time, the years when wages were lowest were also the years when sales played the greatest role in workers' incomes, and, across income groups, the lower the wage category, the greater the role of informal exchange.[16] Monetization and rising wages in the mid-1920s brought urban workers full circle with respect to market vending: as in the prewar period, occasional trade was a familiar enough activity, but for all but the very poor it was no longer habitual or urgent.

The normalization of wages notwithstanding, petty hawkers turned out not to be an oddity of the transition period but a constant feature of NEP private trade. Though no longer universal, street vending, market hawking, and trade from stalls or kiosks continued to account for the lion's share of trade licenses. This was particularly true in rural areas, where the number of stationary private shops barely exceeded thirty thousand until 1926.[17] Rykov's comments on the 1923 investigation of rural trade left little doubt as to the latter's character: "Such Asiatic back-

[14] Kabo, *Ocherki rabochego byta*, 102.
[15] *Biudzhety rabochikh i sluzhashchikh*, 1:14–19, 22.
[16] Ibid., 1:22; Strumilin, *Zarabotnaia plata*, 31; Kabo, *Ocherki rabochego byta*, 138–48.
[17] Strumilin, *Statistiko-ekonomicheskie ocherki*, 694–95.

TABLE 3.1

Trade Licenses by Class, 1912 and 1926 (in thousands, including state and cooperative trade)

Class of license	1912	1926	1926 private
I. Trade from hands, trays, carts	23.6	160.1	158.4
II. Stalls, kiosks	289.0	305.5	292.0
III. Small shops	484.7	259.3	155.2
IV. Stores [magaziny]	148.7	62.3	19.0
V. Wholesale trade	8.3	18.2	4.1

Note: Data from 1912 exclude territory that was not part of the USSR in 1926.
Source: Strumilin, Statistiko-ekonomicheskie ocherki, 692.

wardness [aziatchina] reigns in our villages and counties that, in many places, not only are there no retail shops, there are not even any peddlers. Given such a state of affairs, even a private shop would of course be a step forward compared to what we have now."[18] Three years later, though the number of permanent shops had grown, the bazaar and itinerant categories of trade still accounted for nearly 60 percent of all trade permits and 71 percent of the licenses for private trade (table 3.1).

The typical commercial entity of the NEP was not the small shop characteristic of prerevolutionary Russia, then, but rather a table or stall in an outdoor market. Since nearly half the licenses in the upper three brackets, and almost none in the lower two brackets, fell to the socialist sector, private trade was that much more skewed toward what Strumilin called the "simple commodity," and Lenin, the "petty commodity," as opposed to the "capitalist," socioeconomic stage [uklad]. Merely 4 percent of all private trade permits registered commercial entities larger than a small retail shop.

The size of the petty trade contingent reflected the ongoing problem of poverty. Workers, after all, were only one segment of the laboring poor; if the adequacy of their wages is one important index of poverty, the rates at which citizens dropped out of regular employment is another. Well after 1921, petty trade licenses functioned in lieu of an adequate safety net. Mikhail Kalinin, chairman of the Central Executive Committee (TsIK), tacitly acknowledged this fact in a 1926 circular, when he described free trading licenses for disabled veterans and victims of work-

[18] A. I. Rykov, Khoziaistvennoe polozhenie sovetskikh respublik i ocherednye zadachi ekonomicheskoi politiki (Moscow, 1924), 31; and compare Dzerzhinskii's 1925 comments, cited in Gimpel'son, NEP i sovetskaia politicheskaia sistema, 219.

place accidents as "an equivalent of social security for invalids."[19] Likewise, the number of petty trade licenses continued to rise and fall with the rates of urban unemployment. In 1925–26 lower taxes may have attracted some workers to abandon the socialist factory for the private sector, as Alan Ball has indicated, but mass unemployment also contributed to the movement of one hundred thousand workers into artisanal manufactures and petty trade. This was not a materially advantageous move. Artisans reportedly earned 20 percent as much as industrial workers, and petty traders earned significantly less than the average wage in state and cooperative trade.[20] Like the minimum-wage service sector, worldwide, in the post–World War II era, petty trade was not an occupation of choice for Soviet citizens but rather a meager substitute for a steady blue-collar job.

In this context it is no wonder that when traders addressed themselves to Soviet authorities, a major theme of their letters was material distress. Golfo Alexopoulos, who has studied petitions for the reinstatement of citizenship rights (along with other "class-alien" groups such as former tsarist gendarmes, gentry, and priests, traders were formally disenfranchised until 1936), has found that traders often made emotional appeals to officials' sympathy rather than rational appeals to codified rules.[21] Again and again petitions cast trade as an occupation of last resort. A 1925 letter to the Party's Yiddish-language daily made this point with pathos: "The little Jewish shops have died out: they cannot stand up against state stores, and can't afford to buy wares; taxes are beyond their means. Thousands of people are left with nothing to do. Begging is repugnant; we bang our heads against the wall in the search for a kopeck." Moreover, with the demise of the Jewish shops, Jewish artisans had no outlet for their wares. "Give us factories and plants," the letter-writer pleaded, "and we'll go work in them with our wives and children."[22]

Another collective letter from the Pale, this time from the Ukraine-Romanian border region, provided a concrete description of the small-town trader's milieu. In this Jewish town, 38 of 195 households were employed in trade, with the rest of the population divided among artisans and tradesmen, widows on pensions, and the unemployed. The businesses of the traders had the following complexion:

[19] Arkhiv po khraneniiu strakhovykh fondov (Ialutorovsk), f. 5248, op. 1, d. 1, 1. 50. Many thanks to Golfo Alexopoulos for sharing this document with me.

[20] Ball, *Russia's Last Capitalists*, 30–31, 44–45, 68–69; Strumilin, *Statistiko-ekonomicheskie ocherki*, 712–18; GARF, f. 5446, op. 55, d. 540, ll. 1–3.

[21] Golfo Alexopoulos, *Stalin's Outcasts: Aliens, Citizens, and the Soviet State* (Ithaca, 2003), 97–128 and "Victim Talk: Defense Testimony and Denunciation under Stalin," *Law and Social Inquiry* 24, no. 3 (summer 1999): 637–54.

[22] *Pis'ma vo vlast'*, 1917–1927 (Moscow, 1998), 405–6.

Fifteen families have licenses in rank I, two of whom have nothing but an expenditure sheet to show for it. In each case, they have only five or six rubles' worth of goods on hand: two dozen matches, twenty pounds of salt, one pound of hard candy, twenty sheets of cigarette paper, and several spools of thread. The trader purchases his entire "inventory" at the cooperative shop, and stands with it on the street or spread out on the ground, or he rides to the nearest fair to earn his pound of bread.

Eleven families have licenses in rank II—for us, this means high bourgeois. This class of trader travels to Zhmerinka for miscellaneous wares: a can of herrings, five *puds* of kerosene, twenty pounds of candy, one hundred boxes of matches—all told, some fifty to sixty rubles' worth.

Even the very biggest traders in Kopai-gorod, the twelve families with licenses in rank III, earned little more than a subsistence income. Most of them sold cloth, which required a license in rank III if the business had more than thirty meters in stock, irrespective of whether the exchange venue was an indoor shop. Those traders who had such premises had carved them out of their homes: exactly twenty of the houses in Kopai-gorod had more than one room, and most of these consisted of "a little living room and a little shop," or else a workshop for artisanal trades.[23]

The conditions these letter-writers described were common to many small-town traders. Though the stories of peddlers and hawkers with licenses in rank I must remain obscure, a percentage of traders in rank II petitioned for credit lines from the State Bank (*Gosbank*) or from private or state wholesalers, and thus figure in my database. From Ukraine came a number of instances of traders in rank II, mostly but not exclusively Jewish, who had managed to rent a stall at the market but could barely bring home a subsistence wage. Ioel' Abramovich Serper, an elderly fish-monger from a small town near Odessa, managed to sell 500 rubles a month during the season, but no one knew how he stayed alive in the winter months. Makar Andreevich Tomilin was a petty rural trader both before and after the revolution; throughout the NEP he sold some 250 rubles a month of a miscellaneous selection of petty goods. Nor was this exclusively a small-town phenomenon; in the port city Nikolaev, Meer Iakovlevich Linetskii continued to rent a bazaar stall in the flour and grocery row through at least 1927, though his sales never exceeded 200 rubles a month. These stories could be multiplied, and they obviously extended to other regions.[24] Petty traders everywhere tended to carry a

---

[23] Ibid., 393–98.

[24] The lowest recorded incomes came from a small town near Leningrad, where Zel'man Iakovlevich Bykhovskii (Kb/Sev-zap/Bykhovskii) maintained a selection of just 25 rubles' worth of goods, and in the Kirgiz town Tokmak, where Mir Umar Adilov (Kb/Uzb/Adilov)

standard assortment: tea, flour, candy, salt, tobacco, needles, thread, buttons, nails, all purchased in small quantities from state, cooperative, or private retailers, very often obtained through a trip to a larger city or town. Profits from their sales were probably in the range of 10 to 30 rubles a month.

Though many of these conditions had prevailed in prerevolutionary Russia, small-town traders' perennially poor prospects for earning a living worsened significantly under Soviet rule. The relentless stigmatization of trade as a dishonorable, "non-laboring," occupation poisoned relations between shopkeepers and peasants in the 1920s, as did unfavorable price trends. In early 1924, just after the worst phase of the price scissors, peasants were asked by the newspaper *Bednota* to participate in a write-in discussion of the topic, "Who is a kulak?" The responses revealed a much greater degree of antagonism toward trade than can be documented for the prerevolutionary period. Asked to comment on whether a poor man, who traded "pennies' worth" of goods "exclusively so as not to die of hunger," ought to be considered a kulak and a bourgeois, most respondents answered in the affirmative: "Any person who trades in the peasant milieu, be his business large or small, is an undesirable element"; "any poor person who, not wanting to expand his peasant farm and to live exclusively on it, *trades* in the village should be considered a person seeking easy money, and in him one can identify a future kulak"; "First of all, one should by no means believe that the 'poor man' can actually trade for pennies, since, with today's prices, you can't even buy a shirt or a piglet without a hundred thousand. Anyone who procures the resources to trade, that is easy and even criminal profiteering (as the phrase goes, 'no deception, no sale'), should obviously be considered a social parasite."[25]

Of course, there were successful "kulak" traders in this period,[26] but economic conditions more often pushed traders up against a wall. In the case of the Jews, the irony of the postrevolutionary situation was that they were no longer prevented by law from owning land; but with no capital to obtain it with, all too many continued to eke out a hand-to-mouth existence through petty trade, weighed down by excessive taxes, socialist-sector competition, and the poverty of postrevolutionary con-

---

sold 150 rubles' worth a month. Both had licenses in rank II. Other examples of traders in rank II who were described as "absolutely without resources" and whose sales were less than 700 rubles a month in the years after the monetary reform include Kb/Uk/Khmel'nitskii, Kb/Uk/Tarasenko, Kb/Uk/Sidorenko, Kb/Uk/Podzolkin, Kb/Uk/Markov, Kb/Uk/Leibel', Kb/Uk/Kulik, Kb/Sev-zap/Riskin, Kb/Sev-zap/Baldin.

[25] *Derevnia pri NEP"e. Kogo schitat' kulakom, kogo—truzhenikom* (Moscow, 1924), 19–29.

[26] For example, Kb/Sev-zap/Raichik, Kb/Uk/Transkii and Buianskii.

sumers.[27] For a striking feature of the poorest traders in my database was that they stayed in business: against the constant turnover of the small "permanent" shops, many of the pathetic little businesses of the second rank remained in operation throughout the NEP. Jewish or otherwise, NEP-era private traders were not, in the main, "Russia's last capitalists," in Alan Ball's phrase, but rather the newest incarnation of Russia's urban and small-town poor.

Impoverished petty traders, like starving peasants or the bands of orphaned and abandoned children who roamed the streets of Russian towns, put a human face on the revolution's social dislocations. These same dislocations had an economic face. From an economic perspective, poverty was but one manifestation of the problem of capital exhaustion, perhaps the primary impediment to recovery in the first half of the 1920s. The hyperinflation of the early NEP period wiped out any savings that might have survived seven years of war. Excepting the occasional wealthy bagger, individuals who wanted to start a business had to persuade someone to supply the money or goods on credit. There appears to have been a window of opportunity in 1921–22, before the onset of the price scissors. As we saw in chapter 2, state agencies reacted to marketization by trying to unload their assets, and they were often willing to issue goods to traders on quite favorable terms of repayment. Later, both the marketing syndicates and Gosbank tightened up the requirements for credit, relaxing these terms only briefly in the 1925–26 fiscal year.[28] Kredit-biuro routinely received inquiries about successful prerevolutionary traders who had failed to reopen their business at the start of the NEP but were now, a few years later, petitioning for start-up capital. We cannot know how the banks responded, but credit reports uniformly advised against giving these people loans.[29]

In the parts of the empire where Soviet power had arrived late, capitalization problems were initially less acute. Many Central Asian and Ukrainian merchants remained in business throughout the civil war period or closed down shop "for a very brief interval" without forfeiting

---

[27] Jews were greatly overrepresented in trade—17 percent of the economically active Jewish population was employed in this sector, compared to 1 percent of the economically active population overall—as well as in artisanal work, governmental employment, and the free professions (Z. L. Mindlin, "Sotsial'nyi sostav evreiskogo naseleniia SSSR," in *Evrei v SSSR: Materialy i issledovaniia* [Moscow, 1929], 4:5–31).

[28] See Banerji, *Merchants and Markets*, 73–86.

[29] For example, Kb/Sev-zap/Blokh (10/23), Kb/Uk/Dizhur (2/24), Kb/Sev-zap/Baldin (10/24), Kb/Sev-zap/RumiantsevSA (6/25), Kb/Sev-zap/Rubiazheva (9/25), Kb/Sev-zap/Abramovich (10/26), Kb/Uz/IbragimovMI (9/27), Kb/Uk/Amkhanitskii (10/29).

their assets. Thus Samarkand's leading prerevolutionary fruit merchant, Fishel' Berkovich Erusalimskii, supplied the local market with fruits without a break from 1918 to 1921; the only change in his business after the announcement of the NEP was that he resumed large-scale commercial operations in Leningrad, Moscow, and Siberia, in addition to Tashkent. For a merchant of Erusalimskii's standing, credit remained available well after the introduction of a more restrictive policy.[30] Similar cases from Central Asia included a major Tashkent livestock trader, an Andizhan cloth merchant, and a Poltoratsk flour and "colonial goods" dealer; small-scale traders naturally benefited from the incomplete implementation of war communism in their area as well.[31] This initial advantage did not guarantee a firm's continued success, it must be emphasized. Several cases from Ukraine illustrate the rigidity of certain prerevolutionary merchants who had opened their businesses in the decade or two before the war and refused to alter their practices or objects in response to the new economic and political conditions. Thus, when the Soviet government put a major effort into monopolizing the salt market in 1923, Srul' Shmulevich Kogan, a salt trader in Podol'sk, merely watched as his sales plummeted from the tens of thousands he consistently averaged from 1907 to 1922 to just one thousand rubles a month in 1926.[32]

In the core Soviet territory, those prerevolutionary merchants who had been able to pass themselves off as experts to the Soviet government, and had found employment in the supply agencies, tended to fare best in 1921–22. We have encountered this group before in such characters as Semen Pliatskii, the Leningrad scrap-metal millionaire, and D. A. D'iakov, the rural mill owner turned cooperator and food committee member. The early NEP period saw the resurrection of many of prerevolutionary Russia's lumber barons, cloth merchants, grain dealers, and leather, egg, fruit, meat, wine, and fish traders, and, although their businesses were constrained by the loss of the export market, there was still money to be made at home.[33] As this list suggests, the largest merchants of the period specialized in bulk commodities, for which it was very useful to have connections in the syndicates and at VSNKh. Maiakovskii's tongue-in-cheek description of the Nepman's ideal family—"a fiancée in

[30] Kb/Uz/Erusalimskii.

[31] For example, Kb/Uz/Zakirdzhanov, Kb/Uz/Abdugaliamov, Kkb/Uz/Arustamov, Kb/Uz/Abduzhalidov, and Kb/Uz/Aminov.

[32] Kb/Uk/Kogan. Similar cases include Kb/Uk/Shtern (wine) and Kb/Uk/Stanislavskii (cigarette paper).

[33] For example, Kb/Sev-zap/Rozen, Kb/Sev-zap/Berezin and Chudakov, Kb/Sev-zap/Rukin, Kb/Sev-zap/Rulev, Kb/Sev-zap/Binevich, Kb/Uz/Breslavets, Kb/Uz/Islamov, Kb/Uk/Rivkin, Kb/Uk/Al'tmanKhF, and Kb/Uk/Briskin (among others).

a trust, a godfather at GUM, and a brother in a commissariat" [*nevesta v treste, kum v GUM, brat v narkomat*]—may occasionally have applied to the formation of business networks,[34] but, for the most part, connections derived from prior work as a commission agent or representative. Those same contacts helped with bank credit, until the merchants had amassed sufficient capital reserves of their own; in several cases they also continued to supply goods on a commission basis after the merchant had formally abandoned socialist-sector employment.[35]

Small-business owners inevitably had a harder time mobilizing capital for their shops. Many, including 87 of the 304 traders in my database, pooled the start-up costs, risks, and profits with one or more partners. In a few instances a partner put up the cash without taking an active hand in the management of the business or merely lent the firm his reputation. A young haberdasher in Leningrad, for example, signed on, as a backer, one of the Eliseevs, a famous prerevolutionary retailer, and then used the latter's name to secure a loan.[36] Most partnerships nonetheless involved active collaboration, which presupposed a considerable degree of trust. Partnerships almost never crossed ethnic lines (in fact, none of the partnerships in my database did) and very often rested on kin groups: in-laws, extended family, and, above all, two or three brothers.[37] Somewhat more surprisingly, partnerships sometimes joined together prerevolutionary competitors, whose long-standing familiarity with each other's businesses proved stronger than their traditional rivalry.[38]

Some retailers accumulated capital the hard way: they started as hawkers or traveling peddlers, graduated to renting a table or stall at the market, and finally scraped together enough money to outfit a small shop. This process could be excruciatingly slow, and in fact most traders never moved beyond the second rank. One who did was Vol'f Izrailovich Gamerman, a young shopkeeper in Zhmerinka. It took Gamerman four years of hawking needles, thread, and buttons from a tray before he was able to rent a more permanent space, and, even then, his trading premises were carved out of a stationery shop (the stationer had decided to sublet one counter to help with his own bills). Gamerman must be counted as a success story: his sales more than tripled between September

---

[34] Quoted in Ball, *Russia's Last Capitalists*, 114.

[35] For example, Kb/Uk/Landa, Kb/Sev-zap/Nevel'son, and Kb/Sev-zap/Burin.

[36] Kb/Sev-zap/Rozovskii. The Eliseevs' fancy food shops were eventually taken over by the Stalinist trade establishment as their flagship food stores; see chapter 5. "Silent" partnerships included Kb/Sev-zap/Blokh, Kb/Sev-zap/Bezprozvannaia, Kb/Sev-zap/Burdeinyi, Kb/Sev-zap/Rukin, Kb/Uk/Apriamov, and Kb/Uk/Medvedkovskaia.

[37] Twenty-six firms in my database were partnerships of brothers (plus one of sisters).

[38] Kb/Uk/Tarlovskii and Leonov; Kb/Uk/Shpolianskii, Liberman, and Kleiman.

1927, when he first rented the space, and December 1928.[39] Still, this was not the road to riches. A few traders succeeded in using a small shop as a springboard for large-scale retail or wholesale operations, but they had generally taken this leap by mid-1923.[40] Something similar would happen in the 1990s: it was possible to become very wealthy very fast in the first few years after privatization, but income classes subsequently rigidified. Small shopkeepers could continue to hope for modest success in the mid- and late 1920s, but the "wide perspective" that seemed to spread out before the mid-level trader in 1921–22 was now definitively closed off.

The Logic of Utilization and the Regulatory Context

The Bolsheviks moved quickly to regularize the status of private trade. Licenses and business taxes were introduced at the end of the summer of 1921; income taxes and the five-tiered licensing system in 1922; and, as of January 1, 1923, the new RSFSR Civil Code laid the legal foundations for a market economy.[41] While reaffirming the government's monopoly on foreign exchange, the Civil Code codified a range of property rights, including rights to such intangible goods as trademarks and patents. It also established the principles of contract law; delineated fair business practices; and enumerated the conditions for legal exchange. Possessors of property were permitted to sell virtually anything, excepting only those classes of goods (narcotics, explosives, firearms, and military technology) commonly regulated by modern states. As for the legal subjects of exchange transactions, only soldiers, state functionaries, and government suppliers were barred from engaging in trade. As several commentators have suggested, the formal codification of exchange procedures as civil rights must have increased citizens' confidence that the Bolsheviks had, indeed, adopted the NEP "for a long time and in earnest."[42]

[39] Kb/Uk/Gamerman. Other cases of a gradual consolidation of trade from rank I or II to rank III include Kb/Sev-zap/BarenbaumRE, Kb/Sev-zap/RumiantsevVM, Kb/Uk/BeilinIV, Kb/Uk/Levish, Kb/Uk/Kalantyrskii, Kb/Uk/Shul'man, Kb/Uk/Khaikin, and Kb/Uk/Khinkis.

[40] For example, Kb/Sev-zap/Bezprozvannyi, Kb/Sev-zap/Rozovskii, and Kb/Uk/Gurevich.

[41] For overviews, see Ball, *Russia's Last Capitalists*, 15–30; Banerji, *Merchants and Markets*, 40–44; Carr, *Bolshevik Revolution*, 2:331–37.

[42] Quoted in Lenin, *PSS*, 43:329. On the December 1922 decision to ban trade by state employees, suppliers, and soldiers, see Ball, *Russia's Last Capitalists*, 114–15; on the Civil Code and public confidence, see 23, as well as Banerji, *Merchants and Markets*, 45–46. For an annotated compendium of laws regulating private enterprise, see Ia. A. Kantorovich, *Chastnaia torgovlia i promyshlennost' SSSR po deistvuiushchemu zakonodatel'stvu* (Leningrad, 1925), esp. 25–40.

At odds with the Civil Code's rights-based terminology, Bolshevik publicists, economic analysts, and politicians preferred an instrumental discourse. For them, traders had rights only insofar as they made themselves "useful." This logic of utilization had ramifications for state policy, which sought to channel private enterprise in a constructive direction. I. S. Mingulin, author of a 1927 treatise on "private capital," put this goal particularly bluntly:

> Our task is to regulate and control private capital and its accumulation; not to let it accumulate by thievish means; not to let it operate where it is harmful, and to extirpate it from those areas; to attract it to places where from our point of view there is helpful work for it to do. Our task consists in actually putting private capital to the service of socialism.[43]

Mingulin went further than others in advocating the maximal integration of state, cooperative, and private trade, on the grounds that fostering interdependence would force the private sector into a form of state capitalism. Nearly every commentator could agree, though, that, through a rational policy of regulation and exploitation, the state could "harness" private capital until traders' services were no longer necessary.

In practice, the logic of utilization repeatedly trumped traders' codified civil rights. When the scissors crisis reached its zenith at the start of October 1923, just nine months after the adoption of the Civil Code, policy makers were willing to jettison constitutional protections for private businesses in favor of secret police operations to "restore the economy's health." Between October and December the OGPU arrested and deported 916 "parasites, leeches, corrupt and malicious speculators" from Moscow in a campaign targeting private contractors, wholesalers, money changers, illegal alcohol and drug traders, and also socialist-sector officials, who had putatively connived to elevate the prices of consumer goods. Policing organs in other cities followed suit, producing what a Leningrad paper called "a general panic among the Nepmen."[44] This episode makes clear that extrajudicial "operations" against private businesses were not exclusively a Stalinist phenomenon but were a regular part of the Bolsheviks' administrative repertoire from 1917 on. Ideologically they were compatible with the utilization concept, according to which businesses' rights were supposed to be contingent on their utility for the Soviet state.

Chapter 2 touched on the consequences of the price scissors for Soviet

---

[43] Mingulin, *Puti razvitiia chastnogo kapitala*, 43.
[44] Trifonov, *Klassy i klassovaia bor'ba*, 174–76; *Krasnaia gazeta*, February 9, 1924; Kondurushkin, *Chastnyi kapital*, 111.

trade policy, but a few details may be added. The outcome of the crisis, as indicated above, was re-bureaucratization. In addition to the proliferation of regulatory bodies, price cuts were decreed at every stage of the supply cycle for manufactured goods. The so-called issue [*otpusknye*] prices at which industrial syndicates and trusts sold to wholesalers were capped; shipping tariffs were lowered; wholesale prices in the state and cooperative trade systems were regulated; and "orientational" prices were reintroduced into socialist retail trade. As a rule, the mandated cuts reflected the regime's focus on economic stimulation over solvency. According to Malafeev, the historian of Soviet price policy, the 1923–24 issue prices were fixed below the cost of production in several key areas of the consumer economy. With respect to the strategy of policy makers of using consumer demand as an engine of economic growth, the measures were a success: combined with the introduction of a stable currency in early 1924, the price cuts elicited a surge in demand for manufactured goods.[45]

The crisis inevitably affected the relationship between the public sector and private trade. When policy makers fixed issue prices at a level below cost on textiles, sugar, and a few other consumer staples, they were determined to pass the savings on to consumers and to prevent private traders from pocketing the proceeds. One way of averting this was to raise taxes, giving breaks to cooperatives and state trade; similarly major cities slashed cooperatives' rents.[46] A more potent method was to restrict supplies. Sales by industrial trusts and syndicates had been monitored since early 1922 with an eye to increasing the socialist sector's share of manufactured products.[47] In the wake of the price scissors, monitoring was replaced by stronger measures: the textile syndicate, under political pressure, announced that private wholesalers would no longer be able to obtain goods on credit, and the sugar trust went a step further and declared that it would no longer sell to private traders at all.[48] According to a Leningrad paper, "White Guardist" rumors now prophesied "the end of the NEP"—and, indeed, the paper advocated taking immediate steps to eliminate private businesses from wholesale trade, and to regulate retailers. "For them," the column concluded, "this no doubt does seem like 'the end of the NEP,' but for us—it means its fulfilment."[49]

---

[45] Malafeev, *Istoriia tsenoobrazovaniia*, 53–61; Atlas, *Denezhnaia sistema*, 214–47.

[46] *Krasnaia gazeta*, February 12, 1924; Ball, *Russia's Last Capitalists*, 28–30, 53–54, and Banerji, *Merchants and Markets*, 59–72.

[47] B. Udintsev, "Sootnoshenie gosudarstvennogo, kooperativnogo i chastnogo torgovykh apparatov na otdel'nykh rynkakh," in Miliutin et al., *Na novykh putiakh*, 1:198–239, esp. 229–39.

[48] *Krasnaia gazeta*, May 13, 1924.

[49] Ibid., April 30, 1924.

As it turned out, the 1923–24 regulations created as many problems as they solved. They did effect a permanent decline in the percentage of goods sold directly to private businesses by the nationalized syndicates and trusts: from the 27 percent reported in 1921–22, sales to private traders fell to 5–6 percent in 1926–27 and to 1–2 percent the following year.[50] The regulations also made manufactured goods more affordable to consumers, helping to pull the economy out of the slump. On the debit side, below-cost pricing was hardly a long-term solution to the cost-of-living problem. As Malafeev observed, such a solution would have to include an increase in productivity, without which the lower prices could not be sustained.[51] Sapping manufacturers' profits, below-cost pricing tended only to inhibit production. The cessation of sales to private wholesalers further weakened industrial finances, since the cooperatives were notorious for abusing credit. Arup Banerji, a historian of NEP private trade, reports that 70 percent of the fabric, thread, leather footwear, and galoshes sold by state industry to consumer cooperatives in 1926–27 went onto the cooperatives' credit lines, as did virtually all their purchases of sugar and salt. This contrasted with the private sector, which procured the bulk of its merchandise for cash.[52]

While they dampened production of consumer commodities, price reductions naturally stimulated demand. Below-cost pricing may have closed the price scissors, but it opened up a new set of scissors on the supply side of the graph. The "marketing crisis" was thus scarcely overcome before the "goods famine" set in; and, as any microeconomic textbook would predict, the acuteness of the shortages of a given commodity reflected the size of the gap between the fixed price and the market price. For private traders, the effect of these changes was to increase the risks of doing business dramatically. All at once, supplies of manufactured goods became more difficult to obtain, taxes rose, and the socialist sector was given a huge competitive boost in the form of lower transaction costs. Worse, while the political atmosphere became somewhat more favorable to business in 1924–25 under the influence of Bukharin,[53] intensifying shortages sparked a new round of finger-pointing within a matter of months.

---

[50] Banerji, *Merchants and Markets*, 106–7 (1921–27); GARF, f. 5446, op. 55, d. 1585, l. 43 (1927–28).

[51] Malafeev, *Istoriia tsenoobrazovaniia*, 58–61.

[52] Banerji, *Merchants and Markets*, 106.

[53] Banerji dates the conciliatory "new trade practice" to March 1925 (ibid., 51–54), but earlier commentators placed its inception eight months earlier. See Ia. M. Gol'bert, ed., *Novaia torgovaia praktika* (Moscow, 1925); S. O. Zagorskii, *K sotsializmu ili k kapitalizmu?* (Prague, 1927), 127–29.

The role of taxation in this episode was highly typical of the regime's commercial policy. Explicitly aimed at maximizing the utility of the private sector—milking it of profits without shutting it down—NEP-era fiscal policy subjected retailers to a battery of fees and taxes that could be raised or lowered at will if privateers were deemed "too strong" or, alternatively, if the economy needed a boost.[54] There was the onerous personal income tax, the one tax from which petty traders were exempt; the license fee; a 3 percent tax on sales; rent on a stall or street-corner position, or day-use fees for market-hawking rights; the "bourgeois" education fee for any traders with children; occasional one-time taxes, such as the 1923 famine-relief levy; and a surcharge for the right to sell "luxuries," a category broad enough to cover woolen fabrics, fireworks, and mayonnaise. Even in 1924–25, the fiscal year with the lowest tax rates of the decade, these added up to 21 to 32 percent of private traders' earnings, a substantial increase over the prerevolutionary rates. Not surprisingly, if the number of private traders rose and fell with the level of unemployment, the number also corresponded roughly to the weight of the tax burden in a given year. That burden was heaviest in 1923–24, when so many businesses failed that Soviet officials began to worry about "trade deserts," and from 1927 to 1931, when fiscal and repressive policies had the eradication of private trade as their goal.[55]

Through mid-1927 the regulatory context nonetheless left traders room to maneuver. In keeping with the doctrine of utilization, the stultifying restrictions of war communism were replaced by an assortment of rules that would, in theory, "harness" private trade. All levels of government took part in this effort, municipalities generally regulating the noneconomic side of merchandising and central government organs (Sovnarkom, STO, Narkomfin, and Narkomvnutorg) regulating the financial side. Federal regulations were aimed at impairing the competitiveness of private retailers vis-à-vis the public sector, but they also introduced consumer protections and pointed in the direction of modernizing trade. The 1926 RSFSR Criminal Code, for example, prescribed criminal sanctions for the adulteration of products, price collusion, and fraudulent

---

[54] For example, GARF, f. 5446, op. 55, d. 958, ll. 178–79.

[55] For 1924–25 tax figures, see Strumilin, *Statistiko-ekonomicheskie ocherki*, 704–6; G. P. Paduchev, *Chastnyi torgovets pri novoi ekonomicheskoi politike* (*po dannym biudzhetnogo obsledovaniia*). (Voronezh, 1926), 32–33. Small shopkeepers with class II and III licenses paid the lowest rates at 21 percent, whereas the upper trading licenses were in a 26 to 29 percent bracket. Class I petty traders probably paid the highest percentage of all, given the size of fixed taxes and fees; Strumilin calculated that as much as 32 percent of their earnings went to the government in 1924–25. On the evolution of tax policy, see Ball, *Russia's Last Capitalists*, 28–30, 53–54, 68–69, and Banerji, *Merchants and Markets*, 59–72.

sales under the rubric of "violations of the rules of trade." Consumer interests also benefited from regulations designed to retard "speculation," such as the obligatory posting of prices in a visible spot near the door, and one can hardly fault the government for trying to deter tax evasion and to foster transparency in business practices through the maintenance of accurate books.[56] With rigorous enforcement, these regulations would eventually have effected a break with the haggling, personalism, and informal accounting procedures characteristic of Russia's precapitalist exchange culture.

On a day-to-day basis, traders were "controlled" primarily by regulations and policing at the local level. Shops remained barred from defining their own hours, though the devolution of the authority to establish hours of trade from the central government to provincial and municipal trade departments allowed for some flexibility compared to the situation from 1918 to 1921. In Riazan' Province, for example, the trade department permitted barbershops and certain other businesses in the vicinity of a market to remain open for an extra hour or two. Exceptions derived from governmental objectives rather than from private commercial interests. Most shops for manufactured goods in Riazan' were placed on a nine-to-five schedule; most food shops, seven-to-five, though bread shops were authorized to remain open into the evening. Even hawkers were given a 10:00 P.M. curfew, after which they were told to keep off the streets. All shops were to be closed on Sundays, though bazaars could do business; and, finally, "proletarian holidays" were declared off-limits to any and all trade.[57] In the socialist sector, the system of fixed hours emphasized employee rights over customer convenience, much as it does today in Germany and France, but since the vast majority of private traders did not employ hired labor, the concern there stemmed primarily from the impetus to "control" private trade. Making shopping difficult for anyone on a regular work schedule, restrictions on hours had the paradoxical effect of bolstering the need for street vendors as well as for domestic help and housewives.[58]

Local governments also decided the day-use fees for occasional trade at the market (an important source of municipal revenues throughout the period of this study); established sanitary regulations; oversaw "Committees of Market Traders" and "Mercantile Exchange Committees," the

[56] Kantorovich, *Chastnaia torgovlia i promyshlennost'*, 41–51, 60–62; Banerji, *Merchants and Markets*, 91–93.
[57] GA Riaz. ob., f. R-787, op. 1, d. 48, ll. 1,4.
[58] The importance of housewives, daughters, and domestic help to working-class families emerges clearly from Kabo's *Ocherki rabochego byta*; see esp. 50, 58, 89, 101.

government's liaisons with the private sector; collected taxes; and carried out inspections both to ensure compliance with the myriad local and federal trade regulations and to identify tax fraud. The Market Committees helped with several of these functions; though composed primarily of private businessmen, Market Committees took charge of maintaining the stalls and tables at the outdoor markets; collecting garbage; policing for unlicensed vendors; providing statistics on retail turnover; and even assisting financial departments in establishing particular vendors' sales.[59] Recalling the civic role of manufacturers and merchants during the First World War, the Market Committees represented an unusual example of public-private collaboration during the NEP years. Through the middle part of the decade, their very existence seemed to affirm the possibility that traders could find a common ground with the regime.

Shopkeepers' Stories: The NEP from Below

The ups and downs of state policy had a direct impact on many businesses: a few merchants in my database were arrested during the 1923 roundups, and several shopkeepers deliberately enlarged or reduced the scale of their trade in response to changing tax rates.[60] For the majority of traders, however, policies defined the general parameters of business, while success or failure at a given conjuncture had other ingredients, too. Universal factors, such as the location and initial capitalization of the shop, or the proprietor's acumen, experience, and reputation, played a large role in the Soviet Union as they do throughout the world. As suggested above, the ability to mobilize capital was probably the single most important determinant of success in the first part of the decade. More distinctive features of NEP-era trade included the altered structure of consumer demand and traders' chronic difficulties with supplies. From the time of the scissors crisis on, there was also the intensified, extremely unequal character of commercial competition, as socialist-sector retailers obtained rental, transport, and supply contracts on increasingly advantageous terms and received significant tax breaks. A fourth factor was the degree to which different lines of trade were vulnerable to repression. Taken as a group, these factors underscore the heightened risks created by the legal instability and antibusiness bias of Bolshevik rule. Contem-

[59] Kantorovich, *Chastnaia torgovlia i promyshlennost'*, 49–51, 70–73; GA Riaz. ob., f. R-787, op. 1, d. 25, ll. 1–6; d. 50, l. 69.

[60] Arrests in late 1923–24 included Kb/Uk/Bernshtein, Kb/Sev-zap/Rozenoer, and Kb/Sev-zap/Troshin. Shifts in license category, premises, and sales were specifically ascribed to tax rates in Kb/Sev-zap/Rogovskii, Kb/Uk/Briskin, and Kb/Uk/Barbaumov.

porary commentators tended to identify "flexibility" [*gibkost'*] as the outstanding attribute of the NEP-era "private capitalist,"[61] but an equally salient characteristic of the larger entrepreneurs of the period was simply a stomach for risk.

Reviving, as it did, much of the prerevolutionary legal framework, the 1923 Civil Code appeared to presage a return to normalcy in the commercial sphere. Even in those sectors of trade in which their activities were deemed "useful," merchants and shopkeepers nonetheless faced formidable new obstacles to commercial success. One of the largest changes in the consumer economy vis-à-vis the prewar period was the diminished demand for luxury goods. Economic analysts reasonably attributed this shift to the demise of the aristocracy; wealthy Nepmen, performing artists, "bourgeois specialists," and high-ranking Soviet officials enjoyed a comfortable existence, but they could scarcely sustain a luxury market on the prerevolutionary scale:

> The demands formerly made on the market by the ruling classes have, for the most part, no place today, since there are no aristocratic landowners, no *noblesse de robe* or *noblesse d'épée*. The capitalist stratum of prewar Russia has been replaced by the relatively small buying power of the Nepmen. In a word, three quarters of the parasitical elite of prewar Russia have been consigned to the garbage pit of history, and with them, the specific demands created by a "high society" lifestyle. At their expense the consuming capacity of the laboring social strata has risen, but these strata purchase goods with entirely different qualities in mind: "as many as possible, as cheap as possible." As a result, an identical aggregate demand is far from identical in structure. The relative weight of goods for the mass market (cheap varieties of cloth, clothing, tobacco, shoes, etc.) accordingly must be significantly greater than before.[62]

Compounding these demographic changes was a psychological factor: even among middle-class consumers, sociologists observed that the impact of wartime deprivation on consumption attitudes and habits persisted for two to three years longer than deprivation itself. The standard of living of the middle classes (for the most part, white-collar state functionaries) slowly rose, but they did not revert to their "normal," prewar consumption patterns until 1925. Then, and only then, were the more elastic items of the household budget—cultural expenditures, furnishings

---

[61] Arskii, *Kak borot'sia s chastnym kapitalom*, 28; L. Kolesnikov, *Litso klassovogo vraga* (Moscow, 1928), 28; L. Limanov, "Chastnyi kapital na sel'sko-khoziaistvennom rynke," in Zalkind, *Chastnaia torgovliav SSSR*, 47–70, here, 66.

[62] V. Belenko, "O tovarnom golode," *Bol'shevik*, no. 17 (September 15, 1926): 44–61, here 51.

and household goods, woolen cloth and clothing, luxuries—consumed in anywhere near the quantities of the period before the First World War.[63]

These changes in demand had a considerable impact on retailers' prospects. Even in the capitals, Soviet trade was oriented primarily toward the mass consumer. Travelers to the Soviet Union, naturally themselves of the middle and upper classes, often remarked on the absence of jewelry stores and other luxury retailers in Moscow.[64] In Petrograd only 68 vendors were classified as purveyors of "luxury goods" in February 1923, notwithstanding the Bolsheviks' broad definition of that term; one year later, a review of trade permits showed that 11,300 of 12,700 licensed commercial businesses in the northern capital sold foods (6,800), grains, prepared meals, cloth, metal wares, notions, shoes, chemicals, chandlery, and clothes. Bookstores, pubs, barbershops, jewelers, shops for musical instruments and sporting goods, drugstores, stationers, furriers, harness shops, shops for construction materials and fuels—in short, commercial licenses for the sale of nearly all goods and services other than food and clothing—together numbered just 1,400 three years into the NEP.[65]

Luxury dealers who tried to navigate the passage to the new social landscape often found the transition difficult. In Kiev A. N. Kaliadin's "Fashion House" (known before the revolution as "Mme Daudet") employed fourteen seamstresses, supplied with four sewing machines, to construct ballgowns and expensive daywear and hats. Although Kaliadin continued to serve "a certain segment of the population" as late as December 1923, his business languished; by mid-1924 he was fending off debtors and had had a run-in with the law. The Leningrad ladies' tailor A. S. Portnov lasted only slightly longer. According to a 1923 credit report, Portnov's shop on Troitskaia Street "numbered among Petrograd's most renowned" before the revolution, catering largely to an aristocratic clientele. Portnov revived his business at the old location in early 1922, and followed it shortly thereafter with a second shop in Petrograd's trading arcade [Gostinyi dvor]. Then, however, the scissors crisis hit. Already overstretched by high taxes and a weakened demand for finery, the crisis forced him to close first the new shop and then the old. He continued taking orders for ladies' dresses from his apartment until the goods famine made even that business untenable. By mid-1926 the famous tailor had been reduced to working as a shopclerk in a neighbor's store, a

[63] N. Gumilevskii, *Biudzhet sluzhashchikh v 1922–26 gg.*, ed. and with an introduction by E. O. Kabo (Moscow, 1928), 22–23.

[64] For example, Andrée Viollis, *A Girl in Soviet Russia* (New York, 1929), 38.

[65] *Krasnaia gazeta*, February 14, 1923; January 3, 1924.

122 • Chapter Three

casualty of revolutionary social leveling and the NEP's successive crises in the cloth and clothing sector.[66]

Kaliadin and Portnov can be usefully contrasted with a couple of successful luxury clothiers in the NEP era. Leia Aizikovna Temkina had similarly sold fine clothes in St. Petersburg for more than a decade before the revolution, and in 1922 she, too, reopened her shop in an arcade. Again, there were a number of seamstresses attached to the shop. The difference was that Temkina and her husband had excellent connections in the supply agencies (he frequently traveled to Moscow for textiles because of a connection there) and, above all, that she protected her business against demand fluctuations in the luxury clothes market by contracting to supply uniforms to several state institutions on the side. The result was a thriving business, with sales of ten thousand to twenty thousand rubles a month in 1925–26. Rumiantsev & Co., another Leningrad clothier of prerevolutionary provenance, sold fully twice that from a large shop in *Gostinyi dvor*. Its secret lay in the backgrounds and assets of the three partners: Rumiantsev had taken on, along with his original partner, the prerevolutionary proprietor of a warehouse for woolen and silk cloth. Though Rumiantsev's firm continued to concentrate on the high end of the clothing market, the new partner's stocks had given them a cushion with respect to supplies.[67]

Clothing sales for the mass market were also anchored in the private sector; urban Russians of all classes tended to have their suits, shirts, and dresses sewn to order, which ordinarily meant taking fabric to a custom shop.[68] Only a few large socialist retailers opened up ateliers for individual tailoring in the 1920s, as against the numerous privately employed seamstresses and tailors in every city and town. Outer garments, such as heavy woolen coats, hats, shawls, scarves, neckties, and gloves, were usually bought ready-made, but these, too, were sold primarily at the private shops, which employed a small army of outworkers to sew the garments at home.[69] Examples of successful mass-market clothiers from my database include Iakov Abramovich Borushek and David Abramovich Bezprozvannyi, both Jewish, both Leningraders, and both at least the second generation in their family to concentrate on the garment trades. Aiming at lower-class customers, each man chose to rent a stall at the market

[66] Kb/Uk/Kaliadin; Kb/Sev-zap/Portnov.

[67] Kb/Sev-zap/"Rumiantsev & Co." Kb/Sev-zap/Temkina.

[68] As a caveat, many urban and rural families limited the cost of clothing by making shirts, undergarments, dresses, and especially children's clothes themselves.

[69] Petroodezhda opened up an "atelier des modes" in September 1923 (*Krasnaia gazeta*, September 24, 1923). On ready-to-wear clothing as a province of private trade, see *Biudzhety rabochikh*, 1:46.

rather than a Western-style storefront. They each did a big business. Borushek concentrated on working-class bachelors (on and around payday at the big factories, he reportedly sold one thousand to fifteen hundred rubles' worth a day), whereas Bezprozvannyi targeted residents of the nearby suburbs and small towns. Bezprozvannyi's principal clients were peddlers, whom he met while making his rounds to Leningrad's suburban markets. All told, he sold in the area of twelve thousand rubles a month.[70]

As these examples suggest, cheap clothing could be a lucrative business in the 1920s. Not having replaced worn-out clothes and shoes during the civil war, citizens of modest means spent substantially more on dress in the NEP era than before the First World War. According to a 1923 study, workers would have to have doubled their prewar rates of clothing acquisition for the next three years just to restore their wardrobes to their 1915 to 1917 state.[71] If a study of 128 railroad workers' families was at all typical, the first thing they did in 1921–22 was to buy a new pair of shoes; at the end of 1923, 73 percent of the shoes in these households had been purchased since the announcement of the NEP. Less expensive articles, such as underwear, stockings, and men's shirts, had continued to be purchased during the civil war, but they had a short lifespan, and they, too, needed to be replaced.[72] Certainly not every trader in these sectors grew rich from the heightened demand of the early NEP period; in rural areas, for example, the total sales of all trade in 1922–23 totaled less than the value of one pair of shoes per inhabitant.[73] Urban private traders were less likely to prosper from stockings, socks, or shawls than from sales of shoes or cheap clothes. Like other lower-class retailers, vendors of these articles congregated at outdoor markets; however, they typically lacked the capital and the flexibility of the private clothiers, since they sold only what they knitted themselves.[74]

The organizational structure of shoe, stocking, and clothing businesses was characteristic of many private retailers in the "useful" spheres. Combining sales with production, they paid not only for a commercial license but also for a manufacturing license, usually in the lowest, artisanal bracket. From the perspective of Soviet officialdom, the artisanal component muddied the "class character" of the business and justified a

[70] Kb/Sev-zap/Borushek; Kb/Sev-zap/Bezprozvannyi.

[71] *Biudzhety rabochikh*, 1:45; S. G. Strumilin, *Rabochii byt v tsifrakh, Statistiko-ekonomicheskie etiudy* (Moscow, 1926), 88–92.

[72] Strumilin, *Rabochii byt v tsifrakh*, 84.

[73] Dmitrenko, *Torgovaia politika*, 134.

[74] Kb/Uk/Medvedkovskaia, Kb/Uk/Koshelevskii, Kb/Uk/Kagan, Kb/Sev-zap/Beloritskii, and Kb/Uk/Beirak.

slightly more positive view of the proprietor's expertise. This combination was typical of certain food vendors: candy, *kvas*, sausages, and pastries all tended to be prepared by the vendor and then hawked on street corners or at the bazaar from a kiosk or a tray. Up market and down, it was also common to businesses selling a wide variety of consumer articles in addition to clothes and shoes: toys, clocks, lamps, iron beds, wooden and upholstered furniture, jewelry, embossed stationery, bed linens, harnesses, suitcases, pottery, and paints.[75] The All-Russian Union of Manufacturing Cooperatives claimed, in 1926, that artisans, most of whom were not members of cooperatives, produced an absolute majority of the country's consumer goods: 80 percent of shoes, 56 percent of harnesses and other leather goods, 62 percent of clothes, 62 percent of processed foods, 62 percent of cosmetics and soaps, 82 percent of furs and sheepskin articles, 60 percent of woodworking, and so on.[76] In the later part of the 1920s, when state policy turned against private commerce, these artisan-traders were often able to avoid persecution by surrendering their shops and retreating into artisanal work, the output of which they would sell to cooperatives but also at the market. Thus, mutatis mutandis, artisans of consumer goods remained a visible stratum of private trade in the decades after the NEP.

Food, drink, and entertainment businesses were another stronghold of private trade during the NEP years. Compared to other lines of commerce, the capital requirements for the sale of prepared foods were miniscule; one could purchase the ingredients daily, and equipment commonly consisted of little more than an oven or grill, some pots, and a pushcart or tray. Sweets—hard candy, halvah, and chocolate—attracted an especially large contingent of artisanal petty vendors by virtue of their high turnover and low costs of production. The only difficulty was the sugar syndicate's refusal to sell to private traders, which left candymakers at the mercy of state and cooperative retailers for supplies.[77]

There was clearly a cultural component to the food and drinks business. Central Asia had its teahouses, usually located at the bazaar; Russia had its *traktiry*, or pubs, usually located along a street; Jews stayed away from drinking and eating establishments relative to other kinds of trade.[78]

---

[75] Roughly 60 of the 304 traders in my database fit this description.

[76] RGASPI, f. 17, op. 85, d. 293, ll. 1, 20.

[77] Kb/Uz/Ismailov, Kb/Uz/Akbaraev, Kb/Uk/Smolianskii, Kb/Uk/Gel'brukh, Kb/Uk/Gershanovich, Kb/Uk/Povodator, Kb/Uk/Vykhodets, Kb/Uk/Bokhonskaia, Kb/Uk/Angelov, and Kb/Uk/Riskin.

[78] This is documented clearly by the 1926 census, for example, in Ukraine, where 70 to 78 percent of private traders, depending on the license class, were Jewish, but Jews owned just half of all the bars and eateries (*Vsesoiuznaia perepis'* 1926 g., 18:360–68, 28: 100–103).

Nonetheless, what emerges from the credit reports is the importance of the site, rather than culture, capital, or skill, to the success of an eatery or food shop. Maria Andreevna Anosova, who managed to rent space across from the largest factory in Leningrad, predictably did a bustling business in both prepared foods and groceries; Emil'ian Nikitich Tarasenko, who ran an alehouse from his tiny home in a Ukrainian village, equally unsurprisingly did not.[79] The credit reports expressed amazement when a small-town inn and restaurant stayed in business after the town lost its status as district center.[80] By virtue of their high volume and ready market, train stations were a particularly prized location for a fast-food stand or kiosk; this had presumably been the case before the revolution as well.[81]

No less than clothing shops, the food services industry had to adjust to postrevolutionary demand shifts. Among ethnic Russians, at least, there was no lower- or middle-class tradition of dining out; as soon as subsidies to canteens were discontinued, workers and employees reverted to their prerevolutionary habits and came home for the midday meal. Although it is unclear how fast-food stands fit into this picture, NEP-era working-class households spent less than 1 percent of their total food expenditures on meals away from home.[82] This had ramifications for the retail network, initially by increasing the share of groceries, bread bakeries, and flour and cereal shops in the overall distribution of trade. In 1923 businesses specializing in comestibles garnered up to 60 percent of urban trade licenses; even in Moscow 41 percent of retail outlets were devoted to food as against 28 percent thirty years before.[83] Food sales, other than bread, continued to be concentrated at the outdoor bazaars, which were traditionally subdivided into rows for grains and flour, dairy products, fruits and vegetables, and meat. The oversupply of vendors made the food market extremely competitive in the early 1920s; a number of bread bakers and grocers in my database went under, and others sought out new, sometimes marginal, locations for their stalls. One innovative site in this period was the inner courtyard of a large residential building, pioneered by a Leningrad greengrocer, Vasilii Nikolaevich Rumiantsev; although such stalls later became common, his business remained slow as of 1925.[84] By and large, the most successful food retailers were either

[79] Pubs, eateries, and inns run from a person's home were not uncommon in small towns and villages. See Kb/Uk/Tarasenko and Kb/Uk/Al'tman.

[80] Kb/Uk/Shengof.

[81] Kb/Uk/Svirena (actually, this food stand at a rural station was strikingly unprofitable); Kb/Uk/Mikhnovskii; and Kb/Sev-zap/Tarakanov.

[82] *Biudzhety rabochikh*, 1:44; Kabo, *Ocherki rabochego byta*, 34, 54, 62–63, passim, 149–56.

[83] *Trudy TsSU* 8, no. 2: 263–64, 287–88; Gohstand, "Geography of Trade," 436–37.

[84] Kb/Sev-zap/Rumiantsev. Failed bakeries and groceries included Kb/Sev-zap/Narkevich, Kb/Sev-zap/Bagrachev, and Kb/Sev-zap/Belosel'skii.

bulk flour, wine, fish, or meat merchants, who combined retail with whole-sale trade, and sometimes had a direct supply source (a private vineyard; a fishery), or luxurious Western-style shops selling fresh and dried fruits, cured meats and smoked fish, and other fancy foods.[85]

Urban workers, at least, adhered to the pattern established by prewar budget studies: when incomes rose, so did consumption of both staple and supplementary foods. By December 1922 urban meals still consisted largely of potatoes and rye bread, but workers were eating 30 percent more than had been possible six months earlier. By 1924–25 many felt "sufficient confidence" in the Soviet economy to "liquidate their 'granaries,'" the bags of wheat, rye, and flour almost universally hoarded since the First World War.[86] As household incomes stabilized, urban diets improved in all the ways one would predict from prerevolutionary consumption patterns. Wheat bread supplemented, then displaced, rye bread; animal products—meat, milk, and, in higher-income groups, butter—displaced potatoes and grain; consumption of fruits and sugar rose. These developments had a wider social reach in Moscow than in other parts of the country as a result of higher wages and better supplies; in 1924 a worker in the Urals consumed less than three-quarters of the meat of the average Moscow worker, and just 40 percent of the sugar and butter, making up the caloric difference with potatoes and grains.[87] Everywhere, however, the quantity and quality of food improved, while food expenditures fell from 71 percent of working-class budgetary outlays at their peak in the period from 1918 to 1920 to 44 percent in 1926–27.[88]

Even under the Bolsheviks, middle-class citizens (Soviet employees) enjoyed a richer and more varied diet than industrial workers from the same towns. Nonetheless, it is quite possible that more people could afford gastronomic luxuries than ever before, as humorous sketches began to claim in 1923–24. One such sketch, from Leningrad's evening paper, maintained that workers who barely could have afforded an apple before the revolution could now enjoy imported fruits:

> Today everyone is eating oranges. Even the foyers of movie theaters now sport posters with the warning, "It is forbidden to throw orange seeds and peels onto the floor." In a word, death to sunflower seeds! The orange has rolled

---

[85] Kb/Sev-zap/Bardysheva, Kb/Sev-zap/Nazarov, Kb/Uk/Apriamov, Kb/Uz/Aspiiants, Kb/Uz/Bagiev, Kb/Uk/Shtern, Kb/Uk/Rumiantsev Bros., and Kb/Uk/Briskin, among others.

[86] Kabo, *Ocherki rabochego byta*, esp. 27–123, 149–56.

[87] Kabo, *Pitanie russkogo rabochego*, 112–19, 177–83; *Biudzhety rabochikh*, 1:30–40. Note: Before the war, Baku workers ate better than Moscow workers.

[88] *Biudzhety rabochikh*, 1:27–50.

our way and taken up its rightful place. The "lady with an orange" is already an everyday sight. A boy with an orange, a cabby with an orange, a cashier with an orange —everyone has an orange![89]

While the article went on to poke fun at those petty-minded citizens [*obyvateli*] who judged everything according to the "narrow little window" of material goods, it pointed out, incidentally, that oranges were widely available; that dates had appeared in the cooperative shops; that clothing fashions had improved; and so forth. Articles of this ilk were probably confined to the evening papers and humor magazines, which drew a predominently white-collar, noncommunist audience.[90] Nonetheless, even such an indirect appeal to readers' material well-being suggested that Party leaders understood the propaganda limitations of asceticism. As the country emerged from the extreme privations of the civil war era, a "material abundance" theme played better with readers than a "revolutionary austerity" theme possibly could. In the 1930s and 1940s, after the convulsions of collectivization and war, a similar recognition would propel celebratory articles about consumption onto the front pages of even the Party press.

Be this as it may, is it any surprise that the urban dancehalls, billiard and gambling rooms, and pubs were almost exclusively in the private sector? Individual proprietors had two major advantages over socialist commerce in these areas: a willingness and ability to work long, irregular hours, and a looser attitude toward popular morals. The decision of policy makers to repeal the wartime prohibition on vodka was driven solely by financial considerations; as Iurii Larin put it in a rather typical book on the subject, the state needed the revenue, and vodka was better than *samogon*, the peasantry's potent home-distilled liquor. Like other Bolshevik social commentators, Larin tried to steer a middle course between puritanism and license: workers and peasants needed to find new, cultured varieties of entertainment, such as reading circles or the cinema, he suggested; and, to replace alcohol, what about a state subsidy for sweets?[91] This was not exactly the asceticism sometimes ascribed to the Bolsheviks' value system, but neither was it the best attitude for opening a bar. Drinking, gambling, and promiscuity were, after all, the central compo-

---

[89] E. Gard, "Apel'siny," *Krasnaia gazeta*, March 4, 1924, p. 3.

[90] On the target audiences of different classes of newspapers, see Matthew E. Lenoe, "Agitation, Propaganda, and the 'Stalinization' of the Soviet Press, 1922–1930," *Carl Beck Papers*, no. 1305 (August 1998): 19.

[91] Iu. Larin, *Alkogolizm* (Kharkov, 1930); see also Kabo, who offered a very similar commentary in the family portraits section of *Ocherki rabochego byta*. With respect to the legal framework, vodka sales were legalized in two stages, with 80–proof vodka revived only in late 1925; cf. *Biudzhety rabochikh*, 1:80.

nents of popular entertainment establishments. The occasional socialist corporation became involved in alcohol retailing—a notable example, yet again, was Ukraine's Larek—but the endless regulatory hassles of a billiard hall or a pub, with the high mandatory tax rates on these businesses and, above all, the potential for a police raid, left traditional urban entertainments in private hands.

One final shopkeeper's story illustrates both the phenomenon of the artisan-trader and the punishing competition private traders could face. The shopkeeper in question was Ivan Ivanovich Rozhevskii, Leningrad's principal prewar retailer of academic supplies. In 1922 he took out a license in rank III and reopened the shop. This was the kind of specialized business that cooperatives had never before handled; it included academic books in several languages and all manner of scientific equipment and chemicals, most of which he had managed to salvage during the revolutionary years. By 1924 Rozhevskii's inventory was valued at an impressive 160,000 convertible rubles [*chervontsy*], in addition to which he made chemical equipment in a small workshop behind the store. Rozhevskii was widely regarded as conscientious, hardworking, and knowledgeable, and the chief of one of his four departments was a professor. Naturally this kind of outlet had a slow turnover rate compared to, say, a clothing or food shop, but "Educational Aid" nonetheless sold 40,000 rubles' worth a month and enjoyed a large, regular customer base.

The credit reports from 1925 to 1928 chronicle the decline of this successful business, ending in Rozhevskii's abandonment of the store. The problems began in January 1925, when the municipal commercial agency went on the offensive: directly targeting Educational Aid, Lentorg opened its own, competing shop next door. As of October the new store had had little impact on Rozhevskii's sales, as customers remained devoted to their original supplier. Thereafter things rapidly worsened. Lentorg was able to undercut Rozhevskii's prices by a significant margin, and customers began to defect. Rozhevskii fought back, but at the price of his independence: entering into a contractual arrangement with a cooperative, he agreed to follow the cooperative's price policies and essentially to become an employee on commission (according to the contract, he would receive a monthly salary of 180 rubles, plus 1% of sales). In return he obtained access to supplies at the cooperative rate. Even so, Lentorg's tax advantage was such that, by the end of 1927, Rozhevskii elected to sell his business. The cooperative bought his stocks and equipment for 50,000 rubles—a steal—of which it tendered just 10,000 immediately, agreeing to pay the rest in a year's time. Moreover, it stipulated that Rozhevskii stay on for the first year as the store's "consultant" and de facto manager. Rozhevskii, meanwhile, held onto the workshop in the back, but, though he employed three workers, he sold less than 2,000 rubles' worth of equipment a month to the two retail stores. The final report on his business, dated February 1928, concluded only that he could no longer be described as "a man of means" and that the sole cause for optimism about his future prospects was his enduring reputation as an "agile entrepreneur."

It is tempting to read this story as a tragedy: "energetic, capable individualist falls victim to 'dirty competition' from a corporate machine." The socialist nature of Lentorg adds surprisingly little to this plot line. Rozhevskii's troubles were not so different, in the end, from those of any other shopkeeper confronted by the onslaught of modern commercial techniques. Whenever a department store puts a small clothing shop out of business; when an independent hardware store is transformed into an Ace franchise and then forced under by Home Depot; when the local bookstore loses customers to Barnes & Noble or to Amazon.com—all these changes tend to homogenize the retail environment but also bring economies of scale. Associated with the United States, the global trend-setter in mass retailing, such shifts have characterized retail development for the past one hundred years; the decades before the First World War saw a tremendous proliferation of department stores; the 1920s, retail chains. And although the shopkeepers, and some of their patrons, are sacrificed in the process, many other customers benefit from wider selections and lower distribution costs.[92] In a sense, then, Lentorg's aggressive ploy to capture the academic supplies market can be taken as proof that it had "learned how to trade."

For consumers, the long-term effects of a socialist-sector victory were not always benign. All too frequently state and cooperative retailers' competitive advantage derived less from increased efficiency than from prejudicial tax rates. As will become evident in chapter 4, once the private sector was eliminated, the government had little choice but to raise the sales tax in socialist trade. This upward pressure on consumers' real costs was compounded by monopoly conditions. Sometimes, as in the Educational Aid story, intra-socialist competition could continue to hold down prices, but at other times and places, when a private shop was squeezed out by its socialist competitor, the latter became the sole available retailer for a specific line of goods. The hand that guided Lentorg

[92] Many historians of trade have documented these trends in Western Europe and the United States; see, for example, James B. Jefferys, *Retail Trading in Britain, 1850–1950* (Cambridge, 1965); Jeffreys and Knee, *Retailing in Europe*, esp. 49–71; Benson and Shaw, eds., *Evolution of Retail Systems*.

and its numerous counterparts was the visible hand of state policy; if that visible hand pointed toward the modernization of retailing, nothing prevented it from clenching up, fingering the merchandise, or slamming the door in the customer's face.

Conclusion

The New Economic Policy resurrected both the traditional and Western-style retail businesses characteristic of prerevolutionary Russia. Especially in the early part of the 1920s, however, it did not overcome the conditions that had fostered the "degradation" of trade during the civil war. What emerged, then, was a heterogeneous economy or, as Soviet scholars of the early 1970s put it, a *mnogoukladnaia* economy. *Mnogoukladnost'* connoted not just a multiplicity of "ways of life" [*uklady*] but, more pointedly, the coexistence of different stages of socioeconomic development. When Lenin wrote the text that became the canonic reference on this subject, it was absolutely plain that he imagined the various types of economic organization along a spectrum from "most backward" to "most advanced":

> What do we observe in Russia, from the point of view of real economic relations? We observe at the very least five distinct systems or *uklady*, or economic orders, and, listing them from the bottom to the top, these are the following: first, a patriarchal economy; this is where the peasant household works entirely for itself or where it is in a nomadic or seminomadic state (and there are as many as you'd care to name of those in our country); second, a petty commodity-producing economy, where the peasant household sells products on the market; third, a capitalist economy, that is the appearance of capitalists and modest accumulations of private capital; fourth, state capitalism; and fifth, socialism.[93]

The aim of the NEP was not to celebrate this diversity but to create unity out of heterogeneity—*e pluribus unum*—by bringing the "backward ways of life" into the orbit of the advanced, "socialist way of life." V. P. Danilov, a prominent historian of the Soviet village, articulated this premise in a 1972 article: "NEP, the policy of the transition from capitalism to socialism, had as its main task the creation of a unified socialist economy, which would require the overcoming of the *mnogoukladnost'* that the Soviet regime inherited from bourgeois-landowning Russia."[94]

[93] Lenin, *PSS*, 43:158.
[94] V. P. Danilov, "Sotsial'no-ekonomicheskie uklady v sovetskoi dokolkhoznoi derevne,"

In the Brezhnev era the concept of *mnogoukladnost'* was used to justify collectivization and the frontal assault on the private sector. During the 1920s, however, it underpinned the strategy of "utilizing" private trade. It hovered in the background when Rykov pointed out, with respect to rural trade, that "even a private shop would, of course, be a step forward compared to what we have now," or when an economist quoted Lenin's crude assessment, "Capitalism is bad in relation to socialism. Capitalism is good in relation to medievalism, in relation to petty production."[95] This distinction made it very difficult to establish a uniform trade policy. As early as 1923 the scissors crisis led policy makers to rethink their classification scheme for private traders and to transfer successive contingents from the "good" category into the "bad."

Merchants, shopkeepers, and vendors had a lot to contend with in this context. Even in sectors in which their businesses were initially adjudged "useful," some found themselves taxed beyond the sustainable limit or cut off from essential supplies. Others were simply left behind by the altered demographics of the consuming population; still others had to struggle to defend their turf against a dynamic socialist-sector competitor. On the whole, the traders who fared best in the new economy were those who had gotten into business early (in 1921–22); who proved most willing to enter into dealings with the socialist commercial agencies; who did not depend on scarce materials; and who possessed recognizable, often artisanal, skills. Many of these personal and situational qualities were familiar from prerevolutionary days, but although traders' past experience could facilitate success by conferring credit, connections, and business skills at the outset of the NEP, the transformed political economy rendered their future prospects anything but secure.

The impact of the revolution on consumers was differentiated by class and region. As we saw in chapter 1, the revolution drastically worsened material conditions for virtually all nonagriculturalists, and, even in the period from 1918 to 1920, many peasants also starved. Other peasants benefited from the rising food prices on the free market, though Soviet authorities sought to restrict their profits through the war on trade and through militarized, increasingly successful, procurement campaigns. In the early 1920s much of the countryside suffered the aftereffects of the calamitous 1921–22 famine, but in the later years of the decade rural

in *Novaia ekonomicheskaia politika. Voprosy teorii i istorii* (Moscow, 1974), 58–79. The strong interest in *mnogoukladnost'* seems to have been driven by Party leaders' efforts to prove the relevance of the Soviet revolutionary experience to the Third World. Cf. M. A. Suslov, "Leninizm i revoliutsionnoe preobrazovanie mira," in *Izbrannoe. Rechi i stat'i* (Moscow, 1974), 579.
[95] Rykov, *Khoziaistvennoe polozhenie*, 31; Mingulin, *Puti razvitiia*, 26–27.

consumption rose markedly. Urban consumers returned to their normal, prewar consumption patterns, though with a lag-time vis-à-vis incomes of one to two years. The flight (and murder) of the aristocracy meant that aggregate demand shifted from luxuries to necessities, but, within working-class households, consumption of nonnecessities grew. Citizens did not cling to the new practices of consumption fostered by war communism—workplace pilfering, bazaar hawking and barter, dining at a canteen—but, as chapter 4 makes clear, when shortages again came to grip the nation's food supplies, these practices were revived. In the first decade after the revolution, then, socialism cannot be said to have created a distinctive "consumer culture," but it did alter several aspects of material life. It legitimized illegal survival strategies during the initial crisis; it created new retail venues and expectations; and it pointed toward a more widely shared prosperity in the event the economy would continue to grow.

Crisis: Restructuring

The basis of bureaucratic rule is the poverty of society in objects of consumption, with the resulting struggle of each against all. When there are enough goods in a store, the purchasers can come whenever they want to. When there are few goods, the purchasers are compelled to stand in line. When the lines are very long, it is necessary to appoint a policeman to keep order. Such is the starting point of the Soviet bureaucracy. It "knows" who is to get something and who has to wait.

—Leon Trotsky, *The Revolution Betrayed*

CHAPTER FOUR

War Communism Redux

IN THE SECOND half of the 1920s the tenuous compromise between bureaucratic and market approaches to trade collapsed. Private shopkeepers either fled the market or were forcibly removed, leaving gaping holes in the fabric of trade. Famine returned to southern Ukraine, then spread to other regions as collectivization engulfed the countryside in a virtual civil war. The deteriorating economic and social environment, the intensifying food crisis, and the disappearance of private businesses compelled state and cooperative retailers to modify their hours of trade, methods, relationship to the central administration, and stocks. By 1930 the NEP was a dead letter in the commercial sphere.

Standard accounts of Stalin's abandonment of the NEP have emphasized the primacy of industrialization. The perceived need to progress beyond the limitations of the prerevolutionary industrial infrastructure, the threat of war (regarded as imminent in 1927), and the consolidation of Stalin's personal power, we are told, led the leadership to adopt the "left" program of all-out industrialization in 1928. To finance this program they looked to the agricultural sector, which produced the Soviet Union's principal export commodities. Peasants were pressured to sell their crops at below-market prices, and after two years of increasingly tense, coercive, and unsuccessful grain-collection "campaigns" in 1927 and 1928, Stalin opted for a radical, two-pronged solution. First, peasants were forced into collective farms, which were expected to render them more tractable at the same time as creating efficiencies of scale. Second, the alternative channels for peasants' sales of agricultural products and purchases of manufactured goods were closed. As the momentum of antimarket reforms gathered, push and pull factors became entangled: the dislocations created by each successive intervention into the market seemed to necessitate further restructuring along bureaucratic lines, which in turn stoked the flames of the Communists' revolutionary aspirations. By the end of the decade, a policy of integrating peasants into the economy exclusively on "socialist" terms had begun to seem feasible. In a single revolutionary exertion Stalin and his associates sought to vanquish Russia's twin scourges, "private capital" and "backwardness."[1]

[1] Classic accounts of these developments include Nove, "Was Stalin Really Necessary?"

This sketch of the progression from evolutionary economic "recovery" [*vosstanovlenie*] toward revolutionary "restructuring" [*rekonstruktsiia*]—alternatively, from "Bolshevism" to "Stalinism"—remains fundamentally persuasive. With respect to trade, the forcible eradication of private shops from 1928 to 1931 must indeed be understood in the context of a general economic and social upheaval. Nonetheless, even before trade was swept up in the tidal wave of revolutionary restructuring at the end of the decade, trade policy was already drifting toward a substantial revision of the NEP. Having embraced marketization in 1921 as a life jacket, Soviet leaders held onto this principle only as long as it seemed necessary to keep them afloat. Private businesses continually had to prove their usefulness to the socialist system, while policy makers reserved the right to alter the terms of their activity if circumstances or priorities changed. As we have seen, they began exercising this prerogative as early as 1923, when the scissors crisis provoked the administration to intervene in pricing and the organization of supplies. In the second half of the decade chronic shortages dispelled any residual commitment the Stalinists may have felt toward the NEP compromise and prompted a wholesale reconsideration of the utility of private trade. By 1928–29, when the five-year plan seemed to renew the promise of a socialist revolution in productive relations, the economic establishment was primed to imagine a trade sector "without capitalists," as Stalin later put it, "small or big."[2]

A casualty of the offensive against the "capitalists" was the market, that is, economic mechanisms for the societal allocation of resources, products, and costs. While the declining volume of private retail sales in the later part of the 1920s, and more particularly the diminishing role of private trade in working-class consumption, gave policy makers confidence that they could do without the "privateers," Stalin had little to offer by way of an alternative to the market beyond centralization and bureaucratization—techniques tried, and discarded, in the period from 1918 to 1921. Although the economic policy of the late 1920s was imbued with a new rhetoric of planning, restructuring trade in practice meant disinterring all the old instruments of bureaucratized distribution. Price controls were greatly expanded; "commodity exchange," once again,

---

Economic Rationality and Soviet Politics, 17–39; idem, *An Economic History of the U.S.S.R.* (London, 1969), 126–214; E. H. Carr and R. W. Davies, *Foundations of a Planned Economy*, 1926–1929, 2 vols. (London, 1969), vol. 1.; Moshe Lewin, *The Making of the Soviet System: Essays in the Social History of Interwar Russia* (New York, 1985); R. W. Davies, *The Socialist Offensive* (Cambridge, Mass., 1980); idem, *The Soviet Economy in Turmoil, 1929–1930*. Recent, valuable additions to this literature include Shearer, *Industry, State and Society*; Osokina, *Za fasadom*; and Gimpel'son, *NEP i soverskaia politicheskaia sistema*.

[2] I. V. Stalin, *Sochineniia*, 13 vols. (Moscow, 1952–53), 13:203.

was foisted on peasants in lieu of market equivalents for agricultural products; and the "class ration" was revived for the distribution of foods and manufactured goods in urban areas. Even cooperatives, the cornerstone of socialist trade in the NEP era, were once again purged of their elected leadership and subordinated to the economic bureaucracy. Symbolizing these changes—which were accompanied by intensified repression reminiscent of the revolutionary era—the Commissariat of Foreign and Domestic Trade [Narkomtorg] was folded into a new Commissariat of Provisionment [Narkomsnab], a reincarnation of the powerful food-supply commissariat of the civil war years.

This chapter traces the Stalinists' path toward restructuring trade. I argue that crisis once again became the catalyst for economic radicalism, particularly as policy makers' perception of the crisis extended into the sensitive area of food supplies. Once again, "emergency measures" propelled the socialist economy toward a degree of centralization that was neither sustainable nor, for the most part, desired. Once again, factory managers and other local representatives of Soviet power were faced with the challenge of procuring enough consumer and industrial supplies to keep their "particular little business" in operation, by hook or by crook. Lastly, as the chapter's final section shows, the "statization" of the economy led to a recrudescence of hawking, as shortages and the sharp decline in the number of shops forced citizens to find a means of paying for purchases at the quasi-legal bazaars.

THE NEP FROM ABOVE: TRADE POLICY IN THE SHADOW OF THE GOODS FAMINE

The scissors crisis from 1922 to 1924 was a crisis of stagnation and inflation: high prices on manufactured goods softened demand, which in turn depressed agriculture and threatened socialist factories with bankruptcy. In the *longue durée* of Soviet history, this would prove a unique moment. From mid-1924 on, the characteristic problem of the Soviet economy was not the difficulty of selling manufactured goods but rather the perpetual shortage of these goods at the prevailing regulated price. Shortages of consumer goods eroded the central premise of the utilization thesis and hence of the NEP trade policy, the belief that private traders could make a contribution to the socialist cause. Although the logic of utilization was not abandoned, the revised estimate of the utility of private trade meant that this logic ceased to inhibit the Communists' native impulse to repress private businessmen. Instead, it fostered the migration of the "left" view, which favored eliminating private businesses altogether, into the political mainstream. The story of Soviet trade policy after 1926–27 is, to an even greater extent than previously recognized, a story of an ever-widening war on private trade.

The leading edge of these developments was the market for cotton cloth, the paradigmatic "scarce" [defitsitnyi] commodity of the mid-1920s (and, indeed, for the next twenty-five years). In a society in which every second urban household owned a sewing machine and clothes were sewn at home or by a tailor, cotton cloth was the single most important item in citizens' clothing budgets. Alone, textiles were said to have generated as much as one-third of private trade in 1924–25 and 12 percent of retail sales in the socialist sector in 1928.[3] Not surprisingly, then, when the textile syndicate and state wholesalers began curtailing sales to private businesses in 1923–24, traders made every effort to obtain supplies through alternative channels. One source was artisanal manufacturers, kustari, who wove various styles of coarse cloth on handlooms and marketed them to peasants. Since private retailers were concentrated in towns and cities, however, they had a strong interest in carrying the factory-made textiles preferred by urban consumers. State retail outlets, especially in Moscow, the hub of the textile industry, increasingly took over the wholesale function for private trade. A series of investigations from 1924 to 1926 showed that private retailers in the capital actually had more cloth in stock than the small retail shops of the state and cooperative networks, but almost exclusively in short lengths of three to ten meters. Without doubt, these had been purchased at socialist retail shops. By the summer of 1925, when chronic cloth shortages first gave rise to the term goods famine, private traders were routinely paying agents to keep tabs on state and cooperative outlets and to stand in line if a shipment arrived. Queues formed almost immediately; depending on the length of the queue, cloth was parceled out in three-, five-, or ten-meter lengths. Large private enterprises might retain a small army of invalids for the purpose of queuing, while petty traders stood in line themselves a few times in succession and then carted their wares off to the bazaar. To supply provincial traders, mail-order firms of "queue specialists" sprang up. Cooperatives were also known to obtain supplies from the state shops, it should be noted, but it was private traders' purchases from state retailers that had "indubitably acquired a mass character" by 1926.[4]

---

[3] Banerji, Merchants and Markets, 108; Sovetskaia torgovlia. Statisticheskii sbornik, 46. On sewing machines, see Biudzhety rabochikh, 1:48, 50; Kabo, Ocherki rabochego byta, 183; Strumilin, Rabochii byt v tsifrakh, 12–13, 39–45, 84.

[4] GARF, f. 5446, op. 55, d. 958, ll. 35–36, 100, 225; d. 2537, ll. 46–47; Fabrichnyi, Chastnyi kapital na poroge piatiletki, 30–32.

Queuism [*ocherednichestvo*], the term coined for this practice by its many critics, exemplifies the difficulties of combining a market economy with wholesale price controls. Rising urban wages—and, after the 1925 harvest, rising rural incomes as well—without a concomitant expansion of cloth production or imports meant that the market could support quite high retail prices. Private traders could thus recoup their expenditures on queue specialists for much the same reason that socialist trade organizations continually found it profitable to hire "representatives." In fact, the vices attributed to the private sector's queue agents overlapped with those blamed on the agents of socialist trade: they raised transaction costs, wasted time and labor, contributed to supply bottlenecks, and undermined civic morality by bribing the guardians of supplies. Cloth prices in the private sector soon exceeded those in state and cooperative trade by a considerable margin.[5] Looking at this development from the perspective of a rationalizer, one can easily imagine why queuism excited Soviet administrators' regulatory urge.

Queue specialists were clearly not what Lenin had had in mind when he emphasized the utility of private trade. Even V. V. Novozhilov, the period's most articulate champion of market pricing and competition, called private cloth traders' profits "unjustified" and "speculative" in 1926.[6] Both in public and in closed governmental meetings, most members of the Soviet policy community were less restrained. Works on "private capital" and "private trade" published in or after 1927 cast businessmen as shady, criminal characters—agile in responding to opportunities for "easy money" but parasitical and corrupt.[7] Not surprisingly the government redoubled its efforts to confine cloth, yarn, and thread to the socialist sector, and, indeed, factory-made textiles became still more difficult and expensive for private retailers to obtain. This forced many traders out of business even as it sent others to join the queues. As early as 1926–27, the closure of sixty private cloth shops in Rostov led the head of Rabkrin's (the hard-line state inspectorate's) trade department to muse about the "extremely interesting phenomenon of the *complete eradication* of privateers from the cloth market." Private cloth shops were going under in Saratov, Sverdlovsk, Khar'kov, Tiflis, and Dnepropetrovsk

---

[5] Malafeev, *Istoriia tsenoobrazovaniia*, 40; see also G. Popov, "Tseny i nakidki chastnoi torgovli," in Zalkind, ed., *Chastnyi kapital SSSR*, 136–56; A. Grintser, "Itogi i perspektivy politiki tsen," *Ekonomicheskoe obozrenie*, no. 9 (September 1925): 35–45; V. Makarov, "O manufakturnom golode," *Ekonomicheskoe obozrenie*, no. 10 (October 1925): 101–7.

[6] Novozhilov, "Nedostatok tovarov," 78.

[7] Cf. Kolesnikov, *Litso klassovogo vraga*; Larin, *Chastnyi kapital*; Kondurushkin, *Chastnyi kapital*; Fabrichnyi, *Chastnyi kapital*.

for the lack of factory-made goods.[8] Cloth dealers who wanted to stay in business had to demonstrate their continued utility to the socialist economy on highly unfavorable terms. By the end of 1927 "many privateers" had indicated to the inspectorate's agents that they would "gladly sign a contract with the Commissariat of Trade" in which they would promise to sell cloth for less than the going price in cooperatives or state trade. Indeed, six of the seven cloth traders in my database who were still in business in 1927 had shifted over to these contractual sales.[9] Such arrangements notwithstanding, textiles fell from over 30 percent of private retail sales in 1923–24 to 5 percent in 1928–29.[10]

Queue specialists and their employers began to be arrested as criminals in 1928, but the conditions that fostered queuism did not, in the meantime, disappear.[11] Even in 1930, by which point ration coupons regulated the distribution of cloth in the socialist sector and most private shops had closed down, queuism still nourished the remnants of the private market. A secret memorandum from V. N. Iakovleva, RSFSR Commissar of Finance, to the Politburo that February indicated that the textile market had scarcely improved:

> In the market for manufactured goods private capital has ceased to fulfill any useful function whatsoever. [Private capital's] activity begins in wrongdoings and crimes, and its result is to lower the worker's real wages, since [the capitalist] inflates the prices of scarce goods. This is especially striking in the case of textiles. Tax inspection studies show that in the private shops there are virtually no bolts of cloth; in general, there are only short lengths. It follows that textiles reach the shops of the private trader only because he buys up cloth that individuals obtain on coupons, by speculating and creating queues at state and cooperative stores. In his private shop he then sells them at three times the price, or even higher. The same can be said of haberdashery (needles, spools of thread, etc.). That portion of textiles and haberdashery that the private trader does not obtain through speculation in manufactured goods coupons is obtained by the privateer from state and cooperative shops in an illegal manner, since there are no private manufacturers of these goods. One can say with confidence that only an insignificant portion of the manufactured goods

[8] GARF, f. 374, op. 28, d. 2523, ll. 47–48.
[9] Ibid; Kb/Uk/Vertgeim, Kb/Uk/Serebrier, Kb/Uk/Lipes, Kb/Uk/Khalfin, Kb/Uk/Khasin, and Kb/Uk/Kirievskii.
[10] GARF, f. 5446, op. 55, d. 1941, l. 4.
[11] Arrests began around the start of 1928 as part of an OGPU operation directed primarily against leather and grain traders (see below). By April 2, 631 private cloth traders had been arrested (*Tragediia sovetskoi derevni* [Moscow, 1999], 1:231). Arrests evidently continued; cf. *Krasnaia gazeta*, August 8, 1929.

sold by the private trader was obtained from artisans. The overwhelming majority fell into his hands through illicit means.[12]

If Iakovleva's depiction of cloth traders' methods reiterated the allegations of the previous five years, her conclusion reflected the altered balance of forces in the economy now that restructuring was under way. Rather than limit the aim to "controlling" private capital, as in the past, the commissar suggested that a new policy ought to take into consideration the "character of private capital's activity" as well as "its insignificant percentage of aggregate sales" and strive to effect "the complete liquidation of private capital." Her recommendation was simple: "in the manufactured goods sector private trade may be banned altogether by legislative means."[13]

Shortages thus stripped away the veneer of toleration regulating the government's relationship with private commerce, leaving an underlayer of ingrained distrust. That even a top financial official would insist on the "uselessness" of a large class of private businessmen is particularly striking, when their most obvious use for the government lay in the taxes they paid. In 1926–27 private traders constituted 1.2 percent of the economically active population, earned 4 percent of the national income, and furnished approximately 9 percent of the central government's direct tax revenues. With the addition of various class-specific fees, one-time levies, and indirect taxes, private businesses in particular regions were estimated to have financed up to two-thirds of provincial and municipal government funds.[14] The elimination of the "trade bourgeoisie" meant that these revenues had to be replaced by the "laboring classes" at a time when industrialization was swallowing up state monies at an unprecedented rate. Against the fact of private trade's utility in generating tax revenues, however, evidence of its "parasitical" character increasingly provided a counterweight. The visibility of private agents in textile and other queues; the conspicuous consumption of the thin stratum of affluent Nepmen, whose concentration in Moscow made them difficult to overlook; and the high prices of private shops led policy makers to reconsider their utility for the socialist economy.[15] From 1927 to 1930, as in 1918, the efforts of private traders to extract profits from an increasingly risky context of shortages, price cuts, and escalating taxes came to seem

---

[12] GARF, f. 5446, op. 55, d. 1941, ll. 2–4.

[13] Ibid.

[14] Banerji, *Merchants and Markets*, 210–11; Ball, *Russia's Last Capitalists*, 68–69, 73–75.

[15] On "parasitical" consumption on the part of Nepmen, see V. Belenko, "O tovarnom golode," *Bol'shevik*, no. 17 (September 15, 1926): 44–61.

like the *source* of economic dislocations, rather than their symptom, to policy makers predisposed to view commercial activities in a hostile light.

For all the hubbub over the cloth market, textiles were among the most highly centralized segments of the consumer economy. Though policy makers remained obsessed with the fact that so much as a fraction of the country's factory-produced textiles passed through private shops, the cloth market nonetheless bolstered their confidence that the socialist sector ruled the economy's "commanding heights." Less-centralized sectors of the economy, and especially the markets for agricultural products and raw materials, gave Soviet authorities no such ground for complacency. It was one thing for the state to control a market when it was dealing with nationalized factories; it was another thing altogether when individual peasants furnished the goods. Readers will recall that it was precisely agricultural commodities—grain, meat, fruit, lumber, leather, fish, and wine—that supported the largest private businesses of the NEP. Private traders were able to compete in these markets by offering better inducements to suppliers than policy makers found acceptable. In the end, socialist buying agencies either had to make concessions to peasants' expectations, and match the offers of their private competitors, or resort to coercion, an approach that looked increasingly attractive with spiraling supply costs. Though these commodity markets differed considerably from the market for textiles, here, too, the notion of the utility of private businesses was badly damaged by the goods famine of the second half of the decade. The 1926–27 fiscal year was again a turning point, and again the result was the resurgence of class warfare as the determinant of Soviet policy toward private trade.

The clearest illustration of these dynamics can be found in the market for leather goods, which was dominated by the private sector through most of the NEP. Private artisans produced some 80 percent of shoes and leather goods, marketing these products through cooperatives but, above all, through their own workshops or through private retail shops. In the shoe business, private shops outnumbered shoe outlets in the socialist sector by a ratio of sixteen to one and handled 68 percent of shoe sales.[16] Whereas urban consumers spurned artisanally manufactured cloth in favor of factory-produced goods, surveys carried out in Moscow and Khar'kov in the mid-1920s showed that customers gravitated toward artisanal footwear. Cobblers' products were functional and inexpensive, as

---

[16] *Vnutrenniaia torgovlia SSSR za 1924/25–1925/26 gg.* (Moscow, 1928), 39; RGASPI, f. 17, op. 85, d. 293, l. 1; Banerji, *Merchants and Markets*, 111.

against the "frivolous" styles manufactured by the largest Soviet factory, Skorokhod.[17]

Between peasant suppliers of raw hides and the large number of artisanal tanners and shoemakers, private traders were well positioned to play the role of middleman. In 1925–26 the All-Union Leather Syndicate cornered barely half the circulating raw hides; private dealers, mostly trading on a small scale in a single county, handled 46 percent.[18] What happened to the leather market over the next few years was analogous to trends in other areas of peasant production. In the name of securing the economy's *commanding heights*, a term that embraced the major commodity markets as well as large-scale industry, policy makers annulled all rental contracts for leather factories and redoubled their efforts to monopolize what they called "procurements" [*zagotovki*]—the initial purchase of raw hides. Peasants were pressured into signing contractual agreements to sell the leather syndicate a certain number of hides at a specified price.[19] In the context of intensifying shortages of cloth, hardware supplies, and other staple items of rural consumption, however, the government's low procurement prices weakened peasants' incentive to sell their livestock hides. Shortages ensued. In the end, the state's attempt to monopolize the raw leather market backfired; able to sweeten the deal to the point where peasants became interested, private traders actually captured a larger market share than before.

Quite a lot of information has come to light in the past few years about the repression of leather dealers that resulted from this fiasco. According to one recently published document, the OGPU carried out its first "operation" against private leather traders between November 1926 and May 1927.[20] In Leningrad this initial operation entailed "major arrests among the leathermen," followed by the forcible liquidation of five firms.[21] Although it was deemed a success—the syndicate subsequently overfulfilled its procurement plan by 5 percent—the operation did not prevent "private capital" from reviving its activity "in the guise of speculators/resellers" the following fall. Once again, private traders were pay-

---

[17] Banerji, *Merchants and Markets*, 111; GARF, f. 5446, op. 55, d. 1831, l. 57.

[18] L. Limanov, "Chastnyi kapital na sel'sko-khoziaistvennom rynke," in Zalkind, ed., *Chastnaia torgovlia*, 47–70; here, 50, 55.

[19] Stalin termed these agreements "new mass forms of trade"; see G. Ia. Neiman, *Vnutrenniaia torgovlia SSSR*, ed. E. I. Kviring (Moscow, 1935), 149. On the annulment of rental contracts in the leather industry, see L. F. Morozov, *Reshaiushchii etap bor'by s nepmanskoi burzhuaziei* (Moscow, 1960), 60–61. On the concept of *zagotovki*, see Moshe Lewin, "'Taking Grain': Soviet Policies of Agricultural Procurements Before the War," *Making of the Soviet System*, 142–77.

[20] *Tragediia sovetskoi derevni*, 1:86–88.

[21] GARF, f. 374, op. 28, d. 2523, ll. 54–58.

ing 50 to 100 percent more than the syndicate for hides, "jeopardizing the ability of the All-Union Leather Syndicate to fulfill its procurement program."[22] Accordingly, in September, the OGPU's Economic Administration ordered local policing organs to begin "a detailed and careful study of materials concerning the leather raw materials market" with the aim of identifying private slaughterers, dealers in raw hides, tanners, dealers in tanned hides, dealers in various leather products and their agents, and retail shopkeepers whose wares included leather goods. Even vendors of the chemical salts used in tanning were to be placed on the list.[23] Armed with these names, the Economic Administration proposed a larger, repeat operation to the Supreme Economic Council (VSNKh), which approved the measure but forwarded the proposal to Sovnarkom. By the end of April 1928, 2,964 "privateers" in the leather market had been arrested as "speculative and anti-Soviet elements" in the first "mass operations" of the Stalin era.[24]

Several observations can be made about this incident. With respect to bureaucratic decision making, the episode points up the OGPU as an active player in the development of economic and social policy in 1926–27. The OGPU laid the groundwork for this operation on its own initiative, suggesting it to the traditional policy-making bodies only after it had compiled a list of names. Further, the decision to proceed was authorized not on the Party side of the power structure but in the top levels of the government. It was discussed openly in an enlarged meeting of the Sovnarkom collegium (Rykov's secretary, quizzed some months later about it, mainly recalled Tsiurupa's impassioned speech against the proposal), though Rykov chose not to put the matter to a vote. The session made clear that everyone present was familiar with OGPU methods and did not need to have them spelled out. The scribbled note from VSNKh chair Eismont that opened the discussions at Sovnarkom left all the details ambiguous: "GPU [sic] has worked up and made the preparations for an 'operation' in relation to privateers-procurers of leather raw materials. The state of the market is such that we at VSNKh have approved this 'operation,' but it must be carried out extremely carefully, without unnecessary noise, without large arrests, and with the compliance of local Party committees. The GPU has looked into all of this. But without your

[22] *Tragediia sovetskoi derevni*, 1:86–88; 100–102.
[23] Ibid., 1:86–88.
[24] This incident figures in S. A. Shchitinov, *Rezhim lichnoi vlasti Stalina* (Moscow, 1989), 33; and Osokina, *Za fasadom*, 55. A list of arrests of leather traders as of April 30, 1928, appears in *Sovetskaia derevnia glazami VChK-OGPU-NKVD*, 2:1035–36. A comparison with the OGPU Economic Administration's April 2 report on the "mass operations" against "speculative elements" (*Tragediia sovetskoi derevni*, 1:231) indicates that 40 percent of the leather arrests occurred in April, so the April 30 figures may not be complete.

consent it should not go forward."[25] Finally, the policy makers (and Rykov's secretary, who kept this note "just in case") were fully aware that the proposed operation contravened Soviet law. Tsiurupa notwithstanding, this knowledge did not prevent Mikoian from pressuring Rykov for a positive decision over the telephone nor Rykov from finally giving the nod.[26]

Aside from intrigue, the repression of private leather dealers raises a fundamental question about Soviet economic policy from 1926 to 1928. In 1924 policy makers had promoted consumer demand as the engine of growth. Why did they not interpret high "procurement" prices for leather (or, for that matter, for grain or flax or lumber or eggs) as a vehicle for augmenting peasants' incomes, and thus a stimulant of consumer demand? Why not view them, also, as a stimulant to supplies and hence a "useful" function of private trade? Unfortunately any answer to these questions remains speculative, but it would seem to turn on the urban bias of the country's leaders. Belenko showed conclusively that the shortages of cloth in 1924–25 resulted from increasing urban incomes, not from excess rural demand.[27] After two good harvests in 1925 and 1926, however, peasants surely became a more noticeable presence in the urban queues for manufactured goods. As we shall see, one characteristic response on the part of cooperatives was to refuse to sell to peasants, since the cooperatives' ability to absorb the excess demand through price increases was constrained by regulations and political pressures. Endorsing and systematizing these actions, central policy makers showed that they continued to view peasants more as a source of raw materials than as a potential consumer base.[28] Goods were to be kept affordable to urban workers and functionaries, whose rising expectations would spur the expansion of Soviet industry and bolster support for the regime. Peasants' role in this script, by contrast, was to wait patiently in the wings for the products of industry, while continuing to provide raw materials at a submarket price. Traders, finally, were unceremoniously booted offstage as soon as their understudies—state supply agencies in each sector of the market and consumer cooperatives' retail shops—had mastered their roles.

The campaign against leather dealers, subsequently generalized to other "procurement" markets, and the campaign against cloth merchants flowed into yet another wave of repression in 1929. This time, coercion was

[25] GARF, f. 5446, op. 55, d. 1584, l. 125.

[26] Actually Vepritskaia, Rykov's secretary, did not know whether he agreed but concluded that he must have from the fact that it was carried out. He initially vacillated, putting off the decision until his return from a trip (ibid., 126).

[27] Belenko, "O tovarnom golode."

[28] Anastas Mikoian identified this attitude specifically with Stalin; see Mikoian, *Tak bylo* (Moscow, 1999), 466–67.

intertwined with tax policy, which was increasingly subordinated to the program of curbing, and eventually abolishing, as opposed to utilizing, private trade. In the summer of 1926 an onerous new tax, the surcharge on "superprofits," was introduced for businesses of the highest two license categories, then extended to small shops the following May wherever profit margins exceeded an arbitrarily defined norm. Rents and personal taxes, including children's education fees, utility fees, and income taxes, were also raised; by 1926–27 they alone siphoned off 18.8 percent of profits, a 50 percent increase over the previous year.[29] When private traders received their tax assessments with the new charges, many elected not to renew their licenses and liquidated their shops. By 1929, after a power struggle between the Commissariat of Finance and Rabkrin, these decisions were retroactively redefined as tax evasion. Rabkrin's private trade section joined the OGPU to direct a purge of the Commissariat of Finance, which had putatively "undertaxed" the private sector by failing to wrest payment from traders who went out of business and, at the same time, mounted a campaign against the former traders themselves. A round sum of 150 million rubles was named as the size of the arrears, of which 50 million rubles were attributed to traders and former traders in the city of Moscow alone.[30]

Even more than the 1927–28 arrests of leather dealers, the campaign against "tax dodgers" exemplifies the war on the market at the end of the NEP. Like the simultaneous attack on peasant kulaks, the arrears operation was carefully coordinated among a variety of agencies: Rabkrin and the OGPU, Party committees at all levels, the financial organs, the procuracy, and the investigative arm of the regular police. Rank-and-file citizens, mobilized "from the number of active civic workers, unquestionably firm and disciplined comrades" at major factories, as well as "representatives of military divisions, delegates from the women's departments, the [Komsomol] 'light cavalry' brigades, students, and others," also participated. The number of "public" participants ranged from fifty-four in Makhachkala, the capital of Dagestan, to seven thousand in the textile region of Ivanovo; outside Moscow, for which no numbers are available, some twenty-nine thousand workers and other "activists" assisted in the campaign.[31]

The basic operational unit was the brigade. Led by at least one armed representative of the policing agencies and including, in principle, at least one woman, a brigade consisted of a group of workers, plus as many

---

[29] Ball, *Russia's Last Capitalists*, 68–69.
[30] GARF, f. 374, op. 28s, d. 3111, ll. 166–68.
[31] Ibid., ll. 162–64, 166–68.

officials as local governments could spare. Each brigade received a list of names and addresses of traders and former traders who had failed to keep pace with the tax increases in 1927 to 1929. Despite certain "transportation difficulties" in the smaller cities, brigades were to carry out their "operational work" at night. A typical night's work involved banging on the door at a listed address at some point after midnight, demanding entrance, and then quickly making an inventory of any valuables in the home and placing this property under "arrest" (owners were held criminally accountable if anything subsequently disappeared). A female member of the brigade would, in the meantime, conduct body searches of all residents. Financial documents might be removed. A week or two later, after receiving a go-ahead from the policing organs, a second brigade led by a financial official would come to appraise the estate and to direct its confiscation. Metals and jewels went to the USSR Commissariat of Finance; furs, rugs, artwork, and antiques to the Trade Commissariat's export fund; furniture, dishes, and other household items to consumer cooperatives for sale "to laboring people, first of all to workers." Horses, dairy cows, and other livestock were carted off to nearby collective and state farms; and, finally, titles for the domiciles were transferred to the local housing agency.[32]

In Moscow, where the operation was tested in mid-1929 before being generalized to the Soviet Union as a whole, the targets of the operation ran the gamut from owners of hole-in-the-wall pubs and billiard halls in working-class neighborhoods to former jewelers and hat-makers on Moscow's principal shopping streets. The majority had been traders in the upper three license categories—proprietors of permanent shops subject to the surcharge on superprofits. A few, however, had merely rented a kiosk or market stall, and a handful of former morticians, barbers, meat canners, and small factory owners rounded out the list.[33] The most common outcome for these people was arrest. Of the 112 "tax dodgers" from four wards whose whereabouts were known in the early spring of 1930, 22 were serving time in prison, with terms ranging from one and a half to ten years; 8 had been forcibly exiled to special settlements (typically in the Narym and Enisei regions of the far northeast); and 19 were awaiting trial. The remainder were either unemployed, and dependent on savings or relatives for their subsistence, or working in a cooperative with their wages garnished. One had thrown in the towel and joined the OGPU; several were trying to eke out a living through repair work, sewing, or some other occupation in the relatively unregulated service sector. All

[32] Ibid., ll. 166–68.
[33] Ibid., ll. 142–47.

had had their property confiscated to pay off the arrears—and most were specified to be "under observation" by the financial and security agencies.[34]

The campaign was not as successful as officials had hoped. Begun in late November 1929, a few months after the Moscow trial run, the campaign had succeeded in "recovering" only 32 million rubles of the initially estimated 150 million rubles by early 1930. Rabkrin officials placed the blame for this shortfall squarely on the shoulders of the Commissariat of Finance, which had created the problem in the first place with its culpable leniency, but also on an organizational defect: citizens tapped for the brigades should not have been told what they would be doing, the inspectorate concluded, since traders may have had prior warning from the rumors in circulation before the action began.[35] Rumors were indeed flying in commercial circles once the operation was in swing. Notwithstanding the large number of people mobilized for the action, nighttime raids continued for a period of weeks and even months, and, in the Moscow reports, one-fifth of the people targeted had managed to hide or flee.[36]

That these raids were directed against tax evasion should not obscure the illegality at their root. Finance Commissar Iakovleva acknowledged this in her February 4, 1930, memo to the Politburo, in which she advocated a ban on private sales of manufactured goods. After reviewing the quantitative indexes for private trade in 1928–29, she turned to the arrears campaign:

> Our laws should immediately be revised in such a way as to strengthen repressions in relation to tax defaulters and to expand the practice of property confiscation for these crimes. At the present time the jurisprudence in this area reflects yesterday's norms, and is constructed with a view to limiting the growth of private capital. One can say without hesitation that the entire practice of extracting back tax payments in the past several months contradicts the law, so that the local procuracies have had to devise ways of getting around the laws. The laws, and above all our Criminal Code, should be reviewed from the perspective of eradicating private commercial capital as quickly as possible, not limiting its growth.[37]

Iakovleva, then, can serve as our first illustration of the Stalinists' path toward restructuring trade. In her case, the context was an institutional power struggle at a time when "vigilance," a qualification not normally associated with the Commissariat of Finance, outflanked the prudent

[34] Ibid.
[35] Ibid., ll. 166–68.
[36] Ibid., 142–47.
[37] GARF, f. 5446, op. 55, d. 1941, ll. 2–3.

husbandry of economic resources. At the same time, Iakovleva's proposals reflected the distortions of the market created by shortages of consumer goods. Although it was not illegal for a private trader to offer peasants a high price for raw hides or other agricultural products, or to stand in line at a state shop for cloth, Iakovleva was not alone in interpreting these actions as a violation of the NEP social contract. As the old suspicions of "middlemen" rose to the surface, the ground was laid for a war of annihilation against private trade.

In sum, the effect of the goods famine was to highlight the "parasitical" and "harmful" sides of private trade and to cast doubt on the latter's utility. In debates over the goods famine, the possibility of eliminating private trade altogether repeatedly surfaced along with the idea of a great industrial spurt. Although these proposals were not publicly endorsed by Stalin, the government, or the Party until the end of the decade, the new skepticism as to the utility of private trade was reflected in the increasingly burdensome tax payments extracted from the private sector and, above all, in increasingly frequent and serious incidents of state coercion. Although these new strains eventually broke the private sector, a rupture in policy with the original premises of the NEP should not be posited. As early as 1923–24, after all, some traders had fallen victim to extralegal coercion; the phenomenon of "trade deserts"—districts without any shops—dated to the same year. To the Stalinists, the eradication of the private businesses from 1927 to 1931 did not represent the repudiation of the utilization thesis so much as its culmination: from the beginning, the utility of private traders was intended to become obsolete as soon as the socialist sector "learned how to trade."

For Iakovleva and others, the flip side of the reevaluation of the private sector was their increasing confidence in state and cooperative trade. What led Stalin and his associates to believe that the socialist trade networks were now capable of handling the entirety of distribution on their own? A review of policy discussions from the end of the decade suggests that this confidence rested on a narrow set of quantitative indicators. Qualitative shortcomings remained pronounced in the later 1920s, though, when policy makers considered these failings, they were increasingly inclined to blame the private sector rather than the socialist enterprises themselves.

The first quantitative index was quite a basic one: what percentage of the country's trade went through private retailers? As table 4.1 indicates, that percentage dwindled after 1926. There were, however, enormous regional differences, which these averages elide. In the RSFSR alone, which was the focus of most top-level policy discussions, the role of pri-

TABLE 4.1
Private vs. Socialist-Sector Retail Trade, 1924–1930 (in million rubles at current prices)

Year	State	Co-op	Private	Total	Private as % of Total
1924	938	1,773	3,094	5,805	53.3
1925	1,497	3,352	3,716	8,565	43.4
1926	2,033	5,261	4,988	12,282	40.6
1927	2,225	6,833	4,710	13,768	34.2
1928	2,378	8,976	3,407	14,761	23.1
1929	3,198	11,396	2,273	16,867	13.5
1930	4,283	13,300	1,043	18,626	5.6

Source: Sovetskaia torgovlia. Statisticheskii sbornik, 14.

vate trade in 1928–29 ranged from roughly 5 percent in northern and central European Russia to 38 percent in Kirgizia. Private trade was said to play a larger role in general in the non-Russian regions of the republic as well in the Far East.[38] The important point here is that policy makers drew conclusions about the country's ability to do without private trade on the basis of all-Union and Russian averages, combined with information from Moscow, Leningrad, and a handful of other major cities. This selection of data almost certainly inflated their sense of the adequacy of socialist-sector retailing for residents of the country's eastern and southern periphery and for rural areas everywhere.

The second quantitative index that gave policy makers confidence in state and cooperative trade measured the proportional weights of the socialist and private sectors in household consumption. Numerous analyses of household budgets appeared in print in the 1920s, providing information on incomes and expenditures, and the actual quantities of various goods that citizens obtained and the channels through which they made their purchases.[39] Notwithstanding certain inaccuracies derived from self-reporting, these are, indeed, an essential source for any analysis of consumption or trade in the Soviet Union, and Soviet policy makers treated them as such.

Crucially, and characteristically, the reports floating around the government at the end of the 1920s referred exclusively to the budgets of urban residents, and almost exclusively to those of industrial workers.

[38] Ibid., l. 4; d. 1585; d. 1584; f. 374, op. 28, d. 3862, ll. 35–42. Also cf. *Vsesoiuznaia perepis' naseleniia 1926 goda*, 26:6–17, as against 34:4–7,18:360–87, and 19:384–410.
[39] See online appendix "Household Budget Data and Consumption Trends."

Consistent with the published data from 1922 to 1927, these reports revealed an accelerating shift from private to cooperative retailers in all areas of working-class consumption (see table 4.2). Policy makers were buoyed by the fact that, in November 1929, factory workers were making, on average, just 7.4 percent of their expenditures on nonfoods in the private sector; in Leningrad and Khar'kov private trade fell below 4 percent. Even in the non-Russian republics and regions, the role of private traders as a source of manufactured goods for industrial workers barely exceeded 10 percent of their expenditures on these goods. Moreover, since prices on manufactured consumer goods in the private sector averaged 66.3 percent more than prices in cooperative shops, this meant that in real terms, or what trade statistics termed *physical*, as opposed to *sales* volume, Soviet workers acquired just 4.6 percent of their manufactured goods from private trade.[40]

Private sources remained much more important to workers' food consumption, though, even here, budget surveys charted a progressive decline. In Moscow merely 4.5 percent of workers' food expenditures went to the private market (including peasants as well as professional traders) in November 1929.[41] Outside the major industrial centers, and especially in the more fertile agricultural zones, the private market still absorbed 35 percent of workers' food purchases. A breakdown by food group indicated that urban workers bought almost no bread, sugar, or salt from the private sector, but the majority of fruits and milk (65%) and a substantial percentage of vegetables (38%), other dairy products (36%), and meat (15%). Once again, these percentages were much higher in the Soviet Union's southern and eastern reaches.[42]

This, then, was the backdrop to Iakovleva's February 1930 proposal that private trade in manufactured goods simply be banned. Drawing conclusions from surveys of industrial workers' budgets, she and other policy makers inferred that private businesses played a negligible role in the supply of manufactured goods to consumers and, indeed, mainly served to "depreciate the worker's real wages." Not that this was their primary concern; in the next breath the author of the Rabkrin study of private trade from 1928 to 1930 urged the government to expand sales of scarce manufactured goods "at raised prices (double, triple, etc.)," and sugar and certain textiles were indeed reserved, as of 1929, for higher-

[40] GARF, f. 374, op. 28, d. 3862, ll. 10–14.
[41] Ibid., ll. 13–16. This exceptionally low percentage almost certainly reflected the temporary suppression of outdoor trade in the capital. The closure of Moscow's markets in winter 1929–30 was noted by several foreign observers; see below.
[42] Ibid.

TABLE 4.2
Private, Cooperative, and State Trade as a Source of Goods for Urban Workers, 1923–1929 (data from November)

Class of Goods, Where Acquired	1923	1924	1925	1926	1927	1928	1929
Fuel, lighting							
private traders	50	31.3	35.0	39.0	30.5		
firewood						32.0	21.0
kerosene						16.0	1.7
cooparatives	0	8.2	11.8	16.5	15.5		
state shops	50	18.2	20.9	15.3	17.8		
other		42.3	32.3	29.2	36.2		
Foods							
private traders	62.2	33.2	37.5	37.7	29.7	25.0	18.0
cooperatives		56.0	52.8	56.0	64.4		
state shops	37.8	3.2	3.3	2.0	1.1	75	82
other		7.6	6.4	4.3	4.8		
Alcoholic drinks							
private traders	100	32.4	13.4	13.0	12.0	11.0	3.5
cooperatives	—	42.5	47.1	57.3	60.7		
state shops	—	21.2	39.1	28.6	24.9	89	96.5
other	—	3.9	0.4	1.1	2.2		
Tobacco, matches, etc.							
private traders	73.7	21.6	22.7	17.1	16.0	9.0	2.6
cooperatives		59.4	57.6	67.0	69.0		
state shops	26.3	12.3	19.0	15.7	13.6	81.0	97.4
other		3.7	0.7	0.2	0.8		
Clothes, cloth, shoes							
private traders	52.4	39.8	43.7	37.1	31.4		
clothes						12.0	8.0
shoes						16.0	6.0
cotton cloth						1.2	0.7
woollen cloth							0
cooperatives		40.0	41.3	53.7	57.9		
state shops	47.6	19.0	13.7	8.3	8.6		
other		1.2	1.3	0.9	2.1		
Household goods							
private traders	77.2	58.2	58.2	57.9	38.9	NA	NA
cooperatives		21.6	24.9	28.0	42.8		
state shops	22.8	19.8	16.8	11.2	14.1		
other		0.4	0.1	2.9	4.2		
Total expenditures							
private traders	58.8	35.8	40.0	37.1	29.4		
cooperatives		47.3	45.3	52.5	59.2		
state shops	41.2	9.5	9.1	5.8	5.9		
other		7.4	5.6	4.6	5.5		
Total manufactured goods							
private traders	n.a.	n.a.	n.a.	n.a.	n.a.	13.0	7.4

Sources: *Biudzhety rabochikh*, 1:87, GARF, f. 374, op. 28, d. 3862, ll. 10–14.

priced sales.[43] The fact remains that they judged the adequacy of socialist trade on the basis of a manifestly unrepresentative source. Unlike other social groups, factory workers benefited from the system of workers' co-operatives, the best-functioning component of socialist trade. More important, factory workers numbered just 10 to 12 million out of a total population of 157 million in 1930; they did not represent the majority of urban residents, much less the majority of Russians, and still less the majority of Uzbeks, Kirgiz, Azeris, and other southern and eastern peoples of the Soviet Union. In deciding to eliminate private commercial businesses, Stalin and his associates put the imputed interests of Moscow workers over the evident interests of agrarian and artisanal consumers in the country as a whole.

Though efforts were made to improve state and cooperative trade in the later 1920s, the qualitative aspects of the socialist-sector shops gave policy makers even less to celebrate. By 1930, although the low, fixed prices of cooperatives attracted customers, perpetual shortages had transformed them into an object of general derision. Descriptions of cooperative shops sent to *Pravda*, authored, by and large, by rank-and-file Communists, underscored the shortage of virtually everything except vodka and cosmetics: "there's nothing but empty shelves and flasks of perfume" (Mordovia); "in the cooperatives there's nothing besides vodka and wine" (Rostov); "in our stores there is nothing but wine" (Urals).[44] Inevitably "unconscious" workers concluded that "Soviet power" was to blame for these and other shortcomings in the socialist sector. Party members blamed "privateers." For example, a communist salesclerk at the country's flagship department store analyzed the problems as follows:

> "Someone" created the opinion that you should take whatever there is today, no matter what, because tomorrow there won't be anything and who knows when it will reappear. That's supposedly because of industrialization. Things have reached the point of crowds breaking the display windows and unscrewing metal barriers, of an inhuman mob. In the central department store (in Mostorg's retail system, on Petrovka), the fourth floor could cave in from the violent pushing of this kind of customer. The public has gotten more brazen by the day, while speculative elements stir up antagonism and provoke [the crowd], creating a tense atmosphere.[45]

This "tense atmosphere" was no joke, as numerous episodes from 1928 to 1930 attest. In Novorossiisk the crowd in front of the cooperative

[43] Ibid., ll. 11–12; and d. 3869, l. 1; Neiman, *Vnutrenniaia torgovlia*, 238; R. W. Davies and Oleg Khlevniuk, "The End of Rationing in the Soviet Union, 1934–1935," *Europe-Asia Studies* 51, no. 4 (1999): 561–62.

[44] GARF, f. 5446, op. 55, d. 1973, ll. 18, 120, 122.

[45] Ibid., l. 125.

shop became so unruly when the store received a shipment of cloth that a woman shopper bit a policeman, and her comrades in line began throwing rocks at the guards and stormed the shop; in Moscow a salesgirl was beaten by customers until she passed out; and, in many parts of the country, ethnic fights were a regular occurrence in line.[46]

Was it still plausible, as Iurii Larin had alleged back in 1918, that "when you see 'minor shortcomings in the mechanism'—when, for example, a store in Moscow has only twelve pairs of felt boots and forces the public to line up on the street for twelve hours, only to place a notice in the window that there are just twelve pairs," the source of the socialist sector's moral and organizational deficiencies was "the psyche of private commercial capital"?[47] Even for Party members, the answer was sometimes negative. In a town near Kolomna, for example, a *Pravda* correspondent blamed "bunglers" in the cooperative administration for "incompetent announcements" eerily reminiscent of Larin's example twelve years before. The co-op had posted a sign to the effect that shoes were available for sale, causing the "public" to wait in line through the night, but in the morning the manager merely replaced the first sign with the announcement that shoes would not be sold until the shop received a "special authorization."[48] If the malignant influence of speculators was not specifically adduced, the only other plausible explanation for an incident of this ilk, to communist sympathizers, was that the cooperative manager was personally inept. By 1926 Novozhilov was swimming against the current in his interpretation of the ubiquitous corruption and abuses in state and cooperative trade as a structural effect of Soviet price policy.[49] From this time forward the Kremlin took the position that individuals, especially "class-alien" individuals, rather than policies, general conditions, or economic structures, were the root problem in socialist-sector trade.

BUREAUCRATISM ASCENDANT: THE EFFECTS OF FOOD SHORTAGE ON THE DISTRIBUTION SYSTEM

The goods famine forced consumers to revert to the habits of the revolutionary era in order to purchase manufactured goods. Once again, queues at the state and cooperative shops swallowed up citizens' off-work hours and structured their quotidian lives. Policy makers' refusal to raise prices

---

[46] Ibid., d. 1831, l. 8; Terry Martin, *The Affirmative Action Empire* (Ithaca, 2001), 153–54.
[47] *Trudy II. S"ezda Sovnarkhozov*, 100.
[48] GARF, f. 5446, op. 55, d. 1973, l. 25.
[49] Novozhilov, "Nedostatok tovarov," 78.

notwithstanding, queues were an unintended consequence of scarcity rather than a conscious strategy for managing scarce resources. Presenting a visible reminder of the inadequacies of the consumer-goods sector, they were a cause of some embarrassment to Soviet officials, who increasingly felt obliged to stress their incidental origins. By the end of the 1920s publicists portrayed them, if at all, as the result of poor store management on the part of state and cooperative trade; of conspiratorial attempts to corner the market on scarce goods on the part of speculators; of hoarding on the part of benighted peasants; and of glitches in the organization of supplies. From this perspective, the elimination of queues—on which everyone could agree as a goal—would ultimately depend not on economic forces but on rationalized institutional arrangements, the vigilant prosecution of malfeasants, and the moral enlightenment of the peasant masses.[50] In the short run, however, speculation and hoarding were unlikely to disappear through an appeal to civic virtue alone, leaving officials with only one possible weapon against queues. As a spokesman for the Trade Commissariat wrote to the Politburo, "In our circumstances, the primary means of combating lines for scarce goods is to mete them out to consumers, through the establishment of different ration quotas for different categories of consumers."[51] By limiting the quantity of scarce goods that any one customer could purchase in a day, rationing was expected to preclude hoarding and abuses.

Pressures to re-bureaucratize the distribution system intensified as queues and shortages spilled over into the food sector in 1927–28. Foods were not considered scarce from the 1922 to the 1927 harvest, though it should be emphasized that this assessment was accurate only for the 1925–26 and 1926–27 agricultural years. In the first half of the decade, starvation remained a presence. Although the government's committee for "aid to famine victims" (Pomgol) was reconstituted as a committee on the "consequences of famine" (Posledgol) after the 1922 harvest, urgent telegrams continued to report starvation in certain areas both in the Volga basin and in Turkestan through late 1923.[52] Nor was this the last NEP-era famine. Moscow workers may have consumed their hoards of food in 1924–25 because of a newfound confidence in the future, as government sociologists alleged, but peasants in northwestern Russia and the

---

[50] These were major themes in Party directives from 1928 to 1931, for example, *Direktivy VKP(b) po khoziaistvennym voprosam* (Moscow, 1931), 701–3, 803–5. For the next decade, newspaper articles regurgitated these points whenever they touched on queues, for example, *Molot*, January 11, 1933; *Snabzhenie, kooperatsiia, torgovlia*, November 20, 1932, and October 17, 1933; *Sovetskaia torgovlia* (newspaper), January 26, 1940.

[51] RGAE, f. 8043, op. 11, d. 113v, ll. 225–33.

[52] See GARF, f. 1065.

Central Agricultural Region consumed their grain reserves that year because they had nothing else to eat.[53] By late winter 1925 rural officials in Karelia and in Orel, Riazan', and Kostroma provinces were besieged by daily demonstrations of peasants who had exhausted their food supplies, and in Tambov Province eight hundred thousand to nine hundred thousand people, nearly 30 percent of the population, were reported to be starving and in desperate need of food aid. In these times of hunger peasants resorted to their age-old habits: they ate food surrogates such as bark, grass, goosefoot, and chaff; slaughtered livestock; went begging for handouts from more prosperous neighbors; and fled the region, in the hope of finding better conditions elsewhere.[54]

Until the end of 1927, however, food shortage was largely a regional phenomenon. Although good conditions in one area, and especially in Moscow, the beneficiary of powerful centripetal forces from 1917 on, did not guarantee satiety elsewhere, food shortages did not debilitate the country as a whole. Paradoxically, despite Moscow's disproportionately large share of all kinds of foods and consumer goods, Kremlin officials' tendency to gaze out their own windows for insight into the state of the economy probably heightened their sense of urgency in 1927. A series of consumer panics rocked the capital's food markets, beginning with butter, in the fall of 1926, and followed in close succession by salt, meat, sugar, vegetable oil, and wheat flour. Primed by their experience of interminable queues for cloth and other manufactured goods, some of Stalin's closest associates began, as a result of these episodes, to agitate for the re-bureaucratization of food supplies.

The Soviet Union's top military official, Klimentii Voroshilov, can serve as our second illustration of the Stalinists' path toward "restructuring" trade. Alarmed by the series of food panics in the capital, Voroshilov sent an "especially secret," "urgent" memo to the Politburo during the flour panic of autumn 1927.[55] With the war scare at its height, Voroshilov predictably foregrounded the country's military concerns:

> The recent food difficulties in Moscow, which generated huge queues outside grocery stores, especially in the working-class districts, represent an incontestably dangerous phenomenon. This is so not only because, taken in themselves, these queues reflect some serious shortcomings of our organizations and significant miscalculations in our plans. More important, the *ease* with

---

[53] Kabo, *Ocherki rabochego byta*, 149–56; see also Naum Jasny, *The Socialized Agriculture of the USSR* (Stanford, 1949), 231.

[54] RGASPI, f. 17, op. 87, d. 199, ll. 40–43, 75–79.

[55] GARF, f. 5446, op. 55, d. 1584, ll. 87–91. (Hereafter all citations are from this source.)

which a food panic was sown could make for a grave situation in our country in the event of military complications.

To prepare his memo, Voroshilov had taken a tour of Moscow cooperatives on November 1, in which he "conversed with store directors, grilled salesclerks, and, lastly, tried on my own to investigate the composition and mood of the queues." Happily he was able to report that the mood was "calm": "the crowd did not crush forward, and there were no malicious yells or noisy expressions of discontent." More than half the people in the queues were not members of the cooperative, but the vast majority lived nearby. They stood in line in family groups so as to circumvent the limits universally placed on how much anyone could purchase at one time (six kilograms for co-op members, three for nonmembers). People were obviously hoarding: demand for white flour shot up by a factor of eight during the crisis, to more than seven tons a day.

Voroshilov insisted that flour was not scarce; this was, in his view, a "panic" and not a "crisis." Throughout, Moscow's shops had adequate supplies of rye flour and enough wheat flour to meet ordinary needs. However, this had probably also been true in February 1917, when bread riots in Petrograd toppled the monarchy. There is no doubt that Voroshilov was aware of the precedent ten years on. Once again, panicked queues reflected popular fears for the future, which had been incited this time by newspaper reports on the poor wheat harvest in Ukraine and by the omnipresent rumors of war. Dismissing the press releases as unfounded, Voroshilov blamed the media for the whole episode: "The press itself has sown panic, printing unverified and untrue 'news' about a crop failure and about a shortage of wheat flour." Also to blame, he suggested, were citizens themselves for irrationally hoarding flour.

Voroshilov did acknowledge certain structural problems, which seemed to demand a policy response. A noteworthy feature of the Moscow panics was their restriction to relatively expensive foods: top-grade wheat flour, not rye bread or rye flour; refined sugar; expensive grades of butter and cuts of meat. Musing over this, the general found reason for concern:

Demand for refined sugar as against ordinary granulated sugar, demand for the better grades of meat and the highest grade of white flour in working-class neighborhoods is, on the one hand, a positive development, since it testifies to the growth of the masses' well-being. On the other hand, however, the general economic level isn't such that it can support a shift to such valuable foods. In our conditions, an increase in consumption of top-grade wheat at low, domestic prices undermines our exports, and represents, to a degree unheard of, the most inadmissable profligacy.

One solution, of course, would be to allow prices to rise to soak up the excess demand, but Voroshilov did not broach this option, instead advocating administrative measures to give the central government greater control over the food market. These included the accumulation of a strategic reserve of staple foods in major urban areas; the development and implementation of realistic standards of food consumption; the introduction on an all-Union level of standards for bread and flour, with a strict prohibition against any production or sale of grades of flour not foreseen by these standards; the development of detailed plans for food supplies in the event of a war; and, finally, the establishment of fixed prices on flour in the private market, with criminal punishment for violators. As an aside, he had words of praise for those shop directors who had reacted energetically to the panic, and who had managed to dispel the queues by deploying the entire sales force in the flour section.

Voroshilov did not use the word *rationing*, but it is difficult to imagine how else, in the absence of price hikes, his "realistic standards" could shift consumption away from the higher grades of food. The other recommendations were unambiguous. Crystallizing an emerging orthodoxy in Soviet economic theory, they highlighted the importance of stockpiles as a vehicle for government intervention into the market. This approach has a long pedigree; since time immemorial, as Richard Robbins noted in his study of Russia's 1891 famine, governments have tried to manage and deter food crises by constructing granaries.[56] Given their suspicions of the market, the Bolsheviks not surprisingly favored granary building over the alternative approach to food crises, laissez-faire pricing combined with temporary income relief. They established the first Soviet grain reserve, a permanent reservoir of seed grain called the "untouchable" fund [*neprikosnovennyi*, or *nepfond*], even before the last vestiges of the 1921–22 famine were eliminated. In 1926–27 the expansion of strategic reserves of vital commodities dovetailed with the Stalinists' hardening stance toward private enterprise as well as their increasing sense of an international threat. Accordingly a second grain reserve, the "state grain fund," was organized with the following aims: to feed the population in the event of a famine; to supply the consuming regions in times of temporary shortages; and to enable the government to flood the market in the event of a sharp price increase.[57] Voroshilov's recommendations indicated the

[56] Robbins, *Famine in Russia*, 14–15. As I write (in October 2000), President Clinton has just released thirty million barrels of crude oil from the U.S. Strategic Oil Reserve in the hope of bringing prices down. Clearly the stockpiling approach continues to flourish!

[57] The size of these special funds has been the subject of much debate; cf. E. D. Kazakov, *Gosudarstvennye prodovol'stvennye rezervy. Istoricheskie ocherki* (Moscow, 1956), 145–47,

desirability of creating yet additional reserves, with an eye to possible wartime exigencies. It remains unclear exactly when this recommendation was implemented, but by 1931 "mobilization plans" did indeed scuttle around the bureaucracy every few months, and the government possessed reserves of all staple foods. Sugar and flour; dried vegetables, beans, and nuts; frozen and canned meats, fish, and vegetables were stockpiled in every province and near every major city in a so-called mobilization, or "mobfund," the aim of which was to maintain food supplies during the initial period of a war. Like the other funds supervised by STO's Committee on Reserves, regional Party leaders could and did dip into the mobfund, with authorization from STO or Sovnarkom, as a short-term solution to a food-supply crisis, but regulations stipulated that these stocks be replaced within a month.[58]

If Stalin's army commander recommended stockpiling as a form of insurance against possible military and economic disorders, the security organs characteristically emphasized repression. On October 29, three days before Voroshilov took his tour of shops, G. G. Iagoda, the deputy chair of the OGPU, and G. E. Prokof'ev, the chief of the OGPU's economic administration, sent their own memo in response to Moscow's flour panic.[59] Where Voroshilov held the press and consumers responsible for the panic, Iagoda and Prokof'ev placed the flour problem in a broader context of shortages, for which they unequivocally blamed private trade. The problem, they argued, was "speculation, which has gained a particularly wide grip on the procurement markets (flour, vegetable oil, raw and semiprocessed hides, wool, thread, etc.)." By "screwing up" the procurement prices on grain, for example, private traders were making it impossible for the socialist supply organizations to fulfill their plans. Iagoda and Prokof'ev reiterated their previous arguments for the mass operation against leather traders; announced that they had already taken small-scale "administrative measures" in the cloth market; and suggested a mass operation against traders of grain. A crackdown on "speculation," they felt, could not be entrusted to the judicial system, since "the courts scarcely fight speculation"; even the "insignificant number of cases" forwarded to the courts by the OGPU languished without movement for two or three months. Given the fluidity of the market, these delays made arrests useless as a vehicle for affecting market conditions. What was

149, 169; Holland Hunter, "Soviet Agriculture with or without Collectivization, 1928–1940," *Slavic Review* (summer 1988): 203–16; here, 213; R. W. Davies, M. B. Tauger, and S. G. Wheatcroft, "Stalin, Grain Stocks, and the Famine of 1932–1933," *Slavic Review* 54, no. 3 (fall 1995): 642–57, here, 656–57.

[58] RGAE, f. 8043, op. 11, d. 30, ll. 16–151; d. 82, ll. 26–27.

[59] *Tragediia sovetskoi derevni*, 1:100–101 (all citations are from this source).

needed instead of such "normal court processing," the memo concluded, was "speedy repressions, which will quickly exert a healthy influence on the market."

No less than Voroshilov, the OGPU men eventually got their way. The much-discussed "mass operations" against leather traders paved the way for a wider acceptance, among Stalinist policy makers, of repression in the service of short-term economic goals. With the accumulating evidence of a food crisis, the grain "operation" catapulted over leather traders to the top of the OGPU's agenda at the end of 1927. In subsequent months grain traders and millers were arrested in even larger numbers than leather dealers, totaling 4,930 by the end of April 1928.[60] To supplement the repression of private traders (who were often, in the case of the millers and grain traders, identified as "kulaks"),[61] Iagoda and Prokof'ev stressed the need for vigilance against corruption in cooperatives and state economic agencies, and also for supervision over the mass press. Both recommendations were adopted. Punitive campaigns and show trials had, of course, been a constant feature of socialist trade since 1922, but they intensified during the next several years.[62] As for newspapers, the view that the press was "disorganizing" the market was enshrined two months later in the Politburo's emergency decree on grain collection. Empowering Viacheslav Molotov and Anastas Mikoian "to ensure the publication in the press of such information about the market" as would best promote the regime's "measures to organize the market," this decree marked a major step toward outright falsification, with a mobilizing aim, as against the mixture of genuine information and spin characteristic of the NEP-era newspapers.[63]

In addition, the OGPU officials advised banning any transportation of scarce foods or manufactured goods beyond Moscow's city limits and beyond the borders of Moscow province. It seems unlikely that an embargo of this sort was implemented, given the huge policing effort it would have entailed. As in the civil war era, the OGPU would have had to post "blockade detachments" on every train leading out of the city, and on every major road, evidence of which has not at this point come to

---

[60] Osokina, *Za fasadom*, 54–55; *Derevnia glazami VChK-OGPU-NKVD*, 2:1035–36.

[61] The attack on the grain traders in 1927–28 should probably be incorporated into our general understanding of the attack on kulaks, generally discussed in connection with the collectivization drive. The regime's term for many small-town grain traders and millers was *kulak*, which also appears in the documents in this case.

[62] For reports on the ongoing purge, see, especially, the newspaper *Kooperativnaia zhizn'*, and its successor, as of February 10, 1931, *Snabzhenie, kooperatsiia, torgovlia*.

[63] *Tragediia sovetskoi derevni*, 1:111–13. On the shift in newspapers, see Lenoe, "'Stalinization' of the Soviet Press."

light. Nonetheless, the proposal resonated with measures that were taken over the next five years to shield Moscow residents, or, more precisely, "legitimate" Moscow residents, from the extremity of material hardship. Several of these, described by Timothy Colton, were directed at "unburdening" the capital of unwanted social groups, and thereby reducing the number of people who required provisions: the eviction of many traders, priests, and other disenfranchised residents [*lishentsy*] from municipal housing from 1929 to 1931; the expulsion of "kulaks," gypsies, and other citizens ineligible for residency permits during the passportization campaign between 1932 and 1934.[64] Other measures, reflecting the regime's concern with public opinion in its central power base, included efforts to flood the capital with food and consumer goods during major holidays— most immediately, for the tenth anniversary of the October Revolution, to be celebrated one week after Voroshilov's report.[65]

By the end of 1927 Soviet leaders could no longer deny that this was a food crisis, rather than a mere "panic." The principal cause was a crop failure in the major wheat-producing areas; the result was hoarding and severe inflationary pressures in every part of the country, as well as a large-scale famine in Ukraine.[66] Unwilling either to open the Soviet market to grain imports or to allow food prices to rise, policy makers' options were reduced to devising strategies for increasing the marketed portion of grain and devising strategies for stretching out the available stocks of food. Stockpiling and repression were two outcomes of the first dilemma; collectivization, which falls outside the purview of this study, would eventually be another. The outcome of the second dilemma was the class ration and, with it, the resurrection of the bureaucratized distribution system of the civil war epoch.

Readers will recall from chapter 2 that the distribution policy of war communism rested on three mechanisms: price controls, which increasingly succumbed to pressures for demonetization; rationing, which increasingly differentiated consumers in terms of their ascribed importance and social class; and so-called commodity exchange, which increasingly lost its moral claim to equivalency as the state offered less and less in

[64] Timothy J. Colton, *Moscow: Governing the Socialist Metropolis* (Cambridge, Mass., 1995), 210–11, 223–25, 270–72; on gypsies, cf. Nicolas Werth and Gael Moullec, eds., *Rapports secrets sovietiques, 1921–1991* (Paris, 1994), 43–44.

[65] GARF, f. 5446, op. 55, d. 1584, ll. 109–10.

[66] On the causes of the food crisis, see *Tragediia sovetskoi derevni*, 1:114–16; and Jean Welker, "Climate and the Soviet Grain Crisis of 1928" (Ph.D. diss., University of Maryland, 1995). Both emphasize drought over human factors. On the Ukrainian famine, see GARF, f. 374, op. 28, d. 1569.

return for peasants' crops. From 1928 to 1931 demonetization did not prevail over price controls, though antimoney sentiment flourished in connection with urban distribution. The other two mechanisms not only returned to the center of Soviet distribution policy but recapitulated, with variations, the dynamics that were present from 1918 to 1921. In addition, as in the crisis of the previous decade, these dynamics played out against the backdrop of an intensified war on the private sector and the forcible reorganization of consumer cooperatives.

What set into motion the restructuring of socialist distribution was an altered approach to rural trade. As in 1921, and before that from 1918 to 1920, the Party's response to food shortage was to attempt to circumvent the market at the supply end by linking peasants' opportunities for consumption to their deliveries of grain to the procurement agencies. By the end of December 1927 this strategy had become the centerpiece of the grain-collection campaign: 70 to 80 percent of the available stocks of consumer goods were to be shipped to the grain surplus regions "at the expense of denuding the cities and the non-grain regions."[67] Not unreasonably interpreting this provision to mean a revival of *tovaroobmen*, the war communism policy of "exchanging" manufactured goods (very often, empty promises of manufactured goods) for requisitioned grain, local officials cordoned off village market squares and prevented peasants from shopping at local stores. By February complaints were arriving from all quarters that "in the provinces they aren't selling cloth and such for money, but only for grain."[68] In the meantime, peasants were subjected to illegal door-to-door searches, seizures of grain, and other "extraordinary measures," inevitably condemned after the fact but repeated during the next year's procurement season. Rumors proliferated in this context; peasants rightly suspected that the NEP had come to an end.[69]

The exchange of grain for manufactured goods was carried out on an individualized basis, as in 1921, rather than the collective approach of the original commodity exchange campaigns. Over the next few years, however, collectivization virtually ensured that the war communism model would prevail. Collective responsibility is apparent in the May 1932 de-

---

[67] *Tragediia sovetskoi derevni*, 111–14.

[68] At an agit-prop meeting at the Hammer and Sickle factory on February 13, 1928, one-third of the questions concerned rural trade and procurements, for example, "I've heard from the village that they've fixed hard prices and set up a blockade just like 1921"; "Is there a directive in the provinces that says that grain can be taken from the seller at the bazaars for a fixed price, without the seller's consent?"; "Is it right that blockade detachments are stationed in the villages?" (GARF, f. 374, op. 28, d. 1901, ll. 37–39).

[69] *Direktivy VKP(b) po khoz. voprosam*, 461–65, here, 465; Lewin, "'Taking Grain'"; Carr and Davies, *Foundations of a Planned Economy*, 1:3–105.

crees on the market, which authorized peasants to trade at the market only if their whole district had fulfilled its procurement quotas; it was also evident in the famine zones of 1932–33, where entire villages were barricaded until they met their quotas and cooperatives were forbidden from shipping goods to the shops in those villages.[70] As early as 1929 each province and city was once again assigned the rate of consumption at which its needs would be calculated, and goods shipped out accordingly. Once again, the grain-surplus regions were big winners in the competition for manufactured goods, along with Moscow, Leningrad, and the industrial Donbass.[71]

The resurrection of *tovaroobmen* reflected policy makers' increasing desperation about the state of the economy in the late 1920s. The policy was predicated on two conditions, neither of which had been met during the civil war era, nor were they attainable now: the procurement agencies' possession of significant stocks of desirable consumer products and the peasants' inability to obtain better deals on the side. The OGPU's mass operations against grain traders, which subsequently flowed into "dekulakization," might reduce private-sector competition in the procurement markets, but the complete elimination of private traders was unlikely at best. Moreover, mechanisms were not in place to prevent peasants from shopping for manufactured goods on their own.

On the other hand, state finances and institutions were far stronger at the end of the NEP than at its beginning, and policy makers did succeed in institutionalizing a procedure for *tovaroobmen*. In December 1927 consumer goods were diverted to the grain regions on the basis of an emergency decree, but this practice was regularized over the next few years. In late 1929 planners were already able to allocate stocks for urban areas, grain-producing rural regions, and non-grain rural regions for the entire autumn–winter quarter.[72] One year later, late-fall shipments to the villages were fully integrated into the planned economy and acquired their new name, *stimulirovanie* [stimulation]. Henceforth, each year at harvest time the balance of supplies was tipped a little toward the country, as large shipments of the "rural assortment" of manufactured goods—sugar, *makhorka* (cheap-grade tobacco), knitted underclothes, woolen shawls, felt boots, heavy shoes, inexpensive calico, kerosene, household soap, nails, sheet glass, and agricultural implements—were sent to the villages

[70] Sheila Fitzpatrick, *Stalin's Peasants: Resistance and Survival in the Russian Village after Collectivization* (New York, 1994), 76–77; D'Ann Penner, "The Agrarian 'Strike' of 1932–33," *Kennan Institute Occasional Papers*, no. 269.

[71] Davies, *Soviet Economy in Turmoil*, 291.

[72] Ibid., 286; GARF, f. 374, op. 28, d. 3425.

as a stimulus to increase agricultural deliveries. In an effort to bind peasants' consumption as closely as possible to their official grain marketings,
some of these supplies were conferred as prizes for fulfilled and overfulfilled plans at the discretion of local Party authorities.[73]

Most, however, were sold through the village cooperatives to anyone
who could present evidence of having met the procurement quotas unless
a community was so far behind as to trigger a villagewide ban on sales.
Prices were set extremely high. Sovnarkom periodically issued instructions to impose a surcharge of 25 to 33 percent on goods sold in rural
areas from 1929 to 1931, and by 1932, Malafeev has estimated, village
shops charged an average of 39 percent more than their urban counterparts on basic consumer goods.[74] Thus, although the official data identify
1930 as the all-time high with respect to the rural proportion of socialist-
sector retail sales, and 1935 as the twenty-year low, a consideration of
price trends suggests that the percentage of goods sold in rural areas
declined after 1928 and bottomed out in 1932–33.[75] This would hardly
be surprising, given the decimation of peasant livestock holdings, famine,
peasant resistance, and the low efficiency of the collective farms.

Compared to war communism's *tovaroobmen*, Stalinist stimulation was
more systematic, and it also commanded larger (if still inadequate) quantities of consumer goods. Otherwise, the distinguishing feature of early
1930s stimulation was its reliance on vodka sales, the result of a deliber-
ate and successful policy of "squeezing" peasants not just through submarket procurements but also through their addiction to drink (figure 2).
At the instigation of economic planners, vodka production was quietly
expanded from 22.4 million barrels in 1926 to 65 million barrels in 1931.
Though the absolute quantity of vodka leveled off after that year, vodka
profits continued to grow through successive price hikes. By 1932 vodka
had become the motor of the Soviet economy: 19.4 percent of state and
cooperative trade derived from the state's vodka monopoly, which accounted for a staggering 33 to 39 percent of retail sales in rural areas;
vodka profits supplied one-fifth of the central government's budget the
following year.[76] Whereas tractors, fertilizers, and hardwares remained
scarce, and sewing machines—a major focus of rural as well as urban
consumer aspirations in the prerevolutionary period—were totally unavailable in the early 1930s countryside, planners made sure that, even in

[73] Neiman, *Vnutrenniaia torgovlia*, 174–75; *Direktivy VKP(b) po khoz. voprosam*, 803–5;
RGAE, f. 8043, op. 11, d. 3, l. 93; d. 26, l. 39; d. 27, l. 16; d. 29, l. 42; d. 32, l. 3; f. 7971,
op. 2, d. 662, l. 7.

[74] Ibid., d. 38, l. 16; Malafeev, *Istoriia tsenoobrazovaniia*, 165.

[75] *Sovetskaia torgovlia. Statisticheskii sbornik*, 21; RGAE, f. 7971, op. 2, d. 662a, ll. 2–3.

[76] See online appendix "Vodka Production and Sales."

Figure 2. Small-town vodka queue, early 1930s. *Courtesy of the Russian State Archive for Cinematic and Photographic Documents (RGAKFD).*

the most remote corners of the Soviet Union, vodka supplies never ran low. This was not a new concept in the 1930s; Stalin had recommended such a course in 1923, only to retract the idea a few months later when the economy improved. As he put it in a memo, "I never hid the fact that free trade in alcohol undoubtedly represents a political minus (moral lamentations on this score I considered then, and continue to consider, superfluous), but I considered that, alongside it, this minus would be compensated by an economic plus."[77] This evidently became the planners' manifesto from 1931 to 1933.

In urban areas the 1927–28 crop failure proved severe enough to warrant measures for rationing bread and other foods. Cooperatives had already limited the amount of cloth, hardware supplies, and other scarce manufactured goods that they would sell to a customer at one time; with the escalating food crisis, the natural step was to do the same with bread, flour, and cereal products. Limits on sales to "one set of hands" [*v odni*

[77] RGASPI, f. 82, op. 2, d. 683, l. 8.

Figure 3. Sale of bread by coupons, Moscow, 1929. *Courtesy of the Russian State Archive for Cinematic and Photographic Documents (RGAKFD).*

ruki] were enacted in Moscow during the 1927 flour panic and in many parts of the country in early 1928.[78] The reintroduction of bread cards naturally followed (figure 3). Given the widespread sense of crisis, per-customer limits were not as effective as coupons in controlling commodity flows; customers could purchase more if they stood in line again, with the result that the limits mainly served to lengthen queues. Ration coupons could solve this problem, albeit at a cost: as administrators knew, from their experience from 1917 to 1922, the extra layer of accounting inherent in a rationing system obliged local governments and cooperatives to employ a battalion of ration-card checkers and comptrollers. Undeterred, Omsk, the regional center of Western Siberia's cereal-producing zone, began issuing coupons for bread and flour in May 1928, followed in early summer by the cities of the Ukrainian breadbasket—Odessa, Mariupol, Kherson, Kiev, and Dnepropetrovsk.[79] By the end of 1929 most major cities in the country had followed suit.

As in 1918–19, food shortage set the stage for a showdown between

[78] Cf. Carr and Davies, *Foundations of a Planned Economy*, vol. 1, no. 2: 697–704.
[79] GARF, f. 5446, op. 55, d. 1582, ll. 1, 11, 14, 42.

the Party and the cooperatives. Ever since the restoration of membership fees in December 1923, the elected co-op boards had understood themselves as the custodians of shareholders' interests. When shortages began to affect their operations, the consumer cooperatives accordingly tried to protect supplies for their primary constituency by entitling members to purchase more than nonmembers. Once limits were introduced, however, all the old Bolshevik suspicions of cooperatives resurfaced. A study of rural cooperatives, carried out in 1928, revealed that kulak households were twice as likely as poor peasant households to be members of cooperatives, whereas, in the cities, free professionals and traders were reported to hold a disproportionate number of seats on co-op boards.[80] In light of such information, Communists found it intolerable that bread quotas should be linked to the socially retrograde division between cooperative members and nonmembers. Mikoian, the Party's expert on trade matters, underscored this point in a 1928 report to Tsentrosoiuz: "Why must we supply the full 100 percent of the population? Why must we supply Nepmen? The easiest way is to establish a norm, a ration card."[81] As of July 1929, the Commissariat of Trade prohibited socialist shops from selling any foods or staple manufactured goods to the "nonlaboring" population (traders, kulaks, free professionals, priests, etc.) unless the state had a monopoly, in which case these groups could purchase reduced rations at a raised price.[82]

Like so many decrees promulgated during the zenith of the collectivization drive, this prohibition was eventually softened. In May 1930 Tsentrosoiuz received permission to reinstate certain privileges for co-op members, as against nonmembers, as long as these privileges did not affect the basic food rations.[83] From 1928 to 1931, however, the main developmental tendency of Soviet distribution was in the direction of increasing greater centralization, systematization, and, at the same time, social differentiation of consumption entitlements on terms defined by the state.[84] In 1929 one city after another was incorporated into the centralized supply system, which covered an expanding array of products. In addition to essential foods (bread, flour, cereal grains, meat, butter, vegetable oil, sugar, and tea), the Commissariat of Trade took control of the

[80] Dmitrenko, Morozov, and Pogudin, *Partiia i kooperatsiia*, 255–56.
[81] Cited in Carr and Davies, *Foundations of a Planned Economy*, vol. 1, no. 2: 700–701.
[82] Davies, *Soviet Economy in Turmoil*, 289.
[83] *Direktivy VKP(b) po khoz. voprosam*, 701–3.
[84] Early 1930s rationing has been discussed by two scholars, whose works offer a more detailed picture than I can provide here. For social implications, see Osokina, *Za fasadom*, 89–113; for political and institutional development, see Davies, *Soviet Economy in Turmoil*, 289–300.

manufactured goods subject to the greatest demand (linen, cotton, and woolen textiles, ready-to-wear clothing, footwear, tobacco, and soap).[85] Municipalities' improvised rationing systems were gradually transformed into a uniform national rationing system for both foods and manufactured goods. Eggs, vegetables, apples, and pears were added to the growing list of rationed foods. National "norms" were established for individual consumption of the various categories of food on a daily or monthly basis. Ration cards for individual foods were superseded by comprehensive ration booklets [*zabornye knizhki*] from the local soviets, and these in turn were soon replaced by national ration booklets, issued by Tsentrosoiuz.[86] Finally, the whole system fell under the supervision of the Commissariat of Trade, which was renamed the Commissariat of Provisionment to reflect the nonmarket nature of the restructured economy.

In the process of centralization, it was, of course, the civil war principle of the class ration that prevailed. As in the period from 1918 to 1921, the main goal of rationing was to guarantee provisions for urban workers and state functionaries, as well as for the military (now much smaller than in 1918) and for the expanding contingent of security personnel.[87] Urban residents were once again classified according to their occupational status, and "workers," including engineers, specialists, and managers at mines, factories, and other productive enterprises, were allocated roughly twice as much food as white-collar employees and adult dependents. Compared to the class ration of the revolutionary era, this classification scheme appears, at first glance, to be less finely differentiated; the middle level of enhancement for manual labor (150% of the white-collar urban norm) was collapsed into the higher, 200 percent level, and the minimum, "bourgeois" ration (50% of the norm) dropped out. The difference is more apparent than real, since workers in physically dangerous or exceptionally demanding jobs became eligible for supplements, while the elimination of the bourgeois ration reflected the total disavowal of bourgeois groups.

The real innovation of the 1930s rationing system lay in its formal calibration of ration levels to the economic and political significance of particular enterprises and cities. This had occurred on an ad hoc basis in 1919–20, when trade unions had lobbied for "heavy manual labor" status and factory managers had tried to obtain military supplies. In the early

[85] Davies, *Soviet Economy in Turmoil*, 291; Leonard Hubbard, *Soviet Trade and Distribution* (London, 1938), 108–9.

[86] Davies, *Soviet Economy in Turmoil*, 295–97.

[87] As the supply system coalesced in 1930–32, food supplies for the military and the security organs were routed through a separate channel from civilian supplies. Cf. Osokina, *Ierarkhiia potrebleniia*, 73–89; RGAE, f. 8043, op. 11, d. 32, l. 5; d. 45, l. 62; d. 48, l. 195.

1930s STO drew up a comprehensive ranking for cities, regions, and industries, much as agricultural regions were assigned different consumption rates for manufactured goods. Four lists catalogued Soviet cities and production sites, from the top-priority metropolitan areas and defense enterprises of the "special list" to the low-priority small cities, consumer-goods factories, and agricultural concerns of the "third list." Not only were portions larger for the "special" and "first" lists, the ration coupons for these lists covered a larger number of foods and consumer goods, and came out of the central government's, rather than local, supplies. As in the civil war era, supply obligations were met in order of priority, making it far more likely that the consumers on the higher lists would actually receive their allotted rations. When supplies ran low, dependents of all categories tended to lose their rations, as did the workers and employees of the second and third lists. The whole system codified a precept that would later be enshrined in the 1936 "Stalin Constitution"—not, as Marx had written, "from each according to his abilities, to each according to his needs" but "to each, according to his work."

The bureaucratization of distribution traced a familiar pattern, revealing once again the conflicting tendencies within socialist economic and political culture. If the shortages of the late 1920s led citizens to revert to the crisis mode of consumption, they led Soviet officials to revert to a crisis mode of economic management. The first reflex, evident as early as 1923, was to limit prices; the second, to corner supplies; the third, to wage war on the private sector; and the fourth, to allocate goods to consumers on the basis of consumers' utility to the state. As in the civil war era, most economic administrators understood every such action as constrained by necessity; they could not, after all, allow peasants to jeopardize the industrialization effort, nor could they allow Nepmen and other "undeserving" consumers to eat up vital supplies.[88]

Once under way, however, restructuring emboldened the intransigents in the Party to represent bureaucratizing measures in millenial terms. Iurii Larin took the opportunity to republish in book form a series of articles he had written in 1915–16. In his introduction to the volume, which praised Walther Rathenau's organizational innovations in wartime Germany as the model of a totally planned, totally mobilized, totally rationalized economy, Larin invoked both German and Soviet "war communism" as Lenin's idea of "the highest degree of organization."[89] Themes reminiscent of *The ABC of Communism* riddled the Soviet press in 1929–30: journalists heralded the "transition to a moneyless economy"

[88] On this feeling, see Nove, "Was Stalin Really Necessary?"
[89] Iu. Larin, *Gosudarstvennyi kapitalizm voennogo vremeni v Germanii* (Moscow, 1928).

as the realization of utopian communism, and editorials trumpeted the equitable distribution of goods that the "socialist restructuring of the country" had finally "made possible."[90] Bureaucratization, in sum, still possessed an ideological and psychological resonance for a major segment of the policy community. Despite the fact that restructuring was provoked by crisis rather than prosperity, it reinforced the bureaucratizing impulse of its architects by making a thoroughly rationalized economy appear possible.

The result was a reductio ad absurdum: bureaucratism run amok. By 1930 the top policy-making bodies of the Soviet government—Sovnarkom, STO, the Communist Party's Central Committee—found themselves mired in paperwork concerning consumption rights. Literally barraged with requests to increase the ration designation of enterprises, regions, and occupational groups, these organs became involved in such minutiae as whether subway builders' working conditions were "physically deleterious"; whether "eastern merchants" (mainly Persian and Chinese) qualified for rations and at what level; whether employees of vacation homes ought to be given cafeteria meals along with their elite guests; how resettled kulaks or scholars or children at Pioneer Camps should be provisioned; and whether any subgroups deserved better rations than the group norm.[91] At last, as such archbureaucratizers of the revolutionary era as Lev Kritsman had dreamed, the "anarchy of supplies," no less than the "anarchy of distribution," was replaced with a "conscious determination of needs." The cost, however, was the paralysis of the central government precisely when it had become responsible for the vast majority of economic life.

Rampant bureaucratism inevitably triggered a backlash, as it had in 1921. For one thing, the economic crisis continued to intensify; for another, policy makers once again felt confident that the "question of power" had been resolved. Stalin's March 1930 article, "Dizzy with Success," signaled a tentative step away from war communism as a model. Suddenly the forcible closure of bazaars was declared impermissible, and local Party committees were directed to facilitate peasants' market sales. Two months later the Central Committee criticized consumer cooperatives for "bureaucratization" and an "inability to sell."[92] R. W. Davies has meticulously documented the reforms of the next few years. In May 1931

---

[90] For example, *Za industrializatsiiu*, February 14, 1930; *Na novom etape sotsialisticheskogo stroitel'stva* (Moscow, 1930).

[91] See, for example, RGAE, f. 8043, op. 11, d. 7, ll. 127–31; d. 17, ll. 73–74; d. 28, ll. 204, 215–16; d. 31, l. 79; d. 36, ll. 114–15; d. 56, ll. 8, 25; d. 57, l. 107.

[92] *Direktivy VKP(b) po khoziaistvennym voprosam*, 678–80, 701–3.

coupons for manufactured goods were abruptly canceled in favor of per-customer limits, followed ten months later by most foodstuffs. Policy makers then slashed the number of citizens eligible for rations on the second and third lists. Although the centralized rationing system was not fully dismantled until 1935, reforms of planning, supplies, and state finances in 1931–32 became so far-reaching as to evoke comparisons with 1921.[93]

What they did not do was to alter the system's social discrimination. The reforms of 1931 revived war communism's institution of "special provisionment," according to which high-ranking military staff, executives in the central bureaucracy, high-level OGPU officers, and the "mobilization workers" assigned to each economic agency to prepare for war were supposed to be given rations at the level of workers on the special list, plus significant extras in both food and manufactured goods.[94] "Nomenklatura" elites, the most important Party, state, and industrial leaders in each oblast and district, received a similar dispensation, as did members of the Academy of Sciences, prerevolutionary political prisoners, "personal pensioners," and former Red Guards.[95] In principle, each *raion* was to name twenty leading citizens, along with one or two family members, for a total of fifty consumers, who would be tied to special shops and given access to subsidized goods.[96] In practice, the nomenklatura contingent—already several times larger than in the revolutionary era—ballooned over the next few years; in Moscow alone the number of people tied to special shops grew from twenty three hundred bureaucrats and their families in early 1931 to fourteen thousand households two years later. At the same time, both the quality and the quantity of the goods allotted this upper stratum increased; by 1934 army leaders in the Far East were obtaining fur coats, silk and linen clothing, bicycles, record players, and sewing machines at subsidized rates.[97]

At the other end of the spectrum, centralized distribution threw private traders, priests, former tsarist gendarmes, and other "class enemies" onto the free market at a time when their income was cut off. This was bad enough for the few wealthy Nepmen who managed to escape arrest; for expropriated small shopkeepers, it meant a virtual sentence to pau-

[93] Ibid., 845–48; Davies, *Crisis and Progress*, 58–64, 94–97, 206–8.

[94] RGAE, f. 8043, op. 11, d. 30, 111b; d. 31, l. 78; d. 32, l. 29; d. 36, ll. 89–91; d. 45, l. 62; d. 92, ll. 86–87.

[95] List drawn from GA Odes. ob., f. R-710, op. 1, d. 20, l. 255 (1933). Interestingly, when Odessa authorities were told to make a few cuts in "special provisionment," it was GPU and police officers, not academicians, who got the ax.

[96] RGASPI, f. 17, op. 3, d. 862, ll. 16–18; RGAE, f. 8043, op. 11, d. 31, l. 4.

[97] RGAE, f. 8043, op. 11, d. 92, ll. 86–87.

perization unless they could make a living at the market or could rely on relatives, who were better off, for food.[98] Nor did class warfare escape the ethnic overtones of the revolutionary era, as Jews continued to be greatly overrepresented in private trade throughout the 1920s; in parts of the former Pale of Settlement, dekulakization was basically directed at them. Local officials often drew up the list of kulaks from existing lists of *lishentsy*—people who, by virtue of their class or occupation, were denied citizenship rights. In the Western *oblast'* (Belorussia surely presented a similar picture), Jewish traders constituted up to 80 percent of the names on those lists, a figure totally unacceptable to communist sensibilities, and, in particular districts, as many as 45 percent of all Jews were disenfranchised and hence scheduled for dekulakization. Clarifications followed; the Western *oblast'* obtained a special exemption for petty Jewish traders in early 1930, in view of the "traditions of centuries-long oppression" of Jews by the tsarist government, which had left "its deep imprint on the national minorities' psyche." They were, if at all possible, to be collectivized and given land, and the urban petty traders allowed to join cooperatives and hence become eligible for rations. By 1932 some "improperly dekulakized" Jewish traders had been rehabilitated, but, otherwise, the policy had obtained few positive results. The Jewish *kolkhozy* were few and feeble, the Jewish population for the most part hungry and aggrieved.[99]

Peasants, likewise, had to fend for themselves. From 1928 to 1931 crop failure, collectivization, dekulakization, and unreasonably high procurement quotas left peasants, including those from the country's prime agricultural regions, the most vulnerable stratum of the population. The central supply organs were inundated with reports of food shortages, famine-induced diseases, the consumption of food surrogates, popular unrest over food supplies, and deaths from starvation in rural regions, and not just during the renowned Ukrainian famine of 1932–33. Panicked telegrams from Party leaders in Kazakhstan and Eastern Siberia

[98] These groups were not even allowed to obtain unemployment relief in many cities; the unemployed were purged from the labor exchanges if they had well-paid relatives or the wrong "class face" (*Krasnaia gazeta*, August 5, 1929). Relatives, meanwhile, often feared the possible political repercussions of supporting their disenfranchised relations. This practice was enshrined in law—article 49 of the Law Codes on Marriage, Family, and Guardianship obliged children "to provide sustenance to their needy, incapacitated parents"—but the Central Control Commission's Party collegium felt it necessary to remind local Party organizations not to purge anyone from the Party for aiding disenfranchised relatives (GARF, f. 3316, op. 65, d. 55, l. 6.

[99] GARF, f. 1235, op. 124, d. 45, ll. 7–11, 42, 54, 59, 60–88, 145–48, 168–69; op. 125, d. 60, ll. 22–41; d. 61, ll. 1–16.

reported famine conditions every year from 1929 to 1933, often sec-
onded by OGPU reports on popular "negative attitudes" owing to the
food supply "difficulties"—language straight out of the civil war era.[100]
Other regions were hit once or twice, typically either in 1929 or 1930
and 1933. The center's responses to their pleas generally expressed more
concern for the "political situation" than for the suffering of Soviet peasants. As in 1918 to 1920, 1921–22, and 1924–25, policy makers' reluctance to divert food supplies to the countryside from 1928 to 1933 reveals the attitude that peasants' lives were expendable. Compared to the
Politburo's energetic response to queues in Moscow, where the situation
was far from life-threatening, the failure to alleviate rural famine points
up a second core defect of the bureaucratized economy besides bureaucratism: myopia, or policy makers' undue fixation on conditions close to
home.

Corporatism in the Service of the Plan

The rationing system was introduced as an emergency measure, but,
once in place, policy makers sought to use it in the interests of rationalization. Eliminating "speculative" middlemen, capping prices, and linking consumption entitlements to citizens' residency and employment, the
centralized distribution system funneled scarce goods to Soviet consumers in order of the consumers' value to the industrialization drive.
Needless to say, the system did not operate precisely as planned. It foun-
dered above all on its relations with the peasantry: peasants turned out to
need more food than they were supposed to need, and collectivization
resulted not in a great leap forward in agricultural production but in a
considerable step backward. In addition, for the bureaucratized economy
to function, Soviet leaders had to rely on the cooperation of local Soviet
administrators whose methods, motives, and available resources diverged
from central policy as often as they coincided. Local executives frequently cut rations because their planned food supplies failed to material-
ize, or unilaterally raised rations to defuse popular unrest.[101] Viewed from
the regions, the implementation of the planned economy looks as much

---

[100] RGAE, f. 8043, op. 11, d. 13, ll. 161–64; d. 15, ll. 9, 115; d. 17, ll. 139–41; d. 28, ll.
24–26; d. 34, l. 1; d. 59, l. 24; d. 75, l. 20. On Kazakhstan, see also Alec Nove, "Victims of
Stalinism: How Many?" in *Stalinist Terror: New Perspectives*, ed. J. Arch Getty and Roberta
Manning (Cambridge, 1993), 261–74.

[101] TsGAOD Mos., f. 3, op. 15, d. 84, l. 4; f. 8043, op. 11, d. 16, l. 36; d. 17, l. 89; d. 25,
ll. 82–83. See also the denunciations of "localism" [*mestnichestvo*] in *KPSS v rezoliutsiiakh*,
4:501–2.

like improvisation as the execution of a plan. The Soviet supply administration may well have been epitomized by an incident in the Black Sea port Nikolaev in the early months of the 1932–33 famine. Although it was illegal for a syndicate to issue scarce goods without an official allocation order, the supply chief of Nikolaev cornered the director of a meat syndicate in his office for three to four hours a day for several consecutive days, bullying him and demanding meat. When these methods failed, the city council summoned the police to wrest the meat from him by force. Reshetnikov, the meat syndicate director, complained to the bureau charged with investigating abuses but to no avail. The city government called on its connections and eventually procured an ex post facto allocation order from the Ukrainian meat trust approving the "early issuance of supplies."[102]

As this illustration suggests, if the bureaucratized rationing and supply system consolidated the political culture of planning in the center, its effects on the local authorities onto whose shoulders its administration devolved were very often the reverse. As in 1920, when Rykov had grumbled about administrators' "proprietary psychology," the planned economy of the industrialization era generated a style of management directly at odds with the principles that produced it. Rationing broadened the responsibility of local executives for the citizens under their jurisdiction, for whose sustenance it rendered them accountable. At the same time, since the ostensible purpose of the system was to replace the "anarchy" of the market with conscious control through the plan, bureaucratized distribution diminished the official powers of local authorities to obtain supplies. Not infrequently this quandary led them to resort to unofficial methods. Like planning in the industrial sector, rationing put into place a paradoxical system in which the center allocated but the local executive was nonetheless required to procure.[103] As a counterpoint to the "science of planning" that reigned in Moscow, rationing thus fostered a political culture at the local and provincial levels centered on the arts of procurement.

The other salient element of central distribution policy, the stratification of citizens in relation to consumption rights, was warmly embraced by administrators at the local level. Rationing made them responsible for their constituents' supplies, but local executives had reason to conclude that they were not equally accountable for all citizens' well-being. Understanding the ration lists as an indication from their bosses of whose

---

[102] GA Odes. ob., f. R-710, op. 1, d. 20, ll. 118–22.

[103] Shearer makes a similar point with regard to industrial raw materials; cf. his *Industry, State, and Society*, 53–75, 167–86.

rations were most important, local authorities typically magnified the disparities in provisionment between the higher- and lower-ranked groups. This tendency was exacerbated by the fact that the top rungs on the supply ladder were occupied by local notables: the governing authorities themselves and their social and political confreres. With their own privileged position enshrined in Soviet distribution policy, it was only natural that many local leaders should devote themselves with particular zeal to supplying the upper end of the social hierarchy.

The anomalies in the distribution system that resulted from local biases were criticized vociferously in the early-1930s press, but the center was by no means fundamentally opposed to local authorities' initiatives. Far from it, Stalin and his associates had every interest in placing as much of the burden of provisionment as possible on the backs of executives at the local level. The lesson of 1921 had been that even a socialist economy needed to harness personal initiative; although the lesson of 1927–28 had pointed in the opposite direction by suggesting the dangers of utilizing private agriculture, industry, and trade, this left policy makers all the more dependent on the sources of dynamism within the socialist bureaucracy. The challenge, once again, was to harness that initiative on behalf of centrally defined goals—above all, the industrialization effort. War communism suggested two expedients. First, although the allocation of civilian food supplies was "planned" around the four basic ration lists, Stalinist policy makers retained an element of personal discretion in the classification of cities and factories, and allowed administrators to try to persuade them of the vital importance of one or another local group. Both the benefits and pitfalls of such a system were familiar from the civil war era. On the debit side, the system caused government bureaus to be deluged with petitions; fostered the inflation of the upper end of the supply hierarchy; and made it difficult to detect "dead souls." On the positive side, case-by-case determinations enabled central officials to respond flexibly to crises, and to reshuffle the supply rankings as regional and sectoral needs shifted.

Tacitly encouraged by discretionary procedures, local administrators strenuously lobbied for better supplies. The centralized rationing system opened up new channels of communication with the country's highest authorities, and it was a rare Party secretary or factory director who did not avail himself of these avenues. The net effect was to exert a massive upward pressure on supply designations. The hardships ascribed to particular occupational and regional cohorts were all believable, and accordingly, as in the revolutionary period, the privileged segments of the rationing system expanded to accommodate many petitioners' claims. Over the first few years of centralized rationing, all the ration lists exceeded their planned populations, and had their contingents reconfirmed at a higher level, until the system as a whole had expanded from 26 million people (in 1930) to 40.3 million (in 1932).[104] Much of the increase occurred in the upper lists, setting into motion a chain reaction: with the simultaneous expansion of the higher ration groups and reduction in total food supplies, the center introduced a further distinction at the upper end of the hierarchy, the "list of 150" highest-priority defense enterprises, which were to get their supplies directly from the center, without going through the regional supply agencies.[105]

More vexing to central planners than the petition process was the phenomenon of "dead souls." Since supplies to an enterprise or city were determined by a mechanical multiplication of the number of people in each ration category times the amount of food and other goods allotted to each, local executives negotiated with the center over the size of their "contingent" as well as over the ration list at which supplies would be calculated. What every executive hoped for was a confirmed contingent that exceeded the number of mouths that had to be fed. At factories, a surplus meant both a cushion against an unplanned reduction in supplies and a critical degree of leverage over employees, who, faced with the prospect of better rations, might be induced to work harder or stay longer. Accordingly managers padded their lists, in the lingo of the revolutionary era, with "dead souls": truants and habitually tardy workers from whom rations had been withdrawn, former employees, dead relatives, and dependents.[106] We have no way of ascertaining how prevalent this phenomenon was, but it certainly occurred on a massive scale: in the Urals six factories had 10,495 dead souls on the ration rosters in 1932; at Moscow's Red October factory one-third of the 24,000-person contingent comprised dead souls in 1931.[107] Dead souls had reached epidemic proportions under war communism, as readers may recall; in 1920 some 40 percent of all food rations were said to be redundant.

Along with the flexible approach to the class ration, war communism

---

[104] Neiman, *Vnutrenniaia torgovlia*, 176.

[105] RGAE, f. 8043, op. 11, d. 36, ll. 58–64; Davies, *Crisis and Progress*, 116, 179–80.

[106] Population flux and the high rates of labor turnover during the First Five-Year Plan facilitated such manipulations. The central supply administration continually berated managers for not removing "idlers" from the ration lists. See RGAE, f. 8043, op. 11, d. 36, l. 63; *Snabzhenie, kooperatsiia, torgovlia*, November 20, 1932, July 2, 1933, and October 17, 1933; *Direktivy VKP(b) po khoziaistvennym voprosam*, 803–5; TsAIPD Len., f. 24, op. IV, d. 614, l. 21; TsGAOD Mos., f. 3, op. 15, d. 84, l. 4.

[107] RGASPI, f. 82, op. 2, d. 683, l. 58; d. 690, ll. 31–40, esp. 31; P. Gel'bras, ed., *Potrebitel'skaia kooperatsiia v rekonstruktivnyi period* (Moscow, 1931), 122–25. Neiman asserted in his 1935 monograph (*Vnutrenniaia torgovlia*, 181) that "an enormous gap" opened up between the confirmed contingent and the actual labor force at "many" factories.

indicated a second technique for enlisting parochial interests in the service of productivism: engaging factories directly in the procurement and distribution of food. Like the petition process, factory involvement in food supplies had a mixed history; factory foraging brigades had augmented provisions for the workforce but reduced productivity by taking workers away from their jobs. The only unequivocally successful aspect of workplace provisioning had been the organization of cafeterias, which became, for many workers, the primary source of nourishment from 1919 to 1921. In the 1920s, however, the network of factory cafeterias had shriveled up for lack of customers. Educated socialists attributed this shift to the high price of dining out rather than to a preference for home cooking.[108] If factories could provide affordable dinners on site, this surely would reduce the likelihood of tardiness and absenteeism after the lunch break, raise morale, and keep workers from changing jobs. In 1930, during policy makers' brief flirtation with war communism, cafeterias were even ascribed an ideological value as "the first condition" for what Lenin had called "the transition from a petty, individual, domestic economy to a large-scale socialist economy."[109]

Public dining facilities did, in fact, expand dramatically over the next several years, with factory canteens in the forefront. According to G. Ia. Neiman, author of a 1935 history of Soviet trade, over 70 percent of workers in the "decisive sectors of industry" used cafeterias by the end of 1932; canteens serviced 14.8 million diners a day, as against 750,000 just four years earlier.[110] Retail and consumption statistics corroborate this picture. Public catering rose from 4 percent of state and cooperative trade in 1928 to 13 percent in 1933; from virtually nothing, working-class expenditures on cafeteria meals grew to 18 percent of their food outlays over the same period.[111] The popularity of the canteens undoubtedly had much to do with the policy that held prices roughly constant, as opposed to the rising wages and market costs of the period.[112] Once again, employees of the large, high-priority factories were doubly privileged: first, through their enhanced rations and, second, through access to subsidized meals.

Factory cafeterias were organized by the worker cooperatives, which underwent a significant degree of restructuring between 1928 and 1933. Here, no less than in the wider consumer cooperative system, food short-

---

[108] *Biudzhety rabochikh*, 1:44; Kabo, *Ocherki rabochego byta*, 34, 54, 62–63, passim, 149–56.

[109] *Direktivy VKP(b) po khoziaistvennym voprosam*, 803–5.

[110] Neiman, *Vnutrenniaia torgovlia*, 158.

[111] *Sovetskaia torgovlia. Statisticheskii sbornik*, 20; RGAE, f. 1562, op. 329, d. 62, l. 1; op. 15, d. 791, l. 63.

[112] See Davies, *Crisis and Progress*, 299 f.

ages created pressures to discriminate between classes of consumers. Whereas regular consumer associations naturally elected to privilege their membership in the distribution of scarce goods, the historically militant worker co-ops adopted a "productive" system of discrimination. Starting in 1930 they began opening shops on factory grounds and designating other stores for the exclusive use of the workers and employees of a given plant. Called "closed distributors" [*zakrytye raspredeliteli*], as they were not open to the general public, these shops multiplied rapidly as more and more managers sought out agreements with area cooperatives to set one up.[113] They received a boost from the December 1930 Central Committee plenum, which noted the "extremely important significance" of the "network of closed distributors at factories and plants, which has proved its worth as a new organizational form of class distribution."[114]

The key to the success of a closed distributor was precisely the proprietary psychology: a close working relationship between the cooperative and the sponsoring factory or institution, sealed by a serious commitment from the latter of space, money, and personnel. Some of the most active organizers of closed distributors in 1930 were not, in fact, the railroads, mines, and heavy industrial plants that Party leaders would have preferred as beneficiaries; rather, those most active were light industry and even such strictly white-collar institutions as the Soviet post office.[115] After the December 1930 plenum, however, factory managers in the "leading sectors" could not fail to recognize their new responsibilities in the area of "worker provisionment" [*rabochee snabzhenie*]. In the interests of "proximity to production," the industrial giants of the First Five-Year Plan summarily withdrew their workers from the regional cooperative organizations (gorpo and TsRK) and opened up their own networks of cafeterias and shops on factory premises or in workers' housing compounds. Organizationally these new "closed worker cooperatives," or ZRKs, formed branches of the provincial unions of consumer cooperatives, which were supposed to continue supplying them with goods, but they also functioned semi-autonomously and were, by design, subject to considerable influence from the sponsoring factory. The years 1931 and 1932 saw a push to establish ZRKs at smaller factories, but this proved impracticable; small factories had neither the personnel nor the cash to spare.[116]

---

[113] G. Ia. Blank, A. K. Bykov, and V. G. Gukas'ian, *Potrebitel'skaia kooperatsiia SSSR* (Moscow, 1965), 22–23; Gel'bras, *Potrebitel'skaia kooperatsiia v rekonstruktivnyi period*, 91–93.

[114] *KPSS v rezoliutsiiakh*, 4:503.

[115] *Pravda*, December 15, 1930; *Kooperativnaia zhizn'*, January 3, 1931.

[116] Tsentrosoiuz issued instructions in May 1931 on the "fundamental organizational

Figure 4. Bread distribution at the Trekhgornaia factory. *Courtesy of the Russian State Archive for Cinematic and Photographic Documents (RGAKFD).*

The success of the large factories, by contrast, led the state to draw them yet further into the organization of distribution and supplies. By late 1931 central authorities could point to such models as the cooperative at Leningrad's Red Putilovets factory, which had mobilized a large number of workers' wives into cafeteria work and had pioneered a system of supervision whereby each unit of the factory took charge of a particular canteen or shop.[117] Within a year the supervisory principle had been extended to 373 of the country's largest factories, whose managers were instructed to organize "departments of worker provisionment" [orsy] to oversee the procurement and distribution of goods (figure 4).[118] Transforming ZRK shops and cafeterias into ministerial property, without compensation either to the regional cooperative union or to dues-paying

principles" of ZRKs, indicating that factories of five hundred or more employees ought to have their own ZRK. See Gel'bras, *Potrebitel'skaia kooperatsiia v rekonstruktivnyi period*, 113–17. Trial and error caused this number to be raised; cf. RGAE, f. 8043, op. 11, d. 90, ll. 46–48; TsAIPD, f. 24, op. iv, d. 524, ll. 1–2; *Sbornik ofitsial'nyk i spravochnykh materialov po voprosam rabochego snabzheniia i sovetskoi torgovli* (Leningrad, 1933).

[117] Gel'bras, *Potrebitel'skaia kooperatsiia v rekonstruktivnyi period*, 117–19.

[118] RGAE, f. 8043, op. 11, d. 57, l. 81.

members, the legislation on *orsy* amounted to a transfer of assets on a large scale.[119] In the Kremlin, however, property rights mattered little compared to the question of *whose* proprietary psychology was to be harnessed—and a communist factory director or work brigade was obviously more reliable than the associated consumers themselves.

Among other advantages, closed factory cooperatives and especially *orsy* were exceptionally well suited to the execution of a "class line" in distribution. Factory directors had funds for bonuses; and the class ration notwithstanding, from late 1930 on, they were urged to devote those funds to the struggle against excessive egalitarianism in wages and in the distribution of material goods. The policy of preferential provisionment for award-winning workers [*udarniki*] was announced in October 1930 and subsequently confirmed at the December Central Committee plenum and in several of Stalin's 1931 speeches. The press accordingly waged a campaign for the improvement of *udarnik* provisionment, urging factory cooperatives to "pay attention to the needs of the best workers" and promulgating such slogans as "whoever works better should eat better." A year or so later a similar campaign targeted supplies for engineers and specialists.[120] The upshot was that *udarniki* and specialists acquired a variety of privileges: preferential access to consumer goods at the factory cooperative, especially any in short supply; special ration cards for additional food; rights to circumvent lines; and access to special *udarnik* or ITR stores. By late 1934 a rare archival comparison notes that the engineers and technical personnel of the Krasnouralsk mines were receiving approximately 30 percent more food supplies than workers at the mines.[121]

How could such differentiation occur, when centralized rations for all "workers" were identical? One vehicle was salaries, which were weighted in favor of the educated class and enabled specialists to purchase more and better-quality foods and consumer goods than most workers could afford. The other, however, was the factories' own procurement efforts. As in the revolutionary period, factories and trade unions acquired the license to take direct action to improve food supplies. Some, but not all, methods were conceived as a complement to the planning system and

---

[119] According to the chairman of Tsentrosoiuz from the 1950s to the 1970s, thirty two thousand shops and cafeterias were transferred to the *orsy* by the end of 1933 (A. P. Klimov, *Potrebitel'skaia kooperatsiia v sisteme razvitogo sotsializma* [Moscow, 1980], 73).

[120] *KPSS v rezoliutsiiakh*, 4:503; Stalin, *Sochineniia*, 13:51–80; *Kooperativnaia zhizn'*, January 11, 1931; *Snabzhenie, kooperatsiia, torgovlia*, April 6 and 15, 1931; July 6 and 10, 1933; *Sovetskaia iustitsiia*, no. 21 (July 30, 1932): 3. More broadly on the anti-leveling campaign, see Donald Filtzer, *Soviet Workers and Stalinist Industrialization* (Armonk, N.Y., 1986), 97–100.

[121] RGAE, f. 8043, op. 11, d. 107, l. 179; d. 5, l. 139; d. 42, l. 146.

were instigated by the center on the basis of civil war precedents; for example, *orsy* and factory cooperatives formally obtained the right to send emissaries to purchase meat from collective and state farms. Characteristically Moscow was the major beneficiary of this policy; following the civil war approach of "reserving" certain provinces for factory procurement efforts, central policy makers assigned each major factory in Moscow a particular *oblast'* and enjoined the factory directors to arrange for pork deliveries from collective farmers there.[122] In addition, supply departments everywhere were supposed to seek out contracts with farms in their own vicinity to supplement the food they received from the central supply lines.[123] Known as "decentralized procurement" [*detszagotovki*], such arrangements were conceived as an orderly, nondisruptive version of the factory foraging experiments from the civil war.

Decentralized procurement relied on the proprietary psychology of factory buying agents; "representatives," in other words, remained crucial to business operations through the rationing years. Able to dip into the general factory budget, closed cooperatives and *orsy* kept literally dozens of off-plan buyers, now renamed, in slang, as "pushers" or "expediters" [*tolkachi*], on the factory payroll.[124] Expediters traveled to near and distant villages to purchase foods, but this was only one of their many functions. Just as often they mediated in complex barter agreements between factories—operations having nothing to do with the mutual bond between peasants and industry that decentralized procurement was supposed to foster. Expediters from the ZRK of a canning and pickling plant in Odessa, for example, bartered away one-fifth of their factory's output in 1931 for such goods as work clothes, shoes, flour, sunflower oil, nails, tin, soap, caviar, and lead pipe. During the nine-month period of these exchanges, the agents made a deal with another factory every week or two; sold most of the products in their on-site store; and received healthy bonuses for their efforts. Meanwhile, managers ignored delivery orders from the republican parent trust.[125] This was precisely the kind of "squandering" that had fueled hostility toward representatives under the New Economic Policy; not surprisingly media campaigns against them continued sporad-

[122] Ibid., d. 89, ll. 141–42. Jonathan Bone has informed me that this practice was extremely widespread in the Far East in the 1930s, where factories were often given a whole raion for their private disposal.

[123] Ibid., d. 91, l. 5.

[124] The *ors* at the Stalingrad Tractor Factory is a good example: its 271 employees and agents exceeded the number allotted to it in the labor plan by over 400 percent (*Snabzhenie, kooperatsiia, torgovlia*, October 17, 1933). See also Joseph Berliner, *Factory and Manager in the USSR* (Cambridge, Mass., 1957).

[125] GA Odes. ob., f. 710, op. 1, d. 20, l. 5.

ically for the next fifteen years.[126] In an era of shortages it was never difficult to find examples of abuse: the Leningrad ZRK that paid a guard to steal a ton of potatoes for resale at the shop; the Azerbaijan *ors* agents who were reportedly buying their food supplies at hard-currency stores; the factory expediters in many towns who did their "decentralized procurement" at the local bazaar.[127]

Supplementary sources of food grew increasingly important to the supply system in 1934–35, playing a particularly large role in those segments of the food market still dominated at the end of the 1920s by private trade. By 1934 *orsy* in heavy industry were obtaining 37 percent of their meat, 46 percent of their fish, 94 percent of dairy products, and 75 percent of vegetables through supplementary channels, which included, in addition to decentralized procurement, newly established factory farms. Tested during the revolutionary period, when Petrograd and other cities had made suburban land available to factories for weekend cultivation, factory farms were embraced by central policy makers in the early 1930s as a way out of the collectivization-induced crisis. Once again, fallow land was parceled out to enterprises and institutions for the collective cultivation of vegetables, poultry, and rabbits, and for distribution to individual workers as private plots. Organized by the *orsy* and the trade unions, these gardens and farms took hold; subsidiary farms in heavy industry alone produced 618,000 tons of vegetables, 570,000 tons of potatoes, 84,000 tons of milk, and 10,500 tons of meat in 1934, and both gardens and factory farms would become a critical source of food during the Second World War.[128]

The ideological value ascribed to "proximity to production" in trade, as in education and other areas, did not outlast the early 1930s, but, as the example of factory farms suggests, workplace distribution had long-term consequences for the Soviet system. First, it gave the politically supine trade unions a raison d'être. Given the Bolsheviks' intolerance, and later Stalin's, of any independent leadership, trade unions and factory

[126] The numbers of expediters are noteworthy. A study of twelve large factories in Leningrad and Ukraine revealed that, in 1934, twelve thousand expediters passed through or, more often, camped out for several weeks. Similarly, in 1937 some fifteen hundred *tolkachi* visited the wholesale base in Ivanovo, reportedly staying for weeks or months at a time with nothing to do but play billiards at the local hotels. These practices continued, to judge from a postwar editorial that equated *tolkach* bonuses with bribes (*Krest'ianskaia pravda*, May 9, 1935; *Sovetskaia torgovlia* (newspaper), January 5, 1938; *Sotsialisticheskaia zakonnost'*, no. 9 (September 1946): 1–3.

[127] TsAIPD Len., f. 24, op. iv, d. 615, l. 48; RGAE, f. 8043, op. 11, d. 116, l. 122.

[128] *Snabzhenie, kooperatsiia, torgovlia*, April 6, 1931; October 20, 1933; *Izvestiia*, December 26, 1933; RGAE, f. 7297, op. 38, d. 121, l. 146; TsGAOD Mos., f. 3, op. 15, d. 84, l. 4; d. 85.

committees adopted a corporatist, rather than adversarial, approach to labor-management relations. "Worker provisionment" emerged as one of the few areas in which the trade unions' activism on behalf of increased productivity (the primary role the Party assigned to labor organizations) was at the same time a way of promoting workers' material interests. Organizing factory farms and garden plots (later, dacha cooperatives and vacation homes), distributing seed, and overseeing factory cafeterias and shops were activities the rank and file could appreciate. The unions, accordingly, held onto these functions, much as they held onto the tasks of exposing managerial "bureaucratism" and airing safety concerns. Through the end of the Soviet era, distributing perquisites ranked among the unions' primary activities.[129]

For factory managers, too, the administration of rationing seems to have been a formative experience. Identifying success in provisionment with success in production, the rationing system gave managers a bargaining chip with the central government. At the same time, it raised the stakes of food supplies: if an *ors* or factory cooperative failed to provide sufficient food for its assigned contingent, the factory director could be faulted not just for a careless attitude toward workers' needs [*khalatnost'*] but also for the more serious offense of sabotaging the production plan. As in the civil war period, these pressures were all the greater in that food rations genuinely did affect productivity. Foreign observers, no less than Soviet managers, attributed the massive labor turnover of the early 1930s to food shortages.[130] Food shortages also sparked industrial unrest, most notably in April 1932, when a strike wave crippled the Ivanovo textile industry over a reduction in rations.[131] Factory managers had every interest in avoiding such an outcome and, accordingly, sought to keep provisionment in their own hands as much as possible. *Orsy* outlasted the rationing system by a full year as a result of these efforts, and, even after they were dissolved, managers continued to use expediters to procure foods and consumer goods along with the industrial supplies that were

[129] On the evolution of the dual role of the trade unions as instruments of both increased productivity and the defense of workers' legal and social rights, see Blair A. Ruble, *Soviet Trade Unions* (New York, 1981).

[130] Maurice Hindus, *The Great Offensive* (New York, 1933), 41; TsAIPD Len., f. 24, op. iv, d. 615, l. 56. Labor turnover exceeded 100 percent a year from 1928 to 1934, though the fact that the turnover was lowest in the relatively poorly supplied cotton industry casts doubt on the identification of labor turnover with ration levels. Cf. Nobuaki Shiokawa, "Labor Turnover in the USSR, 1929–33: A Sectoral Analysis," *Annals of the Institute of Social Science* 23 (Tokyo, 1982): 65–94.

[131] Davies, *Crisis and Progress*, 188–89, 368, 374; Jeffrey J. Rossman, "The Teikovo Cotton Workers' Strike of April 1932," *Russian Review* 56, no. 1 (1997): 44–69; *Rapports secrets soviétiques*, 209–16.

the ostensible pretext for their employment.[132] Their continuation of the rationing-era arts of procurement made it possible for Soviet factories to revert to rationing from 1939 to 1941 with scarcely a ripple in their functioning; in a time of crisis, in short, the proprietary psychology of Soviet managers could indeed be put to use.

CRISIS, CONSUMPTION, AND THE MARKET

As in the revolutionary era, the effects of economic crisis were not determined solely by policy makers or by the administrators of state policy in factories and towns. The restructuring of trade was, in the first place, the response of government officials to an emergency that consumers both reacted and contributed to: by hoarding, queuing, and panic buying, shoppers exacerbated the shortages of consumer goods. As restructuring progressed, the dislocations resulting from the planned disequilibrium between wages and prices, a constant feature of the socialist sector since 1923, were overlaid by such new dislocations as the disappearance of private shops and the collapse of agriculture. In the interest of avoiding repetition, I will postpone, until chapter 5, any attempt to quantify the impact of the crisis on average consumption and living standards, and to chart its effects on citizens' attitudes. In the meantime, this section explores a major change in consumer practices between 1928 and 1933.

That change—hardly surprising in light of the civil war pattern—was the amplified role of outdoor trade in citizens' daily lives. Regular and makeshift bazaars, important exchange venues throughout the NEP, became virtually the sole alternative to the socialist sector in 1928–29. As Harry Greenwall, a traveler from Britain, reported of Moscow, "Gradually the whole marketing of the city has been driven into the streets. The suppression of private trading has led to the street hawker competing with the State-owned shops." This had occurred, Greenwall observed, between his previous visit in the summer of 1927 and a repeat visit one year later:

> In the summer of 1927 there were two or three streets lined with hawkers. In the year 1928 every main street in Moscow was lined with these hawkers, standing elbow to elbow along the kerb. So many thousands are there of these kerb-merchants that, as there is no more room on the kerb, they have begun to line up on the other side of the pavement with their backs to the shops, so that the streets of Moscow are just like an Oriental bazaar. Every man,

[132] *Sovetskaia torgovlia* (newspaper), January 8, 1935; January 5, 1938; *Za industrializatsiiu,* April 20, 1935.

woman, and child with something to sell is shouting at the top of his or her voice. . . . It is safe to say that there is no commodity of any sort whatsoever that cannot be bought on the streets of Moscow.[133]

This hubbub turned out to be specific to 1928, when high taxes and repression not only forced shops out of business but caused the remaining businesses to shrink. As in 1918, many shopkeepers abandoned their premises only to take up vending at the bazaar or along the sidewalks. In all likelihood, however, the surge in informal exchange resulted as much from the 1928 Ukrainian famine as from the degradation of the capital's trade network. Flight to near or distant cities was the paradigmatic response of peasants to a subsistence crisis, and, once there, they typically tried to eke out a living through petty outdoor trade. This explanation receives support from a foreigner's reaction to the disappearance of Moscow's street vendors a year and a half later: "The streets presented a strange appearance to one who had become accustomed to throngs of peasant pedlars."[134]

In February 1930, after a successful, if undeclared, war on the capital's private sector, the Moscow provincial government sought to ban private trade in most manufactured goods. The interdiction, which was limited to the territory of the city, affected the same essential goods that had been nationalized in November 1918, plus radios and electrical wares.[135] It was not directed at peasant marketing, and it most certainly did not indicate a general prohibition against petty trade. That very month the RSFSR's Commissariats of Internal Affairs and Finance issued instructions that entitled private citizens to rent shop space or stalls at urban bazaars, railroad stations, and ports. The amount charged was, unsurprisingly, class-specific: peasants selling their own produce or livestock, urban and rural artisans selling their own handicrafts, and persons selling everyday secondhand items were exempted from paying rent, whereas private traders had to pay significantly more than cooperatives and collective farms.[136] If, as many foreigners observed, Moscow blocked off market squares and cracked down on street vendors in the winter of 1929–30, this should thus be understood in light of the tendency to ob-

[133] Greenwall, *Mirrors of Moscow*, 35–38.

[134] Calvin B. Hoover, "The Fate of the New Economic Policy of the Soviet Union," *Economic Journal* 40 (June 1930): 186–87, cited in Ball, *Russia's Last Capitalists*, 79.

[135] Other itemized goods included textiles, clothing, thread, leather, shoes, galoshes, felt boots, metals, construction supplies, cement, chemicals and dyes, soap, kerosene, sugar, salt, matches, tobacco products, window glass, paper, and paper products (GARF, f. 374, op. 28, d. 3862, ll. 39–41).

[136] *Biulleten' finansovogo i khoziaistvennogo zakonodatel'stva*, no. 8 (March 17, 1930): 28–29.

struct peasant marketing at the height of each procurement campaign.[137] The ban was neither universal nor lasting. The sorry plight of peasant hawkers described by Leonard Hubbard as the norm in this period ("Peasants stood on the street kerbs with baskets of fruit, eggs, etc., which they sold under constant threat of being 'moved on' by the police, and even of having their stock-in-trade confiscated") belied the continued functioning of outdoor markets in most cities throughout the restructuring years.[138]

In fact, household budget studies reveal a paradoxical effect of restructuring: even as private shops disappeared, citizens spent an increasing proportion of their incomes on private-sector purchases. According to archival data, urban workers went from spending 18 percent of their food outlays at the market in 1929 to 53 percent in 1932, and whereas workers' market purchases of foods declined slightly in 1933, managers and engineers continued to spend 61 percent of their food outlays at the market that year. A similar trend affected firewood and manufactured goods. In sum, by 1933 workers were making 30 percent, and all urban residents 33 percent, of their purchases, in terms of rubles, "at the market or from private citizens," including 54 percent of food expenditures and 22 percent of nonfood expenditures.[139] This, of course, represented a large increase over the 35 percent of workers' food outlays and 7 percent of nonfood expenditures that statisticians ascribed to the private sector in 1929.

Price inflation naturally accounts for most of this increase; as goods became increasingly scarce in the socialist trade system, market prices rose. By 1932, O. V. Khlevniuk and R. W. Davies have found, urban bazaar prices exceeded those of 1928 by a factor of ten—two and a half times the increase in the money supply.[140] Inflation notwithstanding, even in "physical" terms, the role of the market was far from negligible during the restructuring years. In 1932, which was the high point of the market as a percentage of urban food and consumer goods supplies, the quan-

---

[137] Alan Ball did a survey of the travel literature of this period; for quotes, see *Russia's Last Capitalists*, 78–79.

[138] Leonard Hubbard, *Soviet Trade and Distribution* (London, 1938), 141–42. Even Moscow markets were regularized no later than June 1931; cf. *Biulleten' finansovogo i khoziaistvennogo zakonodatel'stva*, no. 32 (November 17, 1931): 64. Admittedly travel reports on markets make it sound as though they were rather feeble in 1931; cf. Mrs. Cecil Chesterton, *My Russian Venture* (Philadelphia, 1931), 83–84 (description of Minsk); Julian Huxley, *A Scientist among the Soviets* (New York, 1932), 46–48.

[139] For 1928–29 figures, see GARF, f. 374, op. 28, d. 3862, ll. 10–14; for 1932–33, see RGAE, f. 1562, op. 329, d. 62, ll. 15–16. For long-term charts and tables, see website: http://darkwing.uoregon.edu/hessler.

[140] Khlevniuk and Davies, "End of Rationing," 562.

TABLE 4.3
The Private Sector as a Source of Selected Foods and Consumer Goods in
Workers' Annual Per Capita Consumption, 1932

Item	Total Quantity Obtained	Of Which, Market	Market Percentage
Flour	28.3 kg	4.9 kg	17
Bread	149.6 kg	3.1 kg	2
Legumes, pasta, rice	12.6 kg	2.1 kg	17
Potatoes	81.0 kg	38.8 kg	48
Vegetables (incl. canned)	42.6 kg	11.7 kg	27
Fruits, melons	10.2 kg	4.2 kg	41
Milk	23.9 l	15.3 l	64
Butter	0.8 kg	0.4 kg	53
Eggs	11.2 eggs	9.3 eggs	83
Meat (incl. canned)	10.7 kg	2.9 kg	27
Fish (incl. canned)	8.7 kg	0.8 kg	9
Vegetable oil	2.0 kg	0.4 kg	22
Ready-to-wear clothes	4.392 m	0.516 m	11.7
Cloth	4.584 m	0.192 m	4.2
Shoes (leather, rubber)	1.284 pairs	0.228 pairs	17.8
Soap	2.66 kg	0.23 kg	8.6
Wood	n.a.	n.a.	44.9

Source: GARF, f. 1562, op. 329, d. 62, ll. 15–16; op. 15, d. 1119, ll. 75–76, 86.

tities workers were obtaining at the market are shown in table 4.3. These figures are discussed in later chapters in relation to long-term quantitative trends; more important to the present discussion is that if bread and cloth remained concentrated overwhelmingly in socialist-sector distribution, the market was a vital supply source for virtually everything else at the end of the First Five-Year Plan.

The rising cost of living led increasing numbers of urban dwellers to resort to informal trade to make ends meet. While the role of petty sales in working-class family incomes remained well below the 25 to 30 percent level of the civil war era, it nonetheless considerably exceeded the levels recorded during the NEP (table 4.4). In Riazan', roughly one hundred miles southeast of Moscow, it was urbanites' petty sales, not peasant marketing, that elicited stricter policing of the outdoor bazaar during the restructuring period. The provincial financial department went after weekend hawkers with a vengeance, levying fines of up to five thousand rubles for unlicensed transactions and confiscating the vendor's wares. In

Table 4.4
Sales of Foods and Goods as a Percentage of Working-Class
Household Incomes

	Average Annual Income	*Of Which, Sales*	%
1927	1282.92	7.20	0.6
1932	724.44	40.20	5.5
1933	845.16	64.32	7.6

Sources: *Biudzhety rabochikh*, 96; RGAE, f. 1562, op. 15, d. 1119, l. 17.

June 1931 the financial department collected fines from various residents, among them industrial workers, for hawking seven pieces of herring, eight pounds of sugar, one pair of shoes, one pair of galoshes, two pieces of wallpaper, and half a jar of sunflower oil. "Habitual" traders, meanwhile, were exiled from the region as kulaks—a fate met by the disenfranchised and unemployed son of a NEP-era trader, who bought up fruit and eggs in his home village and resold them in Moscow and Riazan'; a group of tobacco traders, who traveled the circuit made popular during the civil war; an old disenfranchised butcher and his wife, who continued to offer peasants their services; and a disenfranchised young mother, who twice traveled to Moscow to buy groceries for resale.[141]

When "party-minded" observers considered the growth of petty exchange, they interpreted it in a moral rather than material light. "Speculation" was no more than one would expect of Nepmen and peasants— as any Leninist knew, "in the soul of every petty proprietor is a little Sukharevka" —but the recrudescence of market hawking among industrial workers indicated a dangerous "wavering" in the mood of the leading class. Writing to the authorities about this development in the summer of 1930, an exasperated salesclerk at Mostorg's main department store suggested that the rationing system itself fostered demoralization:

> Spring has come to the habitués of the Sukharevka, Central, Smolensk, and other markets: resellers have truly been breeding like the devil's mother. Seasonal laborers, milkmaids, invalids, people traveling to and from various construction sites, and a segment of unconscious workers and their wives are now feverishly occupied with reselling. They employ numerous methods: one rubs out the writing in a cooperative ration booklet, another creates a totally false one; one has two or more booklets to his name, another simulates being someone's wife for a certain month; still another abuses business travel and lays

[141] GA Riaz. ob., f. R-300, op. 2, d. 13, ll. 73–79; f. R-3602, op. 1, d. 665, d. 723, d. 732, d. 745.

claim to someone else's booklet. It has reached the point where even a backward worker stands in line for ladies' stockings for the fifth time in a week or two, beating his chest about being a worker, saying, "you give them to speculators, you stinking soul, give them to me."[142]

Could it be that the elimination of the private shops had reactivated the civil war dynamic in which "the psychology of the bagger—the psychology of the petit bourgeois—is absorbed by the whole society"?[143] In view of this danger, when the Party moved to regularize the status of the outdoor markets once and for all in May 1932, it fortified the new legal foundation for market trade with concerted propaganda against "reselling" and "speculation." Bazaars were recast as "collective-farm markets," the embodiment of the renewed social link [smychka] between workers and peasants in the post-collectivization era, whereas the traditional flea market and petty trade aspects of the bazaar were alternatively downplayed or denounced.

It is worth reviewing this propaganda before turning to the substance of the decrees. A 1932 newsreel on Moscow's Semenovskii market can be taken as paradigmatic.[144] Mapping a symbolic geography of the marketplace in its opening frames through contrasting modes of transportation, the film identifies the market as the intersection of rural tradition and socialist modernity. Streetcar tracks arc around the square, sharply dividing the "rural" island of the market from the encompassing city, while the mouth of the U is pierced by a dirt road, seemingly a direct bridge from the market to the village. In the next sequence, the film's allegorical characters, city and country, prepare for their mutual encounter. A "welcome" squad of sales assistants opens up Mostorg's many shops at the market, so as to "greet" the arriving peasants with an array of goods and services, while "kolkhozniki" and "laboring individual peasants" progress along the road to the market in a long, single-file caravan of carts. Their slogan, it would appear, is not personal profit but "Agricultural produce to the centers!"—just as the city's slogan is captioned, "Let us greet the goods of the country with the goods of the city!" In this idealized portrayal, goodwill and gratitude structure the encounter on both sides; not the monetary nexus of the market economy but the moral ties of a gift economy were to form the basis of the smychka at the "collective-farm market."

Against this model exchange between the "laborers of the city and the country," publicists counterposed an image of "speculation"—essentially,

[142] GARF, f. 5446, op. 55, d. 1973, l. 125 (July 1930).
[143] Vasil'ev, Natsionalizatsiia vnutrennei torgovli, 7–8.
[144] RGAKFD 3635 (I–II).

petty private trade. Banners emblazoned with such slogans as "Reseller-speculator BEGONE from the collective farm market!" adorn the market-place, and, indeed, the seemingly bourgeois young man who tries to buy up sacks of parsley and cucumbers is caught in the act. However, as a caption admonishes, "There is also another type of bazaar"—one mired in what a civil war era commentator once termed "darkness, especially popular darkness." At this unnamed and hence potentially universal ba-zaar, peasant children wade barefoot in a muddy pond while their elders sit on the ground to sell their wares or lie prone in a drunken stupor. A door labeled "Legal consultation" stands padlocked, a tacked-up decree left to flutter in the wind. Sales appear to be few; only an old gypsy fortune-teller has drawn a significant crowd. In such a setting, publicists suggested, speculation inevitably flourished. Sukharevka remained Suk-harevka, a newspaper lamented in the summer of 1932: as unhygienic as ever, as crowded as ever, as bereft of services as ever, and infested with petty traders, just as before. To turn it into a "new, authentically Soviet, and authentically cultured" market, Sukharevka had to be "scrubbed, washed, and given a new haircut"—and, of course, policed.[145]

What, in light of this publicity, did the May 1932 decrees on the market accomplish? Perhaps it is easier to enumerate first what they did *not* do. The decrees of May 6 ("On the plan for grain procurement from the 1932 harvest and on the development of collective-farm trade in grain"), May 10 ("On the livestock procurement plan and on collective farmers' and individual laboring peasants' meat trade"), and May 20 ("On the organization of trade by collective farms, collective farmers, and la-boring individual peasants and on the reduction of the tax on sales of agricultural products") did not *establish* farmers' markets, as some of the more outlandish speeches and articles of the period claimed; nor did they, in the language of the May 6 decree, testify to the "victory of col-lectivized and state agriculture over the system of the individual house-hold economy" and to the "uninterrupted growth in the number of man-ufactured goods" available for peasant consumers.[146] They did not actually legalize the market, since resolutions banning the arbitrary clo-sure of outdoor bazaars had been issued each year from 1928 to 1931. Finally, they did not remove bazaars from the realm of ambiguity in which they had functioned since 1917. By linking official support for an idealized "collective-farm market" with official opprobrium toward "spec-

---

[145] *Snabzhenie, kooperatsiia, torgovlia*, August 11, 1932.
[146] For a compendium of speeches and decrees on the market, see *Kolkhoznaia torgovlia. Postanovleniia, rasporiazheniia, instruktsii, tsirkuliary* (Leningrad, 1932). See also Davies, *Crisis and Progress*, 201–28.

ulation" (the penalty for which was increased to a five-year labor-camp sentence a few months later),[147] policymakers left the boundaries negotiable between licit and illicit private trade. Outdoor markets remained, in short, a gray area of the Soviet economy despite the 1932 decrees.

That said, the decrees altered the status of the markets in several respects. First, they placed formal private shops beyond the bounds of negotiation. The May 20 decree was the only published legislation explicitly banning private shops: "10. Private traders will not be allowed to open shops and stores at the market, and resellers and speculators, who try to profit at the expense of workers and peasants, should be eradicated by every means."[148] Second, the decrees on the market extended a welcome measure of tax relief to peasants, lowering obligatory delivery quotas for grain and meat, and within a 100-km radius of Moscow or Leningrad, for vegetables, fruits, and dairy products, lowering market rents, and exempting peasant trade at markets and bazaars from sales and agricultural taxes.[149] Third, not just individuals but collective farms obtained the right to trade at market prices, which had been disallowed as recently as 1931.[150] Finally, although such provisions as the authorization to sell any surplus left over after delivery obligations were met, or the establishment of free pricing on market trade, merely ratified existing practices, they articulated these practices by means of a new language of rights. Signed by the top governing bodies of the country, the decrees were intended to inspire confidence among peasants that, this time, the right to trade was truly established, as Lenin had promised of the NEP, "seriously and for a long time." This would in fact prove to be the case, since the 1932 legislation governed the outdoor markets for more than twenty-five years.

During the revolutionary era, the closure of private stores had sent urban shoppers in three directions: they had joined the queues in front of socialist "distribution points" to redeem their ration coupons; they had shopped at open-air markets; and they had traveled to the villages for unmediated private exchange. As chapter 1 emphasized, despite the Bolsheviks' progressively stricter policing of "speculation" in 1919–20, outdoor markets never ceased to function as the country's main conduit of consumer goods distribution during the revolutionary period. Citizens

[147] August 22, 1932, decree "On the struggle against speculation." *Sovetskaia iustitsiia,* nos. 25–26 (September 10–15, 1932): 9.
[148] *Resheniia partii i pravitel'stva po khoziaistvennym voprosam,* 389.
[149] *Biulleten' finansovogo i khoziaistvennogo zakonodatel'stva,* no. 26 (June 1, 1932): 11.
[150] See Davies, *Crisis and Progress,* 141, 211–16.

resorted to the market to purchase the vast majority of their food, fire-wood, and other necessities, and also eked out a living in no small part through occasional market sales. If one measure of normalization after 1921 was the reestablishment of a network of permanent retail shops, another was the reassertion of a social division of labor with respect to market vending. Trade ceased to function as a universal side occupation in the NEP years; though poor people continued, when strapped for cash, to sell their used belongings at the market, even cigarette, news-paper, and pirogi sales were for the most part reprofessionalized by 1924.

At the end of the 1920s the elimination of private shops reversed this development. The percentage of urban household budgets that went to the private sector increased, while occasional sales returned to the in-come side of the ledger. If these percentages can serve as a rough index of hardship, they confirm the standard view in the Western historiogra-phy that Stalinist restructuring sharply reduced urban, as well as rural, standards of living.[151] By the same measure, the level of duress experi-enced by urban residents from 1928 to 1933 appears to have been con-siderably milder than in the revolutionary era—and milder, too, than the material duress of the Second World War.

Even during the height of restructuring, Stalin did not go as far as Lenin in shutting down market trade. Bazaars were closed in many vil-lages during the contested procurement campaigns of the late 1920s, but they generally reopened within months. In the cities, local officials vacil-lated between cracking down on private exchange and profiting from market fees. One week a market square would be cordoned off and locked; the next week officials would denounce one another for obstruct-ing peasants' sales. One week the police would detain virtually everyone in sight as "speculators"; the next week city officials would merely de-mand payment from vendors of posted rents and selling fees. If trade policy continued to be intertwined with municipal finances and OGPU "operations," as in the 1920s, it also became intertwined, as in the civil war period, with the definition of speculation in criminal law. What Sol-omon has called the "campaign justice" of the period only added to the confusion of officials on the ground.[152]

As we have seen, this confusion did not entirely dissipate after May 1932, when the government publicly declared outdoor bazaars a "social-ist" trade venue. Renaming them "collective-farm markets" did not change the character overnight of Russia's flea markets, peasant fairs, and ba-

---

[151] This is discussed in chapter 5.
[152] Peter H. Solomon, *Soviet Criminal Justice under Stalin* (Cambridge, 1996), 81–110.

zaars.[153] The peasant flavor of the markets was strongly reinforced by the pullout or repression of regular merchants and vendors, but after the 1932 decrees there was little evidence of "socialist" presence for several years. Rather, by offering a legitimate outlet for the drive for profits, the outdoor bazaars nurtured a particular kind of "capitalist" spirit among Soviet peasants and urbanites. As we will see in chapter 6, these bazaars demonstrated the limits of the Stalinist command economy in both its crisis and normalization modes.

Conclusion

The years after 1927 brought an intensive economic crisis, reminiscent in certain respects of the civil war of the previous decade. Their reflexes trained by the revolutionary experience, communist officials responded to the dislocations of the late 1920s by tightening their own control over distribution and supplies. Private traders were arrested with or without a legal pretext; consumer cooperatives were forced to adhere to a productivist, rather than member-oriented, system of entitlements; peasants were forcibly severed from the market; and prices were fixed from above. Food and consumer goods rationing, adopted in every urban area on the war communism model, was eventually integrated into a national distribution plan. As Elena Osokina has argued, the structure of this system was telling: in the name of rationalization, "unimportant" citizens were denied access to affordable food.[154] Related policies, most notably the rural price hikes and the diversion of potatoes and grain to the vodka industry, cast a similarly unflattering light on Soviet economic priorities from 1928 to 1933.

The rationing system and its concomitants should nonetheless not be taken directly to reflect "Stalinist ideology." The product of an emergency, rationing did not represent a positive commitment on Stalin's part. If a few commentators saw in the restructuring of distribution a return to the values of 1917, Stalin and his closest economic advisers disliked the bureaucratism, rigidity, and inefficiency inherent in rationing; when they had the chance to clarify what they wanted, they opted unequivocally for nonrationed trade. Andrei Zhdanov's commentary at a November 1934 Politiburo commission meeting illustrates this strong distaste for rationing among the top leadership: "We are in favor of

[153] Basile Kerblay underscored the continuity of Soviet "kolkhoz markets" with pre-collectivization and prerevolutionary peasant markets in his *Les marchés paysans en U.R.S.S.* (Paris, 1968).

[154] Osokina, *Ierarkhiia potrebleniia* and *Za fasadom*.

changing the system of food distribution for the sake of liquidating the vestiges of a war era in that sector."[155] Soviet leaders had, of course, largely created the war atmosphere through their radical restructuring of agriculture, industry, and commerce.[156] Unlike rationing, the elimination of private traders, the acceleration of industrial development, and the forcible establishment of collective farms were not primarily responses to an emergency but rather were core components of the Communists' long-term agenda. Acting abruptly in the period from 1928 to 1930 to achieve these desiderata, Stalin was willing to tolerate, for the moment, quite severe dislocations. In this choice, and in the incremental actions taken at all levels along the way, restructuring reflected the socialist economic and political culture as it had coalesced during the civil war.

What triggered the restructuring of distribution? The catalyst, as in 1917–18, was a panic over food supplies in the capital, but in both periods food shortage was preceded by shortages of basic manufactured goods. Cotton cloth, wool, and leather were among the first goods to become scarce during the First World War, and they reemerged as perennially scarce commodities during the NEP. What puzzled Soviet economists and policy makers was that consumer-goods shortages, traceable in retrospect to NEP-era price controls, became chronic precisely as economic growth accelerated and standards of living rose. We will see this pattern again. On the whole, the Stalinist establishment took an optimistic view of such shortages as evidence of the "increasing well-being of the population."[157] They nonetheless opted to buttress economic regulations with covert operations to "restore the economy's health," and more specifically sought to restrict peasants' access to particularly scarce goods. When shortages began to affect food supplies, the Soviet leadership was primed for more radical actions along both an economic and a repressive axis.

The restructuring of trade underscored the centrality of Moscow to Soviet policy formation—another pattern we have seen before and will encounter again. Nationalized supplies were shipped to Moscow in disproportionate quantities during the civil war, and this remained the case after 1921. It was not just an effect of market forces (major cities the world over are magnets for both purchasers and goods) but also of the particular solicitude with which policy makers regarded metropolitan

---

[155] *Stalinskoe Politbiuro v 30-e gody* (Moscow, 1995), 55.

[156] Whether, in the absence of such policies, the worldwide depression would have triggered an equally acute crisis is impossible to say.

[157] See, especially, Anastas Mikoian, "Disproportsiia i tovarnyi golod," *Bol'shevik* nos. 23–24 (December 31, 1926): 23–33.

consumers. Kremlin officials, who rarely traveled to the provinces during the NEP,[158] acquired the habit of basing their assessments of economic conditions on what they saw in their own backyard. In 1927–28 their perception of a crisis did not stem primarily from mass starvation in southern Ukraine but rather from the shortages of high-grade meat, sugar, and flour in Moscow—shortages attributable, to a considerable degree, to the artificially lowered prices of these goods. Restructuring gave central administrators greater control over all major classes of goods and thereby enabled them to augment the capital's share of the national product. By 1933 Moscow claimed roughly 2 percent of the USSR's population as its residents, but sold 6 to 12 percent of the nationalized stocks of all major categories of manufactured goods, and as much as 25 percent of nationalized meat and fish supplies. In fact, the only consumer article, barring none, for which the percentage sold in Moscow did not significantly exceed the capital's percentage of the total population was a traditional peasant accessory, the woolen shawl.[159] As we will see in chapter 6, an unintended consequence of the prioritization of the capital was that Moscow shops continued to serve, long after the NEP, as a source of goods for provincial private trade.

In terms of the outcome of restructuring, one significant development described in this chapter was the "degradation of trade." As in the civil war era, the Communists' war on the market resulted in a displacement of trade from the shop to the bazaar. The forcible elimination of the private shops inflicted tremendous damage on the commercial infrastructure; by the end of 1930 the number of retail outlets had dwindled to a mere 196,000 from the 555,000 in business in 1926. Per capita, the density of trade in 1931 was less than one-fifth of the prerevolutionary average, with just 12.5 stores, shops, and stalls to service every ten thousand inhabitants.[160] Shops remained heavily concentrated in European Russia and in urban areas, despite the cooperatives' forays into the villages after the 1923 investigation of rural trade.

In connection with the inadequacy of both the commercial network and supplies, the workplace reemerged as a major locus of distribution. Under centralized rationing, individuals were tied to particular stores for all basic necessities, and, from 1930 on, these stores very often came under the jurisdiction of the factory or institution where they worked. The result was a situation not dissimilar from the American health care

---

[158] On this, see Roger Pethybridge, *One Step Backwards, Two Steps Forward: Soviet Society and Politics in the New Economic Policy* (Oxford, 1990), 117, 173.

[159] Calculated from RGAE, f. 7971, op. 2, d. 662, ll. 11–86.

[160] *Sovetskaia torgovlia. Statisticheskii sbornik*, 14–15, 137.

system: benefits depended on a person's place of employment, with the bigger enterprises generally able to provide better benefits, and smaller, less important places of employment, such as cooperatives or collective farms, unable to provide any benefits at all. The bigger enterprises of the "leading industries" received preferential treatment from the central supply administration, commanded greater financial resources to expend on supplementary provisions, and enjoyed greater clout with the local government than other enterprises or the unaffiliated urban trade networks. This phenomenon can be characterized as a form of corporatism, as the labor organizations collaborated with management both to raise workers' productivity and to improve their supplies of consumer goods. Although policy makers later sought to curb corporatist tendencies in the Party, state, and industrial bureaucracies, the restructuring of distribution reconfirmed the proprietary psychology as a permanent element of Soviet power.

CHAPTER FIVE

Toward a New Model

RESTRUCTURING BROUGHT NOTHING positive to Soviet consumers: the shortages from 1925 to 1927 were not overcome but instead snowballed into a crisis of consumption in both rural and urban areas. The ability of policy makers to alleviate the crisis was constrained by their commitment to industrialization and by the government's diminishing revenue base. The expansion of vodka sales in the early 1930s reflected the extremity of the state's budgetary difficulties; between the collectivization debacle, the loss of private-sector tax revenues, and the collapse of grain and lumber prices on the world market, policy makers had to look to unorthodox means of financing their industrial projects and, indeed, revived the civil war practice of covering budget deficits with the mint. Bureaucratism aside, it is not surprising that the economic administration acted in 1931–32 to trim back the unprofitable rationing system and to reintroduce elements of the market into socialist-sector trade.[1] Famine was thus accompanied by an attempt at normalization based on the policies of 1921. As we saw in chapter 4, procurements were partially decentralized; wage differentials were increased; manufactured goods were removed from the ration; and a ceasefire was declared in the war on the market. These reforms were extended in subsequent years. By 1936 the consumer economy had been purged of nearly every vestige of war communism save the ban on private shops.

Hardship, however, remained, and in this unpropitious context Stalin and his associates struggled to articulate a positive vision of socialist trade. Compared to those of the 1920s, policies of the 1930s placed a new emphasis on the qualitative aspects of retailing. During the NEP socialist trade was universally conceded to be less adept at marketing than the private sector, a disparity particularly evident in sales of luxury goods. Unable to afford the loss of tax revenues from the liquidation of the private luxury purveyors, the central government directed the socialist networks to stock some high value-added items and to fashion a more

---

[1] For two different views of these reforms, see Atlas, *Denezhnaia sistema*, 248–61; and Davies, *Crisis and Progress*, esp. 58–64, 94–97, 206–8. Atlas emphasized the unsustainability of submarket pricing and its impact on the state budget, whereas Davies attributes the reforms to an absolute insufficiency of food and goods.

appealing image. "Cultured Soviet trade" became the Party's watchword for the retail sector. From 1931 to 1934 this slogan's impact was barely discernible outside a few elite cafeterias and the "commercial" shops, which sold high-priced foods and clothing off the ration to the well-heeled segments of the Soviet public. With the end of rationing in 1935 the "cultured trade" agenda was, in a highly publicized campaign, generalized to the retail system as a whole.

The first parts of this chapter trace the development of the cultured trade paradigm in the 1930s: its emergence in luxury retailing outside the rationing system; its extension to a wider range of Soviet stores in connection with a push to modernize the retail sector; and its entanglement with the struggle against bureaucratism, the perennial weakness of socialist-sector trade. The discussion then turns to consumption, exploring the ways in which the organization of trade shaped consumers' attitudes, followed by a brief consideration of quantitative trends in the decade after 1928. The chapter's final section makes use of two episodes involving queues to highlight the tensions experienced by policy makers because of their commitment to nonrationed trade, as a "goods famine" once again came to obstruct retailing in the Soviet Union's major cities.

Socialist Modernization: "Cultured Soviet Trade"

In 1931, when "cultured trade" first surfaced in speeches and resolutions as a policy aim, most retailing remained in the hands of consumer cooperatives. Cataloguing the shortcomings of these associations, the major policy statement on trade from the first part of that year went so far as to characterize the cooperative system as a "monopoly" and insinuated that the failings of Soviet trade stemmed from this fact:

> The main deficiency in the current functioning of consumer cooperatives rests in their clumsiness and bureaucratism, which lead to stagnating sales. This is why shortages are often created artificially, even as commodity stocks accumulate in the warehouses.
>
> These shortcomings in the functioning of consumer cooperatives can be explained primarily by the fact that the cooperatives, having squeezed out the privateer and conquered a monopolistic position in the market, have begun to neglect the bottom line and the tasks of expanding Soviet trade; they mistakenly suppose that conditions are already ripe for an unmediated transition to direct products exchange. In this supposition, consumer cooperatives have forgotten that the elimination of the privateer and of private trade does not yet mean the elimination of all trade. On the contrary, the elimination of *private* trade assumes the multifaceted development of *Soviet* trade and the

expansion of the network of cooperative and state commercial organizations throughout the USSR.[2]

The critique of bureaucratism was, of course, hardly novel; in most respects, the "May address" reiterated the standard Party line. It did, however, announce the Party's commitment to a "trade" rather than "distribution" model of economic relations. This was the directive that withdrew most manufactured goods from the rationing system, and it also ordered cooperatives to stop earmarking goods for particular consumers unless specifically charged with a "stimulation" campaign. Finally, while the May address warned of the dangers inherent in a "monopoly" and indicated the need to "reconstruct the work of consumer cooperatives on a fundamentally new basis," it unequivocally reaffirmed the primacy of cooperatives in socialist retailing. Consumer cooperatives were enjoined to open two thousand new stores in major urban areas, and they received a guarantee that state trade would be limited to 30 percent of urban commodity stocks.

How, in light of this last provision, did it happen that the cooperatives were first sidelined, then plundered, and finally eliminated altogether from urban trade as the reforms progressed from 1931 to 1935? The answer rests in policy makers' gradual decision to identify socialism with the concept of cultured trade, which originated not in the cooperative networks but rather in special venues designated for "commercial" sales. As of October 1931, consumer cooperatives were specifically barred from handling such sales in order to concentrate on basic provisionment.[3] The new shops and retail chains that proliferated in connection with this order were necessarily expensive, but, at their best, they offered a pleasant atmosphere, a selection skewed in favor of luxury goods, and the rudiments of customer service, so utterly lacking in the distribution system as a whole. These positive attributes formed the core of "cultured Soviet trade," an ideal that came to define the Stalinist approach to retailing.

The original loci of cultured trade were Torgsin, the retail chain for foreign tourists, and Glavosobtorg, the agency created to organize commercial trade for the population as a whole. Founded in 1930, Torgsin was in many respects a typical product of the restructuring era. It was conceived in reference to a specific group of consumers, to whom access was initially limited not through the price mechanism but through the stationing of guards at the door. Prices were fixed in such a manner as to maximize the benefits to the industrialization drive, in this case through the requirement that customers pay in foreign currency. As in other areas

---

[2] *Resheniia partii i pravitel'stva po khoziaistvennym voprosam*, 2:301–6, here, 301.
[3] Ibid., 2:365.

of distribution, the interests of the nomenklatura and the needs of the fisc conspired to push the business in new directions. Within a year of its inception, Torgsin was authorized to set up commissaries and bars in port districts for the provisionment of foreign sailors; to sell increasingly valuable antiques in its metropolitan shops; to expand food sales; and, crucially, to open its doors to those Soviet citizens in possession of foreign currency or gold. As Elena Osokina has documented, Soviet citizens became the principal customers of Torgsin, which accordingly reoriented its stocks from souvenirs to survival needs. At the height of the famine, bread generated 54 percent of the chain's sales.[4]

Torgsin shops in most cities and virtually all ports, Osokina tells us, were no different from the rest of Soviet trade: "dirty little shops," characterized by "enormous queues, daily brawls, rudeness."[5] In the capitals, however, Torgsin was used to showcase the best products of the Soviet food and consumer-goods industries, and shops glittered with luxury wares. An Australian visitor to the Torgsin grocery in downtown Leningrad in 1933 captured the chain's image in the metropolitan centers:

> We were diverted by the sight of a brightly lit shop with a crowd of people staring in the windows. It soon became apparent what had attracted them. The windows were filled with every sort of gastronomic luxury: Fortnum & Mason could scarcely rival them, and to the hungry crowd outside that food was as remote and unattainable as the Crown Jewels. Our curiosity aroused, we jostled our way inside and saw an excited crowd that surged around the counters in a frantic effort to be served the butter, ham, sausages, cheese, tinned fruit, chickens, ducks and geese that were so temptingly displayed. There were also many kinds of fancy breads, cakes, confectionery and pastries.[6]

The grocery had a cafe, at which this visitor "sampled some delicious little cakes" and spent a "thoroughly convivial hour." Malcolm Muggeridge, a foreign correspondent, similarly described the "wistful groups" who gathered outside the Torgsin shop in downtown Moscow, looking in through the windows "at tempting pyramids of fruit; at boots and fur coats tastefully displayed; at butter and white bread and other delicacies that are for them unattainable."[7] These descriptions are characteristic in

---

[4] Osokina, "Za zerkal'noi dver'iu Torgsina," 86–104; bread percentage calculated from p. 95.

[5] Ibid., 97–98. This is very much in line with descriptions of the Torgsin shops in Odessa's port district; cf. GA Odes. ob., f. R-710, op. 1, d. 20, ll. 71–86.

[6] Betty Roland, *Caviar for Breakfast* (Sydney, Australia, 1989), 6–7. See 83 also Mikhail Bulgakov's description of the Torgsin store across from Smolensk Market in Moscow at the beginning of his *Master and Margarita*.

[7] Malcolm Muggeridge, *Winter in Moscow* (London, 1934), 146; cited in Sheila

their emphasis on the "unattainability" of Torgsin's goods, but they also show the breadth of the selection of luxury goods and the stores' attention to display.

Glavosobtorg's shops, which sold their inventory for rubles but at "raised" or "sharply raised" prices, reflected the same duality as the Torgsin chain. Like Torgsin, Glavosobtorg's "commercial" stores were opened for budgetary reasons from 1930 to 1934, functioned outside the rationing system, were supplied through a special commodity fund, and targeted, at least initially, elite consumers. Again like Torgsin, however, financial pressures soon occasioned a shift in the direction of low-grade consumer goods. Cotton cloth became the state's most important "commercial" commodity after vodka in the fourth quarter of 1931, with cigarettes and sugar close behind.[8] In the summer of 1933 commercial trade became reliant on yet another staple as Sovnarkom authorized a huge expansion of the commercial network in the form of bread stores, a disproportionate number of which were designated for the famine-stricken south, while grain scheduled for export was reassigned to the commercial fund.[9] At the same time, policy makers progressively narrowed the price gap between commercial and rationed sales, so that by the time ration coupons were finally abolished (in January 1935 for bread, October, 1935, for all other foods, and the end of the year for the few remaining manufactured goods distributed by coupons), the commercial shops had already taken over one-quarter of retail sales.[10]

As the case of the commercial bread shops suggests, the vast majority of Glavosobtorg's shops came to supply the survival needs of citizens who were excluded from the rationing system; we can surmise that they, like the provincial outlets of Torgsin, bore little resemblance to the cultured trade ideal. In downtown Moscow, Leningrad, and a handful of other major cities, however, commercial shops retained the elite orientation of the blueprints. Here Bakaleia, Glavosobtorg's commercial bakery chain, sold cakes, pastries, and expensive varieties of bread, while the Gastronom delicatessens specialized in smoked fish, caviar, fruits, confectionary, and fancy liqueurs. Price lists for the Gastronom fish departments give a sense of this chain's aspirations: a 1931 list enumerated forty-one varieties of frozen and canned fish to be sold at "raised" prices and fully

---

Fitzpatrick, *Everyday Stalinism. Ordinary Lives in Extraordinary Times: Soviet Russia in the 1930s* (New York, 1999), 57–58.

[8] RGAE, f. 8043, op. 11, d. 38, ll. 3, 10. Cotton cloth was originally barred from commercial sales on the grounds of political sensitivity; see d. 24, ll. 7–8.

[9] Ibid., d. 60, ll. 15, 121; d. 61.

[10] See Davies and Khlevniuk, "End of Rationing," esp. 557–58.

sixty-seven kinds of smoked fish and caviar for the highest-price sales.[11] Improbable as it sounds, this was no mere paper boast. The flagship stores of the Gastronom chain in Moscow and Leningrad vaunted a rich assortment of delicacies, albeit for a price. By 1934 customers could select live carp from a special fishtank at these supermarkets or purchase hothouse strawberries for one hundred rubles a kilogram.[12] Trade administrators were extremely proud of the capitals' "food department stores" and invariably pointed to them as the avatars of modern, socialist retailing.[13] Customers appear to have shared their assessment: high prices notwithstanding, Moscow's Gastronom No. 1 attracted sixty thousand to seventy thousand shoppers a day.[14]

The striking feature of Glavosobtorg's big-city retailers was their opulence. The capitals' "food department stores" occupied the premises of the famous prerevolutionary fancy-foods shops, the Eliseev delicatessans; adorned with chandeliers, frescoes, potted palms, and sparkling display cases, they embodied the glamorous aesthetic of the Art Nouveau (figure 5). A glamorous ideal likewise shaped Glavosobtorg's "model department stores," which were organized to cater to elite demand for manufactured goods as of July 1933. Like the premiere Gastronoms, the first model department stores were installed in sumptuous prerevolutionary buildings, refurbished and reequipped with up-to-date cash registers and counters.[15] They served as a focus of civic pride: when the Passazh Department Store opened in Leningrad, for example, city authorities gave speeches, the surrounding streets were hung with festive banners, a local chamber orchestra gave a performance in the central hall, and the gala opening was captured on film. Similar scenes played out a few years later in Tashkent.[16] Of course, it was difficult to live up to the expectations

[11] RGAE, f. 8043, op. 11, d. 24, ll. 2–6.

[12] Sheila Fitzpatrick, "Becoming Cultured: Socialist Realism and the Representation of Privilege and Taste," in idem, *The Cultural Front: Power and Culture in Revolutionary Russia* (Ithaca, 1992), 216–37, here, 224; idem, *Everyday Stalinism*, 90. For reference, the average working-class household had a gross income of 923 rubles a month in 1934 (RGAE, f. 1562, op. 15, d. 1119, l. 17).

[13] For example: "This food department store [referring to Leningrad's flagship Gastronom] . . . represents a truly extraordinary phenomenon in the development of Soviet trade" (A. A. Ivanchenko and V. N. Ge, *Sovetskaia torgovlia Leningrada i Leningradskoi oblasti, 1931–1934 gg.* [Leningrad, 1935], 32).

[14] Khlevniuk and Davies, "End of Rationing," 570.

[15] For Narkomsnab's instructions on "model" [*pokazatel'nyi*, or *obraztsovo-pokazatel'nyi*] department stores, see TsMAM, f. 2458, op. 1, d. 227. The first three were to be Moscow's TsUM and Leningrad's Dom Kooperatsii (both reequipped and redecorated prerevolutionary stores) and a new store to be built in Khar'kov.

[16] RGAKFD, reels 1650a, 2524.

Figure 5. The Eliseev "food department store" in Moscow, 1935. *Courtesy of the Russian State Archive for Cinematic and Photographic Documents (RGAKFD).*

created at a grand inauguration; within months of the postrenovation reopening of TsUM, the department store in Moscow, which was far and away the largest in the country, sales assistants were bemoaning the length of the queues, grumbling that "naturally, we need to trade in a cultured manner, but we also need some cultured goods" and suggesting that Soviet trade might seem more "cultured" if the authorities would heat the store. Then again, perhaps the problem rested with customers; one department manager argued in favor of posting placards on the behavior appropriate to "cultured Soviet trade."[17]

Since they already operated without coupons, the abolition of rationing had little impact on the premiere Soviet stores other than to increase their numbers. Moscow remained the primary beneficiary of new investment in the retail sector; along with the subway and grandiose new government buildings, trade was to "play a significant role in the transformation of the Red Capital into the most cultured and the most beautiful city in the world."[18] In the mid-1930s remnants of "old, merchant Moscow" still survived in the form of the dirty, disorganized stores periodically lambasted in metropolitan trade publications, but Moscow officials informed store managers that that era had come to an end. Now managers had a duty not merely to keep their stores clean but also to make them "pretty, according to the artistic requirements of socialist urban construction, for the external (and internal) layout of a store is at the same time one of the most visible aspects of the city."[19] This contrast between "old merchant Moscow" and civilized modernity led to the valorization of such prerevolutionary "Western" shopping districts as Kuznetskii Most and Tverskaia Street, the latter of which was widened, rebuilt as a grand arterial on the Parisian model, renamed in honor of Maxim Gor'kii, and furnished with a parade of prestigious shops and dwellings.[20] The central Bakaleia and Gastronom No. 1 were soon flanked by other shops in the cultured trade mold. There was the new "Fashion House," which, to a visitor from Philadelphia, "reeked of Paris" with its "pile carpets and velvet curtains of grey."[21] Violet Conolly, a specialist on the

[17] TsMA Moskvy, f. 2458, op. 1, d. 227, l. 63.

[18] Ibid., f. R-346, op. 1, d. 57, l. 1; Colton, *Moscow*, 249–80, 325–38.

[19] TsMA Moskvy, f. R-346, op. 1, d. 57, l. 1. For negative depictions of Moscow shops, see, for example, *Stakhanovets torgovli*, November 18 and December 26, 1936; for the article on the "dirtiest bread shop in Moscow," see *Za kul'turnuiu torgovliu*, April 20, 1937.

[20] See Greg Castillo, "Moscow: Gorki Street and the Design of the Stalin Revolution," in Zeynap Çelik, Diane Favro, and Richard Ingersoll, eds., *Streets: Critical Perspectives on Public Space* (Berkeley, 1994), 57–70; Colton, *Moscow*, 327, 337–38.

[21] Mrs. Cecil Chesterton, *Salute the Soviet* (London, 1940), 16–17.

Soviet East, described another impressive Gor'kii Street shop after a 1936–37 trip:

> Cheek by jowl with the expensive tawdry clothes shops in Moscow, and the lack of proper winter garments for the Russian winter at a moderate price, the gorgeous interior of the T.E.J.E. cosmetic shop daily fascinated and irritated me. Its gilt and stucco walls, amber and alabaster lamps, and luxurious rugs were as fine as anything in the rue de la Paix, and seemed like a stage set in Moscow.[22]

The T.E.J.E. (TEZhE) cosmetics trust, as Conolly noted, was run by the wife of Viacheslav Molotov, which may explain the oft-noted surplus of perfume and powder in Soviet retailing, even in relatively distant reaches of the USSR.[23]

Provincial shops could not match the opulence of TsUM or TEZhE. Still, by the end of 1935, there were eight "all-union" model department stores, with annual sales in the range of sixty million to eighty million rubles; together, they accounted for some 3 percent of the USSR's non-food retail sales.[24] Each republican capital was also charged with establishing a model department store, preferably in the local variant of what we might term *socialist ethnic* architecture.[25] For these model retailers, the major development of the mid-1930s was the socialist trade establishment's exposure for the first time in nearly a decade to foreign commercial techniques. Delegations were dispatched to Great Britain (dismissed contemptuously by the study group as a "realm of small shopkeepers"),[26] to Germany, and especially to the United States, where they took notes on everything from shop layout and displays to customer service, personnel, warehouse location and management, and methods for deterring and detecting shoplifters. Given policy makers' preoccupation with the prestigious or "model" stores, the delegations spent most of their time abroad observing high-end retailers in New York, London, and Berlin, rather than small-town shops or budget chains. The impact of these trips on the Soviet retail agenda was to identify "cultured trade" that much

[22] Violet Conolly, *Soviet Tempo* (New York, 1937), 17.

[23] Fitzroy McLean, then third secretary of the British Embassy, observed of the late 1930s, "In Sverdlovsk as in every other Soviet town half at least of the shop-windows were filled with Soviet-made scent and soaps" (*Eastern Approaches* [New York, 1949], 49). See also James Edward Abbe, *I Photograph Russia* (New York, 1934), 225; Eileen Bigland, *Laughing Odyssey* (London, 1939), 78.

[24] Dikhtiar, *Torgovlia* II, 387, 407; *Sovetskaia torgovlia. Statisticheskii sbornik*, 25. TsUM's sales, at 250 million rubles, were triple its nearest competitor's.

[25] For example, Tashkent's model store, as depicted in RGAKFD, reel 2524.

[26] *Sovetskaia torgovlia* (newspaper), February 20, 1935.

Figure 6. A typical Gastronom, 1935. *Courtesy of the Russian State Archive for Cinematic and Photographic Documents (RGAKFD).*

more firmly with enhanced customer service, qualified employees, and a grandly equipped store.[27]

Following the study trips, Bakaleia, Gastronom, and the model department stores initiated a variety of customer services on the American model: packaging goods with a special store label; taking advance orders for out-of-stock wares; delivering goods to the customer's home; accepting returns on defective items; and providing furniture where customers could sit down (figure 6). Home delivery, practiced by a mere 3 percent of food stores in 1935, received an enormous amount of publicity and was seen as the sine qua non of a model store, largely because the delegation to the United States had reported that 95 percent of American milk was delivered to the home.[28] Similarly, when Passazh hired a music pro-

---

[27] For details on the delegations' reactions to American methods, and their influence on Soviet trade policy, see my "Cultured Trade: The Stalinist Turn towards Consumerism," in Sheila Fitzpatrick, ed., *Stalinism: New Directions* (London, 2000), 182–209, here, 190–93; and see also Mikoian, *Tak bylo*, 300–315.

[28] RGAE, f. 7971, op. 1, d. 246, l. 56. See also M. S. Epshtein, "Kak sdelat' magazin stakhanovskim?" *Stakhanovets torgovli*, November 7, 1936; A. Shtukel', "Kak magazin

fessor for afternoon consultations and lessons, or when other model department stores demonstrated the use of a camera or an enameled pot, their directors consciously stole a leaf from New York's Macy's, the world's largest department store in this period and the subject of several admiring reports by the Soviet study group.[29]

What about the rest of socialist retailing? The 1935 trade census revealed the distance that ordinary trade organizations had yet to travel to attain the cultured trade ideal. No less than in 1930, or, for that matter, 1912, the vast majority of the Soviet Union's retail outlets remained small and poorly equipped. Just over 10 percent of clothing shops had fitting rooms, for example, and not quite 20 percent were outfitted with mirrors.[30] A list of the "principal defects of the trade network," prepared by the Odessa city soviet in December 1934, confirms the rudimentary nature of most administrators' concerns:

a. total lack of glass for counters and displays
b. weak lighting of shops in the evening
c. unrepaired facades
d. shortage of small weights and measures
e. total lack of packaging materials
f. inadequate shop signs (small and hard to see)
g. total lack of standardized work clothes[31]

When the cultured trade paradigm was extended to the whole retail system, it was this kind of problem—not the niceties of customer service—that local administrators preferred to address.

The movement for cultured trade gathered steam in late 1934, forming the subject of a public relations campaign in connection with the cessation of rationing. Bread, taken off the ration in January, was its initial focus. According to newspaper reports, the 13,500 newly opened bread shops were to carry some thirty-five varieties of bread and baked goods, be equipped with accurate weights and sharp knives, their salesclerks outfitted in white smocks and caps, and samples of the bread displayed in glass counters, with prices clearly marked.[32] Institutional

---

zavoeval zvanie peredovogo," *Sovetskaia torgovlia* (journal), no. 2 (March–April 1937): 59; Ivanchenko and Ge, *Sovetskaia torgovlia Leningrada*, 32.

[29] T. Gumnitskii, "Kak zavoevyvaiut pokupatelia," *Sovetskaia torgovlia* (journal), no. 1 (January 1937): 62–72; idem, "Priemka, khranenie i kontrol' v firme Meisi," *Sovetskaia torgovlia* (journal), no. 2 (February 1937): 64–70; *Sovetskaia torgovlia* (newspaper), January 10, 1935; RGAE, f. 7971, op. 1, d. 100, l. 26.

[30] *Roznichnaia torgovaia set' SSSR. Itogi torgovoi perepisi 1935 g.* (Moscow, 1936), vol. 3:292.

[31] GA Odes. ob., f. 1234, op. 1, d. 1955, ll. 16–20.

[32] RGAE, f. 7971, op. 1, d. 105, l. 16; *Izvestiia*, January 1 and 2, 1935.

changes, meanwhile, placed a new premium on customer convenience. The hours of trade, which had increased in 1930 to compensate for the closure of private shops, were extended yet again. Planned deliveries from bread factories were increased to six or more a day, seven days a week, beginning at 4:00 A.M. Stricter sanitary regulations banned sales of warm bread; required salespeople to wash their hands frequently with soap and to handle the bread as little as possible; and stipulated that floors and shelves be cleaned daily. Finally, publicists called on shop managers to take the initiative to make their stores and wares attractive to consumers, whether by ordering white curtains for the display cases, piping in music, decorating the store with plants, or adding benches where tired customers could sit down and rest.[33]

A significant corollary to the "culturedness" crusade was the repudiation of the cooperative tradition, with the latter's unconcern for appearances and emphasis on tools and staple goods as the basis of socialist trade. The campaign for cultured trade concentrated overwhelmingly on the state side of socialist retailing—the premiere chains and, to a lesser extent, the flagship shops of each republican or regional *torg*. Urban cooperatives, already weakened by the confiscation of large factory shops and canteens in 1933, were largely left out, though Tsentrosoiuz did open model department stores in Leningrad, Moscow, Khabarovsk, and Khar'kov. Between September and December 1935 these were forcibly transferred to the state, as were all other urban cooperatives, closed distributors, and the cooperatives of the armed forces.[34] For the most part, their premises were given over to the municipal trade departments for refurbishing, though, in practice, many stores remained boarded up for months.[35] This reorganization pointed up, yet again, the extent to which the "utilization" principle governed policy makers' thinking about cooperatives. Like private shops under the NEP, cooperatives had rights only insofar as they were deemed "useful"; if the Party's appraisal of their

[33] *Biulleten' finansovogo i khoziaistvennogo zakonodatel'stva*, no. 7 (March 10, 1935); RGAE, f. 7971, op. 1, d. 105, l. 16; *Sovetskaia torgovlia* (newspaper), January 4, 1935; *Za industrializatsiiu*, January 2 and 3, 1935; *Izvestiia*, January 2, 1935.

[34] *Biulleten' finansovogo i khoziaistvennogo zakonodatel'stva*, no. 29 (October 10, 1935): 23–26; no. 30 (October 30, 1935): 19–21; *Sobranie postanovlenii pravitel'stva*, no. 56 (November 13, 1935): 817. A few leftovers were definitively transferred to the municipal trade organizations in early 1938. Cf. Klimov, *Potrebitel'skaia kooperatsiia*, 85; RGAE, f. 7971, op. 5, d. 39, l. 4.

[35] For example, TsMA Moskvy, f. 346, op. 1, d. 52. Retail trade statistics indicate the slow rate at which the cooperatives were replaced; cf. *Sovetskaia torgovlia. Statisticheskii sbornik*, 140.

usefulness declined, as it did in the early and mid-1930s, cooperative members were not consulted before their property was reassigned.

Relegated to the villages, cooperatives had to contend with the enfeebled economy of the post-collectivization countryside. One by one they went out of business, in part because of a conscious effort to expand the regional *torg* outlets in rural district centers at their expense. Village cooperatives [*sel'po*] were, admittedly, small and dismal shops. According to G. A. Dikhtiar, the physical condition of most rural shops was "extremely primitive": 70 percent "did not even have normal lighting," which probably means that they relied on kerosene; 55 percent had no space for storage; and 35 percent of village cooperatives had a floor space of twenty square meters or less. Their sales volume reflected these conditions: while the average rural shop sold eight thousand rubles worth of goods per month in 1935, 15 percent had sales in the range of twelve hundred rubles and another 20 percent had twelve hundred to three thousand rubles a month in sales.[36] Not surprisingly, when the center decreed that each store should be self-supporting, a mass closure of rural cooperatives ensued.[37] On the bright side, while peasants had to travel farther for basic items, an attractive new store in the district center could foster optimism that the "prosperous, happy life" predicted by Soviet publicists was, indeed, on its way.[38] Although the transformation would take time, the culturedness drive seemed to promise a permanent break with the disorderly little shops of Russia's past.

One noteworthy element of the cultured trade paradigm was its emphasis on luxury; a second was didacticism, in connection with which policy makers heightened their attention to the qualifications of the staff. Sales assistants, in particular, were increasingly cast in a pedagogical role as the ideal of cultured trade jelled. If one side of their job, as administrators admonished, was to study consumer demands, so as to represent them to manufacturers and thus "fight to bring [needed articles] to the market," their second task was to advise customers about what to buy. I. Ia. Veitser, the mid-1930s Commissar of Domestic Trade, liked to portray the consultative role as the retail worker's calling:

[36] Dikhtiar, *Torgovlia* II, 424.

[37] *Biulleten' finansovogo i khoziaistvennogo zakonodatel'stva*, no. 28 (October 10, 1935): 23–26; see also no. 18 (June 30, 1934): 19–20; *Sovetskaia torgovlia. Statisticheskii sbornik*, 140.

[38] For the use of a small-town department store to symbolize material progress, see A. E. Arina, G. G. Kotov, and K. V. Loseva, *Sotsial'no-ekonomicheskie izmeneniia v derevne. Melitopol'skii raion (1885–1938 gg.)* (Moscow, 1939), 383–85.

How can we serve the customer well? . . . You think that your task is simply to
know what the consumer wants and to satisfy his demand. That is necessary;
you have to know the consumer's demand. . . . But your task is not merely this.
You must educate the taste of the consumer. You trade workers must create
new tastes in the consumer, a new Soviet taste and new wares for the consumer.[39]

With increasing prosperity, Veitser suggested, consumers would need to
be trained in the habits appropriate to a cultured, socialist population.
This, however, would require sales assistants to become considerably
more knowledgeable, since it was only through familiarity with a range
of new products that they could offer informed advice.

In this respect, the study trips abroad underscored the continuing educational deficit of Soviet retail employees vis-à-vis their counterparts in
"model" foreign stores. To the Soviet delegates in New York, Macy's
sales assistants seemed helpful, tasteful, friendly, and well informed. The
study group attributed these qualities less to Macy's in-house training
program than to the store's educational minimum: "In a word, the demands Macy places on its salesclerks are exceedingly high. Only a suffi-
ciently cultured person can quickly accommodate himself to these demands and quickly become familiar with all the complex conditions of
this work. For that reason, Macy does not hire any salespeople who lack
an education."[40] Macy's, however, was still operating in a context of labor
surplus in 1936 and could afford to be selective. This was not true of
retail organizations in the Soviet Union, where the workforce was less
well educated to begin with, and where an acute labor shortage had
gripped the economy since 1930. The prioritization of industry placed
the trade sector at a particular disadvantage when trade employees were
assigned to the "white-collar" class of food rations and had no access to
"decentralized" supplies. Meanwhile, trade-sector wages fell further and
further behind (table 5.1): In the mid-1920s trade had been a high-wage
sector; within a decade it had become one of the lowest. The problem
was most severe in rural areas, where shop employees earned a pitiful
average of seventy-nine rubles a month—42 percent of the national
mean—in 1935.[41]

[39] RGAE, f. 7971, op. 1, d. 105, ll. 59–60. See also ll. 64–65; V. Kuibyshev, *Stat'i i rechi*
(Moscow, 1935), 113; *Sovetskaia torgovlia* (newspaper), February 4, 1935; Petrunin and
Evzovich, "Izuchenie potrebitel'skogo sprosa v Tsentral'nom Univermage Narkomvnutorga
SSSR," *Sovetskaia torgovlia* (journal), no. 3 (March 1937): 51–57.

[40] Gumnitskii, "Kak zavoevyvaiut pokupatelia," 64–65, corroborated in Ralph Hower,
History of Macy's of New York, 1858–1919 (Cambridge, 1943), 378–79, 401–2.

[41] Dikhtiar, *Torgovlia* II, 463.

TABLE 5.1
Average Annual Wages in Trade and Public Catering as against Other Sectors

	1924–25	1928	1932	1935
Average, all sectors of the economy	450	703	1,427	2,269
Trade	641	783	1,351	1,851
Public catering	586	623	1,059	1,552

Source: Dikhtiar, *Torgovlia* II, 463.

With these numbers, educated and ambitious young people were not likely to opt for careers in trade. Although Stalin sought to raise the prestige of the commercial sector by promoting it as "our native Bolshevik business" and "revolutionary Bolshevik work,"[42] trade employees unsurprisingly remained near the bottom of the Soviet social hierarchy. As of November 1938 just 3 percent of urban salesclerks had completed secondary schooling, and even among Gastronom and department-store sales assistants, the figures were only marginally better at 5 percent and 10 percent, respectively. These educational attainments fell far below the average for the working-age population as a whole (15%) and still further below the urban working-age norm (26%).[43] This is not to say that recruitment efforts were a failure—on the contrary, the number of people employed in state and cooperative trade rose fourfold in the decade after 1928[44]—but rather that the labor pool for which trade organizations could compete was poorly educated and unskilled. It included many first-time entrants into the paid workforce, including recent migrants from the countryside and, especially, working-class wives. As Amy Randall has documented, women were specifically channeled into the trade sector from 1931 on, through a recruitment drive linking femininity with "culture."[45] Such efforts can be deemed successful: between 1935 and 1938 alone, women increased from 31 percent to 49 percent of state and cooperative trade employees, and from 45 percent to 62 percent of the sales staff. Elsewhere the product of unplanned social change, the feminization of retailing in the Soviet Union thus resulted to a significant extent from political decisions.[46]

[42] Stalin, *Sochineniia*, 13:341–42. See also Amy Randall, "'Revolutionary Bolshevik Work': Stakhanovism in Retail Trade," *Russian Review* 59 (July 2000): 425–41.
[43] RGAE, f. 7971, op. 2, d. 116, l. 83, as against *Itogi vsesoiuznoi perepisi naseleniia 1959 goda* (Moscow, 1962), 1:81 (educational statistics for 1939 and 1959).
[44] Dikhtiar, *Torgovlia* II, 460; Rubinshtein, *Razvitie vnutrennei torgovli*, 286.
[45] Randall, "Women Workers and the Gendering of Soviet Trade."
[46] In 1926 women had constituted just 23 percent of trade employees. See *Vsesoiuznaia*

Under the circumstances, the most feasible way to raise qualifications was to offer practical instruction in the form of short night courses. Although these courses were organized first by consumer cooperatives—the "May address" had charged Tsentrosoiuz with the task of training 150,000 new employees by the end of 1931[47]—they proliferated on the state side of the retail network in the second half of the 1930s. "Technical minimum" programs and other short courses in the Commissariat of Domestic Trade trained an average of 130,000 trade employees a year. Shop managers and other "responsible workers" were particularly encouraged to enroll in continuing-education programs, since fully 20 percent of these cadres lacked any education whatsoever, much less a technical one. Two trade academies were established in Moscow and Kiev to supplement the existing technicums and institutes, and each had a unit [*fakul'tet osobogo naznacheniia*] dedicated to the training of higher management. Training courses in the trade institutes covered a range of topics from "the system of Soviet trade" to "packaging operations," "rural trade and its peculiarities," and "Soviet advertisement and display."[48] Finally, on an informal level, trade administrators sought to elevate the "culture" of Soviet trade through exhortations, urging salesclerks and cashiers to wash their hands, to address customers with the polite form *vy* instead of the familiar *ty*, and to cultivate an attractive appearance.[49]

Didacticism also colored the trade establishment's approach to marketing in the mid-1930s. In an economy of shortages (the state of affairs throughout the decade), one would not expect administrators to accord advertisement a high priority. As Osokina has pithily observed, goods did not need to seek customers under the circumstances; rather, customers sought goods.[50] On the other hand, the Stalinist leadership believed that material conditions were improving; advertisement could help channel newly awakened consumer aspirations toward officially sanctioned ends. The net effect was that the trade organizations and light industry did not

perepis' naseleniia 1926 goda, 34:2–3, 96; A. G. Kulikov and S. G. Rodin, "Kadry sovetskoi torgovli," in *40 let sovetskoi torgovli* (Moscow, 1957), 169–99, here, 183; RGAE, f. 7971, op. 2, d. 116, l. 82.

[47] *Resheniia partii i pravitel'stva po khoziaistvennym voprosam*, 2:305.

[48] See Kulikov and Rodin, "Kadry sovetskoi torgovli," 181–84; A. Goldin, "O prepodavanii 'organizatsii i tekhniki sovetskoi torgovli,'" *Sovetskaia torgovlia* (journal), no. 3 (1937): 31–36; and the 1938 and 1939 editions of the classified statistical yearbook, *Torgovlia Soiuza SSR* (RGAE, f. 7971, op. 2, d. 116, l. 79; d. 137, ll. 109–10).

[49] *Sovetskaia torgovlia* (newspaper), January 2, February 2, February 20, 1935; *Stakhanovets torgovli*, December 14, 1936.

[50] Osokina, *Za fasadom*, 5.

expend very much money or energy on marketing before the war, but when they did invest in advertisement, they adopted a "public service" stance. Rather than unleashing "irrational desires" by manipulating seductive images, after the manner of capitalist advertisement, Soviet officials hoped to stimulate "rational" demand by transmitting information about new products: what they were, how to use them, their beneficial qualities, their price.[51] With this ideal, trade officials revealed the limits of their adherence to the American commercial model: they continued to conceptualize demand in terms of "needs" (said with approval to be "tempestuously growing"), as against the individualistic, pleasure-oriented consumerism marketed by American industry and trade.

In practice, the didactic vision meant that Soviet commercial advertisement consisted mainly of brand labels and shop window displays. An exhibition of Soviet advertising in 1938 was devoted almost exclusively to exemplars of these two forms—and it was no coincidence that half the display cases featured political themes, such as the twentieth anniversary of the Red Army, instead of consumer goods.[52] Important, too, was that consumers encountered labels and display windows in the context of the store, where their desires could be mediated by salespeople and by the available selection of goods. Print advertisement, surely the most popular method of eliciting demand in the West, was relatively uncommon in the 1930s; radio advertisement was virtually nonexistent until after the war.[53]

Rather like the premiere stores, publicity about consumer goods aimed at advertising the Soviet system as well as stimulating consumer demand. This was always the undercurrent of commodity expositions, which were mounted in many major cities in the mid-1930s by the Commissariats of Light Industry and Domestic Trade. Overtly didactic, expos celebrated Soviet industrial achievements and trumpeted the improved standard of living the new products would bring about. For example, at the blockbuster "Parade of the Best" exposition in Moscow, a gigantic banner pro-

---

[51] *Snabzhenie, kooperatsiia, torgovlia*, December 3, 1932; Gumnitskii, "Kak zavoevyvaiut pokupatelia," 64; RGAE, f. 7971, op. 1, d. 105, ll. 57–58.

[52] *Sovetskaia torgovlia* (newspaper), February 27, 1938 (on the exhibition). More generally, see V. Vinogradov and T. Gunina, "Organizatsiia vitrinnoi reklamy," *Sovetskaia torgovlia* (journal), no. 5 (May 1937): 45–48; Gumnitskii, "Kak zavoevyvaiut pokupatelia," 64; and idem, "Priemka, khranenie i kontrol,'" 68–70.

[53] Cf. RGAE, f. 7971, op. 1, d. 100, l. 29. Newspapers ran rather dry ads for cosmetics and a few other industries, seemingly geared at retail networks rather than consumers. Even women's magazines included very few ads; *Rabotnitsa*, for working-class women, carried one full-page color ad for cosmetics or food products on the back page of about two of every three issues, and *Obshchestvennitsa* ran virtually none.

claimed, "See how production has risen, see how consumer demand has risen!" Graphs and statistics, carefully selected to project a smooth upward slope, strategically documented the growth in the output of consumer goods from 1913 to 1928 to 1935.[54] Commodity expositions targeted a specialist audience—they were one way of apprising retail organizations of the goods that were, in principle, available (as a caveat, a reporter for *Vecherniaia Moskva* in the early 1950s described the typical expo as "a museum of the two or three rarities in existence")[55]—but they also aimed to attract a nonspecialist crowd. They were reportedly well attended by the latter group, whose opinions were often canvassed at accompanying public meetings in an effort to study—and cultivate—consumer demand.[56] Expos also received the kind of press that can only be termed advertising, especially if they featured such modern technologies as Soviet-produced motorcycles, automobiles, radios, and washing machines.[57]

Didactic or not, that there was any advertisement at all reveals the flexibility of the "cultured trade" concept. It linked together two cherished Stalinist goals, material progress and the "construction of socialism." According to the latter, consumption needed to be guided; but according to the former, consumption needed to grow. This linkage was not unique to the trade system. It also informed the publicity surrounding Stakhanovism, in which lavish purchases and prizes served to advertise the rewards for high productivity, the "increasing well-being" of the working class, and the specific complement of goods deemed most appropriate to a newly affluent and cultured population. Stakhanovites were given complete collections of the works of Marx, Lenin, and Stalin; crepe de chine dresses; bicycles and grammophones.[58] "Cultured trade" promoted the same ideal of cultivated leisure in the retail setting; at the same time it lent coherence to projects for improving many aspects of Soviet retailing, from the efficiency and qualifications of the staff to customer service, and from the atmosphere and equipment of shops to the assortment of goods.

In the process, "socialism" became subsumed into a vision of modernization derived largely, if not exclusively, from the West. Of the varieties of prerevolutionary businesses, the Stalinist establishment championed the Western-style shops—which they proceeded to take over and turn

[54] "Vystavka pobedy," *Sovetskaia torgovlia* (newspaper), January 12, 1935.
[55] TsMA Moskvy, f. 1953, op. 2, d. 153, l. 82.
[56] For example, RGAE, f. 7971, op. 1, d. 250, ll. 1–18.
[57] For example, *Za industrializatsiiu*, January 30 and March 5, 1935.
[58] See Lewis Siegelbaum, *Stakhanovism and the Politics of Productivity in the USSR, 1935–1941* (Cambridge, 1988), 226–31; Fitzpatrick, "Becoming Cultured," 226–27.

into their own model stores. Luxuries, not basic necessities, were to form the cornerstone of "cultured Soviet trade"; as for trade methods, Stalinist retailers took their cue not from cooperatives or from the indigenous private sector, now reduced to informal exchange at the bazaar, but from the grand emporia of the capitalist West. By the mid-1930s Soviet endorsements of American retailing methods included only the briefest of caveats to the effect that, since America was a capitalist country, Soviet trade should not adopt the methods of its stores "mechanically."[59] Even pricing, the centerpiece of official claims to the distinctiveness of socialist retailing in the 1920s, took a back seat to modernization and American techniques. Whereas Lenin had accepted the revival of monetized trade, as against "socialist products exchange," as a necessary evil, Stalin made it a desideratum; the reforms associated with his campaign for culturedness would form the institutional and intellectual skeleton of Soviet trade until the collapse of the regime.

Bureaucratism Restrained

Between opulence, didacticism, and what we might call socialist consumerism, the cultured trade paradigm represented a new, "Stalinist" synthesis in economic policy. Nonetheless it is important to note that many features of the older socialist economic culture persisted; in fact, it flowed seamlessly into the new model of cultured trade. Most significant among these was the "struggle against bureaucratism," in which name nearly every reform of the early and mid-1930s was carried out. Policy makers may have used examples of "culturedness" as evidence of the progressive character of the reforms when addressing the general public—when, for example, they discussed trade in speeches intended for reproduction in the mass press or when newspapers, on Central Committee instructions, editorialized about the end of rationing—but when speaking with managers, regional party leaders, and economic officials, they tended to revert to their favorite theme.

As in the 1920s the remedies prescribed for socialist-sector bureaucratism included decentralization, managerial initiative, and an orientation toward the market. The organization of factory *orsy* was the first step in these directions, since it gave factories the ability to respond to their employees' demands, but it was clearly only an interim solution until the actual trade system could return to a commercial approach.

[59] M. Smirnov, "Iz opyta amerikanskoi prodovol'stvennoi torgovli," *Sovetskaia torgovlia* (journal), no. 5 (May 1935): 53–55; RGAE, f. 7971, op. 1, d. 246.

Symbolically this transition was effected in July 1934 when the powerful Commissariat of Provisionment split into two new units, one of them the avowedly commercial Commissariat of Domestic Trade. Commissar Veitser became a cheerleader for a kind of market socialism. In meetings with trade administrators from around the country from 1934 to 1936, he rebuked those who "thought that the rationing system would last for a long time yet, with a minimum of commercial trade," and insisted that the historical meaning of rationing lay in its position in a trajectory of progress—in the fact that it "laid the foundations and created a basis for the future development of free trade."[60] According to the commissariat's journal, "free trade" (the new shorthand for nonrationed distribution and consumer choice) would combat "mechanical distribution" and the "monopoly of the cooperatives" by encouraging competition for customers between different stores, between trade networks, and even between state and cooperative trade and the "collective farm" trade at the bazaar.[61] Here, no less than in the cultured trade agenda, the administration drew on capitalist ideas.

Free trade came with a challenge: how to organize supplies efficiently and without excessive bureaucratism (i.e., without a direct governmental allocation), yet in a manner consistent with socialist modernization. In the 1920s trade organizations had employed agents on a contractual basis to line up supplies, which in turn had tended to come either directly from manufacturers or through the syndicates (marketing divisions of each branch of state industry, or glavk) or through mercantile exchanges. The latter became defunct at the end of the NEP, while the glavki went through a series of reorganizations during the restructuring years.[62] At the end of the day, though, the economic administration reverted to a structure not dissimilar from the one that existed from 1923 to 1929. Once again, retail and marketing organizations were expected to abide by wholesale price controls, but, except for a short list of "planned" goods (twelve nonfoods in 1935, six by 1938), they could enter freely into contracts with each other, with manufacturers, and, under the rubric of decentralized procurement [detszagotovki], with collective farms. The Commissariat of Domestic Trade, like Tsentrosoiuz on the cooperative side, increasingly functioned as a commodity clearinghouse rather than an administrative organ. In January 1936 the operational control of trade was

---

[60] RGAE, f. 7971, op. 1, d. 105, ll. 54–55. Veitser had served as the Soviet Union's trade representative in Berlin in 1931, which may well have influenced his economic outlook.

[61] Sovetskaia torgovlia (journal), no. 1 (January 1935): 5–14. See also Stalin's 1933–34 speeches on these topics.

[62] See Dikhtiar, Torgovlia II, 428–45.

transferred entirely from the central commissariat to the republican, ob-last, and local trade departments, while the commissariat was reorganized around such marketing divisions as Soiuzoptmetiz (for metal wares) or Soiuzkul'ttorg (for school supplies, books, and leisure items).[63] Intermediary distribution centers (interregional wholesale bases, etc.) also proliferated in connection with the antibureaucratic reforms.[64]

Through all these changes, trade remained subject to planning. Every trade organization and shop had a "turnover plan" denominated in rubles, which outlined the volume, quality, and assortment of goods to be sold in a given quarter or year. In addition, the handful of essential commodities that were still "planned," or "mechanically distributed," in the later 1930s (cotton and woolen cloth, kerosene, soap, etc.) formed the mainstay of socialist retailing; in rural areas they constituted fully half of all sales.[65] Where inventories went beyond the survival minimum, however, shops gained the latitude to find supplementary supplies on their own. In the second half of the decade, managers in the premiere networks and emporia reported receiving almost nothing through centralized allocations. Instead, they purchased supplies directly from manufacturers, most often concluding contracts with local artisans and small-scale industry; additionally a few of the model department stores set up their own production units for clothes, furnishings, and luxury goods.[66]

Economic officials hoped that decentralization would foster managerial responsibility. In the larger shops, sales and profits now depended directly on the initiative of the store manager, much as they had depended on the initiative of factory managers in a rationing-era *ors*. Commissar Veitser spent much of his time in the mid-1930s in motivational meetings with shop directors, whom he alternatively browbeat and cajoled to push more aggressively for supplies. Even with regard to planned goods, years of experience had shown that wholesale bases would not necessarily pass things along without pressure from an energetic retailer.[67]

---

[63] *Sobranie postanovlenii pravitel'stva*, no. 2 (January 19, 1936): 17–22. Decentralization was accompanied by demotion: whereas Mikoian was a long-time member of the Central Committee and candidate member of the Politburo during his tenure at Narkomsnab, this was not true of his successors at Narkomvnutorg, who remained, in a sense, his subordinates.

[64] See Dikhtiar, *Torgovlia* II, 430–36; Klimov, *Potrebitel'skaia kooperatsiia*, 84–86.

[65] Hubbard, *Soviet Trade*, 112–15; Dikhtiar, *Torgovlia* II, 443–44.

[66] RGAE, f. 7971, op. 1, d. 105, l. 28. For legislation, see *Biulleten' finansovogo i khoziaistvennogo zakonodatel'stva*, nos. 34–35 (Dececember 20, 1935): 45–46; see also Hubbard, *Soviet Trade*, 120–23. Generally, the larger the store, the more freedom it had to determine its own inventory and to conclude contracts with suppliers.

[67] A headline in *Snabzhenie, kooperatsiia, torgovlia*, on September 21, 1932, summarized this oft-repeated complaint: "A Graveyard for Goods, Not a Base."

Bureaucratism outlasted the reforms, to judge from Veitser's comments at a 1935 conference of retail personnel. Describing store directors' passive interactions with wholesale bases in terms of a "dependency syndrome," Veitser's remarks call to mind NEP-era complaints about managers' reluctance to take decisions:

> Our inspector was investigating Kuibyshev krai, where there is a district called Nizhnii Lomov. . . . He went into the GORT store in Nizhnii Lomov and asked the manager, "Why don't you have this item? They have it at the base, but you don't have any." The manager answered, "There are people above me who worry about which goods I need, and they send them to me."
>
> What is this? A dependent's psychology: things will be sent according to plan, the plan is rigid and unchangeable, and everything is accounted for in the plan. . . . This is a crude example, but in a less crude, more subtle fashion, it exists in a great many stores.[68]

Of course, the wholesale base that failed to notify stores of its stocks in this example had to share the responsibility for the organizational breakdown, but Veitser told the anecdote to apprise store managers of the need for active procurement. Why he wanted to impress this point on them is not hard to appreciate; at a conference a few months earlier nearly every trade network had admitted to not fulfilling its plan, but the managers attributed this to inadequate deliveries, insufficient reserve stocks, and other factors outside their control.[69]

The attempt to decentralize responsibility for distribution was extended to salesclerks, whose fixed wages were replaced with piece rates and who were drawn into "socialist competition" for increased sales.[70] Even consumers were mobilized: much as factory brigades had been charged with the supervision of particular cafeterias, citizens were encouraged to express their concerns over the operation of stores and to take an interest in trade. From 1934 on, stores were expected to hold conferences with their customers; while some of these conferences featured testimonies to increasing well-being, others became a forum for criticism. Complaint books became mandatory and were cited as evidence of a "negligent attitude toward the customer" if managerial responses adopted the wrong tone.[71] In addition, citizen volunteers super-

[68] RGAE, f. 7971, op. 1, d. 105, ll. 66–67. David Shearer shows that virtually identical language was used by Ordzhonikidze as VSNKh chairman and then Commissar of Heavy Industry; cf. Shearer, *Industry, State and Society*, 237.

[69] RGAE, f. 7971, op. 1, d. 84.

[70] Epshtein, "Kak sdelat' magazin stakhanovskim"; Dikhtiar, *Torgovlia* II, 464; Randall, "'Revolutionary Bolshevik Work'"; RGAE, f. 7971, op. 1, d. 100, l. 10.

[71] RGAE, f. 7971, op. 1, d. 363; Stephen Kotkin, *Magnetic Mountain: Stalinism as a*

seded the official inspectorate Rabkrin in the surveillance of industry and trade. Commissar Veitser described this expansion of "consumer control" as compensation to customers for the nationalization of urban cooperatives, which at least in principle were more susceptible to influence from shareholders.[72]

Store managers probably felt less threatened by volunteer inspectors than by Rabkrin deputies, who had the power to instigate criminal prosecution for misdeeds, but a zealous "worker controller" could be a thorn in their side. In Odessa, for example, volunteer inspector Zaslavskii spent his evenings after work touring the city's department stores, questioning customers, and demanding to inspect the warehouse if managers claimed that goods were out of stock. Day after day, Zaslavskii's colorful handwritten reports described overbearing store managers who held back goods when they wanted to close up early; disgruntled customers waiting in increasingly rowdy lines; vociferous heckling about the relations of the sales staff with speculators and the immediate appearance of the "scarce" goods at the bazaar; and sharp confrontations with store managers, which Zaslavskii evidently relished.[73] From the point of view of the bureaucracy, this kind of consumer control served more than one end: it provided information to the bureaucracy at no cost and engaged citizens to adopt an official project as their own. Above all, it focused citizens' indignation on local abuses and organizational shortcomings, reinforcing the Kremlin's position that not policies but people and practices were the source of the economy's failings.

Is it surprising, in this context, that the "struggle against bureaucratism" in the state and cooperative trade networks was accompanied by an intensified "struggle against abuses"? In the 1930s, no less than in the 1920s, trade personnel labored under a cloud of suspicion by virtue of their access to scarce goods. The trials of *ors* managers in Magnitogorsk, described so vividly by Stephen Kotkin, illustrate the regime's continuing tendency to blame individuals for the chronic breakdown of supplies. A lack of ethics, not crop failure, was decried as the source of Magnitogorsk's shortfall of seven hundred tons of grain in the summer of 1933;

Civilization (Berkeley, 1995), 261–63. In Moscow there are many more stenograms of customer conferences from 1945 to 1953, for example, TsMA Moskvy, f. R-216, op. 1, d. 703–4; f. 32, op. 1, d. 50, ll. 104, 141 (though one customer participant refers nostalgically to all the customer conferences of the prewar years).

[72] RGAE, f. 7971, op. 1, d. 100, l. 42. Rabkrin was disbanded in 1934 and its work transferred to the trade unions, except for the State Price Inspection, which was shifted to Narkomvnutorg (*Biulleten' finansovogo i khoziaistvennogo zakonodatel'stva*, nos. 27–28 (October 10, 1934): 37).

[73] GA Odes. ob., f. 1763, op. 1, d. 756, ll. 99–102.

and, following the time-honored practice of the Soviet judicial organs, the "thieves, swindlers, embezzlers, and plunderers of socialist property," who had "established a comfortable nest in Magnitogorsk's *ors*," were accordingly raked over the coals in a month-long show trial at the town circus. Lezhava's 1923 objection notwithstanding, the *ors* director was sentenced to death. As Kotkin notes, this episode was only the most spectacular of a series of arrests of Magnitogorsk's supply officials; from 1930 to 1938 managerial positions in the city's trade system were little more than revolving doors.[74]

The politics of blame was, as we have seen, well established in NEP-era socialist trade, but the deprivation of the early 1930s lent new urgency to the search for scapegoats. Through 1933 "vigilance" was directed primarily against former private traders who had found jobs in state and cooperative trade. Stalin may have deplored the "violations of cooperative democracy" that had become so widespread during the collectivization era, but no Party official was about to leave kulaks on cooperative boards. In 1933 the purge of former privateers was handed off to the Komsomol, which organized a nation-wide "light cavalry" raid and purge modeled on its 1929 operation against private-sector tax evaders.[75] This purge failed to quell accusations about "class aliens" in the trade sector. Through the remainder of the decade, legal commentators suggested that ethical violations (deception of the customer, shortchanging, pilfering, all quite widespread) resulted from the fact that "anyone," including "class enemies" and previously convicted embezzlers, could get a job in trade.[76] Each of these infractions in turn served as the basis for a new criminal justice campaign.

The problem of bureaucratism was real enough. We should nonetheless be aware that it had, like so much of the "Lenin legacy," acquired a certain ritual status in Soviet political culture. Indeed, the "struggle against bureaucratism" became *the* legitimate language of economic reform in the Soviet Union, whether from 1932 to 1935 or in 1947, 1965, or 1986, and while excessive bureaucratism was one of the targets of

---

[74] Kotkin, *Magnetic Mountain*, 257–61; *Snabzhenie, kooperatsiia, torgovlia*, March 21 and April 1, 1931; *Potrebitel'skaia kooperatsiia v rekonstruktivnyi period*, 133–36.

[75] *Snabzhenie, kooperatsiia, torgovlia* issued calls for a general purge of "alien elements" on July 3, 1932, and then covered the purge throughout 1933. See also GA Riaz. ob., f. R-300, op. 2, d. 279; TsMA Moskvy, f. 2458, op. 1, d. 241, l. 78.

[76] N. Lagiover, "Za luchshie tempy i kachestvo raboty," *Sovetskaia iustitsiia*, no. 3 (1934): 8–9; A. Ryskind, "Bor'ba s raskhititeliami sotsialisticheskoi sobstvennosti," *Sovetskaia iustitsiia* nos. 23–24 (1939): 29–31; I. Dikovskii, "O rabote organov prokuratury po bor'be s rastratami i khishcheniiami v sisteme gosudarstvennoi torgovli i kooperatsii," *Sotsialisticheskaia zakonnost'*, no. 7 (July 1940): 17–22.

these various reforms, there were other, equally important motives that could not be publicly articulated. From 1932 to 1935 the reforms of the trade system emphasized efficiency and profitability; they mobilized employees to work harder; and they satisfied the needs of the fisc. Unlike the "struggle against bureaucratism" or "cultured trade," these agendas were not publicized, and they do not even figure prominently in the minutes of meetings sponsored by the Commissariat of Domestic Trade. Profits, in particular, tended to be discussed only at the very top echelons of the power structure, most often in the form of classified memos on specific revenue-generating proposals rather than any general acknowledgment of profits as a primary purpose of trade.

In addition, the institutional, ideological, and psychological limits to any antibureaucratic initiative remained virtually unaltered since 1918. The orientation toward market methods consisted mainly in making socialist retailers pay for themselves and at the same time become more responsive to consumer demand. The top echelons of the government and Party certainly did not abandon the habits of micromanagement. In the later 1930s the Politburo continued to discuss such important matters of policy as whether TsUM should open a children's department or what kind of sneakers were available for sale.[77] Nor did the price bureaucracy have to fear unemployment; the end of rationing was accompanied by yet another round of price fixing, on a more systematic basis than before. During the rationing era, published prices were in a sense "orientational" for the elite trade networks; Torgsin, the commercial stores, and the neighborhood co-op could charge radically different amounts of different currencies (e.g., gold, hard currency, so-called *bony*, or hard-currency account receipts, ration coupons, rubles). This was scheduled to change as of 1935, though, in practice, the elite networks continued to enjoy considerable leeway in the pricing of manufactured goods.[78] The "struggle against bureaucratism," in sum, had definite limits beyond which policy makers were reluctant to go.

In terms of ideas, "cultured trade" marked a new departure for the Soviet establishment. Were there lasting organizational changes in socialist trade vis-à-vis the NEP years as well? Beyond the disappearance of

[77] See the Politburo correspondence with SNK in GARF, f. 5446, op. 18a, d. 309, l. 53; see also Politburo protocols, which are filled with this kind of trivia.

[78] The 1935 price reform divided the country into eight belts, within which every store would charge the same amount for a given item. *Biulleten' finansovogo i khoziaistvennogo zakonodatel'stva*, nos. 34–35 (December 20, 1934): 29; but see also no. 18 (June 30, 1935): 29–30. Elite stores were able to circumvent price regulations because they obtained a large percentage of their wares from artisans or their own production units, and hence invoked the "uniqueness" of their products to set their own prices (Dikhtiar, *Torgovlia* III, 108–9).

private-sector supplies and competition, the developments from 1931 to 1935 largely extended processes of social and economic modernization that had already been under way. As in other countries, the feminization of the trade sector only accelerated after the early 1930s. The expansion of refrigerated storage, the organization of regional wholesale bases, and the improvement of shop equipment likewise represented continuations of NEP-era efforts rather than a sharp break. The one exception was the urban cooperatives, which were permanently eliminated between 1932 and 1935.

STALINISM AND THE CONSUMER, I: URBAN ATTITUDES AND TRENDS

As a public relations campaign, "cultured trade" pointed in two directions. On the one hand, it exhorted employees in the retail system to make customer service and cleanliness a point of honor. On the other hand, it encouraged consumers to believe that the restructuring of the economy would soon yield material benefits to match the putative political benefits of the socialist revolution. This was the theme of Stalin's famous 1935 speech to the First All-Union Congress of Stakhanovites, when he announced, "Life has become better, Comrades. Life has become happier."[79] Especially in the big cities, the new "cultured" stores and the increasing availability of consumer goods from 1934 on were calculated to inspire consumer confidence. Did they succeed? How did citizens' attitudes toward trade and consumption, and, in relation to these, toward the Soviet system, develop in the decade after 1928?

The most consistently available source for such an inquiry is letters to *Pravda* and to Soviet authorities—letters authored largely by Party members and communist sympathizers, mostly urban, Russian, educated, and male.[80] Obviously the expressed views of this cohort, especially as excerpted for the Party leadership in mood reports, cannot be taken to represent those of society as a whole. They did, however, change in interesting ways. What clearly comes through from the letters is that these citizens—unlike most peasants and non-Slavs, for example—identified

[79] Stalin, *Sochineniia*, 3 vols. [14] (Stanford, 1967), 79–101, esp. 81–82, 89–90.

[80] Summary excerpts of these letters [*svodki*] are located in several places. For the years 1928 to 1930, I have used GARF, f. 374, op. 27, d. 1901, ll. 37–39 17–34; d. 1569, ll. 1–12; f. 5446, op. 55, d. 1831, ll. 1–83; d. 1832, ll. 1–161; d. 1835, ll. 1–6; d. 1972, ll. 1–62; d. 1973. After 1930 I have mainly relied on letters to the Leningrad *obkom* and on the discussions of public opinion in Sarah Davies, *Popular Opinion in Stalin's Russia: Terror, Propaganda, and Dissent, 1934–1941* (Cambridge, 1997); Lesley A. Rimmel, "Another Kind of Fear: The Kirov Murder and the End of Bread Rationing in Leningrad," *Slavic Review* 56, no. 3 (fall 1997): 481–99; Fitzpatrick, *Stalin's Peasants*; and idem, *Everyday Stalinism*.

with, and had high expectations of, the Soviet regime as "their own." The disillusionment of pro-Soviet authors, when it occurred, was correspondingly bitter, and their psychological need to tell "the truth" to those in power was equally acute. By 1932–33 some of the harshest denunciations of the system came from writers who identified themselves as Communists. The ongoing crisis in living standards played a major role in their progressive alienation from the government, as did the visible corruption and incompetence of Soviet officialdom on the ground. Far from placating this segment of the public, the campaign for cultured trade contributed to its alienation; specifically the luxury orientation of the campaign fostered social polarization: "us" (workers and peasants, ordinary folk) versus "them" (the elite).[81] Finally, the Party's decision to withhold "disorganizing" information from the press severely damaged the government's credibility with its own core constituency, as many workers came to believe that everything published in the papers was a lie.

Already from 1928 to 1930 letters to *Pravda* highlight a constellation of ideas that might be termed *popular communism*, as opposed to the "general line" transmitted from above. Popular communism was radically egalitarian and hostile to anything considered a luxury. It could serve as the basis of a critique of state policy from the communist rank and file, as, for example, when M. M. Radzinskii read in *Pravda* that Gostorg had just signed contracts for the purchase of lemons and oranges from Italy, Turkey, and Palestine. Radzinskii's reaction to this notice was viscerally negative: "Every worker and peasant would undoubtedly say that, in our current economic state, we could easily do without oranges and lemons. If this is being done for purely diplomatic reasons, then why advertise it in the papers?"[82] Similarly: "Our worker's cooperative has purchased mandolins and balalaikas, when there are no potatoes for the workers." "In our cooperative there often is neither meat nor flour, but you can buy as many powders and expensive hats as you like!"[83] The implication of such criticisms was that socialist trade should guarantee everyone basic necessities before supplying anyone with "luxury" items.

This idea colored "popular communist" perceptions of rationing after 1928. On the whole, those who wrote letters to *Pravda* liked the idea of rationing, in the hope that it might stanch the flow of supplies to "speculators." They also tended to view the class ration as equitable, even if they sometimes quibbled over the classification of artisans or chimney sweeps, or felt that the "bourgeoisie" deserved more or less than it re-

[81] On "us" versus "them," see Davies, *Popular Opinion*, 124–46.
[82] GARF, f. 5446, op. 55, d. 1831, l. 47 (November 1928).
[83] Ibid., ll. 48, 52 (Donbass and Urals, November, 1928).

ceived. The Party's decision to calibrate food rations to sectoral priorities, however, fit much less comfortably within popular need-based notions of fairness. When the centralized ration lists were introduced in 1929–30 letter writers thus protested: "How can it be that even if a metal worker earns 100 to 150 rubles a month, he gets bread, whereas a guard or cleaning woman who earns just 18 rubles is left without it just because they work in trade?"[84] With the worsening material conditions of the early 1930s, hardship only strengthened this cohort's commitment to egalitarianism and consumer staples. In 1932–33, even more than in 1928, the ideal of popular communism was a society in which everyone had a survival portion of bread, potatoes, sugar, and meat; some cotton cloth; a pair of shoes.[85]

The cultured trade paradigm grated harshly against this sensibility. For the remainder of the decade it gave rise to a large number of sarcastic jokes and complaints, and served as a focus of popular resentment. Sarah Davies has catalogued anecdotes and jokes about Torgsin, several of which skewered the Soviet officials who were said to be the chain's chief clientele: instead of "*torg*ovlia *s in*ostrantsami" [trade with foreigners], the acronym Torgsin was translated "*T*ovarishchi *o*pomnites', *R*ossiia *g*ibnet, *S*talin *is*trebliaet *n*arod [Comrades remember, Russia is perishing, Stalin is exterminating the people]; or in a joke popular at the end of rationing, citizens were divided into four categories: (1) *Torgsiane*; (2) *Krasnozvezdiane*; (3) *Zaerkane*; and (4) *Koe-kane* [Torgsiners; "red stars," i.e. generals; ZRKers; and Somehow-or-others]. Inevitably, outside elite circles, the luxury retailers of the early 1930s were viewed through the negative lens of privilege instead of the positive lens of "cultured trade."[86]

The end of food rationing in 1935 was bound to exacerbate these social antagonisms in the major urban centers. Although privilege per se—status discrimination within the urban population—was revoked, normalization necessarily meant an end to the glaring price disparities between urban and rural trade and between the various retail networks. Since prices had to cover costs, urbanites could expect to pay more for staple foods than they had in the previous several years. With the impending elimination of the urban food subsidy, rationing suddenly acquired its defenders among workers in the high-priority industries and cities. In Leningrad, Lesley Rimmel has concluded, popular anger over the upcoming price hikes was so intense that Leningraders interpreted

[84] Ibid., l. 12. These themes ran throughout the letters *svodki* from 1928 to 1930.
[85] For examples, see TsAIPD Len., f. 24, op. iv, d. 614, l. 10; d. 638, ll. 2–4; d. 449, ll. 68–70.
[86] S. Davies, *Popular Opinion*, 141–42; Rimmel, "Another Kind of Fear."

the December 1934 assassination of their Communist Party chief, Sergei Kirov, as an economic protest.[87] Not all their anger derived from the popular communism ideal; even in 1935 a few letter writers were still suggesting a return to private trade. However, they appear to have been in a small and dwindling minority among the populations serviced by the "special" and "first" rationing lists.

Popular communist critiques, by contrast, persisted into the postrationing period; the perception of privilege outlasted closed distributors, Torgsin shops, and other overtly discriminatory structures. Though access to the shops became open, anonymous letters to the authorities continued to rail against poverty, inequality, and official boosterism. Stalin's slogan, "Life has become better," figured in several of these, as when a group of maids complained to the Leningrad Communist Party headquarters about the excessive comforts enjoyed by the Soviet executives who employed them ("For *them* life has become better, life has become happier, Comrades"), or when another letter writer declared, "Those who are well paid shout that life has become better, life has become happier. [Otherwise] this slogan of Comrade Stalin's is pronounced ironically and is used whenever people experience some kind of hardship or difficulty."[88] Letters such as these continued to be written throughout the period before the Second World War. As they show, popular communism, which resonated so strongly with the ideals of pro-Soviet workers and more generally with the views of the urban poor, provided a yardstick against which actual communism—Stalinism—could be gauged.

As it happens, popular communism has had a considerable influence on the historiography of Soviet consumption. The popular communist critique posited, first, a progressive immiseration of the laboring classes from 1928 to 1933, with little or no improvement thereafter; and, second, in relation to this downward trend, a widening gap in living standards between urban and rural laborers and an increasingly affluent, entrenched elite. This should sound familiar to all students of Soviet history: it formed the thesis of one of the foundational texts of the field, *The Revolution Betrayed*. Trotsky framed his 1937 analysis around the ossification of a new, socialist elite comprising well-paid functionaries and worker aristocrats. He—like the anonymous letter writers—also reserved some of his most vitriolic remarks for the manifestations of cultured trade. Here, for example, is his commentary on Polina Zhemchuzhina's (Molotov's wife's) expanding business at TEZhE:

---

[87] Rimmel, "Another Kind of Fear."
[88] TsAIPD Len., f. 24, op. 2v, d. 1748, ll. 166–71; op. 2g, d. 149, ll. 129–32.

When the people's commissar of food industries, Mikoian, boasts that the lowest kind of confections are rapidly being crowded out by the highest, and that "our women" are demanding fine perfumes, this only means that industry, with the transfer to money circulation, is accommodating itself to the better-qualified consumer. Such are the laws of the market, in which by no means the last place is occupied by highly placed wives.[89]

Trotsky's explanations are often debatable—in this case, for example, the expansion of perfume manufacturing far more directly reflected Stalin's partiality for highly placed wives than market forces.[90] Nonetheless, Trotsky's species of popular communism has influenced succeeding generations of historians because it captured an intriguing aspect of Stalinism: the insistence, in a time of survival-threatening scarcity, that material progress be measured in relation to the consumption of luxury goods.[91]

We shall return to this point at the end of the chapter, but let us first examine the other propositions of popular communism. Do they accurately describe urban consumption trends in the decade after 1928? A considerable amount of ink has been spilled over this complicated issue. In general, while new archival data from TsUNKhU's household budget studies confirm popular communism's view of the early 1930s, they suggest important revisions of both the immiseration thesis and the social stratification thesis with respect to the period from 1935 to 1939. The flaws in the sources are significant, however. First, the budget studies reflect the Soviet government's fixation on working-class, managerial, and white-collar standards of living to the neglect of other social strata. Occupational groups outside the state sector, such as *kustar'* artisans, house servants, cab drivers, chimney sweeps, members of manufacturing cooperatives, and other independently employed people, as well as the unemployed, were not surveyed, and as these groups generally numbered among the poor, they would presumably have lowered the averages. Second, the budget surveys asked people to record their income and outlays after the fact, and where the raw data for particular households have been preserved, discrepancies between extremely precise figures for some budgetary items and suspiciously round figures for others are striking. Since the sources of error did not change much from the time the surveys were

[89] Trotsky, *The Revolution Betrayed*, 101.

[90] According to Mikoian, Stalin decided to expand perfume production when Zhemchuzhina persuaded him of its likely profitability and potential for growth. Besides, she argued, it was "greatly needed" by "the people" (*Tak bylo*, 297–99).

[91] A few works for which this insight was crucial might include Milovan Djilas, *The New Class* (New York, 1957); Dunham, *In Stalin's Time*; Fitzpatrick, "'Becoming Cultured'"; and idem, *Everyday Stalinism*.

TABLE 5.2
Workers' Annual Per Capita Food Consumption (in Kilograms/Year)

	1919	1927	1933	1935	1938
Cereals, grain products	176	240	192	245	238
Potatoes	180	127	76	83	84
Vegetables, melons	50	67	48	43	46
Fruits	2.7	N.A.	2.5	8.1	9
Butter, oil, margarine	4.2	9.1	1.8	2.6	4.7
Sugar, sweets	4.0	19.0	9.5	10.1	21.1
Meat, fish	20.6	84.5	15.6	19.8	29.8
Milk, dairy (liters)	43 kg	128 kg	20.6 l	28.0 l	38.7 l
Eggs (number)	24 eggs	94 eggs	3.6 eggs	6.9	30.6

Sources: *Trudy TsSU* 30 (1): 104–15; *Biudzhety rabochikh*, 31, 36; RGAE, f. 1562, op. 15, d. 1119, 1. 75.

initiated to the end of the Stalinist period, however, it is reasonable to assume that household budget studies can provide a fairly accurate portrait of consumption trends on the part of three core urban occupational groups: "workers," construed narrowly to exclude the independently employed or casual labor force; "engineering-technical personnel" (ITR), the managerial class; and "employees," a category broad enough to include doctors, teachers, secretaries, and shopclerks.[92]

The budget investigations confirm the precipitous drop in living standards between 1928 and 1933 from a number of different angles. The most direct evidence concerns consumption of foods and clothing, which were quantified in "physical volume" as well as ruble values. For the consumption norms of workers (industrial, transportation, and mining), see table 5.2. In terms of nutritional content, as the table shows, workers went from a high-calorie, high-protein diet in the mid-1920s to a low-protein, low-calorie diet in 1933. Since the table expresses average values, malnutrition undoubtedly became extremely widespread at the low end of the wage scale. The data also show that although workers' food consumption rebounded after 1933, consumption of animal products never returned to the precollectivization level prior to the Second World War.

Cloth and clothing consumption declined even more precipitously in the restructuring era (table 5.3). Again, 1933 defined the low point, after

[92] For a discussion and critique of these sources in relation to the voluminous literature on Soviet consumption, see the on-line appendix "Household Budget Data."

TABLE 5.3
Workers' Annual Per Capita Cloth, Clothing, and Shoe Consumption

	1924	1927	1933	1936	1939
Total clothes - meters	≥3.453	≥5.055	3.973	5.665	n.a.
cotton	2.864	3.941	3.413	4.639	n.a.
woollen	0.589	1.114	0.414	0.795	n.a.
other	n.a.	n.a.	0.146	0.231	n.a.
Total cloth - meters	≥5.017	≥11.137	4.749	7.697	8.728
cotton	4.699	10.572	4.551	7.219	8.194
woollen	0.318	0.565	0.047	0.129	0.160
other	n.a.	n.a.	0.151	0.349	0.374
Total footwear - pairs	1.243	2.082	≥1.324	2.505	2.601
leather	0.799	1.320	0.869	1.083	1.174
rubber	0.184	0.447	0.455	0.673	0.675
felt, etc.	0.260	0.315	n.a.	0.749	0.752

Sources: Biudzhety rabochikh, 48–49; RGAE, f. 1562, op. 15, d. 1119, ll. 86–87; d. 1077, l. 18.

which consumption rose. In terms of causality, the data are ambiguous. Did workers purchase more felt boots and galoshes in the 1930s, and fewer leather shoes, for example, because of shifts in demand, shifts in availability, or shifts in prices? In this instance, supplies offer the most likely explanation: repression against artisanal tanners, shoe producers, and leather dealers disrupted the market in the leather goods sector, and the mass slaughter of livestock from 1929 to 1932 must have reduced the availability of hides for the remainder of the decade. The production of felt boots and galoshes, in which private artisans were not so ruthlessly repressed, did not experience the same decline.

Real scarcity also contributed to the drop in cloth and clothing consumption in the early 1930s; between 1930 and 1931 alone, the state's "market fund" of cotton cloth for rationed and nonrationed sales declined by 31 percent, a decline evenly distributed between urban and rural supplies.[93] At least equally important, however, were changes in the structure of demand; as in the revolutionary era, clothing proved a more elastic item of the budget than food, which consumed a larger percentage of their incomes in 1933 than at any time since 1921. After 1933 the budget surveys chart a gradual return to normalcy, though again, as in the physical data on clothing and food consumption, the "normal" 1927 expenditure ratios were not restored until after the war: In 1927 and

[93] RGAE, f. 7971, op. 2, d. 662, l. 7.

TABLE 5.4
Working-Class Budgets: A Breakdown of Expenditures

	1922	1927	1933	1937
Food	46.0	43.8	59.0	55.3
Housing	1.7	6.9	4.7	4.2
Heating, lighting materials	12.2	6.2	2.2	1.3
Alcohol	0.4	2.8	2.0	2.6
Tobacco	1.2	1.4	2.1	1.2
Clothing	24.0	21.7	11.2	14.9
Furnishings, household goods	11.1	3.3	1.2	1.7
Hygiene, cosmetics	0.8	0.6	1.7	1.3
Medicine	0.4	0.2	0.2	0.3
Culture, education	1.2	1.8	1.2	1.7
Political expenses (dues)	2.9	2.2	1.9	1.0
Material aid to absent family	0.4	1.2	0.6	1.4
Expenditures on garden/farm	0.4	1.2	0.6	1.8

Sources: Biudzhety rabochikh, 27–28; RGAE, f. 1562, op. 15, d. 1119, ll. 18.

1937, as table 5.4 shows, the proportions of various expenditures shifted in ways that one would predict based on increasing prosperity. It would be difficult, however, to read into any of the data on household purchases and expenditures "an altered consumer—a new consumer, who has grown more cultured," in the words of Commissar Veitser.[94] The 1937 budgetary patterns were still firmly rooted in material necessity, not leisure or pleasure. Cultural outlays may have grown—in fact, only in relation to books and especially movies (a staggering 62% of all workers and their family members had seen *Chapaev* by November 1935) can one discern the outlines of a mass consumer culture in the 1930s.[95] On the whole, though, surveys of the late 1930s indicate quantitative increases (more food, cotton cloth, etc.) rather than major qualitative shifts.

With respect to popular communism's second proposition, the quantitative improvements in working-class consumption were nonetheless sufficient to bring it in line with that of the educated class. The years 1932 to 1934 turned out to be the high water mark for consumption inequality within the state sector (nationalized industry, transportation, etc.); afterward, the consumption gap narrowed, as the disposable incomes of workers rose more rapidly than those of their bosses. This pattern can be seen with respect to every item of the budget. In 1934 work-

[94] Ibid., op. 1, d. 105, l. 55.
[95] Ibid., f. 1562, op. 15, d. 806a, ll. 108–30. See also the celebratory volume *Cultural Progress in the U.S.S.R.: Statistical Returns* (Moscow, 1958).

ing-class households spent roughly half as much on clothing per family member as did ITR households. By 1939 they spent three-fourths as much. In 1934 workers spent 38 percent less on soap per person as did ITR households; by 1939 the gap had narrowed to 20 percent. They went from spending 50 percent to 60 percent as much on furniture; 38 percent to 53 percent as much on health care; 26 percent to 50 percent as much per person on culture and entertainment; and 56 percent to 78 percent as much on food.[96]

Much can be said about the budget survey data, but, for our purposes, the points I have indicated are the most important. First, they chart a sharp deterioration in the consumption of both food and nonfood products in the period from 1929 to 1933, both qualitatively and quantitatively. Second, they suggest a substantial, though incomplete, recovery in the period after 1933 and especially after 1935, as evidenced by the consumption of increasing quantities of virtually everything as well as some modest shifts in the proportional breakdown of expenditures. Third, they support popular communism's, and Trotsky's, critique of Stalinism's putative elite bias through 1935 but also indicate that the social stratification of consumption diminished after 1935. Although one should keep in mind the existence of an underclass excluded from state-sector wages and benefits (houseservants, employees of cooperatives, artisans, etc.), blue-collar workers were gaining, not losing, ground. In this sense, although Stalin was premature in declaring to the 1935 Congress of Stakhanovites that the disparities between "manual" and "mental" laborers would be overcome through increasing prosperity and culture, his announcement did accurately forecast the trend of the late 1930s.[97]

STALINISM AND THE CONSUMER, II:
THE PEASANT CHALLENGE TO CULTURED TRADE

Rural budget data suggest that peasants caught the train of economic recovery a few years later than urban workers, a picture corroborated by the weakness of rural trade. The tractors and fertilizers channeled to the collective farms were not enough to compensate for the catastrophic loss of livestock during and after collectivization, and obligatory procurements continued to siphon off the bulk of the crop.[98] What finally im-

[96] RGAE, f. 1562, op. 15, d. 1119, ll. 90–94.
[97] Stalin, *Sochineniia* [14], 81–82, 89–90.
[98] See, again, the on-line appendix "Household Budget Data and Consumption Trends," as well as Gijs Kessler, "The Peasant and the Town: Rural-Urban Migration in the Soviet

proved peasants' lot was the bumper harvest of 1937—the best in recorded history. That year, for the first time since at least 1928, and quite possibly since 1915, significant quantities of such "cultured" goods as bicycles, grammophones, and sewing machines made their way to village shops.[99] In the end, however, rising incomes in the countryside proved a greater challenge to free, "cultured" trade than peasant poverty. Peasants' increased buying power coincided with the conversion of industry to military production; and, once again, urban shoppers had to compete with throngs of rural visitors for cotton cloth, sturdy shoes, and other basic consumer goods. When these queues undermined public order in Moscow, the commitment of central policy makers to "free trade" was seriously strained. Although the context differed in crucial ways from 1927—there were no private shops—it should come as no surprise that policy-makers eventually chose to attack the problem through repression and administrative restrictions. What followed was again predictable: reduced agricultural production and the rebureaucratization of trade.

An analysis of two episodes involving queues, that scourge of Soviet retailing, may shed light on both the policy dilemmas of the "free trade" interlude and the consumer attitudes and behaviors of the peasants. Interestingly, bureaucratization was not the outcome of queues connected with the 1936 crop failure, which several Western analysts have identified as the worst harvest of the decade and which created severe "food difficulties" the following winter and spring across the northern consuming zones. Peasants responded with their traditional crisis behaviors: hoarding reserves in the form of grain or dried rusks; traveling to near or distant towns in search of food; slaughtering livestock. A. S. Arzhilovskii, a former kulak who recently returned from exile to his home district near Tiumen', recorded in his diary the progressive deterioration of food supplies. A late October entry noted that "people used to shop just once a week, but now you have to chase around looking for bread every day." One month later queues were lengthening; people were "get[ting] into fistfights in the bread lines" and having to wait "six or eight hours at a time." Arzhilovskii's account underscored the poverty of the region's peasants and workers; through the first months of the crisis, expensive varieties of bread continued to languish on the cooperative shelves. The crisis peaked in late February, by which point queues were forming at

Union, 1929–1940" (Ph.D. diss., European University Institute, 2001), chap. 4. For a general portrait of the post-collectivization countryside, see Fitzpatrick, *Stalin's Peasants*.

[99] See *Sovetskaia torgovlia. Statisticheskii sbornik*, 58. Predictably peasants' "rising demand" was a major theme for the Soviet propaganda machine in 1937–38.

2:00 A.M. Rumors flourished in such a context—most often, in the Tiumen' region—of a typhus epidemic (the famine fever) or of a great war.[100]

Secret police reports from Leningrad oblast' provide further information about this episode. In northwestern Russia, too, "food difficulties" emerged in late 1936 in connection with the region's crop failure and intensified in February, when stocks were virtually depleted. Again peasants flocked to the towns, and teachers, workers, and low-level officials skipped work to join them in the long lines outside food shops. Everywhere, bread supplies were insufficient to meet consumer demand. After five to six hours of waiting, large contingents of customers were forced to go home empty-handed each day. The security organs identified one village where only 70 kilograms of bread were issued per day as against "an actual need of 350 kilograms." Lines formed four to six hours before stores opened in the morning at a time when temperatures dipped as low as −35 degrees. Fights broke out in a number of places; pushing, cursing, and noisy arguments were the norm. As in the revolutionary era, mothers brought their infants to the queue during store hours in the hope of persuading people to let them in out of turn. Naturally people tried to buy up as much bread as they could; peasants, in particular, set up camp on the outskirts of town and spent several days going from line to line.[101]

Three factors stand out in the sources on this episode. One is the repertoire of crisis behaviors, which proved unchanged in their essentials since 1917 and, in fact, bore a strong resemblance to crowd behaviors in famines around the world. A second, to be considered below, is the strong pull exerted by the bureaucratizing and repressive strands of socialist political culture on local policing organs, co-op managers, and party chiefs. The third is peasant consumers' attitudes, which stand out in relief as a result of the security organs' efforts to monitor moods in the queues. These attitudes, as in 1918 or 1930, were shaped by poverty and survivalism; peasants in the queues advised one another to buy up bread (and vodka and anything else) "before it's too late," so as to lay in reserves of dried rusks in advance of the rumored war. Peasant consumers also highlighted official discrimination: Arzhilovskii and others interpreted the discrepancy between low procurement prices and high retail prices as a form of "state speculation," and charges of a government conspiracy to starve the peasantry were widespread. Despite twenty years of Soviet enlightenment, peasants' understanding of the food crisis was also shaped

---

[100] "Diary of Andrei Stepanovich Arzhilovsky," in Véronique Garros et al., eds., *Intimacy and Terror* (New York, 1995), 111–65; here, 113, 139, 143–44, 148.

[101] TsAIPD Len., f. 24, op. 2v, d. 2418, ll. 65–74.

by the traditional peasant worldview. Apocalypse, a persistent theme in rural areas from 1929 to 1933, was strongly in evidence (e.g., "It is written in the Bible that in 1937 there will be a war and a great famine"); and with regard to the present, the scuttlebutt in every queue was that elsewhere lines were still longer and shortages more acute. In Belozersk rumor had it that children were freezing to death in the queues of Vologda, in the adjacent Northern oblast; in Pestovo peasants in the outlying districts were said to be starving to death.[102]

The conversations of peasants in the queues suggest a mentality that shared certain elements of urban popular communism—the survival orientation, and the condemnation of luxuries and of grain sales abroad. It was, however, much more openly hostile, showing little or no identification with the Soviet regime. Peasants standing in the February bread lines lashed out at the authorities with denunciations or outright threats: "If the president of the kolkhoz refuses to issue me grain, I'll slit his throat first and then do the same to the other members of the kolkhoz treasury"; or, "If the Communists don't provide us with bread, we'll shoot them all in a trice! If the situation doesn't improve, the people will revolt." In the incubator of an angry queue, speakers like these threw caution to the wind. The atmosphere of the queue encouraged the venting of frustration, anxiety, and antagonism toward the regime by fostering a sense of unanimity. Peasant speakers, in particular, considered hostility to the regime as a given: "the entire peasantry is against Soviet power"; "Not even a billygoat likes Soviet power, all because under Soviet rule there is neither bread nor anything else."[103]

It should be apparent that the 1937 bread lines represented a challenge to the newly enshrined principles of "free trade," not to mention retail "culture." Food shops everywhere reinstated or lowered limits on sales to "one set of hands." In Leningrad oblast' a few towns went further: in Pestovo a bread store was relocated to the grounds of the town's major factory hence was accessible only to employees, and in Olonets, in Karelia, bread stores shifted to distribution "by [social] categories." Even without rationing, that is, when push came to shove, local officials still thought in terms of provisions for their "primary constitutuency" [*osnovnoi kontingent*]—the overwhelmingly urban social groups that had been issued rations during the early 1930s.[104] Responding both to the crisis and

---

[102] Ibid.; Garros et al., *Intimacy and Terror*, 145–50. On apocalyptic rumors, see Fitzpatrick, *Stalin's Peasants*, 45–47; Lynne Viola, "The Peasant Nightmare: Visions of Apocalypse in the Soviet Countryside," *Journal of Modern History* 62, no. 4 (1990): 747–70.

[103] TsAIPD Len., f. 24, op. 2v, d. 2418, ll. 65–74.

[104] For other instances from the late 1930s when local officials protected the privileges of

to these "separatist" actions on the part of localities, the oblast' party organization flailed out in several directions: it ordered local governments to adhere to free trade; sent inspectors around to ensure compliance; scheduled an emergency, all-night meeting of the region's top politicians to discuss possible solutions to the bread problem; and telegraphed the Central Committee and the supply organs in increasingly frantic language for a supplementary grain allocation. No solution materialized, though in other regions the center's contribution was to fire and arrest all the supply officials.[105]

In Leningrad oblast' only the NKVD had a solution, namely, the time-honored approach of the security organs to supply disruptions: "speedy repressions." NKVD special agents who penetrated queues in every town arrested people if their expressions of dissatisfaction crossed the threshold into "terrorist statements," "counterrevolutionary conversations," "provocation," or "rumors about uprisings, war, or famine." Party leaders eventually caved in to this temptation as well. A notable example from Leningrad Province occurred in Sol'tsy, where a standing bread queue appointed a delegation to solicit the raion prosecutor and the local trade administration for more bread. NKVD agents, and eventually the Party, understood these emissaries from the bread line as "alarming signals" of a rebellious mood. They responded to the challenge by arresting petitioners as agitators and forcibly dispersing the queue when regional inspectors came to town.[106] One should note that these arrests, like the arrests of grain and leather dealers in 1927–28, flowed into a larger wave of repression: they formed part of an avalanche of cases of "anti-Soviet agitation" in early 1937, one of the major precedents for the unleashing of mass terror against vagrants, kulaks, and other perennial irritants to the regime in the middle of the year.[107]

Yet, for all that, "free trade" held on as state policy through the 1936–37 crisis.[108] This was very important: "free trade" was socially neutral, which enabled peasants to buy bread. If the 1936 harvest was, in fact, the worst of the decade, it was surely the policy of "free trade" that should be credited with preventing mass starvation. As the crisis ebbed, and especially as rural incomes rose in connection with the bumper crop of 1937, "free trade" also gave peasants the opportunity to seek manufactured consumer goods somewhere other than at their poorly stocked country

---

their *osnovnoi kontingent*, see ibid., d. 1537, l. 32; d. 1547, ll. 36, 41; op. 2g, d. 55, ll. 82–83; d. 89, l.59.

[105] Ibid., d. 2418, ll. 84–160; RGAE, f. 7971, op. 16, d. 29, ll. 13 (Ivanovo), 20 (Sverdlovsk), 52 (Belorussia).

[106] TsAIPD Len., f. 24, op. 2g, d. 57.

[107] See Solomon, *Soviet Criminal Justice*, 332.

[108] See, esp., RGAE, f. 7971, op. 16, d. 29, ll. 7–8.

stores. Shipments of bicycles and wristwatches notwithstanding, letters to the Leningrad obkom from rural areas in late 1937 and 1938 depicted a dysfunctional trade system: general stores with neither cloth nor clothing or with shoes in only one size. To cap it off, rural shops were so poorly organized and so few in number that, even with their dismal selections, they still suffered from queues.[109] The effect of rural prosperity was thus oddly similar to the effect of rural hardship: both encouraged peasants to travel to the city to stock up on essential goods.

During the winter of 1937–38 Moscow, Leningrad, and other major cities became inundated with provincial travelers in search of cotton cloth and other cheap consumer articles. City dwellers complained bitterly about the influx; letters soon reached provincial and central authorities about the migrants' deleterious effects on metropolitan trade:

> Every day between 9:00 and 11:00 A.M.—the opening hours of the Passazh department store on Nevsky Prospect—a crowd consisting of thousands of visitors from Ukraine, Belorussia, the Caucasus, and Central Asia, as well as our own speculators, protrudes from the sidewalk, and, like locusts, they descend on everything in their path, pushing forward in a mass, and taking everything that was on the shelves. A Leningrader goes without trousers, jackets, and underwear, while these locusts eat everything up.[110]

By April, top-level administrators had begun to take notice, not least because the shops most seriously affected were the country's "all-union model department stores": Passazh, TsUM, Dom Kooperatsii, the emporia of Khar'kov, Kiev, Sverdlovsk, Minsk. Policy makers predictably focused their attention on Moscow. A report in Molotov's archive identified February as the beginning of the capital's queue problem, which had since taken on a "scandalous and politically dangerous character." Queues were populated primarily by out-of-town visitors intending to purchase cotton cloth, clothing, and shoes. At TsUM, which opened its doors at 8:40 A.M., lines formed at 6:00 A.M.; by 8:00, some twenty thousand people snaked around the sidewalks of the entire quarter behind the Bol'shoi and Malyi Theaters in a gigantic double queue. As if that were not enough, "several thousand people gathered in clumps" at every street corner in the vicinity. The city placed two hundred policemen on duty outside TsUM each morning, but they found it virtually impossible to prevent the crowds from surging forward in a great crush once TsUM opened for the day.[111]

Again, this was spring 1938, at the midpoint of Stalin's terror. It is

---

[109] TsAIPD Len., f. 24, op. 2g, d. 89, l. 60; d. 149, l. 170.

[110] Ibid., ll. 169–70 (March 1938).

[111] RGASPI, f. 82, op. 2, d. 686, ll. 2–7. For a different version of the following episode, see Osokina, *Za fasadom*, 228–32. On late 1930s queues, see also Fitzpatrick, *Everyday Stalinism*, 45.

difficult to imagine that "administrative measures" were not applied here along with policing of a more routine kind. What we know is that the queues formed at 6:00 A.M. because the Moscow police had an order to prevent the formation of nighttime queues. The police were also authorized to search provincial travelers who had come to the capital for purchases and to seize any "excessive" quantities of goods they might find.[112] Thus the situation remained for months, though the number of visitors dropped with the start of the agricultural season. At the start of December, however, just weeks after Stalin's secret order halting the "mass operations" and, quite possibly, in connection with it,[113] the USSR Procuracy suddenly revoked the standing police warrant to break up overnight queues and banned unwarranted searches and seizures. Henceforth Moscow's police force was to restrict its involvement with nighttime queues to maintaining order. Meanwhile the number of provincial visitors once again began to mount. By the beginning of April 1939 there had been "a whole series of incidents of various kinds of hooliganism" in overnight lines.[114] According to Police Chief Kozyrev, who petitioned the USSR Council of People's Commissars to countermand the Procuracy directive, criminal and counterrevolutionary cases "not infrequently" developed out of nighttime queues; moreover (shades of the NEP!), Moscow's overnight queues had spawned "queuing specialists," who hired themselves out to would-be consumers for twenty to thirty rubles a night. Kozyrev concluded that the situation derived "not only from the shortage of goods" but also from the new restrictions placed on policing.[115]

The policing organs received support the next morning, when a spot check of overnight lines at fourteen department stores revealed that only five thousand of the fourteen thousand people in the queues were Moscow residents.[116] Once again, "speedy repressions" seemed the most efficient way of "restoring the economy's health," so on April 5 Sovnarkom secretly reinstated police powers to intervene in the nighttime queues. Again, the Moscow police force was instructed to prevent the

[112] When this order first came into effect is unclear. It was described in GARF, f. 5446, op. 23a, d. 1450, l. 31.

[113] For the text of the order, dated November 17, see *Moskovskie novosti*, June 21, 1992. The best historical accounts of the 1937–38 mass operations to date are Oleg Khlevniuk's "The Objectives of the Great Terror, 1937–1938," in *Soviet History, 1917–53* (New York, 1995), 158–76; idem, "Les mécanismes de la 'Grande Terreur' des années 1937–1938 au Turkménistan," *Cahiers du Monde russe* 39, nos. 1–2 (January–June 1998): 197–208; idem, *Politbiuro* (Moscow, 1996); Paul M. Hagenloh, "'Socially Harmful Elements' and the Great Terror," in Sheila Fitzpatrick, ed., *Stalinism: New Directions*, 286–308 (London, 2000).

[114] GARF, f. 5446, op. 23a, d. 1450, l. 31.

[115] Ibid., l. 13 (April 2, 1939).

[116] Ibid., l. 31.

formation of queues before the hour stores opened, fining "violators" (who, of course, remained in perfect innocence of this unpublished decree) one hundred rubles and arresting "especially malicious violators"—presumably anyone who put up a fight. The police also received the green light to deport "speculators" and other provincials who had "descended" [*naekhavshie*] on Moscow to buy up cloth, using as their pretext the defense of the passport regime. If a person was found with more than fifty meters of cloth, the whole amount was to be confiscated, albeit with compensation; a criminal investigation would look into a possible prosecution for speculation. The Procuracy was to root out and punish rural officials who issued fictitious documents authorizing travel to Moscow for cloth. Store personnel who aided speculation were to be prosecuted; the NKVD and the railroads were to develop measures to deter shopping trips. After this laundry list of punishments, the decree concluded with a single positive measure: the Moscow city government should open twenty-five new stores in working-class neighborhoods for cloth, clothing, and shoe sales, to be stocked at the expense of the existing trade network; this, presumably, would protect workers' access to goods.[117]

Policy makers' vacillation points up the fragility of the official policy of "free trade." The local police, of course, had every interest in deporting out-of-towners rather than putting up with their queues. Why central executives were willing to violate their own principles of free trade is another matter. As we saw in the first episode, they had not been willing to do so in the small towns outside Leningrad in 1937 and had, in fact, rebuked local authorities who prevented peasants from buying food. Policy makers' capitulation in 1939 surely reflected the special status of Moscow. No less than in the 1920s goods famine, Moscow interests had vocal advocates, who, by virtue of their proximity to the all-union government, had the ear of policy makers there. Stalin, Molotov, and other leaders could see for themselves the effects of nighttime queues. Since the "disorder" caused by out-of-town consumers was in their own courtyards, sidewalks, and streets, central policy makers were swayed by the "social order" logic of the policing organs to sacrifice the "social neutrality" logic of "free trade." In doing so, they opened the floodgates to police lobbying over other cities.[118] As long as manufactured goods were at issue, however, policy makers underlined the capital's exceptionalism.

---

[117] Ibid., ll. 72–74.

[118] The USSR Procuracy immediately petitioned to extend the ban on nighttime queues and authorization to deport out-of-towners to Leningrad, Minsk, Khar'kov, and Kiev (ibid., ll. 42–45).

The only other city to which the deportation order was extended was Leningrad, one month after the Moscow decree.[119]

As with so many "administrative measures" in the economic sphere, the effect of the ordinance was ambiguous. Queues may have become shorter as a result of the ordinance, but by no means did they disappear. Though they formed at a later hour, that, too, was problematic. One of the few criticisms that emerged at an April 9 meeting of department store managers was that although dispersing queues was understandable, "there's no need to create a situation where the people who have gathered before the opening of the store throw themselves at the door in a mob." At Store no. 3 of the Rostektsilshveitorg network, the crowds had "practically broken all the display cases and doors" in the few days since the enactment of the secret decree.[120] A month later queues were generally allowed to form a half-hour before stores opened. In the new stores on the outskirts of town, this kept the number of waiting customers down to a manageable 200 to 250 people, but a few stores continued to report phenomenal lines: up to 7,000 each morning at the USSR Trade Commissariat's Dzerzhinskii and Lenin department stores, and 4,000 at the Danilov dry goods store. The only solution that Moscow's trade department proposed was to eliminate the cotton cloth trade at the premiere stores.[121] In the meantime, a certain amount of finger-pointing went on between the shop managers and the police force, which was accused of exacerbating the confusion by permitting friends to step in at the head of the line or taking bribes or actually buying the goods themselves.[122]

This episode sheds an interesting, though not very flattering, light on the ethos of trade executives in the "cultured" venues. Like the policing organs, store managers monitored developments in the capital's queues for the next month; what stands out most prominently in these discussions and reports is metropolitan chauvinism with a strong anti-peasant tinge. As early as April 9 trade executives expressed their satisfaction with the new ordinance on the grounds that Muscovites now constituted the majority of shoppers. Focusing on the needs of their particular "primary contingent," they were only too happy to protect Moscow consumers' access at the travelers' expense. For the director of Mostorg's Store no. 131, for example, it was a matter of pride that he "pa[id] attention to the

[119] Ibid., l. 34 (SNK post. 591–91s, May 3, 1939).

[120] Ibid., l. 62.

[121] Ibid., ll. 67, 70–71.

[122] These allegations also surfaced in ibid., op. 24a, d. 2833, ll. 44–45; TsAIPD Len., f. 24, op. 2g, d. 215, ll. 2–3; Kotkin, *Magnetic Mountain*, 249.

makeup of the queue. If the first people in line are Moscow consumers, I accordingly issue the best goods." The director's preference notwithstanding, an eyebrow-raising 53 percent of his store's customers were from out of town in a spot check on May 5 (the systemwide norm was said to have declined to 5 to 10 percent).[123]

The changed social composition of the queues in favor of Muscovites elicited a slight shift in their objects: cotton cloth continued to top the list of desired goods, along with tin pots, kerosene lamps, and primus stoves; but more expensive woolen and silk cloth, ready-made clothing, and stylish shoes also generated long queues. Concentrating on store prestige as reflected in a higher-class consumer, store officials proved far more responsive to the latter demands and exerted pressure to expand these product lines. Among other characteristics, the customers for silk dresses were likely to be more "cultured" than their counterparts in the cotton queues. With those "peasants," a store manager, who had "ruined his voice" maintaining order before the implementation of the new decree, sniffed, "You go up to the line and ask, 'What are you waiting for?' and the answer is always the same, 'Whatever they're giving out.'"[124]

Like other city dwellers, the managers tended to equate provincial customers with "speculators"—an allegation notably absent from the secret police reports from the 1937 bread queues. Should we interpret this as a change in exchange practices or a difference in perception? On the one hand, a significant number of out-of-town buyers were, without doubt, planning to resell their cloth. Salesclerks, store managers, and policemen saw the same faces every day, and in the week after the decree the police confiscated 42,650 meters of cloth from provincial travelers who exceeded the 50-meter limit. Some of these travelers may have been hoarding out of fear of war, but most were probably planning to resell the cloth at a provincial bazaar. As we will see in chapter 6, travel to big cities was a major source, even *the* major source, of goods sold at the outdoor markets of provincial Russia. This commerce was actively desired by rural residents, as evidenced by the collective farm chairmen accused of issuing "fictitious documents" for travel to Moscow for cloth. No less than factory managers, collective farm chairmen had their own interest in hiring buying agents; from the provincial angle, this was not seen as speculation at all. So the goal of obtaining wares to resell was indeed common among out-of-town customers; on the other hand, there

[123] GARF, f. 5446, op. 23a, d. 1450, ll. 39, 63, 70–71.
[124] Ibid., ll. 62, 70. Central policy makers were also receptive to these demands, given their vision of cultured trade. In 1936 a secret TsK/SNK decree went into great detail about the manufacture of "fashionable shoes" (ibid., op. 18a, d. 309, ll. 97–101).

is no reason to conclude that that represented a change from 1937. Finally, there is no reason to think that provincial travelers were the only ones with an eye to resale. In Leningrad, in the same year, a group of working mothers attributed the problem of queues to unemployed housewives, "who have nothing else to do; they stand in line from morning to evening, they buy up everything, and then resell it at the market."[125] Moscow working-class customers, meanwhile, had taken to bringing in real or fictitious documents from the local vital registration bureau to the effect that the bearer had just suffered the death of a family member and that the store was obliged to issue ten meters of cloth for a shroud.[126]

G. A. Dikhtiar, the preeminent Soviet-era historian of trade, offered the following analysis of the shortages from 1938 to 1940:

> Notwithstanding the growth of consumption in the years of the prewar five-year plans, the population's effective demand for goods was far from fully satisfied. Not only that, the lagging rate of growth of retail sales vis-à-vis the plan meant that the discrepancy between sales and the population's consumption funds increased still further, since money incomes grew faster than was foreseen by the five-year plan. . . . The actual consumption fund of the country's urban and rural population, according to a calculation by the Commissariat of Trade's Scientific Research Institute, totaled 174 billion rubles in 1939. Retail sales in state and cooperative trade, including public catering, totaled just 166 billion rubles, i.e., considerably less than the public's consumption funds, and that is not even to speak of the fact that a percentage of the goods included in the sales figures were sold to state or public organizations and also to collective farms.[127]

Dikhtiar, in other words, had a clear picture of the root problem, and he also knew very well where the deficit primarily fell: "In connection with the general shortage of commodity resources and the necessity of supplying, in the first place, the laboring people of the most important industrial centers with goods (especially foods), the possibility of supplying the villages with these goods declined."[128] Thus, from 1938 to 1940,

> in the consumer cooperatives' rural trade we observe frequent interruptions in sales of everyday goods. . . . Of 2,717 rural shops investigated in various oblasts in March 1939, 452 did not have salt for sale, 454 lacked matches, and

---

[125] TsAIPD Len., f. 24, op. 2g, d. 149, l. 127. Lest this sound dismissive, housewives do appear to have constituted a large percentage of black market traders.
[126] GARF, f. 5446, op. 23a, d. 1450, l. 68.
[127] Dikhtiar, *Torgovlia* III, 115–16.
[128] Ibid., 116.

507 sugar. In Sverdlovsk oblast' nearly one-third of all rural shops were not selling household soap.[129]

In Dikhtiar's view, again, this was a regrettable, but unavoidable, effect of deteriorating economic conditions at the end of the 1930s, as the optimistic projections of the production of consumer goods during the Third Five-Year Plan were pushed aside by military needs. What we can add, with Elena Osokina, is that the prioritization of the "most important industrial centers" was maintained in part through repression and that it was natural primarily from a Stalinist point of view.[130] We might also add that policy makers reinforced the positive prioritization of metropolitan consumers with a characteristic negative campaign. As in 1927 or 1918, one way of preserving urbanites' privileged access to goods was to suppress peasants' effective demand; it is in this light, I believe, that we should understand the May 1939 decision to lop off one-fifth of the land in peasants' private plots.[131]

Was it inevitable that food shortages would follow these interventions, as in 1918 or 1928? This is a tantalizing, unanswerable question. According to Stephen Wheatcroft's calculations, the 1939 grain yield fell substantially below what one would predict from the meteorological data for that year.[132] Did the lack of incentives lead peasants to slack off? Whatever the case, successive years of mediocre grain harvests, combined with dwindling production from peasants' private plots, left the economic agencies struggling to supply the ballooning army and the major industrial centers. By early 1940 bread shortages yet again plagued the civilian economy—and now a queue and deportation order was extended to forty-one major cities.[133] Here again we see the basic reflexes of socialist crisis management: the centralization of supplies (notably the number of "planned" consumer goods increased from six to thirty between 1938 and 1940);[134] the war on the market, represented in this case by provincial "speculators"; and the prioritization of consumers according to their as-

---

[129] Ibid., 117.

[130] Osokina makes this argument with verve in *Za fasadom*.

[131] On this decision, see V. B. Ostrovskii, *Kolkhoznoe krest'ianstvo SSSR. Politika Partii v derevne i ee sotsial'no-ekonomicheskie rezul'taty* (Sarakov, 1967), 68–69; Fitzpatrick, *Stalin's Peasants*, 135; Osokina, "Liudi i vlast'," 21.

[132] Davies and Wheatcroft, *Economic Transformation*, 291.

[133] GARF, f. 5446, op. 24a, d. 2835, ll. 1–80. See also Osokina, "Liudi i vlast'"; Naum Jasny, *Soviet Industrialization, 1928–1952* (Chicago, 1961), 177–234; Nove, *Economic History*, 247–59; Roberta T. Manning, "The Soviet Economic Crisis of 1936–1940 and the Great Purges," in J. Arch Getty and Roberta T. Manning, eds., *Stalinist Terror: New Perspectives*, 116–41 (Cambridge, 1993).

[134] Dikhtiar, *Torgovlia* III, 102–3.

cribed political or economic importance. Let us return to Trotsky's remarks in the epigraph to part 2: "When the lines are very long, it is
necessary to appoint a policeman to keep order. Such is the starting point
of the Soviet bureaucracy. It 'knows' who is to get something and who
has to wait."

The deportation orders notwithstanding, central policy makers sought
to contain the pressures for bureaucratization. Sovnarkom and the Central Committee authorized the revival of closed trade networks for major
military factories as a sop to the defense industry but, in repeated instructions between 1939 and 1941, insisted that closed trade did not
mean the institution of daily consumption quotas. In fact, inspection reports from 1940 concerning the state of closed trade and catering in the
defense industry made clear that the government's intention was to increase food and clothing supplies to workers in this critical sector by
mobilizing factory managers to assist with provisionment, not to limit
their consumption in any way.[135] Other industries were prohibited from
opening closed distributors, and municipalities were forbidden to confine
inhabitants to any one store or to reduce the officially established limits
on food purchases. A struggle ensued between the center and the periphery; in one case the USSR prosecutor took an entire city executive committee to court for binding citizens to particular stores and restricting
them to six hundred grams of bread, bought once a day at an assigned
place. In another region the central Commissariat of Trade annulled a
decision by the oblast Party committee to institute closed trade and rationing in all towns. The threat of prosecution notwithstanding, local
and provincial authorities had unilaterally approved the reintroduction of
rationing in forty out of fifty republics, oblasts, and krais investigated by
the state trade inspectorate by the fall of 1940.[136]

In every region the machinery of rationing was honed by the centralized systems in place from 1918 to 1922 and from 1929 to 1935, but the
specifically local culture of socialism—the proprietary psychology—left a
strong imprint as well. There was, on the one hand, the effort to channel
supplies to the "primary contingent" of urban workers and functionaries
as against peasants, out-of-towners, and other "less important" consumers; on the other hand, local elites showed their propensity for feath-
ering their own nests. In the later 1930s local officials in many areas had
tried to hold onto their rationing-era prerogatives: instances have been
recorded of former closed distributors blocking entrance to all but their
ration-era clientele or of department stores maintaining lists of local not-

---

[135] GARF, f. 8300, op. 22, d. 1, ll. 1–13.
[136] Osokina, "Liudi i vlast'," 18–19.

ables and holding back the best goods for the wives of the men in power.[137] "Our women," in sum, had identified much more strongly with the glamorous values of "cultured trade" during the post-rationing era than with the democratic values of "free trade." Veitser's successor as Commissar of Trade, A. V. Liubimov, reported, in December 1940, that it was precisely local notables who had benefited most from the resurrection of closed distribution: special cafeterias and stores for nomenklatura had reappeared, with purchase limits significantly higher than those officially promulgated, and, crucially, guaranteed access to the "best goods." As local Party and government leaders were assumed to be behind these and similar "violations of the principles of Soviet trade," Liubimov asked that city executive committees be made criminally responsible for the unauthorized organization of elite closed stores.[138] Yet, who would go after them, when the local prosecutor also had his place at the "feeding trough"?

CONCLUSION

Chapters 4 and 5 have traced the evolution of "Stalinism" in trade and consumption. What have they revealed?

At the level of retail structure, Soviet trade underwent major changes as Stalinism coalesced. First and most striking among these changes was the disappearance of private shops, that is, the disappearance of most of the country's permanent retail network. A second lasting change was the socialist sector's move into luxury sales; as we have seen, this innovation had significant ramifications for how policy makers approached trade. Third, the transfer of consumer cooperatives' urban shops to the municipal or provincial state trade networks created a permanent organizational division between urban and rural lines of supplies. Beyond that, however, most structural changes in Soviet retailing proved temporary. The "restructuring" of trade from 1929 to 1931 produced what Alec Nove liked to call "economic irrationality": a crippling centralization of supplies, allocations, and decision making, combined with a hodgepodge of retail units and prices that collectively undermined confidence in the regime.[139] Policy makers were all too aware of these defects. In the end, socialist-

[137] TsAIPD Len., f. 24, op. 2v, d. 1199, l. 1; *Sovetskaia torgovlia* (newspaper), January 9, 1939; interview with Galina Petrovna, a nomenklatura wife.

[138] Osokina, "Liudi i vlast'," 18–19.

[139] Nove used this term to describe an economic policy based on "arbitrary or noneconomic criteria"—the opposite of one that achieved "maximum results" at "a minimum real cost." See his *Economic Rationality and Soviet Politics*, 51.

sector trade reverted to something very like the NEP structure: shops and networks were constrained with regard to pricing, but they relied heavily on contractual (market-based) agreements with farms and factories for supplies and used "representatives" to conclude most deals.

At the policy level, the major innovation of the 1930s was the concept of cultured trade. With it, Stalin steered his country firmly in the direction of modernization, Westernization, and the money nexus, and away from revolutionary "products exchange." Yet even cultured trade was not completely alien to Bolshevik ideas. Lenin himself, in 1923, wrote of the need to transform cooperatives through the inculcation of "culture." His comments on the subject reveal significant differences with the Stalinist agenda, notably in his emphasis on collective economic decision making as a vehicle for self-actualization. Nonetheless, he explicitly identified socialism with every citizen's ability to "be a cultured trader" [*byt' kul'turnyim torgashom*], which would in turn form the basis for "civilized cooperatives"; he also connected that ability with modernization and the West. "Today he trades in an Asiatic manner," he wrote of the Russian peasant, "but to be a capable trader, he has to trade in a European manner. A whole epoch divides him from that."[140] As we will see in chapter 6, Stalin took up this challenge: his 1932 endorsement of the "collective-farm market" may have appeared a concession to "Asiatic" trading habits, but even bazaars were made subject to modernizing plans.

Stalin's "cultured trade" agenda also resonated with Bolshevik aspirations insofar as it was linked with socialist consumerism. While the glamorous new stores of the capitals have led several scholars, myself among them, to discern in Stalinism the *embourgeoisement* of the revolution—a "Great Retreat," in the phrase of the émigré sociologist Nicholas Timasheff, from the Bolsheviks' revolutionary values to the values held by society at large[141]—I now believe that we overstated the novelty of the mid-1930s policy. Newspaper columns in the early 1920s had sounded a similar note, in part because of the propaganda limitations of asceticism after nearly a decade of war and deprivation, but also in part because the Bolsheviks understood the revolution to promise workers a richer material life. Every Party faction wanted workers to eat better, dress better, live in more spacious and salubrious lodgings, and enjoy the cultivated

[140] Lenin, "O kooperatsii," *PSS*, 45:369–77, here, 373. "Culturedness," "cultural revolution," and "culture" appear numerous times in this essay as the stumbling blocks between Russia and the attainment of socialism.

[141] Nicholas S. Timasheff, *The Great Retreat: The Growth and Decline of Communism in Russia* (New York, 1946); Fitzpatrick, "Becoming Cultured"; Hessler, "Cultured Trade"; Vadim Volkov, "The Concept of *Kul'turnost*,'" in Fitzpatrick, *Stalinism: New Directions*, 210–30. Vera Dunham, in her influential study, *In Stalin's Time*, dated *embourgeoisement* to the postwar 1940s.

leisure that had formerly differentiated the "exploiting classes" from the "laboring masses." If publicity about material progress became muted at the end of the 1920s, this surely reflected the dire economic situation—admittedly to a considerable degree of the Party's own making—rather than a conversion to austerity as an ideal.

The continuities between Bolshevism and Stalinism are much more striking at the level of political culture. Here, as earlier, I use this term to connote something pre-ideological—those "subjective factors" or "psychological" propensities that informed Soviet actions both in the center and on the ground. The elements of Stalinist political culture most salient to distribution and consumption included the dynamic tension between bureaucratization and the "struggle against bureaucratism." They included officials' reactions to a perceived crisis, especially if that crisis involved bread. They included the preference for a modern, industrial, urban economy—and, along with it, a willingness to sacrifice peasants' interests in the short and even medium term. They included the high-handed approach to private and cooperative property; the "proprietary psychology"; the obsession with Moscow. Finally, and perhaps most striking in the decade we have just covered, they included an exceptional proclivity to intertwine commercial policy with mass repression. In every single one of these characteristics, Stalinism was the direct heir of the political culture of the revolution and the NEP. For our story, there is just one important distinction in the Bolshevik and Stalinist political cultures: mendacity, which Lenin's Party had largely abjured.

Finally, what did Stalinism mean at the level of material culture? Like the first postrevolutionary decade, the second decade progressed through a series of stages from survival-threatening scarcity to mundane shortages alongside economic growth. The latter phase, with which this chapter ended, presents an intriguing contrast: on the one hand, there were the indifferent customers of the cotton queues and, on the other, the heightened demand for attractive shoes. Should we, perhaps, interpret this duality as evidence of a global shift in Soviet society—that a survival-oriented material culture had begun to give way to a new interest in fashion and individuation through consumption on the part of a growing consuming elite? This was indeed how Soviet publicists depicted the situation. The late-1930s press was filled with celebratory descriptions of the new, cultured Soviet consumer of the free-trade era. This "new consumer" did not just stand in line for whatever was being offered but thought about his or her purchases and went comparison-shopping for the prettiest teaspoons or the freshest bread.[142] Even in internal discus-

---

[142] For example, *Sovetskaia torgovlia* (newspaper), January 2, 1935; *Za industrializatsiiu*, January 2, 1935; Fitzpatrick, "Becoming Cultured," 224–25.

sions, the trade bureaucracy was intoxicated by this vision. As Commissar Veitser (notorious for his ill-fitting suits and asceticism) announced to a closed meeting in 1935:

> This is an altered consumer—a new consumer, who has grown more cultured; a literate consumer, who lives well, for whom life has become happier and easier; a consumer who has already ceased to think, as he thought before, that all he needs in life are his rations for bread or meat. Now he is already thinking about how to buy a piano, a musical instrument, attractive furniture for his home, a good lamp.[143]

By 1939 peasants were said to have conceived a desire for books and musical instruments; even children, publicists proclaimed, were becoming "more demanding."[144]

Given the rise in consumer expectations and opportunities in the mid-1930s, this depiction does have some merit. It would nonetheless be unwise to accept it without modification, since individuated, self-expressive, luxury-oriented consumption was not, in fact, something new. There had been a thin stratum of luxury consumers before the revolution, and the Soviet Union continued to have them in the 1920s as well. What changed in the 1930s was the social profile of these consumers and where they shopped for goods. Wealthy prerevolutionary merchants and aristocrats, Nepmen, and bourgeois professionals did their shopping at private stores. In the 1930s, by contrast, the people who bought silk dresses were "our" Soviet people, and they shopped at Soviet state stores. What the 1930s did, then, was not to introduce modern consumerism to the Russian context but to democratize it, by making it available to citizens from the popular classes—but only if they lived in the big cities or had connections or happened by some miracle to be in the right place at the right time.

It seems fitting to end this discussion, and this chapter, with the strongest element of continuity between Bolshevism and Stalinism in material culture: the queue. Queues lengthened or shortened, depending on the economic conjuncture, but shortages accompanied every phase of Soviet power in the interwar period with the sole exception of 1922–23. In part, queues resulted from Soviet wage and price policies, which created a disequilibrium between the available "commodity fund" and the population's "consumption fund"—this time, with the exception of 1935. They were also the product of socialist methods of production, whose pres-

---

[143] RGAE, f. 7971, op. 1, d. 105, l. 55. On Veitser's asceticism, see the memoir by his wife, children's theater director Nataliia Sats, *Novelly moei zhizni* (Moscow, 1973), 335–38.

[144] *Sovetskaia torgovlia* (newspaper), January 30, 1939; RGAE, f. 7971, op. 1, d. 250, l. 31.

sures and incentives have been described elsewhere.[145] For Stalinism's "new consumers"—the broad urban strata that emerged out of the extreme poverty of 1932–33 to enjoy a little discretionary income from 1935 to 1939—it was shortages, more than anything, that gave the lie to the linkage of cultured trade with material progress. Advertisements, commodity expositions, and model department stores stimulated demands that were unsatisfiable, as consumers demonstrated vividly at a 1936 conference accompanying an exposition of children's wares. Speaking to interested nonspecialists, the Commissariat of Domestic Trade's representative dutifully recited the Stalinist litany on "culturedness" and the "new consumer":

> We mustn't forget that our life has become better, that "life has become happier," and if just a short time ago our customers accepted everything that they were given, today they don't want to be limited to that. The consumer says, "It's not enough that an item fits, it's not enough that it suits my price range; I want it to be attractive, I want it to be pretty in its external appearance." The same object can be made attractive and festive or crude and ugly. . . . It should be the kind of thing, as one Stakhanovite said, to make the soul rejoice when one buys it or wears it.[146]

Though citizens at the conference expressed their eagerness to supply their children with "cultured," attractive goods, Deputy Commissar Levenson sparked anger and derision for this outrageous assertion of material satisfaction. "Now we've seen that at the exhibition there are all imaginable things, and that's all very well, but they aren't in the stores and you won't find them," one listener jeered. And another added, "You may talk about the soul rejoicing at pretty goods, but the only reason the 'soul rejoices' when we buy things now is that goods are so hard to get."[147]

---

[145] See, esp., Kornai, *Socialist System*.

[146] RGAE, f. 7971, op. 1, d. 250, l. 2.

[147] Ibid., ll. 16, 18.

Crisis: War

This market was none other than the bitter offspring of war, of wartime shortages, high prices, poverty, food-supply problems. Here you could buy everything. Sharp, unshaven, cunning youths, wearing soldiers' greatcoats from other men's backs, could palm off or resell anything imaginable. Here people sold bread and vodka, received first as rations at state stores; here they sold penicillin and lengths of cloth stolen from wholesale bases, American jackets and condoms, "war trophy" bicycles and motorcycles brought in from Germany. Here people sold stylish mackintoshes, cigarette lighters of foreign makes, bay leaves, hand-made rubber boots, German hair-growth treatments, watches and fake diamonds, old furs and false documents and diplomas from every type of institute. Here people sold everything that could possibly be sold, that could possibly be bought, for which one could possibly receive money, which had in turn lost its value. And people paid up with all kinds of cash, from pathetic-looking, soiled chervontsy and red thirty-ruble notes to solidly crackling hundreds. In the narrow alleys of the enormous market people darted about and slithered like eels, all animated, notable for their nervous faces and quick, dully-intoxicated glances. Rings glittered on dirty fingers as their owners muttered hoarsely, secretly offering clandestine wares; at the approach of a policeman they disappeared, dispersing into the crowd, appearing again in gateways that reeked of urine, looking around in all directions, beckoning customers in whispers to the depths of courtyards abutting the market. There, by the garbage bins, gathering in groups, they quickly and furtively showed their wares, cursing excitedly.

The market was flooded with speculators and craftsmen from who knows where, recently demobilized soldiers, collective farmers from the surrounding regions, Moscow thieves, people travelling on business, people buying a scrap of bread to eat, and others trading so as to go home that evening and after a warm, solid meal and a little vodka (after all, they spent the whole day in the cold), to enjoy the sweet feeling of counting, recounting, and hiding away a packet of money.

—Iurii Bondarev, *Silence*

CHAPTER SIX

The Persistent Private Sector

STALIN'S "SOCIALIST RESTRUCTURING" aimed, among other goals, at modernizing the Soviet economy. Industry, which swallowed up unprecedented rates of capital investment in the decades after 1928, is the textbook example, but other sectors registered the modernizing impulse as
well. Collectivization was supposed to facilitate the adoption of tractors
and other labor-saving machines; promote agronomic science; and eliminate inefficiencies connected with farming on a small scale. Even trade
became subject to a modernizing agenda in the early 1930s, as exem-
plified by the campaign for "culturedness" and the closure of particularly
"primitive" village cooperatives. In light of Stalin's strong identification
with socialist modernization, his endorsement of the peasant market in
May 1932 seems aberrant. Outdoor bazaars were a vestige less of capitalism than of Eurasia's traditional economy—the "petty commodity-pro-
ducing *uklad*." Policy makers' approach to the bazaar after 1932 was defined by the familiar logic of "utilization", that is, they deemed it a
necessary supplement to socialist-sector food supplies, but they also
hoped to transform the markets along the lines of socialist modernization. However, these projects met with structural impediments for
the remainder of the Stalin era, and they were jettisoned entirely during
the war.

Readers should be alerted to one of the themes of this chapter,
namely, the expanded role of the bazaar in the war period. The epigraph
to part 3, taken from a novel set in 1945–46, describes one of Moscow's
busiest and most renowned wartime bazaars—essentially the Sukharevka
of the 1940s. While peasant marketing declined precipitously after the
German invasion for all the reasons one might expect (the occupation of
much of the country's best agricultural land; the loss of men and draft
animals to the army; the conversion of agricultural machinery plants to
the production of tanks, and so forth), the *tolkuchki*, or flea markets,
flourished as citizens once again found themselves pressed to sell off surplus possessions to pay for essential foods. At the same time, the other
gray areas on the margins of socialism—small-scale, service-sector businesses and artisanal trades—expanded as the war progressed. All in all,
the role played by petty private enterprise at the end of the Great Patri-

otic War can be compared only to what Lev Kritsman called the "heroic period of the Great Russian Revolution," 1918 to 1921, and also to the first year or so of the NEP.

As we have seen, policing and extralegal repression were the usual reactions of the Stalinist establishment to undesirable forms of exchange. It should come as no surprise that they continued to be applied to the markets after 1932. In striking contrast to previous crises, however, the war elicited a softer approach to illegal and quasi-legal marketing. Having learned his lesson in 1931–32, Stalin did not want to repeat his, and before him Lenin's, mistake of "going too far ... in the direction of shutting down local sales" in a period of national emergency. The relaxation of punishment both fueled the expansion of informal trade and strengthened its openly transgressive features.

This chapter traces the evolution of private trade after 1932 with respect to its social forms, economic functions, and relationship to the state. The first section explores the development of Stalin-era bazaars from their permanent legalization in 1932 to the years after the Second World War. These bazaars had two guises: peasant markets, which were clearly endorsed by the regime and which officials constantly sought to channel in a socialist direction, and flea markets, which combined legal and illegal transactions in a more problematic way. The second section considers the revival of "bagging" during the war against a constant backdrop of unauthorized travels in small-town market trade. Next, the chapter outlines the revitalization of private enterprise at the end of the war. The chapter's final section attempts to provide a longer-term perspective by comparing the social organization of the informal private sector of the Stalin era with the formal enterprises of the NEP.

STALIN-ERA BAZAARS

For historians outside economic history, where this is familiar knowledge, surely what is most remarkable about the Stalin-era "kolkhoz market" is that it continued to purvey such a substantial portion of urban food supplies. Since socialized agriculture was not much of a presence at the markets in this period, peasants' market trade should be understood as a legal private sector in Soviet agriculture.[1] In 1939—ten years after collectivization—this private sector furnished 33 percent (in kilograms) of white-collar households' potatoes, 46 percent of other vegetables, 60 percent of fruits and berries, 54 percent of milk, 27 percent of butter, and

---

[1] See Karl-Eugen Wädekin, *The Private Sector in Soviet Agriculture*, trans. Keith Bush, ed. George F. Karcz (Berkeley, 1973), 10–19.

46 percent of meat and meat products, including 58 percent of fresh meat. Workers, who were more likely to receive food packages from relatives in the country and to cultivate vegetable gardens, got a slightly lower percentage of most foods there. These are all-union averages; the percentages were much lower in the capitals, but the nonagrarian population of large swaths of the country bought virtually all food besides bread, rice, and grain products at the market.[2]

Socialist restructuring clearly did not erase the "multiplicity of ways of life" [mnogoukladnost'] that ideologues identified as the defining feature of the NEP. Based on individual peasants' farms and, increasingly, collectivized peasants' personal plots and livestock, kolkhoz markets retained what Basile Kerblay called "their traditional visage as peasant markets."[3] Policy makers' willingness to accept peasant marketing as a component of socialist trade rested on the belief that this "traditional visage" could be supplanted by an updated, socialist visage: one dominated by socialized farms, offering abundant food at a low price, and sharing the attributes of "cultured Soviet trade." These goals shaped central policy toward the market as early as 1932, though, for the duration of the famine, they were routinely shunted aside in favor of temporary market closures, "administrative measures," and the Soviet polity's standard repertoire of techniques for displacing food from the market to the procurement agencies.[4]

Cultured trade, as applied to the bazaar, had little to do with the opulence of Gastronom No. 1. At most, it included a range of services for peasant vendors; on a more rudimentary level, a "cultured" market had the garbage cleared out at the end of each day. Predictably markets in most cities did not measure up to either standard; throughout the prewar period trade officials deplored their "uncultured" state. From 1932 to 1934 these complaints registered the continuing role of private dealers and independent peasants, who often proved more willing to comply with sanitary regulations than did collectivized peasants or collective farms.[5] As of 1935 "resellers" and "private traders" no longer figured prominently in administrators' discussions of peasant marketing, but sanitary problems persisted. At a conference on kolkhoz markets at the Commissariat of Domestic Trade, the occasional deputy bragged about the "snow-white smocks" and order of his markets, but most expressed

[2] RGAE, f. 1562, op. 15, d. 1077, ll. 64, 36; f. 7971, op. 5, d. 2, ll. 39–40.

[3] Kerblay, Les marchés paysans, 131. On the role of the "personal subsidiary farm" (i.e., private plot and livestock) in peasants' marketing and consumption, see Ostrovskii, Kolkhoznoe krest'ianstvo, 68–83, and Kessler, "The Peasant and the Town," 107–13, 174–9.

[4] For temporary decrees relating to the market from 1932 to 1934, see O bor'be so spekuliatsiei (Moscow, 1942), 3–7, 19, and Kerblay, Les marchés paysans, 128–32.

[5] GA Odes. ob., f. R-710, op. 1, d. 263, ll. 4–6; GARF, f. 5446, op. 15a, d. 1071, l. 14.

Figure 7. Peasant bazaar in Bashkiria, 1932. *Courtesy of the Russian State Archive for Cinematic and Photographic Documents (RGAKFD).*

embarrassment about poor facilities, inadequate trash cleanup, and, especially in small-town markets, ankle-deep mud (figure 7). Even the Arbat market in Moscow, where "diplomats shop," suffered from a deficit of low-level culturedness. Because of an iron shortage, peasant stalls were roofless against the rain and snow, and as late as November 1936 a foreign visitor described the "cold, ragged, underfed men and women" at the Arbat market, who "sat on the stone floor all day trying to sell their dirty sacks of meat."[6]

In the first half of the decade the more ambitious goal for the outdoor markets was to enable peasant vendors to obtain all necessary goods and services on site. Two instructions were sent down to the localities on this subject in the summer of 1932, ordering municipal soviets to open barbershops, veterinary offices, smithies, bootmakers, and legal offices. In Odessa administrators talked endlessly that summer about opening up "cultured cafés" with spigots for peasants to wash their hands.[7] Inns and

[6] RGAE, f. 7971, op. 1, d. 88, ll. 2, 6–8, 15–16, 25–26; *Stakhanovets torgovli,* December 14, 1936 ("Griaz', beskul'tur'e"); Connolly, *Soviet Tempo,* 19.

[7] GA Odes. ob., f. R-710, op. 1, d. 263, ll. 4–6; *Biulleten' finansovogo i khoziaistvennogo zakonodatel'stva,* no. 43 (September 13, 1932): 29–30.

flophouses in the environs of bazaars were to be converted into peasant hostels (Doma Krest'ianina) with a range of conveniences: a secure spot for horses and carts; indoor plumbing; nourishing, inexpensive meals; a movie theater; a library; and regularly scheduled lectures on agricultural themes.[8] Not surprisingly the hostels did not always meet these standards, and where they did, the proprietary psychology could divert them to other uses. Odessa's newly refurbished Dom Krest'ianina housed actors, business travelers, and city officials in 1933, and similar conditions prevailed in Sverdlovsk, Samara, and Kursk.[9] The center's impractical announcement that an array of services should instantaneously appear at the markets thus elicited an equally typical sequence of reactions: sluggish, partial, and occasionally deceptive implementation on the part of local officials, who had more pressing priorities to worry about, followed by a volley of accusations over who was to blame.

The provisionment of new socialist-sector shops at the marketplace was subject to a similar set of contradictory pressures in 1932–33. Now that the market's private shops had gone out of business, central authorities instructed state and cooperative trade organizations to increase the number of their outlets at the markets and to orient their business toward the peasant consumer. These outlets, referred to as the "greeting trade" [vstrechnaia torgovlia], were intended to serve a function similar to the "stimulation" campaigns, that is, to induce peasants to market a larger share of their produce through the promise of desirable goods.[10] What, in fact, occurred in 1932–33 was that the food crisis inhibited peasant marketing while the financial crisis inhibited the expansion of the trade network. Trade organizations procrastinated about organizing shops at the markets, and, when they did, the new shops were all too often either undersupplied (as in the case of Odessa, where the municipal cooperative issued just one-tenth as many manufactured goods to these shops as it was supposed to) or supplied with overstock luxuries: expensive perfumes, silks, fashionable shoes, hats "that the city population had already rejected," all totally unappealing to the peasant consumer.[11]

To add insult to injury, socialist trade organizations did not immediately disavow the discriminatory practices that they had adopted, with

[8] For an ideal depiction, see the newsreel on Moscow's Dom Krest'ianina, RGAKFD 2616; see also M. I. Kalinin, *O sovetskoi torgovle* (Moscow, 1932), 13.

[9] *Biulleten' finansovogo i khoziaistvennogo zakonodatel'stva*, no. 43 (September 13, 1932): 29–30; GA Odes. ob., f. R-710, op. 1, d. 263, ll. 4–6; f. 1234, op. 1, d. 1655, ll. 2–4, 6–8; *Snabzhenie, kooperatsiia, torgovlia*, October 14, 1932.

[10] Cf. *KPSS v rezoliutsiiakh*, 5:46–52; Kalinin, *O sovetskoi torgovle*, 13.

[11] GA Odes. ob., f. 1234, op. 1, d. 1655, l. 2; *Snabzhenie, kooperatsiia, torgovlia*, July 1, 6, and 20, 1932; August 10, 1932.

official backing, at the end of the NEP. Although the greeting trade was supposed to encourage all farmers to market their crops for cash, many shops refused to sell to peasants without certification of membership in a collective farm; others charged them a certain number of eggs or butter over and above the list price. Still another common practice (chronic in Soviet shops since the revolutionary period) was the "compulsory assortment" [*prinuditel'nyi assortiment*], or refusal to sell a popular item without the customer also agreeing to purchase articles that would otherwise sit on the shelf.[12] Classed in the press under the rubric of "distortions of Soviet price policy," these practices reflected the low profit margins of the greeting trade, which was supposed to sell at a discount.[13]

Policy statements attributed the weak performance of "collective farm trade" in 1932–33 to the unavailability of lodging, services, and manufactured goods at the bazaar, and also to the activities of private middlemen.[14] This was obfuscation: the steep price increases and feeble deliveries of 1932–33 can be explained by reference to scarcity alone. As soon as the famine ended, peasants greatly increased the volume of food that they carted to the markets, whether or not the greeting trade had improved. Deliveries to the country's largest cities were estimated to have grown by 70 percent between 1933 and 1934 and by a factor of four and a half or five between 1932 and 1937.[15] Nonetheless, the dearth of manufactured goods and the service deficit were genuine failings, which might, in ordinary times, affect the volume of trade. As such, they continued to be highlighted as a brake on peasants' marketing through 1935.[16]

The trade organizations eventually did establish a variety of shops at the markets, but the waning of political interest in the greeting trade derived only in part from the achievement of this aim. Equally important, the economic expansion of the mid-1930s evoked a new optimism over the possibility of transforming peasant marketing along socialist lines. Although they did not renege on the promise implicit in the 1932 legislation and outlaw peasants' private sales, policy makers sought to supplant autonomous peasant trade, at market prices, with contractual deliveries [*kontraktatsiia*] at a lower, predetermined price. The economic administration thus put much more energy in the later 1930s into "commoditizing" these contracts with manufactured goods [*otovarivanie*] than

[12] *Snabzhenie, kooperatsiia, torgovlia*, July 3 and 20; August 1, 1932; TsAIPD Len., f. 24, op. iv, d. 411, l. 40; GA Odes. ob., f. 1234, op. 1, d. 1655, l. 2.

[13] Cf. *Snabzhenie, kooperatsiia, torgovlia*, August 17 and 24, 1932.

[14] See, esp., *KPSS v rezoliutsiiakh*, 5:49, Kalinin, *O sovetskoi torgovli*.

[15] On the increase in volume, see *Kolkhoznaia torgovlia* (Moscow, 1935), 16; and Dikhtiar, *Torgovlia* II, 389, 414–15. On prices, see Malafeev, *Istoriia tsenoobrazovaniia*, 194–196, and Kerblay, *Les marchés paysans*, 132–36.

[16] RGAE, f. 7971, op. 1, d. 88, l. 28 and passim.

into the provisioning of market shops.[17] In 1927 Stalin had identified *kontraktatsiia* as the vanguard of "new mass forms of trade"; its revival after 1934 illustrates the extent to which 1930s trade policy was conceived as an extension of the socialist-sector policy of the NEP.

Likewise, economic administrators hoped to increase the proportional role of socialized agriculture. In this aim they failed, in large part because the kolkhozy preferred to distribute marketable surpluses to their members either as wages for labor-days or in the form of discounted sales.[18] Published sources indicate that collective farms accounted for roughly 10 percent of total market sales in 1935 and 16 percent in 1937, but an unpublished report maintained that collective farms instituted regular deliveries only in 1939. That year, Leningrad had one of the higher recorded rates of kolkhoz participation at 5 percent of sales; in Moscow the percentage ranged from 2–4 percent each month. Gor'kii, Stalino, and many other cities reported that collective farms traded no more than "periodically."[19] All in all, the "kolkhoz" component of "kolkhoz trade" was conspicuous mainly for its absence in the period before the Second World War.

Trade inspectors ascribed the reluctance of collective farms to trade at the markets to the lack of stationary booths and stalls or, where these existed, to high rents. The construction of new stalls figured prominently in the late-1930s plan for infrastructural improvements at the markets. Unfortunately, with the exception of Moscow and a few other metropolitan centers, this plan regularly went unfulfilled.[20] Explanations of sanitary lapses and other shortcomings in the administration of bazaars meanwhile shifted to reflect the poisoned political climate of the period. When the Trade Commissariat's market administration surveyed eighty republican and provincial capitals in April 1938 and found that 40 percent of the marketplaces of these cities were unpaved, 50 percent lacked hygienic stations for testing milk and meat or both, and 50 percent lacked overnight refrigeration or storage, bureaucrats were no longer inclined to blame shortages or other impersonal causes. Rather, the report ascribed the problems to saboteurs:

> Wreckers in charge of the trade organs deliberately tried to reduce the space for collective farms and kolkhozniks, creating conditions whereby a collective farmer has to wait in line for a trading spot and in the meantime to trade from the bare earth. . . . Wreckers from the financial agencies used every means to

[17] Kerblay, *Les marchés paysans*, 131; Neiman, *Vnutrenniaia torgovlia*, 149.
[18] Ostrovskii, *Kolkhoznoe krest'ianstvo*, 57–61; Whitman, "Kolkhoz Market," 388–89.
[19] Whitman, "Kolkhoz Market," 388; Kerblay, *Les marchés paysans*, 145; RGAE, f. 7971, op. 5, d. 2, ll. 39–47; d. 10, ll. 5–10.
[20] Ibid., d. 4, l. 34.

hold up the markets' assets for a whole fiscal year, and then assigned them to the local governments' general funds (Iaroslavl', Omsk, and Cheliabinsk oblasts, Armenian SSR, Krasnoiar krai, etc.). Wreckers from the agriculture and health organs obstructed the expansion of the network of meat and milk control stations, deliberately creating queues at the existing control stations and forcing kolkhozniks to wait in line a full day and more just to have their produce checked.[21]

This list went on, but the difficulty was that neither municipalities nor collective farms had an incentive to invest in structural improvements at the markets. They were highly profitable as it was; between licensed peasant and artisanal traders and the numerous citizens paying one-time hawkers' fees, the bazaars brought hundreds of thousands of rubles a year into municipal coffers (more than three million in Moscow in 1934).[22]

The focus on the negative in official documents makes it easy to overlook those modernizing changes that did occur over the course of the decade. In Moscow, the showcase city, downtown markets undoubtedly become more "cultured" in the sense that indoor trading halls were constructed and sanitation standards improved.[23] Another very noticeable change, not unrelated to sanitation, was the disappearance of livestock from most urban markets after 1935. Whereas the mass slaughter of livestock in from 1929 to 1932 did not prevent live animals from generating one-quarter of market sales through the middle of the decade, this quotient declined very rapidly thereafter in connection with several discrete trends. The first was the regime's successful elimination of private livestock traders [skupshchiki] in the middle of the decade—an achievement that should presumably be attributed to repression. Second, the considerable increase in refrigeration capacity at the markets facilitated the sale of meat, which was easier for peasants to transport. Third, while urban workers may have actually renewed their ties to farming in the 1930s through factory farms and allotments, trade unions typically supplied the chicks or rabbits for these ends. Finally, this may be an area in which material culture was shifting in the big cities. Surely, by the late 1930s, one was less likely to see a cow in an urban courtyard than a decade before.[24]

The socialist transformation of the farmers' markets would have been difficult enough, but outdoor bazaars traditionally nourished other types

---

[21] Ibid., d. 40, ll. 1–2.

[22] GARF, f. 5446, op. 16a, d. 404, l. 16.

[23] RGAE, f. 7971, op. 5, d. 4, l. 34.

[24] Dikhtiar, Torgovlia II, 415; Kerblay, Les marchés paysans, 143. See Kabo, Ocherki rabochego byta, 36, for cows in Moscow in the mid-1920s.

of petty trade as well. In particular, urban residents had relied on bazaars as a source of used clothing and inexpensive household articles since time immemorial, and, as we have seen, they also used the bazaars to supplement their incomes during periods of financial stress. Acknowledging this function, the 1932 legislation had permitted citizens to sell their used possessions at the market, ordinarily in an unequipped space to the side of the main trading area, for a twenty-kopeck day-use fee. In the later 1930s bazaar sales dropped back from nearly 8 percent of working-class household incomes to 2 percent,[25] but flea markets remained a hub of life and activity, and they continued to furnish citizens with an appreciable percentage of their consumer goods (figure 8). In 1935 urban workers were getting 28 percent of their shoes and ready-to-wear clothing "from private citizens or at the market," according to TsUNKhU's budget surveys,[26] and there were indications—probably less reliable than the budget surveys but taken seriously at the top echelons of power—that this may have understated the market's role. One example that circulated in policy reports came from a working-class dormitory in Cheliabinsk, where an in-depth study of consumption habits showed that of 706 inhabitants, 512 had purchased their most recent pair of shoes at the bazaar.[27] Moscow's gigantic outdoor flea market, Iaroslavskii Market, was in all likelihood the USSR's most widely visited attraction in the 1930s, drawing an estimated three hundred thousand shoppers on a typical Saturday in 1935.[28]

It should not be difficult to conjure up an image of the 1930s bazaar. In atmosphere, what impressed official observers most forcibly was the "crush" of people [tolcheia], the shoving, jostling, and lack of breathing space [tolkotnia], and the general confusion that together gave the flea market its traditional name, tolkuchka [Ukr., tolchok].[29] Otherwise, its distinguishing feature was the throngs of hawkers who, like the 1928 "kerb-merchants" described in chapter 4, stood in rows or in any open space, holding out for inspection a small number of wares. It is unclear whether they loudly accosted shoppers, as in the 1920s, or stood silently, as in 1991, but they inevitably spilled out of the confines of the area designated for "trade from the hands" [torgovlia s ruk] onto neighboring alleys

[25] Calculated from RGAE, f. 1562, op. 15, d. 1445, l. 2; d. 1119, l. 17.

[26] Ibid., l. 86.

[27] GARF, f. 5446, op. 16a, d. 404, l. 12.

[28] David Shearer, "Crime and Social Disorder in Stalin's Russia: A Reassessment of the Great Retreat and the Origins of Mass Repression," Cahiers du Monde russe 39, nos. 1–2 (January–June 1998): 119–48, here, 124. For comparison, Gastronom No. 1 was said to have drawn sixty thousand to seventy thousand, and TsUM two hundred thousand.

[29] See, esp., GARF, f. 5446, op. 16a, d. 404, l. 11.

Figure 8. Market day in the Central Agricultural Region, 1933. *Courtesy of the Russian State Archive for Cinematic and Photographic Documents (RGAKFD).*

and streets.[30] Poor old men and women congregated outside every bazaar selling sunflower seeds and used cutlery; but beyond that, hawkers sold literally everything. Here is how Arzhilovskii, the ex-kulak diarist from the Tiumen' area, described his town's bazaar:

> *January 12, 1937.* Because of the town's concern about our progress toward socialism, the flea market was moved to the outskirts of town, and the private property system is now living out its last days there. People go out there, dragging with them anything that could possibly be sold. If you have money you can buy whatever you want. Life is free there, there are no lines. No matter how you look at it, this market is good both for supply and demand.[31]

Except for the famine zones in 1921–22 and from 1931 to 1933, Arzhilovsky's portrait matches descriptions of flea markets throughout the first forty years of Soviet rule.

It seems apparent that precisely what repelled Soviet officials gave the flea market much of its popular appeal. In the later 1930s, as survival concerns faded, Soviet citizens went to the market not just out of necessity but also for fun. Local authorities tried to capitalize on this entertainment function, but they also tried to keep it within officially sanctioned, "cultured," bounds. Market supervisors in Moldavia, Magnitogorsk, and Dnepropetrovsk could thus point with pride to the cabarets, Punch and Judy shows, and circuses that regularly made their appearance on the local market stage.[32] These performances were cheap, and surely attracted spectators; but it was also the spontaneous, freewheeling atmosphere created by the hawkers that led people to spend a day at the bazaar. It was there that consuming subcultures took root among Stalinism's "new consumers"—notably in the youth market for jazz records.[33] There, too, one could laugh at, or profit from, the new market for Soviet kitsch. No one personified the anarchical, carnivalesque quality of the markets more strikingly than I. A. Slavkin, a habitué of Iaroslavskii Market in the years before the war. Slavkin had quit his job as a lawyer in order to pose for the burgeoning art industry of Lenin busts and portraits. Earning up to fifty rubles an hour modeling in his homemade Lenin suit and cap for the most renowned artists of the period, Slavkin spent his weekends at the market, impersonating Lenin and hawking photographs of himself to passersby. Should he be permitted to develop a Lenin postcard series, as Slavkin petitioned to do in 1940, or should he

[30] Ibid., l. 11; TsMA Mos., f. 46, op. 1, d. 8, ll. 79–80.

[31] *Intimacy and Terror,* Garros et al., eds., 137.

[32] RGAE, f. 7971, op. 1, d. 88, l. 3; op. 5, d. 1, l. 25.

[33] TsMA Moskvy, f. 46, op. 1, d. 8, l. 22; GARF, f. f. 8131, op. 15, d. 89, ll. 24, 30; op. 37, d. 332, l. 139.

be sent to the Gulag for shirking "socially useful work"? For Soviet authorities, this was the kind of dilemma the flea market posed; and when the NKVD finally opted for repression, other "Lenins" surfaced to take Slavkin's place.[34]

As Slavkin's example shows, hawkers sold more than berries and secondhand clothes. This was to some extent a matter of policy; though opening a private shop was prohibited, it was still possible, in the mid-1930s, to obtain a full-time vending license for sales of a variety of goods from one's hands or from a tray. Acceptable objects of these businesses included traditional prepared foods (cold drinks, sweets, farmer's cheese, fermented whey, and a baked dairy product called *varenets*); fruits, nuts, sunflower seeds, and berries; wax, soda, putty, bleach, and petty household supplies; toys; and haberdashery (thread, needles, etc.).[35] The hawkers' ranks were also swelled by private artisans, who were permitted to sell their handicrafts at the market as of the 1932 decrees; indeed, more than two thousand artisans registered with Moscow's municipal financial department in 1935 for Iaroslavskii Market alone.[36]

As a matter of policy, these concessions to the private sector were not destined to last. For one thing, artisans and other licensed vendors blended into the mass of hawkers. As a Party inspector concluded in 1935, "The flea market, where people formerly sold secondhand things for personal use, has been transformed in the present day into a sort of department store. . . . Here it is difficult to distinguish the honest laborer from the speculator, and the pseudo-artisan from the real artisan."[37] Such concerns dovetailed with the goal, articulated at the Communist Party's "Congress of Victors" in 1934, of achieving the "final liquidation" of independent artisans, "capitalist elements," and *mnogoukladnost'* by the end of the Second Five-Year Plan.[38] Accordingly, the sphere of legal private enterprise was once again restricted. By March 1936 independent artisans were prohibited from manufacturing many kinds of consumer goods: clothes and clothing accessories, linens, hats, and leather shoes; saddles and harnesses; goods made out of nonferrous metals; and, in perhaps the most striking deviation from previous practice, any prepared foods. The "liquidation" of the private artisan thus began with goods manufactured from perennially scarce materials (textiles, leather, metal,

---

[34] *Rodina*, no. 12 (December 1993): 38–40.

[35] Narkomfin instructions of June 10, 1934, discussed in GARF, f. 5446, op. 15a, d. 1071, l. 14; f. 8131, op. 12, d. 43, l. 6. In Kiev, where they were said to be particularly numerous, petty vendors of these items grossed two hundred to three hundred rubles a day.

[36] GARF, f. 5446, op. 16a, d. 404, l. 11.

[37] Ibid., l. 11.

[38] *KPSS v rezoliutsiiakh*, 5:148.

food), leaving only such articles as toys, furniture, glassware, pottery, barrels, goods made from straw, candy, and felt boots, all produced from abundant materials, to private artisanal trade.[39]

It would seem that the March 1936 "Rules on the registration of manufactures and trades" should have eliminated sales of new clothes, shoes, and most other manufactured consumer goods at the bazaar, but in the later 1930s flea markets continued to traffic in "everything that could possibly be sold." Three months after the promulgation of the new rules, an edict on bazaar trade reported that its complexion had scarcely changed: "In the markets of many cities, private citizens can be seen selling new manufactured goods (cotton, wool, silk, and linen cloth; shoes; bicycles; clothing, shirts, linens, and clothing accessories; household goods; phonographs, phonograph records, etc.)." As in the "goods famine" of the late 1920s, most of these goods were of state or cooperative manufacture; most had been obtained through the socialist retail system; and most were being sold for a price that significantly exceeded the state price.[40] Inevitably central policy makers and their watchdogs interpreted such sales as "parasitical" or "speculative"—and in light of the August 22, 1932, decree on speculation, which established a five-year minimum sentence for sales above the going state price "with the intention of profiting," they incontestably were.

The decree on speculation grew directly out of the May 20, 1932, legislation on market trade. According to the latter, local authorities were instructed to use "every means" against "resellers and speculators, who try to profit at the expense of workers and peasants."[41] A rough division of labor soon emerged from this mandate, whereby local financial departments battled unlicensed trade while the police maintained order at the markets and, with the help of the procuracy, prosecuted the "war on speculation." The municipal soviet's trade department, the third administrative pillar on which the markets rested, named market directors, established sales plans, looked after the physical upkeep of the market, and oversaw the collection of daily fees from unlicensed hawkers.[42] Each of these local agencies had links to the central bureaucracy; municipal trade departments, for example, fell under the jurisdiction of the Commissariat of Domestic Trade, from which they periodically received instructions and to which they were obliged to file reports. At the same time, the

---

[39] See *Sovetskaia iustitsiia*, no. 21 (July 8, 1936):21–22.

[40] TsMA Moskvy, f. 46, op. 1, d. 8, l. 22; GARF, f. 5446, op. 18a, d. 309, ll. 97–101.

[41] *Resheniia partii i pravitel'stva po khoziaistvennym voprosam*, 389.

[42] GARF, f. 5446, op. 16a, d. 404, l. 11. Kolkhoz markets were transferred to municipal trade departments from communal economy departments in 1935.

police, procuracy, financial departments, and trade departments took orders from the local soviets, and, in the case of speculation, the central
and local lines of authority frequently crossed. A 1935 report on bazaars
in five major cities (Moscow, Leningrad, Khar'kov, Rostov, and Minsk)
indicated that none of the relevant local agencies wanted to apply a full
five-year labor-camp sentence to everyone found in violation of the law.[43]

Not surprisingly, given the extent to which local governments depended on the markets for their revenues, a major impediment to the
war on speculation was financial. An episode was reported from Khar'kov
in which the financial department's fee collector got into an argument
over the detention of petty traders: "If you chase away all the speculators,
we won't have anyone left to pay the daily fee."[44] Moreover, municipal
police departments could significantly augment their budgets by fining,
rather than arresting, unlicensed traders, and by working with the market
administration. In many cities, market administrators signed contracts in
which they promised to pay the police department for its services—in
Khar'kov, 30 percent of the income from booth and stall rentals; at Moscow's biggest flea market, a flat fee of 156,978 rubles. Police departments
regularly petitioned their superiors in the central administration for ap-
probation of these and similar deals.[45]

As in the civil war period, enforcement of the decree on speculation
was also hampered by a sense of fairness, which made law enforcement
officers reluctant to go after petty traders in force. In the words of a
Dnepropetrovsk prosecutor, "I'm not going to lock someone up for small
change—selling a pair of boots or a couple of meters of cord!"[46] The
Commissariat of Justice and the USSR Procuracy tried to overcome this
aversion to mandatory sentencing by issuing a series of clarifications:
buying and reselling vodka or schoolbooks or coins or state bonds did,
indeed, qualify as speculation and were to be prosecuted accordingly.[47]
Some officials took these instructions at face value; a subsequent report
to the Procuracy on these practices indicates considerable regional variation in official acceptance of private exchange.[48] Still, one thing seems to
have been universal: after the abolition of Rabkrin in 1934, none of the
agencies directly involved in policing the informal economy wanted pri-

---

[43] GARF, f. 5446, op. 16a, d. 404, ll. 11–12.

[44] Ibid., 16.

[45] Ibid.; Shearer, "Crime and Social Disorder," 124–25.

[46] GARF, f. 8131, op. 12, d. 43, l. 5; see also GARF, f. 5446, op. 16a, d. 404, ll. 4–5.
Solomon shows that this was a common procuratorial reaction to mandatory sentencing; cf.
his *Soviet Criminal Justice*, 114–17, 388–89, 408–9.

[47] Cf. *O bor'be so spekuliatsiei*, 8–9, 20–21, 27.

[48] GARF, f. 8131, op. 12, d. 43, l. 5.

mary responsibility for its eradication. The police and the procuracy argued for taxation as the state's principal weapon against the black market, and they typically tried to relocate bazaars to sites beyond their jurisdiction at the outskirts of town. Market officials and municipal financial departments, by contrast, tended either to call for a tougher police struggle against informal trade or to throw in the towel and neglect law enforcement in favor of the collection of fees.[49]

The limitations of criminal prosecution predictably rallied the political leadership around its time-honored alternative, extrajudicial repression. Between 1932 and the German invasion, big-city markets were subjected to repeated raids and "administrative" operations, which culminated in the murderous "mass operations" of 1937–38. In the first half of 1934, for example, 58,314 individuals were arrested for speculation, but, in addition, some 53,000 unemployed petty traders, "whom one could not possibly prosecute under the law of August 22, 1932," were deported from the Soviet Union's "largest cities."[50] In late 1935 the Commissariats of Finance and Domestic Trade were agitating for another round of "special temporary measures and administrative repressions" in order to rid the major cities of "malicious speculators, who so capably evade criminal responsibility."[51] In July 1936 Sovnarkom secretly authorized the NKVD to deport up to 5,000 "speculators" apiece from Moscow, Leningrad, Kiev, Minsk, and (after a plea from the regional Party organization) Dnepropetrovsk to "distant parts of the Union."[52] Like their counterparts of the late 1920s, the mass operations of 1937–38, in which petty traders and other down-and-out types who frequented the bazaars were sent to labor camps or shot, were thus preceded by successive episodes of terror on a smaller, less murderous, "administrative" scale.[53]

And yet, for all that, taxation, toleration, and "socialist modernization" remained as significant as repression in defining the regime's approach to urban hawkers. An example from 1938 to 1940 was the effort, revived with great enthusiasm by Moscow administrators after the war, to ratio-

---

[49] TsMA Moskvy, f. 46, op. 1, d. 8, ll. 5, 60; GARF, f. 5446, op. 16a, d. 404, l. 16; f. 8131, op. 12, d. 43, l. 6; RGAE, f. 7971, op. 5, d. 40, l. 5.

[50] GARF, f. 5446, op. 15a, d. 1071, ll. 16–21, here, 16; cited in Shearer, "Crime and Social Disorder," 123.

[51] GARF, f. 5446, op. 16a, d. 404, ll. 4–5.

[52] Ibid., op. 18a, d. 309, ll. 1–8, 97–101.

[53] Shearer ("Crime and Social Disorder") and Hagenloh ("'Socially Harmful Elements'"), have drawn attention to mid-1930s police operations as a precedent for the "mass operations" of 1937–38. As a caveat, Shearer's conflation of petty trade with "speculation" and that in turn with "social disobedience" is problematic, and his argument that social disorder was on the rise from 1934 to 1936 (as against 1932–33!) defies belief.

nalize the flea market by dividing it into distinct departments.[54] Then again, officials sought to divert would-be hawkers by providing alternative channels for the disposal of unwanted goods. Bureaucrats repeatedly called for the organization of more "buying-up points" and "commission" stores, which sold citizens' personal property for a commission, and they also attempted to force stores to accept returns.[55] These measures worked from the premise that people traded at the flea market because they had things they wanted to get rid of; they aimed, that is, at the "honest" hawker, and not at the speculator who bought things for the purpose of resale. However, while "buying-up points" and commission stores were organized at the largest flea markets in the late 1930s, they accepted only reluctantly, if at all, the petty domestic goods that formed the staple of the flea market.[56]

The measures aimed at substituting other arenas for the flea market also assumed that people resorted to the flea market, as buyers or sellers, only out of necessity, and would prefer a more cut-and-dried exchange atmosphere—an assumption not supported by any evidence. The flea market prevailed because it offered both buyers and sellers the opportunity, if not the likelihood, of making good on subjective differences in valuation. Although the network of buying-up points was scheduled to expand from 1939 on, it, in fact, contracted dramatically in the early 1940s because of the increasing gap between fixed purchase prices at the points and market prices. In early 1945 the state raised commission store prices to reflect market prices but continued to offer the same low prices at the buying-up points. Not surprisingly these places received commodities at the rate of a slow trickle. By 1946 there were said to be just five hundred underutilized commission stores in the country, as "significant numbers of citizens sell their belongings at the market."[57]

Bazaars, no less than stores, were affected by the shortages from 1938 to 1941. The widening gap between citizens' "consumption fund" and the ruble value, in current prices, of available goods in socialist-sector trade inevitably caused market prices of both foods and nonfoods to rise. Accordingly markets consumed an increasing proportion of consumer outlays, a trend reinforced not just by the excess money in circulation but

[54] TsMA Moskvy, f. 46, op. 1, d. 8, ll. 5, 53, 56, 60.
[55] Ibid., l. 56; GARF, f. 8131, op. 15, d. 89, ll. 2, 7; op. 37, d. 2825, ll. 237–49; f. 5446, op. 23a, d. 1450, l. 67. Commission stores were not yet authorized to sell agricultural produce, which became one of their major functions after 1953.
[56] Ibid., l. 67; TsMA Moskvy, f. 46, op. 1, d. 8, ll. 48, 60.
[57] GARF, f. 8131, op. 37, d. 2825, l. 244; TsMA Moskvy, f. 46, op. 1, d.8, ll. 109–10; see also TsAIPD Len., f. 24, op. 2v, d. 1382, l. 1.

also by the outbreak of war.[58] The USSR's aggressive war against Finland both heightened the country's economic difficulties and fueled fears of a "great famine," never far from the surface among the urban and rural poor. A long report on speculation prepared by the USSR Procuracy indicated that citizens had begun stockpiling foods, particularly such nonperishable staples as grains, sugar, salt, and oil, from the first days of mobilization. By 1940 hoarding food or feeding food grains to livestock was enough to land a person in prison. In a case in Riazan' *oblast'*, a middle-aged peasant was sentenced to seven years for laying in reserves of kerosene, soap, sugar, salt, and thread, and thereby "creating queues in front of the village co-op [*sel'po*]."[59]

As we saw in chapter 5, the perception of a crisis triggered efforts to centralize control over essential foods and consumer goods, and also to shelter the welfare of metropolitan consumers at provincial consumers' expense. The same concern for consumer access and social order in Moscow that resulted in the April 1939 secret decree on overnight queues found expression in several orders limiting hawking at the capital's bazaars. By August 1940 the Central Committee and Sovnarkom had weighed in with a decree "on the liquidation of hand trade in manufactured goods at Moscow markets." This order, which does not appear to have been extended to other cities, banned all sales of manufactured goods "from the hands," though the Moscow city government issued clarifications four days later that limited the ban to sales of new clothing, cloth, galoshes, and shoes.[60] As the epigraph to part 3 describing Tishinskii Market should make clear, this ban did not have a great deal of force during the war years. Nonetheless, until 1946, when the city successfully petitioned to restore the 1930s compromise whereby hawkers could sell new goods as long as they paid the daily fee and did not charge a "speculative" price or trade "systematically" without a license, the largest flea markets of the area were, indeed, located in the suburbs. There they may have continued to serve as a "gathering place for criminal elements," as administrators alleged, but they were unlikely to disrupt the business of state.[61]

Farmers' deliveries to the market increased after the 1940 harvest, but the German invasion in June 1941 blocked any recovery from the dislocations of the previous few years. Throughout the country, food sup-

[58] RGAE, f. 7971, op. 5, d. 4, l. 34; Kerblay, *Les marchés paysans*, 138–42; *Sotsialisticheskoe narodnoe khoziaistvo SSSR v 1933–1940 gg.* (Moscow, 1963), 562.

[59] GARF, f. 8131, op. 37, d. 332, ll. 288–302, here, 288–9; GA Riaz. ob., f. R-4800, op. 1, d. 36.

[60] TsMA Moskvy, f. 46, op. 1, d. 8, ll. 57–58, 85.

[61] Ibid., ll. 1, 5, 60.

plies dried up. Echoing his predecessors, Commissar of Trade Liubimov attributed the low rates of peasant marketing to the inability of peasants to obtain manufactured consumer goods in state and cooperative shops, "in connection with which collective farmers are not materially interested in delivering foods to the market." Some peasants, he wrote in a February 1942 memo, were refusing to sell foods for cash and instead were demanding, in exchange, clothes, shoes, matches, salt, soap, and household supplies from the procurement agencies. Here was a new twist: peasants wanted *tovaroobmen*, albeit on their own terms, whereas the economic establishment insisted on adhering to monetized relations and the principles of trade. From a policy perspective, this reflected, in other words, the crisis of 1931–32, not that from 1927 to 1930, and Liubimov's main suggestion was to revitalize the greeting trade by supplying manufactured goods of a "peasant assortment" for commercial sales. Local authorities, by contrast, continued to react to the crisis as they had in 1918 or 1928. Some tried to control prices: in many localities Party officials posted price limits on privately sold foods. Others tried to corner supplies. "Localist sentiments" led not only to an unauthorized reintroduction of food rations, as we saw in chapter 5, but also, as in the revolutionary era, to various kinds of embargoes to prevent shipments of food from leaving the district.[62]

In fact, the expansion of the greeting trade was not a viable alternative, as the conversion of industry to military ends left the government with miniscule stocks of consumer goods. At the nadir (in most cases, 1943), the socialist distribution system handled the following volume of centralized supplies relative to the 1940 amounts: cotton cloth, 7 percent; woolen cloth, 25 percent; shawls and scarves, 13 percent; clothes, 10 percent; leather shoes, 8 percent; household soap, 20 percent; bath soap, 8 percent; sugar, 7 percent; low-grade tobacco [*makhorka*] 0.5 percent; matches, 12 percent; and kerosene, 8 percent.[63] Under the circumstances Moscow's ban on sales of new cloth, clothing, and shoes at the market became moot. New factory-made goods virtually disappeared from circulation everywhere until 1945, and much of the country reverted to barter, as had occurred during the civil war. In the main agricultural areas (the middle and lower Volga, the North Caucasus, the Central Agricultural District, Viatka, and Western Siberia) peasants increasingly demanded

[62] RGASPI, f. 82, op. 2, d. 688, ll. 69–71, 77; GA Riaz. ob. (party doc. div.), f. 220, op. 1, d. 227, l. 84. See also RGAE, f. 7971, op. 5, d. 60, ll. 2–3.

[63] Calculated from *Narodnoe khoziaistvo SSSR v Velikoi Otechestvennoi Voine* (Moscow, 1990), 189–90. Nove has a slightly different list in his *Economic History*, 271.

manufactured goods of would-be purchasers, according to a region-by-region survey of the farm markets; whereas in the enormous region from Vladivostok to Sverdlovsk, and especially from Khabarovsk to Chita, "peasants were unwilling to exchange their limited produce for anything other than bread."[64]

In the industrial provinces the situation was more complicated. Certainly, as William Moskoff contends, barter operations formed an essential part of market and off-market trade there as well, but more important than barter were occasional sales. The handful of people I interviewed in connection with this project all had something to say on this subject. To my query as to what sorts of people engaged in hawking during the war, I received the following answers: "Just about everyone!" "If that's a crime, the whole nation is guilty!" "Every family without exception." Nearly all could report someone in the household having served as the family vendor: one sold embroidered baby clothes, another traded bread for milk, one engaged in ration-card speculation, one speculated in shoes, one sold old clothes, another sold her rations of manufactured goods, and so forth. Usually the older women of the household performed this function but not always: teenage children assisted their mothers, and one man speculated in ration cards as a university student, having learned how to manipulate the different types of cards to his advantage. In each case the remembered purpose of hawking was very simple: hawking enabled the household to supplement its food supplies both quantitatively (a few kilos of potatoes) and qualitatively (milk for the baby, otherwise inaccessible). In the words of one informant, "We had to live."[65]

Household budget studies from the war period underscore the universality of petty trade as a survival strategy. From 2 percent of household incomes from 1937 to 1940, occasional sales soared to the 25 to 30 percent characteristic of the civil war. Meanwhile, the disappearance of goods from the shops meant that purchases were also concentrated at the bazaar during the war years. Working-class households spent an average of 2,099 rubles on food in 1943, of which 1,775 rubles "were spent at the market or paid to private individuals." So, too, were 236 of 312 rubles spent on cloth, clothing, and shoes; 25 of 33 rubles on heating and light-

[64] William Moskoff, *The Bread of Affliction: The Food Supply in the U.S.S.R. during World War II* (Cambridge, 1990), 161–64; RGAE, f. 7971, op. 5, d. 60.

[65] Interviews with Eleanora Semenovna (March 1993), Aleksandr L'vovich (September 1993), Galina Alekseevna (April 1993), Galina Petrovna (March 1993), Liliana Isaevna (March 1993), and Ruben Artemevich (March 1993).

ing materials; 75 of 90 rubles spent on leisure goods, hygiene, and cosmetics; and so on. In all, 82 percent of the households' total expenditures on goods (as opposed to housing, services, taxes, and other noncommodity outlays) went to the private sector, a figure roughly in line with the budget data for all republics and social groups.[66] In light of these figures, the published estimates of market sales, which indicated a shift from 14 percent of retail sales, as measured in rubles, in 1940, to 46 percent in 1945, may well have understated the role of the markets in the wartime consumer economy.[67]

Physically the expansion of the flea market considerably undermined the "cultured trade" ideal. Such infrastructural improvements as had been completed before the outbreak of war were supposed to serve hygienic ends: at the newly constructed "modern" farmers' markets of Moscow and Leningrad, pavilions were designed to isolate meat and milk from unsanitary goods, and even in ordinary markets, hawking was always relegated to a separate space. During the war period the flea market essentially took over the bazaar. As the official year's end survey of the markets in 1943 reported:

> Many significant violations of the established rules can be observed in collective farm trade at the markets. The main culprit is trade from the hands by the general public—sales of everyday articles and other goods. This kind of trade is carried out not in the specially designated sections of the market territory but in direct proximity to sales of foods, which disorganizes kolkhoz trade and makes it unsanitary to an impermissable degree.[68]

In Moscow this was a constant complaint of market administrators from late 1941 through at least 1946. Meat and milk pavilions became so "choked up" [zabity] with hawkers selling used clothes and other personal effects, according to the head of the trade department's market administration, that "collective farmers cannot make their way through the crowds to their assigned trading place." Sanitary standards went out the window, especially since some of the hawkers sold pirogis, pies, bottles of milk, and home-grown fruits and vegetables, which naturally did not undergo the hygienic tests to which farmers' milk, meat, and produce were subjected.[69] As a caveat, by no means could all the sanitary lapses at the

---

[66] RGAE, f. 1562, op. 15, d. 1573 (unnumbered file); d. 1445, l. 2; d. 1872, ll. 74–75. Urban households obtained an average of 28 percent of their income from sales in 1943.

[67] *Sovetskaia torgovlia. Statisticheskii sbornik*, 19; *SSSR v tsifrakh. Statisticheskii sbornik* (Moscow, 1958), 427.

[68] RGAE, f. 7971, op. 5, d. 60, ll. 2–3.

[69] TsMA Moskvy, f. 46, op. 1, d. 8, ll. 60, 79–80; d. 10, l. 66. See also RGAE, f. 7971, op. 5, d. 60; Jeffrey Wade Jones, "'In my opinion this is all a fraud!': Concrete, Culture,

markets be blamed on hawkers. At the huge bazaar in front of the railway station in Gor'kii (Nizhnii Novgorod), the Italian Communist Ettore Vanni was struck by the "row of filthy, half-open latrines" near one of the entrances, which attracted "clouds of flies," gave off an "insupportable stench," and was always surrounded by a "sea" of muck.[70]

Vanni's description of this bazaar is one of the most vivid from the war period and deserves to be quoted at greater length. At the least it makes clear that the carnivalesque quality of the markets did not become submerged in the citizens' drab struggle for survival. As in the 1930s,

> everything is sold, including the most absurd things. . . . Here you could find all kinds of tobacco, white bread, and everything the human fantasy could imagine: from bras to electric springs, from a metal camp bed to military decorations with all the corresponding documents, regularly stamped and signed, that the purchaser could register in his own name. As if obeying a tacit accord, the crowd has instinctively established zones or departments: here shoes are sold, further on men's clothing, then old keys for hypothetical locks. Two steps further, people are playing cards; another half-meter and a gambling house is functioning; then there is the place for vodka, the one for canned goods and American egg powder and then for Soviet internal passports.[71]

"Cultured entertainments" may have disappeared from the wartime bazaar, but popular entertainments persisted. So, evidently, did the trangressive aspects of the bazaar: the gathering of "criminal elements," epitomized by the traffic in military decorations and stolen passports, was a problem at many bazaars.[72]

How did the policing organs adjust to the veritable explosion of informal exchange in 1942–43? Given these agencies' usual reaction to a crisis, we might expect them to have tightened the screws. Indeed, in July 1941, the Commissariat of Justice and the USSR Procuracy had issued a directive extending the application of article 107 (speculation) and article 169, part 2 (fraud), to cover the purchase or sale of ration coupons. As more and more citizens resorted to petty trade, however, moral reservations about its criminalization mounted. By 1943 top officials in both agencies were pressing for a more liberal policy, not simply or even primarily because the wartime manpower shortage made enforcement im-

---

and Class in the 'Reconstruction' of Rostov-on-the-Don, 1943–1948" (Ph.D. dissertation, University of North Carolina at Chapel Hill, 2000), 208.

[70] Ettore Vanni, *Io, Comunista in Russia* (Bologna, 1949), 130–31.

[71] Ibid., 131–32.

[72] See Moskoff, *Bread of Affliction*, 161; K. S. Karol, *Between Two Worlds* (New York, 1983), 206.

possible but because they believed that privation altered the requirements of justice. Here, for example, is what the Deputy Commissar of
Justice, I. A. Basavin, had to say about ration-card offenses:

> Article 169, part 2, of the RSFSR Criminal Code is applied to such incidents
> as the sale of a citizen's own ration card. While this action may not be re-
> garded as legal, nonetheless it contains no signs of fraud. Similarly the pur-
> chase of food cards is frequently perpetrated by workers in connection with
> the fact that their own coupons are canceled for cafeteria meals, and they are
> then left without enough coupons to dine at the cafeteria through the end of
> the month. These actions are likewise impossible to regard as legal, but except
> for those cases when the ration card was acquired illegally for the purchaser,
> or ought to revert to the government, the purchaser surely does not merit
> criminal prosecution for fraud.[73]

Basavin's argument proved persuasive; criminal sanctions were replaced
with fines, not to exceed three hundred rubles, for all but the most serious infractions, and the courts' caseload of ration-card offenses dropped
from eighteen hundred to three hundred a month.[74] It must be observed
that lenience had its price: from 1943 to 1946, when criminal sanctions
were revived, ration cards were the most widely sold commodity at the
RSFSR's twenty-six hundred bazaars.[75]

Speculation was also prosecuted much more sparingly as the war
progressed. At first this occurred inconsistently and with no central coor-
dination; a person apprehended for selling personal belongings, bartering
possessions for food, or obtaining more food than necessary for personal
consumption could receive a reprimand, a small or large fee, a one-year
prison sentence for "violation of the rules of trade" (article 105), or a
five-year prison sentence for "speculation" (article 107). The trend, however, was clear: as the number of hawkers ballooned, criminal prosecution gave way to fines or the more vigorous collection of daily fees or
both.[76] By mid-1943 police officers were instructed to ignore many kinds
of petty sales, irrespective of the price. Barter exchanges, sales of foods
received as rations or of home-grown produce, sales of personal possessions (used or new), and possession of surplus foods and goods were,
within limits, to be tolerated, leaving the police to concentrate on the
struggle against "genuine speculators"—that "nonlaboring element,"

[73] GARF, f. 8131, op. 22, d. 274, ll. 2–3.
[74] Ibid., l. 5; f. R-9401 s/ch, op. 2, d. 139, ll. 234–43.
[75] Ibid.; RGAE, f. 7971, op. 5, d. 60, ll. 1–3; TsMA Moskvy, f. 46, op. 1, d. 8, ll. 110–11.
[76] GARF, f. 8131, op. 37, d. 1433, ll. 1–4.

which, despite a decade of repression, continued to supply 25 to 40 percent of the vendors at the wartime bazaar.[77]

Travel, Bagging, and the Survivalist Consensus

Both during the war and in the 1930s, the bazaars of provincial cities and towns were affected by the uneven geography of trade. The influx of provincial shoppers into Moscow from 1937 to 1941 was just one indication of the disparity in provisionment between the major cities and everywhere else. As noted in chapter 5, this was not unique to the Soviet Union; larger, wealthier markets always offer a wider selection of goods, and especially of specialty items and luxuries, than smaller, less wealthy towns. Still, several features of the Soviet economy tended to exaggerate geographical disparities and to extend them to basic consumer goods. To start with, provincial consumers remained too poor, even in the late 1930s, to support a high volume of trade. Low sales volume, in turn, translated more directly than usual into a low density of retail outlets, since the ban on private shops precluded taking advantage of small businesspeople's traditional willingness to work for meager returns. Finally, the unusual centralization of the economy meant that policy makers' prejudices concerning the "political importance" of one city or region or another had a direct impact on the opening of new shops and the allocation of supplies. The following joke, which circulated in the postwar period, caricatured the end result: "A famous American economist came to Russia for a conference. Chatting with a Russian colleague, he said, 'America is a big country, but your country is immeasurably bigger. It must require a tremendous mobilization of resources to supply so many towns across such great distances. How do you do it?' The Russian economist replied, 'Very simply. We bring everything to Moscow, and let the rest of the country come to us!'"[78]

What becomes clear when we turn to provincial sources is that this was not just a joke. Throughout the Stalin period, a large percentage of the goods sold at provincial flea markets originated in vendors' unofficial supply trips to Moscow and other major cities. This commerce was sometimes suppressed at the supply end, as we know from the late-1930s queue and deportation decrees. Its persistence, however, suggests a provocative conclusion regarding Soviet economic life. Is it possible that Stalinist restructuring was less violent and abrupt in its impact on provin-

[77] Ibid., ll. 1–4, 6–19; d. 332, ll. 57, 86, 138–45, 148–49; TsMA Moskvy, f. 46, op. 1, d. 8, ll. 110–11.

[78] Interview with Aleksandr L'vovich; cf. Karol, *Between Two Worlds*, 263.

274 • Chapter Six

cial towns than on villages or major cities? Both kulak traders and urban
shopkeepers were persecuted at the end of the 1920s, as we know; but at
small-town bazaars, the practices of petty traders in the lowest two license classes plainly outlasted the NEP.

Some examples from the market town of Kasimov (Riazan' *oblast'*) will
help to illustrate the business activities of provincial hawkers, and thus of
an important segment of small-town trade. Again, unofficial buying trips
furnished most of their wares. There was, for instance, the former horse
trader who ran an informal cloth business from 1933 to 1935. Officially
unemployed, this man was a kind of traveling salesman: he stocked up on
cloth in Moscow's commercial stores, hawked it on market days in Kasimov and nearby Shilovo, and went door to door in neighboring villages. Or there was the family shoe and galoshes business, also based in
Kasimov, in 1936–37; the fifty-five-year-old parents packaged up shoes,
galoshes, and children's boots and hawked them at the market, and the
twenty-five-year-old daughter, who lived in Moscow, procured the shoes
from various metropolitan stores. A woman from the nearby village of
Syntul traded cloth and knitted wear, all purchased in Moscow, for five
years at Kasimov's market before she was apprehended in 1941. Similar
informal businesses, centered on cotton cloth, shoes, galoshes, wool
scarves, and occasionally clothing, predominated at all of the province's
bazaars in the prewar period. The vendors almost invariably purchased
supplies in the capital, some 160 km away, though a few traveled to
Leningrad or Saratov for their wares or bought articles in other towns
while visiting relatives.[79]

If buying trips linked provincial market towns with the metropolitan
economy, they also forged ties to the rural hinterland. Many small-town
vendors traveled a circuit of farms and villages, from whom they procured agricultural products and rural handicrafts to sell at the bazaar. In
the later 1930s, when peasants largely stopped herding livestock to the
market themselves, slaughterers formed a distinct subgroup within this
class of trade. Professional slaughterers traveled around to the farmhouses and bought livestock from peasants, which they then slaughtered,
carved into recognizable cuts of meat, and sold at the bazaar.[80] Others
purchased sunflower seeds, tobacco, or cranberries in bulk by going
around to the farmhouses, and then selling them by the glass in Riazan'
or in the market towns. Handwoven cloth, a traditional handicraft in one
corner of the province, was also bought up and sold in this manner, as

[79] GA Riaz. ob., f. R-4407, op. 1, dd. 2, 16, 19; f. R-4387, op. 2, d. 23; f. R-3602, op. 1,
d. 1171.
[80] Ibid., f. 4480, op. 1, d. 101; f. 4800, op. 1, d. 88; d. 111.

Figure 9. Artisanal trade in Arzamas, 1930s. *Courtesy of the Russian State Archive for Cinematic and Photographic Documents (RGAKFD).*

were birchbark sandals (*lapti*), onions, eggs, vegetable oil, and honey (figure 9).[81] A few more ambitious traders followed the example of the civil war baggers, and sold agricultural products in Moscow, which, in turn, financed the purchase of manufactured goods for sale at home. A father-and-son team thus made a habit of buying up and slaughtering lambs, selling the meat in the capital, and returning with nails, wire, and roofing materials for the local bazaar; a woman systematically bought apples and other foods in Riazan' to sell at her hometown market, traveled to Moscow for string and calico, and sold knitted stockings in each place. One entrepreneur went so far as to rent a booth at Moscow's Arbat Market, identifying himself as a "kolkhoz representative" to the market administration and as the "manager of a shop at the Arbat Market" to peasants in the various villages whose vegetables he bought.[82]

I have detailed information only about the Riazan' area, but there is strong reason to believe that purchasing trips played a large role in the

---

[81] Ibid., f. R-4387, op. 1, dd. 13, 62, 108; f. R-4407, op. 1, dd. 9, 13, 20; f. R-3602, op. 1, d. 1216; f. R-4480, op. 1, d. 26. A particularly large number of tobacco cases dated from the war years (f. R-4387, op. 2, dd. 19, 26, 34, 46, 84).

[82] Ibid., dd. 99, 101; f. 4387, op. 1, d. 99.

bazaar trade of most provinces. Stephen Kotkin offers examples from
Magnitogorsk, a mid-sized city with an underdeveloped trade network:
Guzeeva, the wife of a railroad worker, who, according to the local paper,
"used her husband's right to free transport and, together with her friend,
Kozhevnikova, traveled to the Donbas, to Rostov, and to the gold mines
of the Kucharskii region" to buy cloth, shoes, coats, and butter to sell at
the Magnitogorsk bazaar; a group of workers who traveled around to the
villages to exchange manufactured goods for flour, which they then sold
in town. Kotkin concludes, "Most everyone who traveled outside the city
took advantage of the opportunity to purchase whatever they could and
bring it back to Magnitogorsk, sometimes for personal use, sometimes
for friends, and often for resale, or at least barter."[83] From Western Siberia a 1938 report observed that speculation cases were becoming pet-
tier by the year; the prototypical example was now F. E. Trofimov, who
spent seven years after the liquidation of his farm buying and selling
consumer goods. In 1936, when he was arrested, he made a living from
periodic trips to Sverdlovsk. There he bought up a selection of goods
that can only be termed random (e.g., buckets, enamel basins, fabric, and
buckles for use on a raincoat) and then sold these at the market in Slav-
gorod, where he resided at the time, and at a nearby state farm.[84] Similar
cases illustrate every report on speculation in the later part of the decade.[85]

What conclusions can be drawn about unauthorized travels in the informal economy of the 1930s? First, a unifying feature was the very modest quantity of goods purchased and transported at one time. Not only
was it difficult for provincial travelers to buy goods in bulk from metropolitan stores, the wares thus obtained could not take up so much space
on the train as to arouse suspicion. Second, hawkers' purchasing trips
focused not on luxuries and specialty items but on basic, everyday goods.
Above all, people traveled to acquire, for consumption as well as resale,
those articles that independent artisans were prohibited from manufacturing as of the 1936 rules. In other words, these were articles that could
not enter the provincial bazaars by strictly legal means. Third, the commerce based on these trips was often ongoing: though a few hawkers
were apprehended after a single purchasing trip, many others traveled
repeatedly and essentially operated a business for a period of months or
even years. Finally, this commerce was no less likely than in the NEP

[83] Kotkin, *Magnetic Mountain*, 251.
[84] GARF, f. 8131, op. 15, d. 89, ll. 1–13, here, 7.
[85] The most important archival file on late-1930s speculation is probably GARF, f. 8131,
op. 37, d. 332; cf. A. Sergeeva, "Rabota sudebnykh organov Kirgizii po delam o spekuliatsii," *Sovetskaia iustitsiia*, 1937 no. 19 (October 1937): 14; Gukov, "Praktika sudov Be-
lorusskoi SSR po delam o spekuliatsii," *Sovetskaia iustitsiia*, no. 6 (March 1939): 43–47.

period to be spurred by poverty rather than an entrepreneurial impulse. Traders' motives are admittedly difficult to judge from the sources: scattered reports make clear that a large percentage of hawkers were "non-laboring elements," but were they unemployed because they found petty trade more lucrative or convenient than employment in the socialist sector or because they could not get a job? In the case of housewives, a sizable contingent at the markets throughout the Stalin period, the former motive may have predominated; but recently released ex-traders and kulaks, for example, the "socially dangerous element" who "looked like a pauper" and walked from village to village selling combs, buttons, scissors, and *lapti* in the Kasimov hinterland in 1937–38, were almost certainly pushed by hardship into peddling as a way of life.[86]

After the outbreak of war the geography of supplies was reordered. Though provisioning trips to the big cities continued to take place in 1940, and again, more insistently, from early 1942 on, food shortage reversed the flow of traffic and the terms of urban-rural trade. As Commissar Liubimov reported to the Politburo that February, "Thousands of citizens are rushing to the countryside to exchange secondhand clothes and goods for agricultural products."[87] Market towns within a fifty-kilometer radius of a major city became overrun by urban foragers, despite the increasingly stringent passport controls on travel in and out of the cities (figure 10). In Moscow a black market in travel permits arose in response to this problem: as of the spring of 1942, the price of a counterfeit exit-reentry pass for the capital ranged from a half-liter of wine to a half-liter of vodka plus five kilograms of potatoes, according to the trial report on a travel-permit ring.[88] People obviously would not have paid for the passes unless they believed that they could recoup this cost, but the disintegration of the economy made such calculations risky. One could travel to a market thirty-five kilometers from the city only to find the same prices for milk and potatoes being charged in town.[89]

Despite passport regulations, citizens also traveled farther afield to purchase foods and consumer goods. Policy makers tried to stanch this flow through a series of restrictions on the use of the railways: the Supreme Soviet's April 9, 1941, ukase, which criminalized unauthorized travel on freight trains, under penalty of a year's incarceration; the State

[86] GA Riaz. ob., f. R-4407, op. 1, d. 14. Housewives ranged from 5 percent in Moscow (1937) to 23 percent in Stalingrad *oblast'* (1938) to 36 percent in Stalino *oblast'* (1944) (GARF, f. 8131, op. 15, d. 89, ll. 5, 29; op. 37, d. 332, l. 57; d. 1433, ll. 16, 49).

[87] RGASPI, f. 82, op. 2, d. 688, l. 69 (February 1942).

[88] TsMA Moskvy, f. 819, op. 2, d. 61 (city court).

[89] Moskoff, *Bread of Affliction*, 156–57; see also TsMA Moskvy, f. 819, op. 2, d. 61, 71a; f. 1889, op. 1, d. 66.

Figure 10. German army photograph of a peasant market, 1941.

Defense Committee's September 25, 1942, decree on the "struggle against bagging," a phrase that had largely disappeared from the Soviet lexicon during two decades of disuse; and, finally, the January 22, 1943, decree, also issued by GOKO, against "illegal transport of foods and goods for the purpose of speculation."[90] The railroad police confiscated nearly five thousand tons of food from baggers in 1944; threw 1.5 million baggers off Soviet trains; arrested eighty-eight thousand; and sent thirteen thousand to prison for terms of one to five years.[91] As in the civil war period these measures were unpopular and occasionally met with resistance—most notably in a rash of fights between soldiers and policemen in the summer of 1944. In scenes reminiscent of "the first war of the Soviet power—the war with the railway passengers," soldiers and sailors repeatedly attacked police officers when the latter tried to eject crowds of baggers from passenger and freight trains. Wielding weapons, the soldiers wrested confiscated sacks of food from the policemen, and returned them to their owners. In a few such episodes, the fight escalated into a

[90] GARF, f. 7523, op. 4, d. 48, l. 86; f. 8131, op. 37, d. 1433, ll. 77, 88–97. I have not been able to gain access to the GOKO decrees.
[91] GARF, f. 8131, op. 37, d. 1433, ll. 125–27.

pitched battle between servicemen armed with machine guns and a hastily summoned "operational group" of the NKVD.[92]

What these incidents suggest is the very wide popular acceptance of law evasion in the interests of survival. This attitude can be traced to the first years of Soviet power, when it was virtually universal, but it persisted in parts of the country where citizens had reason to feel deprived. When there was no woolen cloth to be had in Kasimov, why should one not bring some back from Moscow and sell it at the market? What could the state say about it anyhow, when *it* obviously "speculated" in its pricing of bread? It is impossible to ascertain the prevalence of this attitude, but it must have resonated with many people who were left out of, or left behind by, the system, especially in the villages and smaller towns.[93] The impact of the war was to bring it back to the cities; although what I have termed *popular communism* of the prewar Stalin era was survival-oriented, its adherents were idealists who wanted an egalitarian rule of law. From 1942 on (1941 in the occupied territory), however, they, too, adopted survivalism as their moral standard (figure 11). This has been observed by several recent scholars of the Soviet home front, both in the occupied areas and in the rear. Richard Bidlack has documented the crystallization of a survival-based consensus in Leningrad over the course of the first winter of the siege; Uwe Gartenschläger has tracked it in occupied Minsk; Jeffrey Jones, in liberated Rostov.[94] There were, of course, limits to the survivalist ethic; Bidlack, for example, has observed that many Leningraders "made a moral distinction between theft from a food store or warehouse and from an individual."[95] Whether in peacetime or during the war, however, violating travel restrictions was not the kind of behavior likely to evoke popular moral censure. Until at least the early 1950s, when food supplies stabilized, the regime would face an uphill battle in its efforts to restrict self-procurement by rail.

The Revitalization of the Private Sector

With respect to the consumer economy, the USSR's war with Germany can be divided into two stages. The first, from 1941 to 1943, was charac-

[92] GARF, f. R-9401 s/ch., op. 2, d. 66, ll. 40–53 (Stalin's *osobaia papka*).

[93] Arzhilovskii, the diarist, evinces this attitude at a number of points.

[94] Jones, "'Reconstruction' of Rostov," 231–35; Uwe Gartenschläger, "Living and Surviving in Occupied Minsk," in Robert Thurston and Bernd Bonwetsch, ed., *The People's War* (Urbana, 2000), 13–28; Richard Bidlack, "Survival Strategies in Leningrad during the First Year of the Soviet-German War," in Thurston and Bonwetsch, *The People's War*, 84–107.

[95] Bidlack, "Survival Strategies," 98; cf. David Dallin, "The Black Market in Russia," *The American Mercury* 69 (December, 1949): 676–84; here, 679–80.

Figure 11. Shoppers at a flea market under the German occupation.

terized by the chaotic transfer of economic life from the west to the east, the collapse of civilian manufacturing, and the catastrophic reduction in food supplies in both the industrialized center and the occupied west. As we have seen, these conditions altered prevailing consumption norms, especially in the cities, where the optimistic consumerism of the later 1930s gave way to a grim survivalism, comparable to that of 1918 to 1921 or 1932 to 1933. As in the revolutionary period, city dwellers sought to overcome the disintegration of the economy through individual foraging trips to the villages, and, once again, they were compelled to join the ranks of hawkers to supplement their earnings from work. Increasing numbers resorted to pilfering.[96] By 1943, when these tendencies had reached their zenith, urban households derived a quarter to a third of their incomes from informal (in not a few cases, illegal) transactions. In the first period of the war, then, the main developmental tendency was the universalization of survival-oriented petty exchange, against a backdrop of constantly worsening supplies of foods and consumer goods.

Fire sales and looting were especially characteristic of this period. As

[96] Rates of theft from trade and consumer goods factories rose sharply during the war, after declining from 1933 to 1939. Cf. GARF, f. 5446, op. 48, d. 1819, ll. 31–33; f. 8131, op. 22, d. 101, ll. 13–16; RGASPI f. 17, op. 88, d. 707, ll. 3–22.

rumors of the German advance crescendoed, state and cooperative store managers sometimes succumbed to the temptation to parcel out the wares of their stores. A case from Moscow, which resulted in the execution of the managers, illustrates the panicked atmosphere in which such a decision could be taken. The venue in this episode was a custom tailoring shop, or *atelier*, located on the first floor of a large workers' dormitory. On October 16, 1941, when the German offensive was directly threatening the capital, the manager of the shop piled forty suits from the store into his car, authorized his assistant manager to distribute the rest of the clothes to employees, and ordered his chauffeur to drive east until they were safely out of town. The employees spent much of the afternoon trying on clothes and selecting what they wanted (the store's accountant, for example, acquired a winter coat with a fur collar and a woolen skirt) and then sold off the remainder by going up and down the halls of the dormitory and offering clothes at a discounted price. When the smoke cleared, the custom shop was short by more than one hundred thousand rubles. Not surprisingly the purchasers, who would not have been able to afford these clothes under normal circumstances, could not be induced to give them back.[97] Similar scenes played out in Minsk[98] and presumably in many other cities in the days before the Wehrmacht's arrival; they epitomize the pandemonium that accompanied the German advance.

The second period of the war, from 1943 to 1945, was distinguished by its much more positive military and economic backdrop. The volume of goods sold in state and cooperative trade bottomed out in 1942–43 at some 15 to 20 percent of the 1940 level (per capita, 22 to 30 percent), after which it slowly climbed, reaching 40 percent of the prewar level in 1945.[99] Meanwhile, the western and southern parts of the country slowly came back under Soviet control. Somewhat surprisingly, albeit in keeping with the civil war pattern, these successes resulted not in a reduction of private economic activity but in its revitalization. Private ventures became untethered from survival: provisioning trips became longer and more profit-oriented, thefts larger, transactions more ambitious, more official, and more overt. Small businesses of a relatively formal variety also made their appearance. All these tendencies continued and expanded through the immediate postwar period until 1947–48, when the policing organs reined them in.

One spur to the private sector from 1943 to 1945, as in 1920–21, was

[97] TsMA Moskvy, f. 819, op. 2, d. 46.
[98] Gartenschläger, "Living and Surviving in Occupied Minsk," 23.
[99] Calculated from Malafeev, *Istoriia tsenoobrazovaniia*, 222, 407; U. G. Cherniavskii, *Voina i prodovol'stvie. Snabzhenie gorodskogo naseleniia (1941–1945)* (Moscow, 1964), 16.

the Red Army's reconquest of the lower Volga, North Caucasus, and Ukrainian breadbaskets. As numerous scholars have documented, the German occupation of these areas was murderously exploitative; the Germans retained Stalin's coercive structure for food procurement in the countryside and essentially let the cities starve. Rations, if occupation authorities issued them at all, covered no more than a fraction of a subsistence diet.[100] Nevertheless, the Nazis took a much looser attitude toward private trade than did the Communists, and private shops, no longer even nominally deterred by Soviet interdictions, soon sprang up to meet citizens' demand. In Odessa, for example, Soviet financial agents estimated in 1945 that there were twenty-five hundred private traders, of whom more than eleven hundred had their own permanent shops, and that a further six hundred artisans had set up private manufactures in the city.[101] Not surprisingly toleration of private trade in a traditional grain-surplus region acted as a magnet. In 1944–45 it was precisely the railway lines to the south and southwest that were inundated with baggers, who streamed in from all parts of the country to purchase grain and other foods.[102]

Individual foraging trips remained a mass phenomenon during the second half of the war, but, alongside them, bagging increasingly acquired an institutional base. Nearly three decades after the revolution, baggers still spread across a continuum, and it was no simpler now to distinguish "legitimate" agents and consumers than it had been during the civil war. As a top police official complained in 1945, the forms and methods of speculation had shifted; now the main culprits were "miscellaneous representatives from various organizations, [who] buy up foods in distant regions and transport them to the industrial centers, where they sell them for a speculative price."[103] By 1944 large-scale buyers were invariably furnished, as in 1918, with "some kind of a document from an organization"—a factory, rural soviet, university, or collective farm. Not all were authentic, of course; counterfeit travel and procurement papers became a widespread, lucrative business, and spot checks up and down

---

[100] See Theo J. Schulte, *The German Army and Nazi Policies in Occupied Russia* (Oxford, 1989), 87–89, 101; Moskoff, *Bread of Affliction*, 50–65; Alexander Dallin, *German Rule in Russia, 1941–1945. A Study of Occupation Policies*, rev. ed. Boulder, 1981 [1957]), 310–313; Bohdan Krawchenko, "Soviet Ukraine under Nazi Occupation, 1941–44," in *Ukraine during World War II* (Edmonton, 1986), 15–38; Gartenschläger, "Living and Surviving in Occupied Minsk."

[101] RGAE, f. 7733, op. 30, d. 19, ll. 35–36.

[102] GARF, f. 8131, op. 37, d. 1433, l. 88.

[103] Ibid., d. 2264, l. 7.

the rails yielded numerous false papers in the later years of the war.[104] More significant, even when buying agents' documents were in order, they and their institutional sponsors often skirted the law. D. G. Simkin, a *tolkach* for an electrical factory in the Moscow suburb Liubertsy, affords an example: when Simkin attracted scrutiny for the private railroad car that he had managed to attach to a southbound train, investigators found not one but a sheaf of stamped and signed travel permits from his factory director. The latter intervened with an explanation: since Simkin had to arrange with railway officials to hook up the car, he might end up traveling to an unplanned destination; it was in the factory's best interest to facilitate the trip.[105]

Simkin's story illustrates particularly vividly the freewheeling side of the wartime corporate culture. In a period when supply functions once again devolved onto employers and institutions, the proprietary psychology reasserted itself with a vengeance. Irregularities proliferated, not least because railway workers often had to be bribed if one wanted to bring on extra luggage, to travel with one's wares in a freight car, or, like Simkin, to hook up an extra car.[106] Nor did the irregularities stop there. In Dnepropetrovsk, an affiliate of Simkin's factory allowed him to leave the freight car on its grounds while its *ors* director chauffeured him around to exchange the flashlights, clothes, shoes, underwear, basins, buckets, baking soda, toys, and ribbons that he had brought with him for food. In return for this favor, which enabled him to trade substantial quantities of goods in nearby villages for vegetables, wheat, dried beans, and sunflower seeds, Simkin transferred some of the wares to his associate's kiosks. He also acquired—this was probably what did him in—two grand pianos, one for himself and one for his boss. During the police interrogation, Simkin explained the contents of his freight car in terms of "decentralized procurement." This was indeed his job; but in his execution of it, the policing organs could readily identify a whole series of criminal violations, and, despite a glowing reference from his factory director, Simkin was sentenced to prison for violations of the rules of trade.[107]

The freewheeling wartime corporate culture had an effect on representatives' dealings: in at least a few cases, their trips became more daring in destination or scale or in both. In Riazan' oblast, the most noteworthy case from 1944–45 was that of E. G. Bragin, who used stolen

---

[104] GARF, f. 8131, op. 37, d. 1433, ll. 82, 88–89.

[105] TsMA Moskvy, f. 953, op. 1, d. 7.

[106] A total of 2,155 railroad workers were reportedly prosecuted, and many more fined, for abetting speculators in 1944 (GARF, f. 8131, op. 37, d. 1433, l. 90).

[107] TsMA Moskvy, f. 953, op. 1, d. 7.

order forms from a local textile cooperative to ship consignments of shawls to his hometown. When Bragin was arrested, he had squirreled away 130,000 rubles from a three-month series of orders and had bank-rolled half his relatives for helping him sell the goods.[108] Central government documents list various other examples: the wife and sister-in-law of a Stalino supply official, who gave them travel permits to purchase two thousand notebooks and school uniforms, which they then sold for their own profit at the local bazaar; and the woman who cut a deal with a border guard to travel back and forth to Romania for cloth and other goods.[109] Business travels on this new scale jeopardized the wartime consensus; it was difficult to attribute them to personal hardship when profits went so far beyond survival needs.

Private marketing, likewise, became more entrepreneurial toward the end of the war. Though most hawkers continued to buy and sell only occasionally, bazaars increasingly supported regular, full-time vendors as well. In the spring of 1945 this was a major theme in reports of local and regional tax collectors from every part of the USSR.[110] As the Armenian Republic's chief tax administrator put it:

> Many collective farmers, and also workers and employees with vegetable gardens, are not in a position to sell their surplus produce at the market themselves. Whether out of a lack of time or merely for the sake of convenience, they resort to assistance from other people. In this way, there emerges a class of individuals who systematically engage in buying and reselling goods.[111]

A factor he did not mention was the large number of disabled veterans, which the socialist economy could not immediately absorb. In Rostov, as Jeffrey Jones has found, war invalids often remained unemployed for months after their discharge from the army, "preferring," in the words of local officials, to make their living through "trade and speculation."[112] At Moscow's markets disabled veterans were the chief vendors of goods from "commercial" stores, since they were eligible for a 35 percent discount (as in the years 1932 to 1935, high-priced off-ration shops were opened in major cities from 1944 to 1947; see chapter 7). War invalids also figured prominently, along with children and adolescents, in sales of ration cards, vodka, tobacco, and cigarettes.[113] We might recall Mikhail Kalinin's 1926 advocacy of petty trading licenses as "an equivalent of

[108] GA Riaz. ob., f. R-4387, op. 2, d. 8.
[109] GARF, f. 8131, op. 37, d. 2264, ll. 7–10.
[110] For a detailed discussion of this episode, see my "A Postwar Perestroika?"
[111] RGASPI, f. 17, op. 121, d. 584, l. 65.
[112] Jones, "'Reconstruction' of Rostov," 218–20.
[113] TsMA Moskvy, f. 46, op. 1, d. 8, ll. 110–11.

social security for invalids." In the 1940s, no less than the 1920s, the human flotsam of industrial warfare overwhelmed the country's social services. Prostheses were late in arriving, pensions inadequate, job training minimal—and so, not surprisingly, disabled veterans sought to look after their needs by begging or trading at the bazaar.[114]

Private trade found new venues between 1944 and 1948. To the consternation of trade officials, one such venue was, in fact, the commercial stores. When TsUM reopened in 1945, it was positively flooded with private vendors; for the better part of the next decade, administrators would complain that it "more closely resembles a bazaar than a model department store."[115] Private traders came to the same department each day with a suitcase full of goods: shoe sellers to the shoe department, dish sellers to the china department, and so forth. If the wares were too bulky to bring into the store, as in the case of furniture, vendors loitered by the counter; whenever someone wanted to buy a furniture item, three or four vendors would descend on the customer with offers of the same item at a lower price. According to managers, hawkers congregated primarily in departments selling scarce goods (woolen cloth, ready-to-wear clothing, shoes); near the freight elevators (a source of information about goods in stock); and in the women's restrooms (out of earshot of the police).[116] Most sold the same wares advertised in the given department, at a steep discount. Others sold related items of their own manufacture: homemade food in the grocery department, hand-knitted sweaters in the children's clothing department, homemade leather jackets in the coat department.[117] One manager claimed that only a permanent force of eighty to one hundred plainclothes policemen could deter private trade in the store.[118]

A second incongruous cover for private trade in the mid-1940s was provided by cooperatives, which thereby confirmed the Party's long-standing suspicions of them as "less proletarian than bourgeois." Expanding an occasional practice from the 1930s (as Elena Osokina has shown, a few cooperatives, theaters, and branches of the Red Cross hired private citizens to run cafes through 1935),[119] the cooperative would obtain a patent from the municipal or provincial financial department to run, say, a billiard hall, but instead of opening the business itself, it would farm it

[114] Jones, "'Reconstruction' of Rostov," 50, 70; GA Riaz. ob. (Party doc. div.), f. 3, op. 3, dd. 237, 239.
[115] TsMA Moskvy, f. 1953, op. 2, d. 73, l. 16.
[116] Ibid., ll. 16, 25, 45; op. 2, d. 153, ll. 31–34.
[117] TsMA Moskvy, f. 1889, op. 1, d. 2118; d. 2371; d. 1910.
[118] Ibid., f. 1953, op. 2, d. 73, l. 45.
[119] Osokina, Za fasadom, 154–56.

out to someone else. This person then paid the cooperative a fixed monthly fee, and sometimes also rent, for the right to operate the concession, but otherwise ran the business independently: he or she supplied equipment and raw materials; personally provided the product or service or hired enough helpers to do so; priced labor at will; and pocketed all proceeds beyond the predetermined fee. Popular businesses for concessions included photography, portraiture, rag-collection, watch making, barbershops, restaurants, billiard halls, and repair shops of all kinds. Some privateers opened up regular stores under the umbrella of a cooperative. For the privateers, affiliation with a cooperative offered some shelter against harassment from financial agents or the police. For cooperatives, the concessions served the dual ends of bringing in a steady income and providing services that members desired.[120]

Fast-food stands and cafeterias were a particularly widespread and lucrative concession from 1944 to 1948. In Rostov a number of snack shops were reported by the local newspaper to be privately owned and operated. In Georgia privateer Kal'diashvili grossed 106,000 rubles a month in 1947 from a bar and snack shop, after paying 13,000 rubles each month to the sponsoring artel. Teahouses run by private citizens sprouted up throughout Central Asia and Kazakhstan; million-ruble fortunes were made from ice cream, nougat, and fried fish.[121] Again, despite their affiliation with a cooperative, these shops must be considered private enterprises. Owners made an initial capital investment in cooking equipment, flatware, and dishes, and if they had not received a separate space from the cooperative, they spent time and money remodeling their homes. After opening their enterprise, they bought groceries at the bazaar, employed hired labor, and prepared and served customers' food. The success of their business rose and fell with customer demand. Given the paucity of palatable alternatives in the immediate postwar years, private eateries flourished until forced to close shop.

Bazaars also continued to thrive, nourished in part by the influx of southern peasants into the cities during the 1946–47 famine,[122] but also

[120] See my "A Postwar Perestroika?" GA Riaz. ob. (Party doc. div.), f. 3, op. 3, d. 613, ll. 103–6; see also GA Kursk. obl., f. 4850, op. 1, d. 253, ll. 18–38; d. 263, l. 38; f. 3761, op. 1, d. 7, ll. 207–8; d. 20, ll. 198–203; f. 4910, op. 1, d. 35, ll. 1–5.

[121] Jones, "'Reconstruction' of Rostov," 211; RGASPI, f. 17, op. 121, d. 584, ll. 11–16; V. Navozov, "Ochistit' potrebitel'skuiu kooperatsiiu ot chastnikov i spekuliantov," *Pravda Vostoka*, June 4, 1948. Ice cream was also quite lucrative in Kursk (GA Kursk. ob., f. 3761, d. 20, l. 200).

[122] Speculation cases involving refugees include TsMA Moskvy, f. 1889, op. 1, dd. 668, 670, 767; see also f. 46, op. 1, d. 8; RGAE, f. 7971, op. 16 s/ch, d. 472, ll. 126–27, 157–73; op. 5, d. 65. On the famine, see Zima, *Golod v SSSR*.

by an upsurge in artisanal manufacturing at the end of the war. Sokolov and Nazarov, co-authors of an early history of postwar trade, wrote that artisanal cooperatives increased their output by 47 percent between 1942 and 1944.[123] In the subsequent period, however, artisanal production shifted decisively toward the private sector. Bel'kovskii *raion*, a rural district in the northeast corner of Riazan' *oblast'*, was an extreme case in point. In 1944–45 the peasants of this area greatly expanded their traditional cottage industry, the weaving of a coarse cotton cloth. By 1946, 40 percent of the households in the district had taken up this trade. The 1936 "Rules on the registration of manufactures and trades" notwithstanding, Bel'kovskii peasants bought thread from textile workers in the neighboring provinces of Ivanovo and Vladimir, where factories had resorted to compensating overtime with wages in kind; wove the thread on handlooms; and sent out agents to sell the cloth at markets all around the USSR. On a single loom a family could weave twenty-two to twenty-five meters of cloth a day, for a daily profit of 350 rubles. Many households had set up a second loom; nearly all had abandoned work in their cooperatives and collective farms.[124]

Though the Bel'kovskii case attracted national attention, there is reason to conclude that it was not unique. Tax officials reported on private artisanal manufacturing as a "mass phenomenon" from 1945 to 1948, and, as I have written elsewhere, they accordingly urged the government to widen the legal—and taxable—bounds.[125] The Armenian tax chief described the situation particularly bluntly:

> Manufacturing cooperatives and local industry are not yet in a condition to satisfy the growing needs of the population for [such goods as clothing, linens, hats, and leather shoes]. The population is thus compelled to resort to privateers, whose number has grown incredibly. In keeping with paragraph 20 of the "Rules for the registration of manufactures and trades," these privateers are not subject to taxation; but for its part, the Procuracy does not press [the prescribed] criminal charges against them.
>
> This creates a situation where not only the rural artisan ceases to work according to his registered permit, but even members of manufacturing cooperatives, disabled veterans' artels, and workers in other productive enterprises set aside their cooperative work and take their business underground—that is, they start working on a private basis.[126]

[123] V. Sokolov and R. Nazarov, *Sovetskaia torgovlia v poslevoennyi period* (Moscow, 1954), 38. Unfortunately they did not provide figures for either date.
[124] GARF, f. 8131, op. 23, d. 105, ll. 1–9.
[125] See Hessler, "A Postwar Perestroika?"
[126] RGASPI, f. 17, op. 121, d. 584, l. 65.

Their sales typically took place at the bazaars, which accordingly overflowed with goods manufactured by private artisans and artisanal outworkers—members of manufacturing cooperatives who worked at home
and were obliged only to deliver a certain number of units each month to
the cooperative store. By 1948, when this issue had been festering for
three years, an investigation concluded that outworkers tended to ignore
their delivery obligations, and to sell their products for higher prices on
their own. In the Kursk area, for example, soapmakers from the "Buden-
nyi" artel took their soap to out-of-town markets rather than adhering to
the cooperative agreement; hatmakers associated with "New Way" delivered only 250 rubles' worth of hats to the cooperative, but earned 10,000
rubles a month by fulfilling private orders on the side; cobblers from the
"Stalin" artel failed to deliver a single shoe to the cooperative until
threatened with the confiscation of their sewing machines; and so forth.[127]
Outworkers privately manufactured and sold permissable items—soap,
baskets, barrels, bricks and construction materials, toys, furniture, and
candy—but they also produced all the goods that independent artisans
were prohibited from manufacturing according to the 1936 Rules. In
Kursk alone, there were private artisanal sales at the market of clothes,
hats, leather shoes, and felt boots; knitted socks, mittens, and underwear;
sausages and other food products; and leather saddles and harnesses.
Clothing, felt boots, and candy, the three most common products of
outworking in the Kursk and Riazan' regions, literally inundated area
bazaars until 1948.[128]

Nationally the flea market reached its zenith in connection with the
December 1947 monetary reform. Announced together with the cessation of rationing, the monetary reform required citizens to trade in old
rubles for new rubles over the course of the next week. The differential
rates of exchange were aimed at confiscating savings from anyone who
might have prospered from the war: the first three thousand rubles in
state savings accounts would be exchanged on a one-to-one basis; pre-
1947 state bonds would be denominated at one new ruble to three old
rubles; and all other savings or cash would be subject to a one-to-ten
exchange rate. Wages would remain the same, though paid in new rubles.[129]
Elena Zubkova has described the "holiday" atmosphere fostered first by
the rumors of this reform and subsequently by its announcement: citi-

[127] GA Kursk. ob., f. 3761, op. 1, d. 7, l. 208; d. 20, ll. 198–203.
[128] Ibid., ll. 207–8, 272–74; d. 20, ll. 198–203; f. R-4850, op. 1, d. 218, ll. 37–49; d. 253,
ll. 18–38; d. 263, ll. 38–39; GA Riaz. ob. (party doc. div.), f. 3, op. 3, d. 613, ll. 107–16.
[129] *Izvestiia*, December 15, 1947. On the politics of the monetary reform, see Popov,
Ekonomicheskaia politika sovetskogo gosudarstva, 77–98.

zens' response to the imminent confiscation of their savings was to go on a wild spending spree.[130] In the words of an older Muscovite, "tout le monde" spent the evening of December 15 at the market so as to exchange old rubles for goods before their money lost its value. To meet this demand, goods appeared at the market as never before—with prices as never before, even during the worst period of the war. Among my interview subjects, one woman's family bought a cow, two pigs, and a gold pocketwatch during the week of the 16th to the 22nd; another informant bought a bookshelf full of prerevolutionary books.[131] Although extreme shortages were not yet over—many regions experienced food crises throughout 1948—this free-for-all marked a turning point after which popular buying and selling at the market gradually ebbed back to prewar levels.[132]

PRIVATE TRADE AS A SOCIAL FORMATION: CONTINUITY AND CHANGE

Private trade did not, of course, disappear after the monetary reform or the April 1948 crackdown on "privateer penetration" in cooperatives and state trade. As the well-developed scholarly literature on the Soviet "second economy" attests, an informal private sector continued to furnish goods and services in subsequent decades, though its proportional weight in the consumer economy probably declined.[133] Was it structurally analogous to what we have been discussing? Yes and no. The concept of the second economy has connotations that are problematic for the Stalin period: specifically, the second economy is often portrayed as having piggybacked on the socialist sector for equipment and supplies. This certainly happened, as evidenced by the ubiquity of petty workplace theft. During the Stalin period, however, one can, with equal and often greater justice, describe the socialist sector as having piggybacked on the private. Not only collective farms but manufacturing cooperatives obtained their basic tools and machinery when individual private artisans were pres-

[130] Zubkova, *Russia after the War*, 51–55; idem, *Obshchestvo i reformy*, 1945–1964 (Moscow, 1993), 41–64; and idem, *Poslevoennoe sovetskoe obshchestvo. Politika i povsednevnost'*, 1945–1953 (Moscow, 1999), 78–88.
[131] Interviews with Galina Petrovna and Aleksandr L'vovich (1993).
[132] This can be traced through an archival file on Soviet markets in 1948–49: RGAE, f. 7971, op. 5, d. 65.
[133] For the post-Stalin second economy, see Gregory Grossman, "The 'Second Economy' of the USSR," *Problems of Communism* 26, no. 5 (September–October 1977): 25–40; and Aron Katsenelinboigen, "Coloured Markets in the Soviet Union," *Soviet Studies* 29, no. 1 (January, 1977): 62–85. For a bibliography of literature on the subject, see *Berkeley-Duke Papers on the Second Economy in the USSR*, no. 21.

sured into joining. When these same former private artisans used their equipment to manufacture goods for the market, can we really accept the Soviet government's assessment that "socialist property" was misused?

Cooperative members did not always accept this view. An intriguing case from the 1948 investigations of "privateer penetration" concerned N. I. Konorev, a member of Kursk's "Krupskaia" sewing cooperative who essentially worked as a private tailor. The cooperative's general assembly refused to go along when a state inspector tried to force Konorev to "socialize" his sewing machine and move his work to the cooperative space; as the inspector had to report to her supervisor, "the members of the artel stated that the wives of local executives [*otvetstvennykh rabotnikov*] all have sewing machines and sew on the side, and the financial department takes no measures against them."[134] Rather than pointing ahead to the post-Stalin second economy, Konorev's business is best understood as a vestige of the NEP. Like many of its 1920s counterparts, it was a family enterprise, employing Konorev's daughter in addition to himself. Konorev's patrons were drawn not from personal connections, in the characteristic manner of an informal or second economy, but from that segment of local society that had money to spare. Nearly all the Kursk *nomenklatura* bought clothes from Konorev, but he socialized with other artisans—not with his clientele. This is the kind of small tailoring business, in short, that could have existed at any time between 1900 and 1948. With two crucial exceptions—his formal membership in a cooperative and the fact that he was not licensed as a private tailor—it was not identifiably a product of the socialist regime.

Unlike Konorev's business, other cases from the postwar Stalin period have a more distinctive "second economy" look. Liliana Isaevna, an elderly Russian Jew whom I interviewed in 1993, ran two such businesses in the decade after the war. L. I.'s resumé revealed a flamboyant, freewheeling personality; she had spent the late 1930s in a theatrical troupe that traveled from market to market, in which capacity she had met, and eventually married, a Dagestani prince. After the war she tried to make some money by manufacturing cosmetics. Having learned a recipe for mascara from an acquaintance in Tashkent, where she spent the war, she mobilized her relatives to help set this business on its feet. Her uncle, a professional photographer, used his business connections to buy small industrial glass bottles by the lot, and designed a label for the mascara in French, to give it a classy image. Her brother helped out by marketing the mascara—taking it around to high-class department stores and hawking it to customers there. After a couple of profitable months, L. I. hired

---

[134] GA Kursk. ob., f. R-4850, op. 1, d. 253, ll. 33–38.

two employees to help with both manufacture and sales, while she increasingly devoted herself to managing the business. The lucrative enterprise screeched to a halt in 1949, when an employee became disgruntled over low wages and notified the police bureau for economic crimes of the underground operation. As its organizer, Liliana Isaevna was arrested and jailed, but a timely call to an influential army general, a one-time acquaintance, resulted in her release two days later.

Though this type of activity was clearly laden with risks, the lure of profits drew L. I. back into business less than two years later. Seeing a female acquaintance enjoy material success with an underground millinery for the wives of Party elites, she approached her and asked to be taken on as an apprentice. The acquaintance initially demanded one thousand rubles for the instruction but then finally agreed to teach her for free, as a special favor. After a brief apprenticeship, Liliana Isaevna decided to specialize in the feather decorations then popular on hats, which would keep her out of direct competition with her friend. The difficulty was obtaining supplies: she needed to find a source of feathers. In the hope of cutting a deal with a devout Jewish butcher, she decided to go to the synagogue for the first time in twenty years. There, she broke the rules of the service and sat in the men's section so as to introduce herself to this man. The combination of ethnic ties and the profit motive evidently overcame his religious orthodoxy; giving her a favorable deal on chicken feathers, he also set her up with an acquaintance at the Aragvi restaurant for feathers from wildfowl. L. I.'s hat decorations became extremely popular and profitable; she was soon supplying most of the underground milliners in Moscow and had taken on three employees. Unlike the mascara operation, it died a natural death when feathers on hats went out of style some years later.

How do these businesses compare to those in the private sector of the NEP? There are, of course, details that date them to the immediate postwar period: the hawking of mascara at TsUM and other premiere department stores; the prevailing fashion in hats. In terms of objects, Liliana Isaevna's activities were nonetheless consistent with those of the private sector from the NEP period on. Both mascara and feather decorations were consumer, rather than industrial, goods, and both combined artisanal production with sales. If we consider the other private businesses that flourished in the late 1940s, it is clear that many were more or less in the NEP mold. Along with artisanal manufacturing and marketing, the fast-food stands, eateries, and billiard halls of the postwar years followed directly in the footsteps of the NEP-era privateers. So, too, did peasant sales of surplus produce, the constant base of market trade. The one component that permanently disappeared from the Soviet economic landscape was private trade in bulk commodities, which had been the most lucrative line of commerce during the NEP period and the one most vulnerable to repression. In the late 1940s and 1950s, as, for that matter, in the 1930s, cotton cloth continued to motivate purchasing trips to the big cities, but large-scale underground dealers of wine, meat, flour, or lumber, much less factory-made cloth, were exceptional at best.[135]

The most distinctive feature of Liliana Isaevna's enterprises was their social organization, though here, too, continuities with the past can be discerned. Readers will recall that a major impediment to commercial recovery in the early 1920s was the exhaustion of citizens' capital reserves. Entrepreneurs' solutions to this problem included applying for credit, combining work for a socialist entity with a spinoff business, and entering into a partnership. In the 1940s and 1950s bank credit was not an option, but the Simkin case shows that socialist-sector representatives still occasionally cut their own deals alongside official business, and partnerships, at least in the illegal private sector, were still very much the norm. Forty-four of the 210 black market criminal cases I have examined from Riazan' *oblast'* and Moscow involved the collaboration of family members, and another 73 were based on partnerships between associates or friends. As in the NEP period, these partners were almost invariably members of the same ethnic group, and they were, more often than not, acquaintances from work.

Liliana Isaevna, more than most of these "speculators," acted as an entrepreneur in her social relations. As she indicated in the interview, the combination of instrumental and affective reasoning pervaded both her decisions and those of her contacts: she felt sorry for her unemployed brother and wanted to help him, but she also knew that he could be trusted not to inform the police and that he would take over the retailing side of the business, which she found distasteful. The milliner friend took her on as an apprentice both out of sympathy and out of the expectation of a few months' unpaid assistance. The Jewish butcher liked the idea of assisting a fellow member of his ethnic community while at the same time calculating that he would profit from the otherwise wasted by-products of his occupation. Without written contracts but with obligations on all sides that could be breached, this network shared aspects of a moral economy, based primarily on favors, with those of a market economy,

---

[135] MVD operatives did uncover a large-scale wine business in 1956, centered in Moldavia and southern Ukraine; cf. GARF, f. 7971, op. 16, d. 1140, ll. 52–56. The following postwar court cases involved speculative purchasing trips for cloth: GA Riaz. ob., f. 4433, dd. 96, 126; TsMA Moskvy, f. 901, op. 1, d. 117; f. 1919, op. 1, d. 58; f. 1889, op. 1, dd. 5, 39, 232, 617, 734, 926, 951, 1284, 1665.

based primarily on cash. Unfulfilled expectations could lead to ruptured alliances, as in the case of the employee who bolted. In the context of an "underground" enterprise, coalitions were inherently unstable, subject to reformation or dissolution if the basis for individual or group profits disappeared.

The structuring of businesses around interpersonal networks has been identified as a distinctive feature of informal economies, whether in the Soviet Union or in other parts of the world.[136] In the Soviet case, however, some of these same networks were mobilized during the NEP period, when private businesses were legal but supplies were difficult to obtain. Are they not also typical of many aboveboard businesses in the capitalist world? In Western Europe and the United States the past few decades have whittled down the role of "old boy networks" in personnel decisions, but personal references and school connections have by no means disappeared. Businesses organized around kinship, ethnic ties, and social networks were typical, but not distinctive, of the Soviet second economy. What identified Liliana Isaevna's businesses with the second economy was a different attribute, namely, that it was organized with the evasion of taxes and regulations as a primary goal. The hiring ("exploitation") of labor and the failure to obtain a license—not the actual manufactures, both of which were permissable under the 1936 Rules— were what placed her outside the law.

Conclusion

One of the purposes of this chapter, and indeed of this book, is to demonstrate the persistence of private trade in the decades after the NEP. Though its precise role in the consumer economy fluctuated in relation to overall economic trends, private trade—both peasant marketing and private sales of manufactured goods—provided an appreciable percentage of what citizens consumed throughout the Stalin era. This is by no means to deny the significant structural differences between the private trade of the 1920s and the private trade of the period from the 1930s to the early 1950s. Excepting the unofficial arrangements with cooperatives at the end of the war, private traders were unable to rent an enclosed shop after 1931. They could legally sell only certain kinds of articles of their own manufacture—goods made from abundant materials, such as

---

[136] Cf. Jeremy Boissevain, *Friends of Friends. Networks, Manipulators, and Coalitions* (New York, 1974); Larissa Adler Lomnitz, "Informal Exchange Networks in Formal Systems: A Theoretical Model," *American Anthropology* 90 (1988): 42–55; Teodor Shanin, ed., *Neformal'naia ekonomika: Rossiia i mir* (Moscow, 1999).

wood, straw, or clay—and they had the right to sell them only in certain, restricted ways (hawking at the market or, for a slightly larger circle of objects, taking advance orders). Except during the Second World War, they were also permitted to resell articles that they had purchased at state or cooperative shops, but "excessive profits" from such sales were disallowed. The effect of these restrictions in a period of chronic scarcity was not to eliminate private trade but rather to transform much of it into an informal economy or black market.

Whether licensed or unlicensed, private trade was concentrated at the bazaars, whose centrality to the retail structure was strongly reinforced during the Stalin period. In the nineteenth century educated "Westernizers" had continually predicted the demise of the outdoor markets, which never came; the fact was that Russians liked bazaars, which also served as a kind of cheap amusement. This remained true in the communist era. Especially in the smaller towns, where the socialist retail system was woefully underdeveloped, the markets were almost the only source of consumer goods and foods; even in the cities, outdoor flea markets attracted huge crowds. Again they provided entertainment, and they gave shoppers a respite from queues as well as from the cold formality of the official Soviet shops. During the Second World War the overwhelming preponderance of the marketplace in the country's informal trade distinguished the Soviet Union from its continental European neighbors; whereas every part of German-controlled Europe had a black market, venues in other countries ranged from the bazaar and street corner to the school or café.[137] A brief comparison with Europe's wartime black markets may shed light on the Soviet situation. By and large, wherever food rations, which were adopted in every country "for the duration," fell below a survival minimum (e.g., Poland throughout the war period or Germany in 1945–46), informal exchange closely resembled the Soviet pattern. The price of foods rose sharply in relation to both money and manufactured goods; urban dwellers increasingly relied on foraging trips to the countryside for food, and on hawking for income support; workplace theft burgeoned; and personal connections, especially in the retail network, were activated for goods that were difficult to obtain. The difference lay in the military, political, and psychological context: black markets thrived in defeated, occupied countries, whose governments lacked legitimacy and whose civilians exhibited low morale. In occupied Poland and Vichy France, for example, citizens viewed illegal trade as

---

[137] Cf. David, *Le marché noir*; J. Debû-Bridel, *Histoire du marché noir (1939–1947)* (Paris, 1947); Wyka, "The Excluded Economy," 55; Wildt, *Der Traum vom Sattwerden*, esp. 101–14.

practically a civic duty; in Germany, black market activity was connected to defeatism fostered by the 1944–45 strategic bombing campaign.[138] These links with morale and governmental legitimacy raise interesting questions in the Soviet case. One can speculate that the Soviet government's arbitrariness and brutality did nothing to bolster popular legal consciousness in the Stalin era. In this sense, the government surely contributed to the acceptance of survivalism as an alternative moral code.

The other crucial difference between war-torn Europe and the USSR was the relationship of wartime economic behavior to normal, prewar life. In the Soviet Union this *was* normal life: the wartime market and its attendant practices represented the continuation and expansion of the informal economy of the 1930s, overlaid with that repertoire of crisis behaviors that citizens had been honing, by intervals, since 1917. I have suggested that the private sector gradually underwent a shift, which gathered steam in the period from 1943 to 1948, from the forms connoted by "survivalism," "vestiges of tradition," and "vestiges of the NEP," to the more familiar "second economy" of the Brezhnev years. This shift was, however, very subtle, perceptible only in such innovations as the rise of the department store as an informal exchange venue or the enhanced role of tax evasion as an organizing principle, rather than a by-product, of informal trade.

[138] *U.S. Strategic Bombing Survey* (Washington, D.C., 1946–47), 64:90–91.

CHAPTER SEVEN

Postwar Normalization and Its Limits

THE ORGANIZATION OF distribution of foods and consumer goods was strikingly similar during each of the great economic crises of the Lenin and Stalin epochs. In each instance, supplies were centralized and bureaucratized; urban consumption was regulated by coupons on the principle of the class ration; distribution was displaced to the workplace; and peasants' access to consumer goods was made contingent on their fulfillment of the procurement plan. These measures, which dated to the revolutionary period, were adopted as a matter of course during the Second World War.

With respect to state policy, the war years nonetheless registered the political developments of the early 1930s, when Stalin had so clearly repudiated "socialist products exchange" in favor of socialist trade. Thus, whereas economic officials, from 1918 to 1920 and from 1928 to 1930, had embraced the bureaucratization of trade even as they found themselves pushed in that direction by an agricultural crisis, policy makers in the period from 1939 to 1941 held onto the trade model for as long as they possibly could. This period witnessed no revival of the notion of war communism as the "highest stage of economic organization" or of utopian projects for "Taylorism in distribution" or the abolition of money; bureaucratization was not portrayed as an end in itself. Like their counterparts in other countries, Soviet leaders made clear that the regimentation of distribution would apply only "for the duration." Stalin's wartime addresses invoked a mood of solidarity and patriotic sacrifice, not class warfare, and, as we saw in chapter 6, these ideas found expression in a softer approach to policing citizens' survival-oriented exchange.

Committed, as it was, to the normalization program of the 1930s, the economic establishment did not have to grope around for a new policy at the end of the war. As in the 1930s, plans for the reconstruction of Soviet trade called for restoring the commercial networks, dismantling *orsy*, progressively decentralizing supplies, and improving the retail atmosphere. As in the 1930s, too, famine intensified through the first steps of this reorganization. The 1946–47 famine is not, however, the principal focus of this chapter. More surprising about the postwar Stalin period is that, by the early 1950s, something genuinely appears to have changed.

Although the retail system still had its defects—there were often queues for consumer necessities, and small-town residents still had to travel for goods—nonetheless there seems not to have been a repeat of what occurred in 1939–40 following the cessation of rationing in December 1947. At least in the prewar Soviet territories, there were no overnight queues; there was no famine. In this fundamental respect, the period from 1949 to 1953 had more in common with the Khrushchev and Brezhnev periods than with the era that preceded it: as against the virtually perpetual food crises and famines of the first thirty years of Soviet power, the subsequent forty years had none. Of course, it is possible that the kind of severe shortage that merits the term *crisis* will come to light as archives from the 1950s, 1960s, and 1970s are declassified and explored. In general terms, though, I think that this picture will hold and that Soviet economic history can be divided into two broad eras: one of perpetual, subsistence-threatening crises, ending in 1948–49, and a second of relatively "normal" development from 1949 on.[1]

Looking at the late Stalin period in this light—as a transitional time divided by a major watershed—raises questions about the resilience and capacity for change of the Stalinist economic system, and the inherent viability of the 1930s model. This chapter approaches these questions by examining the relationship between trade policy and both quantitative and qualitative developments from 1945 to 1953. Both trade policy and retail structures naturally reflected the economic conjuncture: crisis or progress, before or after 1948. However, first economic crisis, and then economic growth, was refracted through the prism of Soviet leaders' reactions and priorities, and through consumers' and trade employees' expectations as well. As in the 1930s, Soviet goals for trade were not just narrowly economic. The measure of success was also moral and "cultural," in the sense indicated by the concept of "cultured Soviet trade." By the time of Stalin's death, genuine progress had been achieved in each of these areas, but the idiosyncrasies of Soviet leaders' economic agenda precluded full normalization. Indeed, the early 1950s brought troubling reminders of the goods famines of the late-1920s and late-1930s, though dislocations never reached the crisis point.

This final chapter explores the perception of policy makers that an era of crisis had come to an end. The first two sections provide a brief overview of wartime distribution, and then identify the evidence that informed policy makers' growing optimism in such areas as sales figures,

---

[1] Donald Filtzer has recently made a similar point about 1948; see his "Standard of Living of Soviet Industrial Workers in the Immediate Postwar Period, 1945–1948," *Europe-Asia Studies* 51, no. 6 (summer 1999): 1013–38; here, 1031.

market prices, and rates of employee theft. The chapter's third, and final, section is devoted to the implementation of "cultured trade" in two disparate settings after 1945. My aim is to provide a balance sheet for Stalinist trade policy in the postwar, and post-crisis, era: what was new, what was old; what worked, what failed. Was there, at last, a new relationship between "Stalinism" and Soviet consumers?

FROM WARTIME "ABNORMALITIES" TO THE PARADOX OF GROWTH

Chapter 5 described the spontaneous revival of food rationing in Soviet cities from 1939 to 1941, after a hiatus of just four or five years. Though the loss of the Caucasian oilfields and the suspension of civilian manufacturing during the war meant that fuels and manufactured consumer goods were also extremely scarce, public officials focused their energies on food. Food stocks were drastically reduced by the German invasion without a concomitant reduction in the number of mouths to be fed: the Soviet Union is estimated to have lost 47 percent of its prewar sown acreage, 45 percent of its livestock, and half its food-processing enterprises to the occupation, but just 33 percent of its population.[2] Within a few months of the invasion, local rationing measures were incorporated into a national distribution system after the pattern of the early 1930s and the civil war. Initially regulating only the distribution of bread and flour, centralized rations soon governed sales of sugar and sweets, meat and fish products, fats, cereals, and pasta in forty-three major metropolitan areas; as of February 1942, they were extended to basic manufactured goods.[3] By 1945 the centralized rationing system supplied bread to more than 80 million people, roughly half the population. This contingent, already double the number in the early 1930s, continued to expand, reaching 87.8 million at its peak in September 1946. In the end, 65.4 million were entitled to rations of other foods, and some 60 million people received coupons for manufactured goods.[4]

In keeping with Stalin's solidaristic rhetoric, food rations were not just more inclusive but somewhat more egalitarian than in the rationing systems of the past. The class ration continued to structure entitlements, with "workers" officially allotted 25 to 33 percent more food than white-collar "employees" in a given factory or town, but, over the course of the war, the white-collar category virtually disappeared. More and more oc-

---

[2] Cherniavskii, *Voina i prodovol'stvie*, 16.

[3] Ibid., 70–71; A. V. Liubimov, *Torgovlia i snabzhenie v gody Velikoi Otechestvennoi Voiny* (Moscow, 1968), 21.

[4] *Narodnoe khoziaistvo SSSR v Velikoi Otechesvennoi Voine, 1941–1945 gg.*, 202–5.

cupations were transferred into the "worker" class until, by 1944, the ratio of "workers" to "employees" was eleven to one.[5] The rationing system did continue to discriminate against the nonworking population; dependents' rations provided fewer than eight hundred calories a day, and, as of February 1942, no able-bodied man between the ages of sixteen and fifty-five, or woman between sixteen and forty-five, excepting students and mothers of young children, was eligible for rations without holding a job. Meanwhile, food supplements were used to promote "patriotic" behavior: having babies, donating blood.[6]

Even more than before, the most significant dividing line fell between the large, high-priority enterprises and smaller, less important concerns. The former received preferential provisionment from the center, as in the early 1930s, and their rights of supplementary provisionment were considerably enhanced. Factory *orsy*, resuscitated in 1942, consolidated their control over "subsidiary farms," which had gone into decline after 1935 and had, in many cases, reverted to the status of independent *sovkhozy*. In 1939–40, and especially from 1941 to 1943, regional authorities transferred these farms back to the factories, which became responsible for supplying fuel, transportation, and extra labor during the sowing and harvesting periods, but received 50 percent of the farm's grain, meat, and fish output, and all vegetables and other crops.[7] These directly benefited workers in the form of supplementary meals. In Moscow Party delegates reported in 1943 that factory farms had "essentially ceased to be subsidiary and have come to represent almost the primary resources" for factory food supplies.[8] *Orsy* and trade unions also organized group excursions to pick berries and mushrooms growing in the wild, as well as nettles and even pine needles, recently discovered to contain considerable quantities of vitamin C. Even the army became involved in the "subsidiary farm" movement, which became an important source of food for the military in 1944–45.[9]

Factories, and more particularly trade unions, were also involved in organizing gardening on suburban tracts. By 1945 half the urban population took part in vegetable gardening, which formed the most important local food source after the markets. In the 1930s planners had targeted

[5] Cherniavskii, *Voina i prodovol'stvie*, 84.

[6] Ibid., 79–81, 111; Liubimov, *Torgovlia i snabzhenie*, 32, 37–38; Moskoff, *Bread of Affliction*, 148–50; GARF, f. 8009, op. 22, d. 69, ll. 57–58.

[7] Cherniavskii, *Voina i prodovol'stvie*, 131–34.

[8] TsGAOD Moskvy, f. 1244, op. 2, d. 10, l. 61.

[9] D. V. Pavlov, *Stoikost'* (Moscow, 1983), 138–39; Moskoff, *Bread of Affliction*, 113–34; *Tyl sovetskikh vooruzhennykh sil v Velikoi Otechestvennoi Voine* (Moscow, 1977), 206–7; Cherniavskii, *Voina i prodovol'stvie*, 139–40.

six regions, Moscow and Ivanovo oblasts, Kazakhstan, the Ukraine, West Siberia, and the Urals, for individual gardening under the aegis of area factories. After the outbreak of war, officials in the first three of these regions had occasion to regret having neglected to make suburban plots available to urban gardeners. Kemerovo *oblast'* in West Siberia, in which more than half the urban population already had a sizable vegetable garden in 1939, obtained 230 kilograms of potatoes and vegetables for every urban inhabitant of the region in 1943. In Moscow, by contrast, very few people gardened until well into the war, and those who did had less than one-sixth as much space; not surprisingly these plots were able to provide only 38 kilograms of vegetables per person.[10] Urban vegetable gardening flourished in proportion to the energy expended by employers in lobbying the authorities for land. In November 1942 the central government acceded to these pressures and issued a decree that simultaneously guaranteed workers' garden plots against redistribution for five to seven years, and subjected their plots to confiscation by the factory or institutional administration if they left work for any reason other than to join the army.[11]

Inevitably the wartime rationing system gave rise to the same abuses and accounting difficulties as its predecessors. In Riazan', residential building administrators were supposed to provide lists of inhabitants and distribute ration cards; in 1943 random checks of several buildings yielded dozens of fictitious names, whose rations the administrators had either sold at the market or distributed to their family members.[12] Dead souls also turned up at factories, though the more common complaint was that factories were failing to enforce the tough wartime labor laws. A survey of leading industrial enterprises in Kuibyshev *oblast'* showed that every factory forgave the majority of worker infractions: Factory No. 42 had 458 absentees but docked the rations of only 37; Factory No. 525 had 317 absentees and cut rations for 121; Factory No. 1 had 1,713 absentees before the promulgation of the law, all of whom went unpunished, but even afterward it docked the rations of only 37 percent of its "loafers." Reregistration of ration cards, intended to root out absentees in the middle of each month, took place nowhere.[13]

The proprietary psychology, as usual, had its benefits and disadvantages. On the positive side, factories used extra food as an incentive,

[10] Cherniavskii, *Voina i prodovol'stvie* 145–47. The national average in 1944 was ninety-four kilograms per urban inhabitant from individual gardening, and fifty-three kilograms from factory farms.

[11] Ibid., 139–40.

[12] GA Riaz. ob. (Party docs. div.), f. 220, op. 1, d. 509, l. 29.

[13] RGASPI, f. 17, op. 88, d. 133, ll. 81–2.

whether by unilaterally increasing the most productive workers' bread rations or by singling them out for decentralized supplies. Many factories served a second hot meal to their "best workers," above and beyond the basic rations; some (seemingly at odds with the productivist agenda) issued one hundred grams of vodka to Stakhanovites with their lunch.[14] Less beneficially, the special cafeterias, restaurants, and commissaries that sprang up to accommodate high-ranking military officers, Party and state bureaucrats, factory managers, and the intelligentsia proved highly susceptible to abuse. After threatening local authorities with lawsuits for reviving the elite cafeterias in 1939–40, the Kremlin made its peace with preferential provisionment from 1941 to 1945. Elite restaurants and cafeterias were nothing spectacular, but they did provide heavily subsidized, multicourse meals, and if those in Riazan' are any indication, they serviced large numbers of hangers-on. As in the civil war period, their very inaccessibility bred rumors, many of them justified, and undermined the regime's public utterances about the wartime community of sacrifice. Notably, a *nomenklatura* memoirist identified the war years as the high point of string-pulling on the part of elite wives.[15]

Privileges were more marked with regard to manufactured goods, which were less sensitive than food and could be conferred with a freer hand. By early 1942 the price bureaucracy had assigned every basic consumption article a certain number of coupons, in addition to the ruble price. "Workers" received 125 coupons per six-to-nine month period; this was enough to purchase, say, three cotton dresses or two men's suits. "Employees" and "dependents" received, respectively, 20 percent and 36 percent less, and rural areas received shipments for "stimulation" but very little else.[16] In addition, in July 1943, the center issued regulations on nonfood perquisites for Party and state *nomenklatura* at the local, provincial, and national or all-union level. Each member of this elite was allotted two "limit booklets" [*limitnye knizhki*], equivalent to one thousand rubles apiece, for the purchase of manufactured goods above the ration. Closed stores for elites were authorized to maintain stocks of luxury cloth, clothing, and shoes, marked at relatively low ration prices. At the same time, the decree prohibited localities from supplementing these

[14] Cherniavskii, *Voina i prodovol'stvie*, 75; GA Riaz. ob. (Party div.), f. 220, op. 2, d. 50, l. 19.
[15] GA Riaz. ob. (Party div.), f. 220, op. 2, d. 229, ll. 47–49 (17% of meals at this higher officers' canteen went to wives and children, and 13% had obtained passes *po blatu* from local officials or the staff). Cf. Moskoff, *Bread of Affliction*, 177; and Shatunovskaia, *Zhizn' v Kremle*, 136–39.
[16] Cf. Liubimov, *Torgovlia i snabzhenie*, 40–44; GA Riaz. ob. (Party div.), f. 220, op. 1, d. 509, l. 43.

perquisites in any way. Once again, the motivation for the decree may have stemmed less from a perceived need to grant perquisites to local elites than from a perceived need to keep those prerogatives within reasonable bounds.[17]

Investigations into elite perquisites in Moscow and Leningrad after the war revealed that local officials bestowed on themselves a variety of additional privileges. As early as 1943, when the city was still under siege, the Leningrad city council printed up special manufactured goods cards for the *nomenklatura*, whereby ranking municipal and Party bureaucrats received five thousand to six thousand extra rubles' worth of subsidized goods a year. More egregiously, the city executive committee entitled its own members to receive unlimited clothing supplies through the select custom-shop designated for limit-booklet sales.[18] After the war privileges expanded in both Leningrad and Moscow. Moscow municipal elites were acquiring up to two thousand rubles' worth of subsidized manufactured goods a month in 1946; the deputy chairman of the Moscow Soviet, T. A. Selivanov, used special perquisites to amass five overcoats, three suits, six women's dresses, six children's outfits, ten dress shirts, ten pairs of shoes, eleven pairs of underwear, 35 meters of cotton cloth, 8 meters of silk, 3.5 meters of woolen cloth, as well as other items.[19] All in all, the rationing system was an extremely rigid, bureaucratic, inegalitarian, and inefficient system. Although a stratified rationing system gave Soviet officials a lever of social control, they were as eager as their counterparts in other countries to return to nonrationed trade.

Not unconnected to elite perquisites, a structural abnormality of the rationing period was the distorted price system. While it is not true, as Voznesenskii claimed, that rationed food prices remained unchanged for the duration of the war, the Soviet government clearly made an effort to keep the basic food rations affordable.[20] Nonetheless, the state's budgetary needs, combined with the relatively successful precedent from the years 1932 to 1935, led the regime to reopen the Gastronom network of luxury grocery stores and certain other "commercial" and "special" stores for nonrationed sales in 1944–45. In these stores foods were priced at roughly thirty times the prices of the rationing system, and manufactured goods were roughly double; but the comparison was moot, since most of what they sold—butter, milk, eggs, high-quality sausages, cookies; high-quality manufactured goods—was otherwise available only at the market.

[17] RGASPI, f. 17, op. 121, d. 584, ll. 24–34.

[18] Ibid., ll. 30–34.

[19] Ibid., l. 26. This quantity of clothing would have been enough to send an ordinary citizen to labor camp for the intention to speculate.

[20] N. A. Voznesenskii, *Voennaia ekonomika SSSR v period otechestvennoi voiny* (Moscow, 1948), 110–18; Malafeev, *Istoriia tsenoobrazovaniia*, 229.

The high prices of commercial trade were mitigated for some 6 percent of the population, including "leading personnel," veterans, and manual workers with three years' experience on the job, who became eligible for discounts of 10 to 40 percent off the listed price.[21] Even so, commercial trade remained prohibitively expensive for all but the best-paid households. It was, in fact, instituted with this group in mind; the 1944 decree that launched "commercial" trade targeted "scientists, artists, and writers," who traditionally defined the top of the income scale, as well as senior military officers, as their likeliest customers.[22]

Connected to the bifurcated price structure, an additional abnormality worth mentioning was the renewed dependence of Soviet retailing on vodka sales. Economic planners had intentionally reduced the government's reliance on vodka revenues after the early 1930s, but they fell back onto vodka during the war as a relatively painless way to extract revenues from Soviet citizens, without raising prices on essential foods. Vodka prices were progressively hiked from 11 rubles, 50 kopecks per half liter in 1940 to 80 rubles, 50 kopecks three years later within the rationing system, and to 250 rubles in the newly opened commercial shops in 1944. Planners continued to tinker with the prices and output to try to maximize revenues; commercial prices on vodka were lowered in late 1944 and again in 1945, while production dramatically rose. The result was fairly extraordinary: from 12 percent of the total ruble intake of trade in 1940–41, vodka sales' share of trade increased to 21 percent in 1942, 28 percent in 1943, 35 percent in 1944, and 38 percent in 1945. As in the early 1930s, then, both the wartime distribution system and the Soviet government more generally took their sustenance from the Russian national vice. Providing some fifty billion rubles in pure profit, vodka sales supplied one-sixth of state income in 1944–45, making them, once again, the state's single biggest revenue source.[23]

The final, and in some regions decisive, abnormality of the Soviet trade at the end of the war was the shortage of shops. The war had decimated the retail network: of 407,000 state and cooperative retail outlets functioning at the end of 1940, 245,000 remained. Several provinces had lost 75 percent or 85 percent of their stores under the occupation, and even in the rear the retail network had shrunk by one-quarter. Warehouses, depots, grain elevators, and refrigerated storage had all suffered proportionately, with 26,000 of these facilities irreparably destroyed.[24]

---

[21] Moskoff, *Bread of Affliction*, 178–79; Zima, *Golod*, 56.

[22] GARF, f. 5446, op. 48a, d. 1962 and d. 2068, ll. 49–50.

[23] See on-line appendix "Vodka Production and Sales."

[24] *Narodnoe khoziaistvo SSSR*, 191; Sokolov and Nazarov, *Sovetskaia torgovlia*, 44; Cherniavskii, *Voina i prodovol'stvie*, 108.

The first, truly pressing need for the Soviet trade system was simply reconstruction—for which stores had to compete with other, equally urgent rebuilding projects for labor and materials.

These, then, were the indexes and circumstances that confronted postwar planners in the sphere of distribution. They all represented abnormal and undesirable conditions, and, indeed, most governments would likewise have considered them disabilities to overcome. At the end of the war, Soviet policy makers' agenda for retail trade concentrated on returning to normalcy in each respect. "Normalcy" meant the retail system that was in place from 1936 to 1939—a system structured, at least in principle, around nonrationed trade; open admission to stores; a reduced role for distribution at the workplace; unified pricing from one outlet to another within each region; a "normal" structure of sales; and adequate, or at least increasing, quantities of consumer items. By 1950 the economic administration had basically accomplished this agenda. Stores were slowly rebuilt and resumed their position of overwhelming dominance over market trade.[25] Rationing was eliminated—earlier, in fact, than in any other major European belligerent except Italy, where it simply fell apart. Vodka returned to the "normal" 10 to 12 percent of retail sales; cloth, clothing, and shoe supplies increased; and, by the early 1950s, even consumer durables were being sold in greater numbers than before the war. Sales of food lagged somewhat behind those of manufactured goods, which, by 1950, outdistanced the 1940 volume (in real quantities) by 40 percent; but in 1951 real food sales, too, exceeded prewar sales.[26] The early 1950s brought nothing but smoothly rising curves for each of the indexes that had appeared most important in 1945. Given such successes, it is no wonder that triumphant graphs dominate the Soviet-era historiography of postwar trade.[27]

Two observations are in order before we abandon quantitative trends for qualitative developments. First, the famine of 1946–47 had very little impact on the normalization agenda, though it evidently affected the timetable. At the start of 1946, Stalin publicly heralded the abolition of ration cards "in the very near future"; famine led him to postpone this step until December 1947.[28] Famine nonetheless slowed the normalization process much more than it altered it. As several recent works have observed, policy makers took their first step toward dismantling the ra-

---

[25] *Sovetskaia torgovlia. Statisticheskii sbornik*, 19, 137; also registered in budget studies.

[26] Ibid., 9, 53. In 1950 the actual quantity of food distributed by state and cooperative trade was 94 percent of the 1940 amount, but in 1951 it climbed to 110 percent.

[27] See, for example, Dikhtiar, *Torgovlia* III, 238–303; Sokolov and Nazarov, *Sovetskaia torgovlia*.

[28] Stalin, *Sochineniia*, 3 [XVI]: 19; *Pravda*, December 9, 1947.

tioning system when the postwar famine was clearly on its way. Stressing the material privations that resulted from these reforms, both Filtzer and Zima have attributed the price hikes on rationed foods and the withdrawal of rations from twenty-seven million citizens in September 1946 to the regime's awareness of the inadequacy of centralized food stocks.[29] With regard to pricing, however, it is difficult to reconcile this interpretation with archival discussions of trade. The September 1946 reforms adhered to the same policy that had governed distribution since the introduction of "commercial" food sales in 1944. Predicated on the idea that postwar distribution would advance through the stages laid out during the previous transition to nonrationed trade, the policy called for a progressive narrowing of the price gap between rationed and commercial sales, and a progressive increase in the latter's proportion of all retail trade. Projections of how the restructured prices (higher in the rationing system, lower in commercial trade) would affect various social groups bounced around the government for months before September 1946, along with summaries of what had happened in 1934–35.[30]

Famine probably contributed to the decisions to restrict eligibility for food rations and to reorient the commercial network to high-priced bread sales, but, even here, its influence is difficult to isolate from the general policy at the end of the war. With regard to commercial bread sales, famine reinforced the normalization agenda, rather than undermining it. In the absence of universal rations, which policy makers by no means felt capable of supplying, commercial bread sales represented a step in the desired direction of divorcing access to goods from social or political status, as opposed to ability to pay, the deciding factor in "normal" trade. As a consequence, commercial bread sales increased the amount of food available to peasants, the primary victims of the famine. They also emancipated the government from vodka revenues, another desideratum from the standpoint of normalization, by reducing the state's subsidy of bread. Defensible during the war, the regime's reliance on vodka placed it in an awkward predicament in 1946: financially it could ill afford to curtail vodka sales, but, with hunger escalating, the diversion of potatoes and grain to the vodka industry must have troubled a few consciences and carried political risks. Unpublished trade statistics tell the story: from 38 percent of retail sales in 1945, vodka dropped to 23

[29] Filtzer makes this point most effectively in "Standard of Living," 1020–22. See also Zima, *Golod*, 51–52; Zubkova, *Russia after the War*, 40–50.

[30] GARF, f. 5446, op. 48a, d. 2068, esp. ll. 3–4, 11–13, 25–27, 96. A similar interpretation of the 1946 reform can be found in Nove, *Economic History*, 307–8; and Popov, *Ekonomicheskaia politika*, 79.

percent in 1946, 13 percent in 1947, and to an unprecedented (and unrepeated) 6 percent in 1948. Bread sales charted the reverse course, jumping from 7 percent of sales in 1945 to 15 percent in 1946 and to 18 percent two years later.[31] This change notwithstanding, trade policy in 1946–47 remains much more striking for its continuity with the wartime blueprints than for its famine-inspired deviations from them.

A second observation vis-à-vis quantitative questions is that trade policy became increasingly ideosyncratic as the wartime abnormalities disappeared. Starting in 1949, planners' attention shifted from "eliminating abnormalities" to fostering economic growth, on the one hand, and to lowering prices, on the other. Alongside smooth upward curves of supplies and sales, and in part to elicit sales, Soviet leaders wanted to be able to chart a smooth downward curve of price movements both in the open market and in socialist-sector trade. With regard to the open market, the administration could influence prices on either the supply side or the demand side: it could increase production to the point where supplies offered at the state price sufficed to satisfy demand, or it could reduce demand, as it did in December 1947, when the "surplus mass of money" was, in the approving words of Z. V. Atlas, removed by means of a "surgical operation."[32] In combination with the stronger harvest of 1947, the monetary reform had its desired effect; the price index for market food sales in the first quarter of 1948 declined by a factor of three vis-à-vis the previous year.[33] More generally, though, Soviet policy was oriented toward the supply side of the equation. During the late 1940s supply-side thinking even led policy makers to take the extraordinary measure of allowing consumer cooperatives to buy agricultural products, and to open up special shops in which to sell them, at *market* prices. This policy, which began in the aftermath of the 1946 crop failure and lasted only until 1949, clearly aimed to increase the amount of marketed food.[34]

From 1948 on, Soviet leaders' desire to cut prices in state and cooperative trade conflicted with the goal of lowering prices on the private market. In the spring of 1948 some reduction of the official price level was probably necessary; state and cooperative sales were unusually flat after the monetary reform, both because citizens had made so many purchases at the end of 1947 and because they had too little money to fulfill

---

[31] RGAE, f. 7971, op. 2, d. 221, ll. 14, 61; d. 251, ll. 15, 66; d. 264, ll. 14–15, 74–75; d. 288, ll. 95–96; d. 310, ll. 106–7; d. 347, ll. 110–11. See also on-line appendix "Vodka Production and Sales."

[32] Atlas, *Sotsialisticheskaia denezhnaia sistema*, 295.

[33] Ibid., 302; Sokolov and Nazarov, *Sovetskaia torgovlia*, 61; RGAE, f. 7971, op. 5, d. 65.

[34] See Sh. Ia. Turetskii, *Ocherki planovogo tsenoobrazovaniia*, 59, 226; Dikhtiar, *Torgovlia* III, 277.

the retail trade plans.[35] Over the course of the next several years, how-ever, price cuts in state and cooperative trade bore little relationship to costs or to citizens' expanding consumption resources. As late as 1955 the Soviet representative to the United Nations Economic Council boasted about the price cuts that had been carried out annually for the previous seven years: "In the Soviet Union, prices are lowered even on goods that are still in short supply, if these goods are important to mass consumption. This provokes further demand and pressures industry to increase its production of essential scarce goods more rapidly."[36] As Russian economists have acknowledged since 1959, however, the result of such an approach was mixed. Alongside the tremendous growth of consumer goods supplies, and indeed of the "material well-being of the population," artificially depressed prices in the socialist sector fostered shortages and queues. We can see this in the price gap between state and market prices; at its peak in 1943 the ratio of state to market prices was 100:1300; it fell to 100:400 by 1946, and then rose during the famine; it dropped to 100:110 in 1950 but then rose again, slowly but steadily, to 100:134 in 1954. Malafeev observed of this price gap, "the kolkhoz market (and also the 'underground' trade in manufactured goods) established a kind of monopoly pricing, which to a certain degree was utilized by speculative elements for the redistribution of part of the national income for their own ends."[37]

Obviously, the price gap of the early 1950s was nothing like that of the war era—and neither were the goods that were most scarce. Although bread shortages continued to dominate the secret correspondence on trade through the middle of 1950, and meat, butter, flour, and fish shortages cropped up briefly in 1951, one can already catch glimmers of a recovery in the consumer economy in the minutes of low-level trade meetings in 1948–49. That year, provincial stores outside Kursk started reporting a high, unsatisfied demand for high-heeled shoes; or witness the following list of shortages in the small towns of Riazan' *oblast'*: musical instruments, fashionable [*model'naia*] men's and women's shoes, cosmetics, winter sporting goods, soap, razors, stockings, socks, gloves, needles, ribbons, tea, lamps, lightbulbs, sleds, flashlights, wire, nonalcoholic

[35] Dikhtiar, *Torgovlia III*, 270; RGAE, f. 7971, op. 16, d. 471, l. 159 and passim.

[36] RGAE, f. 7971, op. 5, d. 76, ll. 19–20.

[37] Malafeev, *Istoriia tsenoobrazovaniia*, 265. See also Dikhtiar, *Torgovlia III*, 266–73; Turetskii, *Ocherki planovogo tsenoobrazovaniia*, 415. The market price of grain rose from eight to fourteen rubles a kilogram in 1946 to fifty to seventy rubles in 1947—which is still substantially lower than the market price of grain between January 1943 and June 1944. Zima, *Golod*, 55; cf. *Narodnoe khoziaistvo SSSR*, 198–99.

Figure 12. Queue for cloth and shoes in the Leningrad suburbs, 1947. *Courtesy of the Russian State Archive for Cinematic and Photographic Documents (RGAKFD).*

drinks, and milk (figure 12).[38] While "primary necessities" [*predmety pervoi neobkhodimosti*] figured prominently in this list, the addition of such items as musical instruments, sporting goods, and fashionable shoes indicate that bare survival no longer exhausted consumer expectations. Khrushchev explained this development in 1954, in language straight out of late-1930s (or, indeed, 1920s) discussions of trade: "Demand for high-quality goods has embraced wide circles of the population."[39]

The tendency to view shortages as a sign of prosperity inhibited any effort to overcome them, but Khrushchev was correct to a point. As in the late 1930s but still more so, postwar household budget studies reveal a notable diminution in the social stratification of urban consumption. Urban working-class, white-collar, and managerial households effectively achieved parity in consumption by 1952. Once again, the best quantitative information concerns cloth and shoe consumption (table 7.1). Although I have not located such direct quantitative data for other items,

[38] GA Kursk. ob., f. R-207, op. 1, d. 13, l. 31; GA Riaz. ob., Party archives div., f. 3, op. 3, d. 999, l. 22. On 1951 food shortages, see GARF, f. 5446, op. 81, d. 2269, ll. 72–193.
[39] *Pravda*, December 24, 1954.

TABLE 7.1
Urban Per Capita Cloth and Shoe Consumption, 1934 vs. 1952

	1934		1952	
	Worker	*ITR*	*Worker*	*ITR*
Cloth (meters)	5.248	8.516	12.64	12.80
Cotton	5.101	7.988	10.86	10.08
Woollen	0.050	0.178	0.56	0.72
Silk, other	0.097	0.350	1.24	1.96
Shoes (pairs)	1.948	2.726	2.5	2.4
Leather	0.956	1.301	1.3	1.3
Rubber	0.560	0.780	0.8	0.7
Felt, other	0.432	0.645	0.4	0.4

Source: RGAE, f. 1562, op. 15, d. 1119, ll. 86, 88; op. 26, d. 80, l. 14.

expenditure breakdowns make clear that virtually all consumption patterns of the urban social groups converged. Even with respect to such typically class-segmented items of consumption as books and newspapers (a middle-class consumer item) and alcohol (the working-class item par excellence), the difference in consumption between workers, white-collar employees, and managers amounted to little more than one ruble per month. This was owing in part to rising working-class incomes (by the early 1950s, the income gap between even an unskilled worker and a technically or university-educated engineer or manager had narrowed to a mere 25 percent) and in part to the tendency of working-class, but not managerial-class, wives to hold jobs.[40] Geographical disparities in provisionment—between villages and cities, between the various republics, and between Moscow and everywhere else—did not disappear in the post-crisis period, by contrast; on the contrary, Moscow's share of the total goods increased significantly between 1933 and 1951, and in 1955 the Soviet Union's five largest stores alone, all located in either Moscow or Leningrad, made fully 1.2 percent of the country's sales.[41]

The late Stalin era formed a transitional phase between the extreme, survival-threatening privations and crises of the period from 1917 to 1948 and the mundane shortage economy of later years. Though at the

[40] RGAE, f. 1562, op. 26, d. 80, ll. 9–10. It remains to be seen whether this flattening of the social landscape in the early 1950s was a lasting or temporary trend—and this is not to say anything about the much thinner stratum of best-selling authors, ballet dancers, and *nomenklatura* elites, as well as professors, whose perquisites appear to have increased in the decade following the war. Cf. Matthews, *Privilege*, 97–98.

[41] *Sovetskaia torgovlia. Statitischeskii sbornik*, 203, compared to 20.

most abstract level, the shortages of the 1940s and the 1950s alike expressed a disequilibrium between supply and demand, the disequilibrium of the 1940s stemmed from the inadequacy of supplies relative to absolute human needs, whereas that of the 1950s reflected shortcomings in pricing, bureaucratized production, and the organization of trade. The abnormalities caused by the war were thus successfully overcome by the end of the 1940s, but the abnormalities caused by the postwar price policy remained a problem through 1953 and beyond. Khrushchev seemed to be groping toward a solution when he acknowledged that "today, when prices have been significantly lowered for successive years, one observes an inadequate supply of certain goods."[42] His ideas were constrained, however, by the optimistic, Stalinist interpretation of shortages. As a result of this blindness, and of the idiosyncratic feeling that prices mattered more than manufacturing or retail profits, consumer convenience, choice, or time, normalization was doomed to remain partial despite substantial economic growth.

Cadres Policy in Postwar Trade

Quantifiable growth was not the only salient development in postwar Soviet trade, but it underpinned all other changes. Trade policy registered the shift, from 1948 to 1950, from economic recovery to economic growth not just in the new emphasis placed on price cuts and expanding sales but also in its noneconomic goals. No less than in the quantitative sphere, political interest in the qualitative dimensions of trade was initially confined to the negative goal of "eliminating abnormalities"—above all, employee misconduct, which was said to have burgeoned as a result of the wartime and postwar economic crises. After 1948, though misconduct did not disappear, the crusade against it was subsumed into a positive program of "culturedness," an agenda that once again included improved customer service, better-trained employees, greater efficiency, wider selections, and better-quality goods. In emphasizing a positive agenda for improving the quality of trade in the early 1950s, policy makers expressed a renewed sense of optimism about the future. This attitude contrasted sharply with their suspicious, secretive, repressive orientation of the immediate postwar years.

The negative campaign exemplifies a continuity in policy not just since the late 1930s but since the beginning of communist rule. By the early 1920s Soviet leaders had transferred their distrust of private busi-

---

[42] *Pravda*, December 24, 1954.

nessmen to employees in state and cooperative trade. The approaches adopted at that time to combat misconduct—show trials, executions, purges, and education—remained unchanged for the next thirty years. In the meantime, the relentless media stigmatization of "scoundrels behind the sales counter" appears to have shaped public perceptions of trade employees. As we saw in chapter 2, trials staged to showcase bribe taking in the socialist trade sector had elicited negative reactions in the 1920s on the grounds that taking bribes was by no means limited to the commercial sphere, and that it was unreasonable to "use the death penalty to wage a struggle against a centuries-old, mundane fixture of Russian life." By the 1940s, however, citizens almost universally identified trade as the breeding ground of theft, bribery, speculation, and other economic violations, an identification that went well beyond the documented scale of wrongdoing.[43]

Trade-sector misconduct resumed its place on the political agenda in the postwar era as a result of the famine of 1946–47 and the attempt, in 1947–48, to reestablish prewar political controls. Reaching its zenith between September 1946, when rural residents and some urbanites lost their food rations, and December 1948, one year after the transition to "free" trade, the campaign not surprisingly targeted the distribution of food.[44] The philosophy of the period was encapsulated by a contemporary comment in the legal press: "the state is less interested in payment for goods than in their correct distribution."[45] Rationing facilitated "correct distribution" in a time of scarcity not just by securing specific, limited quantities of foods and consumer goods for each consumer but also by imposing additional accounting procedures on stores. This made it more difficult for trade personnel to profit from their proximity to scarce goods when they had to balance sales against canceled ration coupons as well as cash. This may account for the low rates of employee theft revealed by an audit of the Ministry of Trade's retail network, a mere 0.15 percent to 0.22 percent of sales from 1944 to 46.[46] On the other hand, it

[43] Cf. Zubkova, *Russia after the War*, 42, 78.

[44] Stalin's "*osobaia papka*" communications from the NKVD/MVD, a rough barometer of political interest in various topics, were literally dominated by reports on crimes and misdemeanors in the trade sector from late 1946 through 1948. See *Osobaia papka I. V. Stalina. Katalog dokumentov* (Moscow, 1994).

[45] G. Smolitskii, "Praktika Verkhovnogo suda SSSR po delam o sluzhebnykh zloupotrebleniiakh," *Sotsialisticheskaia zakonnost'*, no. 6 (June 1946): 23.

[46] RGASPI, f. 17, op. 88, d. 707, l. 7; GARF, f. 5446, op. 48, d. 1819, ll. 31–33. Consumer cooperatives had significantly higher rates, according to a 1946 report—some 0.8 percent of sales. If these estimates are accurate, the rates would seem to be surprisingly low by international standards, and also in comparison with those of 1933, when 1.1 percent of

seems certain that many violations eluded detection. Store managers, salesclerks, and cashiers often paid for things that they appropriated; after carting off the store's most desirable wares to sell on the side, they would ring up the sales at the official price, and return that amount— perhaps one-fifth of what they yielded on the black market—to the cash register.[47] Rationing simply meant that it was prudent to obtain coupons to cancel as well. When the government once again tightened up its policing of the market trade in ration coupons in 1946, it turned out that store and cafeteria employees were the principal buyers.[48]

The year 1947 brought several new assaults on wrongdoings in the trade sector: tough mandatory sentences for theft, the beginnings of a purge of "privateers," a campaign against shortchanging customers, and a major effort to prevent trade employees from abusing the December monetary reform. The June 4 law on theft of public property, like its August 7, 1932, precursor, was framed very broadly, but trade employees were definitely among the intended quarry. Although the rate of em- ployee theft from trade may have been modest in terms of the value of the stolen goods, fragmentary evidence suggests the opposite with re- spect to levels of participation. Trade personnel were responsible for more than one-quarter of all theft convictions between September 1945 and April 1946, and occasional regional reports suggest truly huge num- bers of infractions: nearly four thousand trade and cafeteria employees in the Bashkir ASSR were arrested for theft in the first three months of 1944 (a famine period); two thousand were apprehended in Vladimir ob- last in the first eleven months of 1947.[49] The picture that emerges from these scattered reports is of an epidemic of petty pilfering from consumer goods factories and trade.

State and cooperative trade were also burdened with the purge of "pri- vateers" in 1947–48. As chapter 6 indicated, the socialist trade networks had been affected by the revitalization of private trade not just through the emergence of private-sector competition but also through their own

---

the cooperatives' turnover was stolen, as calculated from A. Shliapnikov, "Okhrana ob- shchestvennoi (sotsialisticheskoi) sobstvennosti," *Sotsialisticheskaia zakonnost'* 2, no. 1 (Janu- ary, 1935): 16.

[47] Examples of this practice can be found in criminal cases from the 1940s, e.g. TsMA Moskvy f. 819, op. 2, d. 71a; f. 1889, op. 1, d. 920, d. 1347. See also Smolitskii, "Praktika Verkhovnogo suda," 19–24.

[48] GARF, f. 8131, op. 22, d. 274, ll. 2–3, 5; f. R-9401 s/ch, op. 2, d. 139, ll. 234–43, 361– 67; d. 168, ll. 135–42; d. 169, ll. 12–25, 322–29; d. 170, ll. 1–8; see also S. Baksheev and Shemelevich, "Usilit' bor'bu s raskhishcheniem prodovol'stvennykh i promtovarnykh kar- tochek," *Sotsialisticheskaia zakonnost'*, nos. 11–12 (December 1946): 24–26.

[49] RGASPI, f. 17, op. 88, d. 707, l. 3; f. 17, op. 125, d. 596, l. 5; GARF, f. R-9501 s/ch., op. 2, d. 64, ll. 182–84. For reference, Vladimir oblast' probably had about sixteen thou- sand trade employees at any given time in 1947, and Bashkiria had about thirty thousand.

entrance into contractual relations with private businesspeople. Store managers cut deals with local artisans and factories to sell products off the books at a mutually agreed-on price; kiosks featured privately obtained fruit; cooperatives approached private individuals to set up restaurants, barbershops, and photography studios, for those individuals' profit—in short, many "combinations" were possible, and many developed from 1944 to 1947. Cooperatives, which went further than state trade in their relations with private trade and services, attracted scrutiny for these practices in September 1947; a series of investigations and condemnations ensued, which eventually spilled over into the state sector, and resulted in a purge in the spring of 1948.[50] The entire process recapitulated purges of former privateers from state and cooperative trade in the early 1930s and, before that, in the 1920s. Like the June 4 law on theft, the purge of private-sector contacts showed that policy makers' reflexive reaction to economic and social crisis was a crackdown. V. M. Molotov's widely publicized 1947 speech, attributing economic crime to "vestiges of capitalism in people's consciousness," provides further testimony to the sterility of the Party line.[51]

Yet another revival of a 1930s campaign was the August 1947 "verification" of trade organizations' "accuracy in issuing food products and manufactured goods to consumers." Carried out by the State Trade Inspectorate in conjunction with the MVD, this undercover operation targeted deception in the trade sector. By falsifying weights and measures, manipulating labels, and diluting or adulterating foods and cosmetics, salesclerks could steal the difference between what customers paid for and what they received. The verification confirmed the prevalence of shortchanging, exposing deceptions at more than one-fifth of the 21,358 retail or public dining outlets subjected to the check, and catching in the act 15,737 individual trade workers, several of whom tried to bribe their way out of their predicament. Unfortunately the verification had no discernible deterrent effect. As the MVD was obliged to report to Stalin, the Trade Inspectorate had bungled the action; only 1,755 of the culprits were placed under investigation, and the remaining 14,000 were merely slapped with a fine—with the result that one year later a repeat operation revealed similar rates of noncompliance.[52]

<hr/>

[50] State trade, which I did not discuss in "A Postwar Perestroika?" was drawn into the fray by the Ministry of Trade's *prikaz* no. 482 (October, 20, 1947), "Ob izvrashcheniiakh v torgovle i proizvodstvennoi deiatel'nosti torgovykh organizatsii," discussed in RGAE, f. 7971, op. 16, d. 472, ll. 109–10.

[51] Cited in *Sotsialisticheskaia zakonnost'*, no. 6 (June 1949): 1–5.

[52] GARF, f. R-9501 s/ch, op. 2, d. 170, ll. 352–61; d. 200, ll. 346–51. Such leniency may have evaporated in subsequent years; cf. TsMA Moskvy f. 1889, op. 1, d. 2209; f. 1921, op. 1, d. 56.

Given the state of workplace ethics in Soviet trade, it was inevitable that second-economy schemes would proliferate when the end of rationing was combined with a one-time, 90 percent tax on savings—the monetary reform. Store managers, bookkeepers, and other trade employees were in a unique position to launder money in this period by virtue of their privileged access to goods. Cleaning out their stores with their savings, unscrupulous trade employees hoped to resell the wares either at the market or in their own stores for a favorable price in new rubles. Not surprisingly such machinations became the focus of yet another campaign against trade-sector misconduct. Monitoring of the trade network sharply increased during and immediately following the reform, with the result that some 3,000 trade employees were arrested for abuses connected to the monetary reform in the last two weeks of December, including 1,100 store directors and nearly 900 Party members; similar numbers were reported for each two-week interval throughout January and February.[53] At the local level these abuses significantly accelerated the turnover of leading trade cadres: in Riazan' *oblast'* 761 of the 5,068 "materially responsible workers" in trade were fired in 1948 for abuse of office, compared to some 400 the following year.[54]

How much money was laundered through the trade sector in 1947–48 is impossible to gauge. As with employee theft more generally, most violations were probably minor. Nonetheless there were exceptions. In the Moscow suburb of Tushino two store directors, both Communists, together bought up a staggering 296 pairs of women's shoes, 1,248 suits, 6,750 pairs of women's stockings, 239 pairs of pants, 56 ladies' dresses, 236 children's blankets, 29 ladies' blouses and jackets, 140 pairs of children's shorts, 600 meters of window tape, 117 fur pieces, 60 pairs of mittens, 38 table runners, 28 tablecloths, 5,400 spools of thread, 150 meters of lace, 170 bottles of perfume, 11,800 razor blades, and an unspecified quantity of "other goods" for the purpose of resale in new rubles, at the new, raised state prices. Having hidden these goods in the basement of the stores in December, they slowly siphoned them off to the market through a couple of unemployed speculators, and also sold them in their own stores. This was certainly money laundering on a grand scale.[55]

Through mid-1948, when cases of abuses connected to the monetary reform began to taper off, there was clearly no ethical normalization in

---

[53] GARF, f. R-9501 s/ch, op. 2, d. 199, ll. 3–12, 63–64, 140–48, 249–60, 344–51; d. 171, ll. 332–36, 343–47, 354–59, 440–64, 471–86, 499–509; d. 200, ll. 102–6.
[54] GA Riaz. ob. (Party doc. div.), f. 3, op. 3, d. 999, l. 13; d. 626, ll. 9–24.
[55] GARF, f. R-9501 s/ch, op. 2, d. 199, ll. 63–64.

Soviet trade. Afterward, the picture becomes more ambiguous. Political interest in trade-sector misconduct receded—or at least high-level sources dried up. We know that conviction rates for theft, presumably including theft from trade, declined sharply in the early 1950s, but, as Peter Solomon has argued, this could have more to do with changes in prosecution than with any behavioral alteration on the part of employees.[56] Criminal convictions for shortchanging and overcharging appear to have stayed roughly in line with the numbers from the late 1940s.[57] Some types of misconduct were simplified by the end of rationing: sales through the back door [*chernyi khod*] became easier when all a store manager had to do was ring up the requisite number of small sales. Still, a police report on speculation in 1954 maintained that such misconduct had "unquestionably" declined "since the first postwar years"—though a few months later the same office suggested that the dimensions of theft, especially in the trade system, in the consumer goods industries, and in the food procurement organizations, continued unchanged, and likewise that petty speculation "at markets, in shops, and on the street" had not declined.[58] Finally, noncriminal misconduct—holding back choice items for acquaintances or improper communication about shipments of scarce goods—remained chronic as long as there were shortages, that is, well past 1953.

If neither ethical violations nor the struggle against them disappeared in from 1949 to 1953, they did become less urgent. Economic and political stabilization enabled the leadership to look beyond campaign justice and to embed criminal sanctions in a broad program for improvement. The conclusion to a February 1949 pamphlet on trade-sector theft hinted at this shift by invoking Stalin's most positive words about trade: "Trade workers should constantly remember Great Stalin's indication that 'Soviet trade is our native, Bolshevik business [*delo*], and trade workers, including sales workers, if only they do their work honestly, are the conduits of our revolutionary, Bolshevik business.'"[59] With respect to employees, political aspirations for higher quality once again led to the proliferation of training programs. The wartime labor shortage had forced administrators to accept an influx of housewives and adolescents into the sales force, thereby confirming the feminized and unskilled pro-

[56] Solomon, *Soviet Criminal Justice*, 435.

[57] The police division for economic crimes, OBKhSS, reported convictions of 2,803 trade employees for "deception of the customer" and another 712 for "violations of the rules of trade" in 1953 (GARF, f. 9415 s/ch, op. 3s, d. 840, ll. 67–73).

[58] Ibid., ll. 2, 67–73.

[59] G. Aleksandrov and L. Mariupol'skii, *Okhrana sotsialisticheskoi sobstvennosti v sisteme sovetskoi torgovli* (Moscow, 1949), 21.

file of shop employees. If in 1935 women had constituted 31 percent of the trade-sector workforce, they constituted 72 percent ten years later; adolescents made up 8 percent.[60] Short "technical minimum" courses were soon reinstated to instruct them in basic skills, and the advanced commercial institutes reopened for the training of managers and commodity experts. By 1950 all these programs were turning out several times as many graduates as they had in the 1930s.[61]

As an addendum, the shift of emphasis from punishment to long-term improvement through education came at the cost of high-level interest in trade. The postwar punishment and purge of trade employees had preoccupied the very top echelons of the power structure: the central Ministry of Trade, the Procuracy, the Council of Ministers, the Central Committee of the Communist Party, the Party Control Commission, the MVD, and ultimately Stalin himself. By contrast, the training of trade cadres and other incremental improvements were entrusted to the lowest rungs of the Soviet power structure: branches of the salesclerks' professional association, provincial cooperative unions, and local or provincial departments of trade. The Ministry of Trade sought to show progress in its annual personnel statistics, but, beyond that, little attention was paid. When policy makers relaxed the campaign against trade-sector misconduct, the qualitative aspects of trade—in fact, all aspects besides price movements and the volume of sales—fell off their radar screen.

POSTWAR "CULTURED TRADE": A BALANCE SHEET

So the end of rationing, rising sales, and the perceived reduction in misconduct assured policy makers that they had turned the corner. Henceforth they could delegate the supervision of trade to lower, apolitical authorities, namely, the local trade administrations. Using trade archives from Moscow and Kursk, this final section will consider the extent to which the concerns of local cadres—shop managers, trade department officials, union activists—affirmed the Kremlin's perception that a new era had dawned. On the whole they did reveal such a sentiment in their increasing attentiveness to retail atmosphere and marketing. It was not that they, or their political superiors, simply abandoned punishment but

[60] *Vsesoiuznaia torgovaia perepis' 1935 g.* Vol. 2: *Kadry sovetskoi torgovli* (Moscow, 1936); *Narodnoe khoziaistvo SSSR,* 182. These percentages declined somewhat in subsequent years (teenagers, in particular, dropped out), but women continued to fill the lower-ranking positions in retail trade and food services.

[61] Kulikov and Rodin, "Kadry sovetskoi torgovli"; *50 let potrebitel'skoi kooperatsii* (Moscow, 1967), 163; Sokolov and Nazarov, *Sovetskaia torgovlia v poslevoennyi period,* 58.

that emphasis shifted from the negative to the positive components of trade policy as the privations of the immediate postwar period receded. In the process, the prewar concept of "cultured trade" once again provided the blueprints for refashioning Soviet stores.

Retail "culturedness" was a quintessential example of what Terry Martin has called a "soft" policy.[62] In the postwar period, as in the 1930s, low-level trade officials received frequent, consistent instructions regarding such questions as customer service, the "minimum assortment" of consumer goods, and employee training. These directives reached store managers through such "soft" channels as the provincial trade department or the local soviet, to which the managers were obliged to file periodic reports. They were not backed by force. As opposed to the punitive campaigns, which went through such hardline agencies as the Party, the Procuracy, and the MVD, and which placed careers on the line, failure to meet a target for culturedness barely merited a rebuke. Nonetheless, although no one went to jail for running a shop inefficiently or for neglecting to install mirrors, soft policies could have an impact. Operating through honor rather than fear, the campaign for cultured trade proved popular with the salesclerks' union and with civic-minded employees. It made them feel valued, surely a rare gratification in a sector that afforded few psychological rewards.

Like other "soft" initiatives, results faded with increasing distance from the center. In Moscow, the campaign for culturedness had on occasion obtained hardline backing, as in the case of the queue and deportation orders of 1939. This was unthinkable in other parts of the country. Even during December 1947, when the end of rationing topped the hardline political agenda, regional Party organizations put much more effort into punishment than into trade. Twelve out of fifteen regions surveyed for a report to the Central Committee had omitted to conclude supply contracts or arrange for deliveries and, as a result, were "absolutely unprepared" on December 16. They knew from experience how to limit the damages. In at least six of the regions, provincial cooperatives had shipped all their food supplies to the cities for the first days of nonrationed trade, while major cities mobilized their resources to supply the big downtown stores. Working-class districts on the periphery of town, not to mention villages, were less likely to garner publicity and were hence more easily ignored.[63]

It is doubtful whether anyone was disciplined for such decisions, since central planners largely endorsed a policy of preferential provisionment.

[62] Martin, *Affirmative Action Empire*, 21–22, 76.
[63] RGASPI, f. 17, op. 125, d. 596, ll. 1–5.

They cared mostly about Moscow, the focus of a series of high-level reports.[64] Aware of this interest, the Moscow municipal government issued a flurry of directives in December 1947: store managers were to carry out repairs within a month; to post their store's hours and a list of available goods on the door; to sell goods only with the proper packaging; to make sure that the store was cleaned daily; to "liquidate" lines; and to decorate stores with display cases and other civilizing adornments. An almost nauseating degree of publicity memorialized the transition to nonrationed trade in the capital, portraying food shipments as so many "gifts" from well-wishers in the national republics, and declaring stores an integral element of the campaign to turn Moscow into "the most beautiful, most well-built, and most cultured city in the world."[65]

Culturedness thus played differently in Moscow and in the provinces; it also played differently depending on the shop. Because its archives offer a unique window into trade concerns at the store level, let us look for a moment at the pinnacle of culturedness—the Soviet Union's flagship department store, TsUM—before returning to ordinary provincial trade.[66] The busiest, most prominent store in the country, TsUM naturally embraced the agenda of cultured trade earlier and more warmly than other stores.[67] TsUM's managers viewed the emporium as a symbolic standard-bearer; they constantly had the sense that their efforts reflected not only on themselves or their departments or even their own store but on the condition of Soviet trade in general and on the prestige of the Soviet state. This sentiment echoed in meetings throughout the postwar Stalin period in a dozen formulations: "The Central Department Store is a special department store; both here and abroad it is customary to judge all Soviet trade on the basis of our store." "Our store is an all-union store, and, if for no other reason than that, it should have a proper appearance." In 1949 TsUM's director went so far as to insist that cus-

[64] Ibid., op. 121, d. 584, ll. 125–28, 131–34; GARF, f. 9401, op. 2, s/ch, d. 171, ll. 332–36, 343–47, 354–59, 412–21; d. 199, ll. 46–52, 213–16.

[65] These were constant themes in *Vecherniaia Moskva*, especially during the week of December 15–21, but they also appear in the national press. Quote, October 1, 1947.

[66] TsUM's archive, TsMA Moskvy, f. 1953, is the only archive of a single store that I have found. It begins in the mid-1930s, breaks off during the war, and resumes with much more material in 1945.

[67] TsUM had 1.7 billion rubles in sales in 1955; it handled a far higher volume of trade than any other store except GUM, which reopened after a fifteen-year hiatus in 1954. *Sovetskaia torgovlia. Statitischeskii sbornik*, 203. Some 120,000 customers visited the store each day, according to the director's 1953 estimate (TsMA Moskvy, f. 1953, op. 2, d. 153, l. 70)—down from the estimated 200,000 before the war.

tomer service and "culturedness" transcended plan fulfilment as the store's top priority.[68]

Administrators' image of culturedness informed both the selection of goods they carried and the organization and services of the store. As in the prewar period, TsUM modeled itself after department stores in other countries. The store subscribed to American trade journals, from which managers were supposed to cull applicable ideas.[69] For a more proximate paradigm, they referred to conditions before the war. TsUM administrators considered their store less cultured than it had been in the 1930s, when its equipment was purportedly better, when it was "warm, clean, and pleasant," and when speculators did not roam freely through its floors.[70] Trying to re-create the original exclusive atmosphere, managers reintroduced the full range of customer services that the store had offered in the years before the war. They also restricted its selection to expensive luxury products. Through the end of the 1940s, when customers inquired after basic commodities like cotton cloth, salesclerks had to refer them to Tishinskii market.[71] Managers elected to safeguard the prestige of the store's label by promoting goods manufactured in small quantities by TsUM's own production unit, and hence unavailable to other stores. In this decision, they catered to shoppers who viewed consumption as a means of individuation or self-expression—an approach far removed from most consumers' concerns (figure 13).[72]

In its quest for exclusivity, TsUM benefited from the trickle of imported consumer goods from Czechoslovakia and East Germany, a new development of the postwar years.[73] Imported products had tremendous cachet in the aftermath of the war, whether at high-end department stores or at the bazaars and commission shops trading in so-called trophy articles. In the TsUM archives, imported hosiery stands out as the object of desire; at the height of the famine in the spring of 1947 nylon pantyhose attracted crowds of female customers, who clustered around the

[68] TsMA Moskvy, f. 1953, op. 2, d. 42, l. 13; d. 73, ll. 34, 73; d. 98, l. 108.

[69] Ibid., d. 73, l. 28.

[70] Ibid., ll. 5, 60, 189, and elsewhere. This characterization of the late 1930s should be taken with a grain of salt, given the enormous queues of 1938–39.

[71] Ibid., l. 186. Much of the expansion of consumer goods production from 1948 to 1950 came in the area of such relative luxuries as silk and woolen cloth, clocks and watches, bicycles, sewing machines, radios, motorcycles, and record players. Cotton cloth was scarce. *Narodnoe khoziaistvo SSSR*, 221; *Sovetskaia torgovlia. Statitischeskii sbornik*, 57.

[72] Cf. director's comments in TsMA Moskvy, f. 1593, op. 2, d. 73, l. 191.

[73] See Paul Marer, *Soviet and East European Foreign Trade, 1946–1969* (Bloomington, 1972), 111, 128–43.

Figure 13. The lace department at TsUM, 1948. *Courtesy of the Russian State Archive for Cinematic and Photographic Documents (RGAKFD).*

sales counter, pinched and pulled at display models, and bought up these stockings as soon as a shipment appeared.[74] Expanded offerings of European imports suited TsUM's high-class profile, but they gave rise to a certain consternation. The idea of cultured trade had always been connected with a notion of *socialist* modernity and prosperity, the patriotic content of which was, if anything, strengthened at the end of the war. Committed to this conceptual framework, TsUM managers would have liked for "Moscow goods" to be "no worse than anything from London or Paris." In fact, every department complained that even the Baltics managed to produce better goods. The best one could say about Soviet clothing was that it was sometimes solidly constructed; but since it tended to be ugly and unimaginative, customers always preferred foreign brands. This made it extremely difficult for salesclerks to serve as "agitators" or "propagandists" for Soviet-made items, as repeated directives suggested they should, and it exacerbated the awareness of foreign prosperity that soldiers had brought home from the war.[75]

Certain exclusive Soviet products also did a good business. TsUM began stocking expensive furnishings, typically inaugurating a new line of products with banners and fanfare. Central Asian rugs, for example, were introduced in connection with the thirtieth anniversary of the October Revolution; luxury furniture sets arrived just in time for the thirty-third. Except for the dubious assertion that these had "unquestionably improved the daily life of the Soviet people," the archives give no indication of whether the items actually sold.[76] Televisions, however, sold out as fast as they arrived; according to the manager of the electronics department, customers insisted on buying even defective models. By 1950, judging from the prevalence of speculators in that department, televisions were already the object of a thriving black market. Automobiles likewise began to be sold to private individuals, and a secondary market for their resale emerged.[77] Demand for other modern conveniences—washing machines, refrigerators, and vacuum cleaners—likewise outpaced supplies, assisted, no doubt, by preferential pricing.[78]

So much for the successes of "cultured trade" at TsUM. It should be clear that TsUM's managers paid attention to "soft" policy directives;

[74] TsMA Moskvy, f. 1953, op. 2, d. 73, l. 65.

[75] Ibid., d. 42, l. 5; d. 73, l. 24; d. 153, ll. 24, 70, 73.

[76] Ibid., d. 73, ll. 24, 47; d. 111, l. 146; d. 125, l. 10.

[77] Ibid., d. 111, l. 146; d. 125, l. 10. This evidently changed in the later 1950s, since prices on televisions had to be lowered in 1958, while prices on refrigerators, sewing machines, and automobiles were raised (Marshall I. Goldman, *Soviet Marketing* [London, 1963], 89, 94).

[78] Philip Hanson, *The Consumer in the Soviet Economy* (Evanston, 1968), 112.

they identified with the cultured trade agenda and made it the central policy of their store. Even at TsUM, however, the endeavor to make trade more cultured collided with the economic realities and priorities of the late Stalin era. Rosy sales projections needed to be fulfilled, for example. In periods of unusually sluggish sales, such as the spring of 1947 or the winter of 1948, TsUM's sales plans challenged its cultivation of a cultured image. For the first time, managerial meetings identified other stores as competitors, not to mention the hawkers who sold similar wares at a discount in their own aisles. However, TsUM's emphasis on high-quality merchandise prevented it from expanding its selection of cheaper wares that might appeal to customers in straitened circumstances. At other times, however, these imperatives worked in tandem. Many of the store's innovations in customer service and advertising in the postwar period—areas traditionally understood under the rubric of "cultured-ness"—stemmed from efforts directed primarily at increasing sales. One manager made the startling discovery that smiling salesclerks sell more; another found that he could boost sales of unpopular items by dressing pretty young salesgirls in them. In such profit-oriented innovations, the educational component of selling, so prominent in managerial discussions of the 1930s, tended to be absent. Now, salespeople might still advise customers, but their more immediate concern was to elicit demands and to cater to the customers' tastes.[79]

Even at TsUM, salesclerks fell short of administrators' expectations. Truly egregious demonstrations of "culturedlessness" [beskul'tur'e] were rare, as in an instance when a salesclerk assisted a customer to her bicycle, but then slashed its tires when she refused to tender him a tip.[80] On a more routine level, however, salespeople were often rude to poorly dressed customers, though this was said to be still more of a problem at other stores; they continued to respond to queries with such helpful answers as "Stand in line and find out!"; and they continued to spend the first half-hour of each workday buying up goods for themselves and squirreling away scarce items for acquaintances and friends.[81] Such problems were almost inevitable given the persistence of shortages and the weakness of labor regulations. Administrators wanted to wield their authority through fear on the part of the sales staff; as one manager put it, "If you walk around the floor and the salesclerk doesn't feel flustered and nervous, that is very bad!" However, the worst that the management actually

---

[79] Ibid., l. 48; d. 98, l. 47; d. 125, ll. 4–5; d. 153, ll. 10, 24, 82.

[80] Ibid., d. 111, l. 146.

[81] This last practice was the bane of managers from the 1930s on (ibid., op. 1, d. 15, ll. 9–10; op. 2, d. 111, l. 136–39; d. 125, ll. 14, 168). On rudeness to poorly dressed customers, see d. 73, l. 42; d. 153, l. 58; f. 32, d. 50, l. 141.

could do to a recalcitrant employee was to demote that employee to the warehouse. For salesclerks with an orientation toward the second economy, this was a mild threat indeed.[82]

For all its shortcomings TsUM was, at best, a distorted "mirror" of Soviet trade from 1945 to 1953. Located in the center of the capital, patronized by "many bosses" and foreign dignitaries, given a virtual monopoly over novelties, imports, and luxury products, the Ministry of Trade's flagship store was sheltered from the supply "difficulties" that afflicted ordinary trade venues. Though it had to take some goods from the bureaucratic pipeline, about which managers complained endlessly, it could obtain most of its wares through independently arranged contracts and from its own workshops. If funds ran low, the government could be expected to keep it afloat. Such advantages freed TsUM's managers to concentrate on the store's "cultured" image. Their mixed success gives an inkling of the obstacles ordinary stores faced when they tried to implement a program of cultured trade.

Ordinary stores were much more vulnerable to market vicissitudes. TsUM's modus operandi barely changed after the end of rationing; it had been an exclusive commercial store in from 1945 to 1947, and remained much the same from 1948 to 1953. For the vast majority of the country's retail outlets, by contrast, December 1947 brought dramatic modifications. So, too, did the famine of 1946–47, as well as the amelioration of conditions after 1948. Whereas TsUM department heads, buyers, and senior salesclerks discussed the same range of problems in 1947 as in 1953, provincial trade archives—in this case, from the province of Kursk—throw the events, changes, and hardline campaigns of the different parts of the postwar Stalin period into relief.

From 1945 to 1947 provincial trade department meetings centered on the food crisis: on "interruptions," especially of flour supplies, and on who was shortchanged in the distribution of bread. Not surprisingly the rural population, including teachers and medics, lost out whenever supplies ran short. Vodka, however, was available at every rural trading outlet during the "interruptions" of 1945 and 1946, and, according to a regional report, it sold briskly.[83] Administrators were also interested in maintaining order in the food lines, which persisted through the fall of 1948 and occasionally thereafter; in monitoring market prices; in arresting "speculators"; and in preventing abuses with ration cards.[84] Finally, they were very much interested in making arrangements for the redemption of local elites' "limit booklets," ordering that goods of an "improved

[82] TsMA Moskvy, f. 1953, op. 2, d. 73, ll. 134, 137.
[83] GA Kursk. ob., f. R-207, op. 1, d. 67, l. 60–75; d. 69, ll. 1–6.
[84] Ibid., d. 7, ll. 4, 19, 78–81, 86; d. 13, ll. 13, 120; d. 67, l. 60.

assortment" be reserved for these subsidized sales. At the local level, perquisites increasingly viewed as "abnormal" by central administrators thus
continued to garner enthusiastic support.[85]

The "abnormality" that preoccupied provincial authorities at the end
of rationing was the shortage of shops; site of the hugely destructive
1943 battle that bears its name, Kursk had much more than its quota of
reconstruction to do. In April 1949 a report on the retail network indicated that the province still had one thousand (25 percent) fewer stores
and nearly four hundred (31 percent) fewer kiosks than had been in operation in 1941.[86] Identifying the consumer cooperative network as the
source of the deficit, the report trumpeted the return of state trade to its
prewar strength. The disparity between state trade and cooperatives suggests that provincial authorities had focused on rebuilding urban stores
from 1947 to 1949 and had accomplished this objective with relative
speed. Thereafter progress stalled. Between 1950 and 1953 the number
of stores and kiosks in the province remained constant; even four years
later Kursk's retail network was 10 percent less dense than before the
Second World War.[87] Once urban trade had returned to normal, local
officials evidently stopped worrying about opening new shops.

Provincial administrators were also concerned with the key quantitative indexes and devoted many a session to the question of how to increase sales. This concern did not, however, extend very far in the direction of widening the selection of goods or eliminating queues. Consumer
cooperatives had been obliged since the 1920s to keep a specified "minimum assortment" of basic necessities constantly in stock. In Riazan'
Province, a 1949 survey of shops in one rural county revealed that not a
single store met the minimum standard.[88] While "rising expectations"
may have contributed to this problem, so, too, did administrators' awareness that their performance would be judged on their fulfillment of the
sales plan, not on the availability of any particular article. In a period of
increasing incomes, this was not generally so difficult to achieve.

It should come as no surprise that culturedness made much less head-
way in the provincial context than at TsUM, though, even here, it de-

[85] Ibid., d. 7, ll. 34, 137.

[86] GA Kursk. ob., f. R-207, op. 1, d. 67, l. 4. These numbers may be inaccurate; a
published statistical handbook painted a roughly similar picture of the relative decline in
retail outlets in Kursk oblast', but it listed completely different numbers of shops for both
the end of 1940 and the later period. Cf. *Sovetskaia torgovlia v RSFSR. Statisticheskii sbornik*
(Moscow, 1958), 128.

[87] *Sovetskaia torgovlia v RSFSR*, 128.

[88] GA Riaz. ob. (Party doc. div.), f. 3, op. 3, d. 999, l. 22. Sokolov and Nazarov estimated
that 40 percent of all co-ops adhered to the minimum assortment.

pended on the venue. With regard to markets, Kursk's trade department mainly hoped to clear out the garbage and the speculators; with regard to bread shops, the hope was to clear out the speculators, the dirt, and the queues. The first directives that invoked any standards of culture beyond rudimentary hygiene concerned shops for "commercial" trade in manufactured goods. Opened in four provincial cities in 1947, these were supposed to provide fitting rooms, mirrors, and seats; to advertise on the radio; and to employ salesclerks who were "cultured, highly qualified, and polite."[89] Whether the directives were fulfilled can only be conjectured; but certainly some salespeople and managers in the prestigious networks identified with the cultured trade agenda. In Kursk the most eloquent champion of culturedness in the late 1940s was a saleswoman at the *Gastronom*.[90] What comes across in these documents is Martin's hard/soft distinction. Educated and polite salesclerks, beguiling or even decent surroundings, home delivery: all these garnered lip service, especially when economic conditions became better, as the official desiderata for trade. If the salesclerks' trade union took them up, so much the better! But both the urban and provincial trade caucuses had more pressing problems on their minds throughout the late Stalin period—among them, Stalin's punitive campaigns.[91]

Did things improve at all in the provincial setting? One aspect is quite noticeable in the sources for provincial trade. Even in 1946–47 Soviet newspapers did not hesitate to trumpet the country's "achievements" in "raising the well-being of the population," but archival sources, including such mundane archives as provincial trade department meetings, make clear that officials were well aware of the famine and perceived the whole economy in terms of an acute, ongoing crisis. From 1948 on, pronouncements in closed meetings gradually came to resemble the boosterism of the controlled press. If misconduct and shortages continued to raise questions, they were no longer so crippling as to pose a political threat. By the mid-1950s, Kursk trade department concerns were barely distinguishable from those of a capitalist firm.

CONCLUSION

This chapter began with an assertion about normalization: that in retail trade, and more generally in the consumer economy, the late Stalin period brought a measure of normalization in the economic and social

[89] GA Kursk. ob., f. R-207, op. 1, d. 7, ll. 40–41, 78–81.
[90] See, esp., ibid., d. 19, l. 35.
[91] For example, ibid., d. 29, ll. 82–83.

spheres. ("Normalization") accurately describes the overcoming of wartime "abnormalities" by the end of the 1940s, and the corresponding reorientation of policy toward economic growth. (Normalization can also be discerned in the regime's shift in emphasis regarding the qualitative aspects of trade. Brighter economic prospects led policy makers to modulate from a minor to a major key. By the time of Stalin's death, Soviet government and Party leaders felt that they had something to brag about in the retail sector. This was an unmistakable change vis-à-vis the immediate postwar years.

Was Stalinist policy responsible for the country's emergence from the famine era? Without a doubt, many of the food crises and famines in the period from 1917 to 1948 had resulted directly from Soviet policies; it is equally clear that Soviet policies in the post-Stalin period prevented starvation from recurring then. Milestones from 1954 to 1964 included the radical increase in the state's purchasing price for agricultural products, which spurred peasants to intensify their efforts in collective fields; the end of obligatory deliveries, or the system that Moshe Lewin called "taking grain"; and, perhaps above all, the decision to import essential foods. Technological progress played its part as well: the mass production of penicillin from 1949 on made it possible to control infectious diseases, which in turn would render hunger less lethal. Also, modern fertilizers and agricultural equipment led to a dramatic increase in harvest yields. As to Stalinist policy itself, the evidence remains ambiguous. Policy makers deserve credit for favoring universal access to stores over codified status privileges and also for embracing economic growth. Nonetheless, there is no evidence that Stalin's pathological indifference to short-term human hardships altered in the period after 1948, and this was particularly true of his attitude to peasants.[92] To this extent, the 1948–49 watershed was as much a product of good weather as of conscious direction. If a drought had occurred in 1951 or 1952, the era of starvation may well have persisted until the innovations in agricultural policy of the Khrushchev years.

Below the policy level, projects for improvement encountered obstacles that did not preclude all economic, moral, and "cultural" progress in Soviet trade but that impeded such progress beyond a certain point. Reviving an interpretation prevalent during the Thaw era, I have argued that the chief obstacle to normalization in 1949 to 1954 was politicians' obsession with the prices of foods and consumer goods. Successive price

---

[92] Mikoian discussed this explicitly in his memoirs (*Tak bylo*, 513–14), describing himself as "disillusioned" by Stalin's refusal to raise procurement prices in the period from 1948 to 1953.

cuts led to a situation where the total "consumption fund" of money available for consumer purchases significantly exceeded the ruble value of the total "commercial fund" of consumer goods. In other words, demand exceeded supply; and although supplies dramatically increased during this period, bringing about a genuine improvement in living standards, the disequilibrium between supply and demand guaranteed that shortages and queues would persist, and that goods would continue to be displaced from the official to the "second" economy.

The development of trade policy exemplifies a trend toward narrower frames of accountability in the Soviet bureaucracy after 1948–49. Observed by Yoram Gorlizki with respect to the legal agencies, late Stalinist management increasingly focused on a few, easily quantifiable measures of success.[93] In the case of trade, the indexes that mattered in the early 1950s were "physical volume" [*fizicheskii ob"em*], or the actual quantity of goods available for sale; retail volume, or the ruble value, in current prices, of the goods that were actually sold; and price movements, particularly though not exclusively in the socialist sector. None of these was as "hard" a concern as the punishment of ration-card abuses and employee theft from 1945 to 1948, since the threat of force was not implied. Nonetheless, high-level officials paid attention to these indexes, and if the policing organs directed their energies elsewhere, central and regional Party organizations certainly monitored them along with the central administration of trade. Efforts to elevate "culture" received still "softer" political support, though, as the examples of TsUM and the Kursk *Gastronom* suggest, a "model" trade venue might privilege the qualitative agenda over the prevailing quantitative goals.

Postwar trade evokes one final historical theme, at least to this author: a theme of "missed opportunities." Given the enormous prestige of the Soviet Union both at home and abroad at the end of the war, the immediate postwar years offered the regime a unique opportunity to develop a new, freer and more open, relationship with its citizens in every sphere of public life. Stalin had a chance to pay peasants a living wage for their work on the collective farms; to introduce contested elections; to curtail political punishment; to free up the labor market and the press; and to introduce any number of other liberalizing reforms.[94] In trade I would point to the purge of private-sector businesses as a missed opportunity to harness individuals' initiative in the consumer economy. More generally,

---

[93] Yoram Gorlizki, "Rules, Incentives, and Soviet Campaign Justice after World War II," *Europe-Asia Studies* 51, no. 7 (November 1999): 1245–65.

[94] This theme resonates throughout the work of Elena Zubkova; in English, see her *Russia after the War*.

the revival of the 1930s "cultured trade" paradigm, and the fixation on a narrow set of economic indexes, showed the failure of Soviet leaders to respond to the changes of the postwar world. Soviet policy makers accepted, as they had in the late 1930s, the idea of Soviet citizens as consumers. They proved unable and unwilling, however, to imagine the autonomous formation of desires that inevitably accompanied the country's emergence from survival-threatening need. If, as Vera Dunham suggested,[95] the promulgation of a prewar concept of cultured consumerism consolidated the regime's alliance with middle-class (and, I might add, middle-aged) Russian functionaries, it could only alienate young people and other individualistic consumers as time went on.

[95] Dunham, *In Stalin's Time*, esp. 3–24.

Conclusion

In the summer of 1917 Lenin took time away from political organization and oratory to write a theoretical treatise on communism, revolution, and the state. His point of departure was a passage that had already attracted attention within the small community of international Marxist theoreticians, namely, Engels's comments in *Anti-Dühring* on the "withering away of the state." According to Engels, when "the proletariat seizes power, and then transforms the means of production into state property . . . it puts an end to all class differences and class antagonisms, it puts an end also to the state as the state. . . . Government over persons is replaced by the administration of things and the direction of the processes of production. The state is not 'abolished,' *it withers away*." Lenin's most immediate aim in discussing this passage was to reconcile the mild and incremental-sounding concept of the "withering away of the state" with the political strategy of violent revolution. Logically his approach was to draw out the chronology of the future socialist transformation, distinguishing a revolutionary moment ("the proletarian seizure of power"), a state-building moment (the "substitution of one [proletarian] 'special repressive force' for another [bourgeois] 'special repressive force'"), and, finally, a state-dismantling moment (the end of repression and the reduction of "the great majority of functions of the old 'state power' . . . to such simple operations of registration, filing, and checking that they will be quite within the reach of every literate person").[1]

What has tended to strike historians about *State and Revolution* is the lack of correspondence between Lenin's theory and the actual historical development of the USSR. It failed to foresee that "class substitution" would so greatly increase the state's reliance on its capacity as a "special repressive force"; it grossly underestimated the complexity of "directing the processes of production"; and it failed to anticipate the problem of bureaucratism, which is to say that "registration, filing, and checking" amplified and extended the state instead of trimming it back. Engels's and Lenin's other proposition, that "government over persons" would in time be replaced by "the administration of things," was similarly distant from Soviet reality in the Lenin and Stalin eras. Through at least the

[1] V. I. Lenin, *State and Revolution* (New York, 1943), 15–20, 37–38.

1940s, the relationship between the communist state and its citizens—in our case, private traders, socialist-sector trade workers, and consumers—was characterized by abrasive assaults, sudden shifts, opacity of purpose, and the systemic favoring of particular groups over others. This was, without doubt, "government over persons" in the specific, Leninist sense. In the protracted era of crisis that extended from the revolution through the reconstruction after the Second World War, the Soviet system was constituted not through the offices of the clerks or the technocrats, much less rank-and-file literate workers, but through the state police, the Party, and the Komsomol.

As I tried to show in chapter 7, this political system began to change even before Stalin's death. One certainly cannot speak of an end to the state as an instrument of repression; the terror campaigns against "cosmopolitans" and Jews, not to mention Stalin's continuing use of secret decrees, absolutely disallow such an interpretation. One can, however, speak of its rollback, as discrete policy areas were handed off to the bureaucrats. In the commercial sphere, "government" (and with it, the "special repressive force") *did* give way to "administration" in the early 1950s: "vigilance" was replaced by the monitoring of quantitative performance indicators, and such preeminently political organs as the Party Central Committee, the MVD, KPK, or Sovmin increasingly left the formulation of trade policy to the competency of the Ministry of Trade.

The decentralization of decision making within this ministry was another expression of the same trend. I have proposed a reason for the rollback: at least in the economic realm, Soviet policy makers felt themselves to have emerged from an era of crisis. At long last, utopian dreams might actually be realized: in the words of the NEP-era economist A. Z. Gol'tsman, "after the difficult journey in the snowy and rainy spirals of our ascent we will reach the summit, and above us, on the other side of the mountain, the warm sun of socialism will shine."[2] Gol'tsman's effusiveness would have seemed quaint and out of place in the early 1950s, but his sentiment was not. Policy makers believed in the future, and accordingly returned to the positive agenda of "socialist construction," associated in the consumer economy with "cultured Soviet trade."

Of course, many of these same changes had occurred in the mid-1930s, when for a short time (from 1936 to 1938) the USSR Commissariat of Domestic Trade functioned as little more than a commodity clearinghouse for the provincial and municipal *torgi* and for the premiere stores and chains. Does this imply that then, too, trade policy was moving in a rational, apolitical, administrative direction? I would argue that

[2] Gol'tsman, introduction to Mingulin, *Puti razvitiia*, 11.

the development of trade paralleled the better-known development of Stalinist legal culture, to which the mid-1930s brought a forceful repudiation of the "anti-law" theory of socialist justice; a promise of legal stability in the form of the 1936 Constitution; and a concerted attempt to professionalize legal officials—but, at the same time, it brought "mass operations," torture, and secret decrees.[3] In the case of trade, the "anti-trade" theory of socialism was likewise firmly rejected, and the popular demand for an egalitarian, necessities-only economy was judiciously spurned in the interests of governmental solvency and economic growth. Central policy sought to make the trade system profitable and efficient, both responsive to consumer demands and able to channel and stimulate them. Tying these aims together with occupational training, the concept of "cultured trade" presaged an improved atmosphere in Soviet shops and a wider range of goods. Outside a few "model" venues, this promise remained unfulfilled. It was stymied by the resurgent terror of the later 1930s, and also by militarization, which left the civilian economy even less able than usual to satisfy the aggregate demand.

In the late 1930s, as in the late 1920s and the revolutionary years, shortages propelled the trade system in the direction of bureaucratized distribution. I have tried to describe this process and also to explain why it occurred. With regard to *what* happened, this study has highlighted a recurrent pattern. Cotton cloth, an article manufactured almost exclusively by socialized factories and marketed at a controlled price, was in each case the leading edge of the crisis, followed by woolen textiles and various agricultural raw materials. Shortages intensified during periods of rising incomes and, more specifically, of increased peasant demand. They began to obstruct trade in Moscow. Policy makers intervened on behalf of the metropolitan consumers, limiting rural consumers' access to goods. Those same rural consumers responded by reducing their agricultural marketings, a tendency reinforced in many areas by crop failure, to which Russian agriculture had always been prone. Shortages began to cripple the food market, beginning (at least in 1927 and 1939) with the higher-grade foods that displaced cheaper staples as urban incomes rose. Limits on purchases were introduced by cooperatives and local authorities, while the policing organs successfully promoted the prophylactic benefits of "speedy repressions," whether against unruly or obstreperous consumers, "speculators," peasants, or socialist-sector "wreckers." The

---

[3] Roger Sharlet, "Stalinism and Soviet Legal Culture," in R. Tucker, ed., *Stalinism: Essays in Historical Interpretation* (New York, 1977), 155–79; Eugene Huskey, "Vyshinskii, Krylenko, and the Shaping of the Soviet Legal Order," *Slavic Review* 46, nos. 3–4 (fall–winter 1987): 414–28; Solomon, *Soviet Criminal Justice*, 153–98.

economy nonetheless continued to deteriorate, until rationing had to be reintroduced.

Why did one step always lead to the next? I have put forward two explanations: the first involving the concept of political culture; and the second, the specific weaknesses in the Soviet approach to trade. "Political culture" is, in any case, a slippery term, and readers may have found my distinction between it and "policy" artificial. I have used policy to signify government actions directed at achieving articulated objectives, and political culture to connote the psychological makeup of Soviet officials—the values, mentalities, and impulses that shaped their responses to circumstances on the ground. The effect of this distinction for the overall interpretation is twofold. It explains the contradictions in the state's economic management during the 1920s and 1930s by attributing the "struggle against bureaucratism," say, or the acceptance of the market, to policy, while ascribing bureaucratism itself, or the easy recourse to repression, to a political culture derived from the civil war. It also explains the unfolding of each economic crisis, as policy makers' initial perception of a crisis brought to the fore all the old civil war reflexes, which produced a predictable series of dislocations and elicited another reflexive response. If Soviet policy and political culture pulled in the opposite directions on the adoption of "normalizing" reforms, they cleaved together during the early phases of each crisis, when policy was temporarily realigned.

This realignment was more complete during the revolutionary era than subsequently. In 1919–20 left-wing ideologues dominated economic policy; the regime's public and private position was that socialism required a radically new form of distribution, from which not just the private traders but also money and the market would disappear. Although these ideologues were still around in the late 1920s, they did not have the same sway over state policy, and they certainly did not have it in 1941. Even during the collectivization period, the restructuring of socialist distribution around ration coupons and the workplace was utilized by policy makers for the short term, without being envisioned as permanent. This distinguished the rationing of food and consumer goods from other components of Stalin's "restructuring of the national economy": collectivization, forced-pace industrialization, and the elimination of private trade may also have been triggered by a sense of emergency, but they were conceived in the first years after the revolution, were initiated at the top of the power structure, and corresponded to long-term ideological goals. There, Soviet policy and political culture coincided, whereas in socialist retailing they rapidly moved apart.

My second explanation for the downward spirals that occurred from

1917 to 1922, 1927 to 1933, and (albeit to a lesser extent) 1939 to 1947 involves another debilitating legacy of the revolution: the conceptualization of trade in social, rather than narrowly economic, terms. Trade, for the Bolsheviks, was "the economic form of the *smychka* in the transition period." This understanding of trade as a regulator of urban and rural group interests meant that, from a Leninist standpoint, trade policy was *intrinsically* a matter of "government over persons" rather than "the administration of things." Trade policy was a social policy, a class policy; hence prices were understood to gauge the "deployment of class forces," not the intensity of consumer demand, much less marginal cost. This conception had manifold ramifications during the Lenin and Stalin periods, the most important being to justify, especially at the onset of a crisis, socially discriminatory interventions into pricing and a discriminatory allocation of goods. Alec Nove concluded his survey of Soviet economic history with the comment that "the new men were remarkably indifferent to the welfare of the masses."[4] This study has suggested that they had some concern for the welfare of urban workers, but Lenin's and especially Stalin's unremitting willingness to sacrifice peasant and small-town interests to the well-being of metropolitan consumers, via the diverse mechanisms of outright coercion, "commodity exchange," exclusion from urban retail establishments, and price, was one of the defining features of the age. While the concept of the *smychka* lost currency in the postwar period, discriminatory, sub-market procurement prices remained in place. Urbanites, the beneficiaries of this putative zero-sum game, came to view low food prices as an entitlement; witness the response of the Novocherkassk workers when the social equation finally changed.

Besides its detrimental impact on peasants' welfare, the other major problem with the social interpretation of trade was its analytical crudity. From the revolutionary period on, economic policy makers imagined consumers as comprising two, or at most three, great blocs—Stalin's "two classes and a stratum," workers, peasants, and intelligentsia, the latter of which was broadened to include "the best Stakhanovites." Though this rudimentary breakdown bore some relationship to consumption patterns at moments of complete economic collapse, it gave policy makers and trade organizations a grossly oversimplified picture of the consumer economy during more ordinary times. Particularly at the end of our period, when urban incomes were converging and on the rise, the tendency of economic officials to conceptualize demand in reductive, normative ways inhibited retail innovation. The Soviet economy was very slow to respond to the emerging youth market, and although I cannot cite Soviet

[4] Nove, *Economic History*, 386.

planners from the Brezhnev era, their counterparts in East Germany were still conflating demand and "needs" in language straight out of our period as late as the 1970s.[5]

Despite these cultural and conceptual limitations, the development of Soviet retailing had more in common with contemporary Western trends than might have been supposed. Though Soviet trade had its peculiarities—among others, the dominant role of the state in organizing distribution, the severe restrictions on private trade, the trade sector's chronic shortages, bureaucratic pricing, even the reluctance to replace the *kassa* system with self-service shops, which occurred in the United States in the 1930s and in Western Europe in the 1950s and 1960s[6]—it conformed in certain respects to a standard pattern. Here, as in the West, retail chains became more numerous and integrated, shops became bigger and more cost-efficient, prices grew more transparent, novel wares were introduced, and tastes became both increasingly homogenized across class, ethnic, and regional divisions and individuated in connection with the expansion of discretionary spending and a widening of consumer choice. Some of these developments resulted from policy makers' conscious efforts to modernize retailing on an American model; in the mid-1930s, when the Soviet government sent delegations to Western Europe and the United States to study retailing, they dismissed British businesses as petty and dated. The same could be said of most continental European trade until its Americanization in the decades of the *Wirtschaftswunder*. This is not to say that the Soviet leadership's interest in rationalization meant that the new mass retailing techniques were assimilated with any great speed. As late as 1956 the vast majority of rural shops still employed just one person, and the overall average of 1.59 employees per shop across the entire retail system was scarcely an impressive increase over the 1913 average of 1.32.[7]

However slow the modernization of Soviet trade, the surprise from a comparative perspective is just how great a role the small-scale and inefficient vestiges of the private sector, mostly concentrated at the markets, continued to play in consumer purchases and lifestyles after 1928. In part, this was an effect of poverty: in times of hardship, citizens supplemented their incomes through market hawking, a pattern documented for several regions of Europe and North America in the nineteenth century and common throughout occupied Europe during the Second World

---

[5] Cf. Jonathan Zatlin, "The Vehicle of Desire: The Trabant, the Wartburg, and the End of the GDR," *German History* 15, no. 3 (1997): 358–80.

[6] Jeffreys and Knee, *Retailing in Europe*, 105–8.

[7] *Sovetskaia torgovlia. Statitischeskii sbornik*, 171, as against Strumilin, *Izbrannye*, 1:436.

War.[8] Then again, the importance of the bazaar reflected the unusual
sparseness of the Soviet retail network, which intensified the geographical disparities in the availability of consumer goods that exist in every
society and made a redistributive mechanism a practical imperative. Beyond these structural factors, however, the cultural factor should not be
disregarded. The tenacity with which consumers and vendors clung to
the marketplace as a retail venue links the Soviet republics to a broad
swath of Eurasia and North Africa that at one time or another fell under
Turkic, Persian, or Inner Asian influence. From North India to the Balk-
ans, and from Russia to Morocco, *bazaars* (a Persian term adopted in
most of the area's languages) appear to have occupied a special place both
in the consumer economy and in ethnic cultures and consciousness. Despite the Bolsheviks' explicit modernizing and Westernizing intentions,
the Soviet regime only strengthened the role of the bazaars. This had
long-term effects on Soviet society, preserving a traditional, face-to-face
culture of exchange alongside the bureaucratized modernity of the Soviet
shop; and, as any visitor to the former Soviet Union can attest, the marketplace continues to hold its own in the region's retail structure and
consumption habits today.

A final implication of this study has to do with the broad course of
Soviet history, and, specifically, with the nature, role, and consequences
of the NEP. From many angles—cultural, social, economic, and political—the Western historiography of the 1970s through the 1980s brack-
eted the NEP off from the main line of Soviet development; it was, after
all, defined by its creative diversity, its cacophony of competing ideas,
styles, and economic systems (*mnogoukladnost'*!), which was subsequently
reduced to monotone. Some, arguing that famine forced the Bolsheviks
to accept a temporary deviation from the route to socialism implicit in
their ideology, attributed the relative permissiveness of the NEP interlude strictly to circumstance; others imputed the moral and cultural superiority of the revolutionary intellectuals to the Stalinist managers who
took their place.[9] Without rejecting the NEP's exceptionalism altogether,
this study reflects the trend of the past decade and paints a darker picture
of the NEP.[10] It also suggests that the spectacular rupture represented by

[8] On nineteenth-century hawking and itinerant trading, see Benson and Shaw, eds., *Evolution of Retail Systems*, 51–52, 54–56, 79–82, 90–92.
[9] For historiographical overviews, see Stephen Cohen, *Rethinking the Soviet Experience*
(New York, 1985), esp. chap. 3; Robert H. McNeal, "Trotskyist Interpretations of Stalinism," in *Stalinism: Essays*; and the roundtable discussion "Kruglyi stol: Sovetskii Soiuz v 20-e
gody," *Voprosy istorii* 9 (1988): 3–58.
[10] See, esp., the essay collection *NEP: Priobreteniia i poteri* (Moscow, 1994); Shishkin,
Vlast'. Politika. Ekonomika; Gimpel'son, *Formirovanie sovetskoi politicheskoi sistemy. 20-e gody*;

the "socialist offensive" in agriculture and industry may have obscured the threads of continuity that stretched between the NEP and the 1930s in other spheres of life) Politically the "administrative" repressions of 1921–22, 1923–24, and 1926–27 prepared the ground for what were explicitly termed *mass operations* from 1927 to 1930 and anticipated the buildup to 1937–38. Economically the socialist sector of the 1920s, with its reliance on representatives, contracts, and regional and sectoral commercial agencies only loosely integrated into the national trade bureaucracy, and also its counterproductive pricing, prefigured the socialist trade of the later 1930s and the decades after the war. Socially the persistence through the entire period of this study of petty trade, bazaars, small-scale purchasing trips from the market towns to the big cities, and also farm-to-farm "procurement" circuits underscores not just the chronic poverty of the Soviet Union but, more generally, the structural impediments to radical social change. In important ways, then, the NEP was not simply a dead end but rather a bridge between the socialist aspirations of the revolutionary epoch and the "real-existing socialism" of later years.

idem, *NEP i sovetskaia politicheskaia sistema*; Lewis H. Siegelbaum, *Soviet State and Society between Revolutions, 1918–1929* (Cambridge, 1992).

Bibliography

A note on sources: Like most works published in the past decade, this study grew out of the author's encounter with newly available Soviet archives. The sources on trade, distribution, and consumption are so numerous that I cannot pretend to have consulted all the relevant archival locations, but I did use a wide variety of primary sources, which I would classify as follows:

A. Statistical sources, both published and archival, concerning trade, prices, and household incomes and expenditures. Whether published or unpublished, these sources were most often generated by the Ministry of Trade and its predecessor commissariats; the Central Statistical Administration; and, for the NEP era, the regional economic soviets, or Ekoso.

B. Policy sources, including published and unpublished laws (*postanovleniia, dekrety, zakony, and ukazy*), executive orders (*prikazy, rasporiazheniia, and direktivy*), lower-level circulars and instructions, and, finally, materials connected to the formulation of policy (recommendations, draft decree proposals, interbureaucratic correspondence, and policy discussions). Along with the standard compendia of Soviet legislation, these sources tended to be concentrated in the archives of the Council of People's Commissars (Sovnarkom) and its various committees and secretariats; the Ministry of Trade and its predecessors, notably the Food Supply Committee (Komprod) for the revolutionary period and the People's Commissariat of Provisionment (Narkomsnab) for the period from 1930 to 1934; and also the Communist Party's Politburo.

C. Descriptive and analytical sources generated from within the bureaucracy, including "materials" gathered for the purposes of policy formation and reports to all the above-cited agencies, as well as to the municipal and provincial governmental offices of several regions singled out for research trips (Moscow, Leningrad, Odessa, Riazan', and Kursk). NEP-era publications on trade prepared for one or another bureaucracy fell into this category, as did reports drawn up by inspection agencies (notably the Workers' and Peasants' Inspection, Rabkrin, until its disbandment in 1934) and many items in Soviet newspapers. Reports by the policing agencies (the USSR Prokuratura, the GPU/NKVD, and the postwar police division for economic crimes, or OBKhSS) form an important subcategory of documents in this group for reconstructing informal trade.

D. Descriptive sources generated outside the system: travelers' accounts, diaries, and memoirs, as well as an in-between source, the *svodki* or excerpted synopses of citizens' opinions as expressed in letters to authorities or to the newspapers, in comments at public assemblies, and in conversations recorded by secret police agents and informers.

E. Criminal cases concerning particular illegal transactions, another essential source on unofficial trade. Many such cases appear in Prokuratura and other high-level reports, but, more particularly, this study rests on 210 cases from the province of Riazan' and from the city of Moscow (elsewhere, the filing system for criminal cases made them virtually impossible to use).

F. Credit reports from the Kredit-biuro, used to develop a database of 304 NEP-era private traders.

Several of these sources are described in greater detail in the online appendixes at http://darkwing.uoregon.edu/~hessler.

ARCHIVAL COLLECTIONS CONSULTED

Asterisk indicates systematic and extensive, as opposed to selective, use of a given collection. Dates indicate dates consulted, again, selectively unless indicated by the asterisk. Abbreviations: f. = *fond* = collection, op. = *opis'* = inventory, d. = *delo* = file, and ll. = *listy* = pages.

RGAE—Rossiiskii Gosudarstvennyi Arkhiv po Ekonomike
 f. 484 Tsentrosoiuz, 1918–53
 *f. 1562 Tsentral'noe statisticheskoe upravlenie (TsSU)
 f. 1943 Narodnyi komissariat po prodovol'stviiu, 1917–24
 *f. 7624 Kredit-biuro, 1922–31
 f. 7733 Narodnyi komissariat finansov, Ministerstvo finansov, 1945–50
 *f. 7971 Narodnyi komissariat vnutrennei torgovli, Narodnyi komissariat torgovli, Ministerstvo torgovli, 1934–52
 *f. 8043 Narodnyi komissariat snabzheniia, 1929–34
 f. 8090 Glavnoe upravlenie po delam promyslovoi i potrebitel'skoi kooperatsii pri SM SSSR, 1947–52
GARF—Gosudarstvennyi Arkhiv Rossiiskoi Federatsii
 f. 130 Sovet Narodnykh Komissarov (SNK), 1917–21
 *f. 374 Workers' and Peasants' Inspection (Rabkrin), 1928–34; esp. op. 27s–28s
 *f. 393 Narodnyi komissariat vnutrennykh del RSFSR (Internal Affairs), 1918–20
 f. 1064 Komissiia pomoshchi golodaiushchikh pri VTsIK (Pomgol), 1921–22
 f. 1235 Vserossiisskii tsentral'nyi ispolnitel'nyi komitet (VTsIK)
 f. 3316 Tsentral'nyi ispol'nitel'nyi komitet
 *f. 5446 Sovet Narodnykh Komissarov, Sovet Ministrov (SNK, Sovmin), 1921–50; esp. op. 55, Rykov's secretariat, and many annual opisi
 f. 7523 Verkhovnyi Sovet
 f. 8300 Ministerstvo gosudarstvennogo kontrolia
 *f. 8131 Prokuratura, 1929–53
 *f. 9401s, Narodnyi komissariat vnutrennykh del, op. 2 Osobaia papka Stalina, 1944–53
 f. 9415s Militsiia, esp. op. 3s Otdel po bor'be s khishcheniiami sotsialisticheskoi sobstvennosti, 1942–59

RGASPI—Rossiiskii Gosudarstvennyi Arkhiv Sotsial'no-Politicheskoi Istorii (formerly RTsKhIDNI)
    f. 5 Lenin (op. 1, Sekretariat, 1918–22)
    f. 17 Central Committee (op. 84, Biuro sekretariata, 1918–23; op. 85 Sekretnyi otdel 1925–28; op. 88; op. 121, Tekhsekretariat Orgbiuro, 1939–48; op. 125 Upravlenie propagandy i agitatsii TsK)
    f. 82 Molotov's secretariat, 1922–45
RGAKFD—Rossiiskii Gosudarstvennyi Arkhiv Kino-Foto Dokumentov
Newreels on trade and consumption, 1927–55; photographs of trade
TsAIPD Len.—Tsentral'nyi Gosudarstvennyi Arkhiv Istoriko-Partiinykh Dokumentov (Leningrad)
    *f. 24 Obkom (op. 1v, 1g, 2a, 2b, 2v, 2g), 1931–41
TsMA Moskvy—Tsentral'nyi Munitsipal'nyi Arkhiv Moskvy
    f. 32 Mostorg
    *f. 46 Upravlenie rynkami, 1933–47
    f. 216 Upravlenie torgami po torgovli prodovol'stvennymi tovarami goroda Moskvy, 1942–51
    f. 297 Upravlenie promtovarami g. Moskvy pri Min. Torgovli RSFSR, 1947–53
    f. 346 Glavnoe upravlenie torgovlei Mosgorispolkoma
    f. 819 Gorodskoi sud g. Moskvy, 1941–1952
    f. 901 Narodnyi sud Leningradskogo raiona g. Moskvy, 1942–51
    f. 953 Lineinyi sud Moskovsko-Riazanskoi zheleznoi dorogi, 1941–47
    f. 1078 Narodnyi sud Sovetskogo raiona g. Moskvy, 1948–52
    f. 1536 Narodnyi sud Zamoskvoretskogo raiona g. Moskvy, 1919–23
    f. 1546 Narodnyi sud Pervomaiskogo raiona g. Moskvy, 1947–53
    *f. 1889 Narodnyi sud Kievskogo raiona g. Moskvy, 1945–52
    f. 1919 Narodnyi sud Zheleznodorozhnogo raiona, 1947–50
    f. 1920 Narodnyi sud Moskvorctskogo raiona g. Moskvy, 1942–43
    f. 1921 Narodnyi sud Sokol'nichcskogo raiona g. Moskvy, 1947–52
    *f. 1953 Tsentral'nyi Universal'nyi Magazin (TsUM), 1936–53
    f. 2458 Profsoiuz rabotnikov kooperatsii i gostorgovli, 1933–51
TsGAOD Moskvy—Tsentral'nyi Gosudarstvennyi Arkhiv Obshchestvennykh Dvizhenii g. Moskvy
    f. 3 gorkom
GA Odes. ob.—Gosudarstvennyi Arkhiv Odesskoi oblasti (State archive of Odessa oblast')
    f. R-710 Odes. ob. Workers' and Peasants' Inspection (Rabkrin), 1932–34
    f. R-1763 Trade unions, 1930s
    f. R-1234 Gorsovet, 1925–40
    f. R-1217 Okr. Rabkrin, 1925–28
GA Kursk. ob.—Gosudarstvennyi Arkhiv Kurskoi oblasti
    f. R-192 Gubsnab/Kurtorg/Kurgubtorg, 1921–25
    f. R-207 Kurskii obl. otdel torgovli, 1945–61
    f. R-367 Kurskoe gorodskoe mnogolavochnoe obshchestvo potrebitelei/ EPO/TsRK, 1918–35

f. R-3761 Glav. upr. po delam prom. i potreb. koop. pri Sov. Min. SSSR, Starshii inspektor po Kurskoi ob, 1947–52
f. R-4850 Oblstrompromsoiuz, 1947–50
GA Riaz. ob.—Gosudarstvennyi Arkhiv Riazanskoi oblast
f. R-298 Rabkrin Riaz. gubernii, 1924–29
f. R-299 Rabkrin Riaz. okruga, 1929–30
f. R-300 Rabkrin Riaz. raiona, 1924–31
f. R-787 Riaz. gubvnutorg/gubtorgotdel, 1922–28
f. R-3602 Nar. sud Mikhailovskogo raiona, 1931–34
f. R-4335 Nar. sud Bol'she-Koroveshskogo raiona, 1941–48
f. R-4387 Nar. sud Klepikovskogo raiona, 1931–45
f. R-4407 Nar. sud Bel'kovskogo raiona, 1934–44
f. R-4433 Nar. sud Riazanskogo raiona, 1947–49
f. R-4480 Nar. sud Rybnovskogo raiona, 1933–41
f. R-4800 Nar. sud Mozharskogo raiona, 1936–45
Party documents division:
f. 3 obkom, 1946–50
f. 24 gorkom, 1941–45

NEWSPAPERS, WITH DATES CONSULTED

Biulleten' Prodovol'stvennogo otdela Moskovskogo Soveta Rabochikh i Krasnoarmeiskikh Deputatov (byvshevo Moskovskogo gorodskogo prodovol'stvennogo komiteta), 1918–20
Ekonomicheskaia zhizn', 1920–31
Izvestiia, 1929–48
Kommersant, 1909–17
Kooperativnaia zhizn', 1926–31
Krasnaia gazeta, 1918–29
Pravda, 1922–50
Snabzhenie, koperatsiia, torgovlia, 1931–34
Sovetskaia torgovlia, 1935–41
Stakhanovets torgovli, 1935–38
Vecherniaia Moskva, 1945–48
Za industrializatsiiu
Za kul'turnuiu torgovliu, 1934–38

JOURNALS AND PERIODICALS, WITH DATES CONSULTED

Bol'shevik, 1924–28
Ekonomicheskoe obozrenie, 1923–30
Ezhenedel'nik Chrezvychainykh komissii po bor'be s kontr-revoliutsiei i spekuliatsiei, 1918
Izvestiia Narodnogo Komissariata po Prodovol'stviiu, 1918–20

Kooperativnaia zhizn', 1912–17
Materialy po statistike truda
Narodnoe khoziaistvo, 1918–22
Obshchestvennitsa, 1935–41
Planovoe khoziaistvo, 1923–41
Prodovol'stvennoe delo, 1917–18
Rabotnitsa, 1934–40
Soiuz potrebitelei, 1903–30
Sotsialisticheskaia zakonnost', 1934–42, 1944–53
Sovetskaia iustitsiia, 1922–41
Sovetskaia torgovlia, 1926–41
Statistika truda, 1918–20
Vestnik finansov, 1925–27

PUBLISHED COMPENDIA OF LAWS AND DECREES

Biulleten' finansovogo i khoziaistvennogo zakonodatel'stva. Moscow, 1925–49.

Denezhnoe obrashchenie i kreditnaia sistema Soiuza SSR za 20 let: Sbornik vazhneishikh zakonodatel'nykh materialov za 1917–1937 gg. Edited by V. P. Diachenko and N. N. Rovinskii. Moscow: Gosfinizdat, 1939.

Direktivy KPSS i Sovetskogo pravitel'stva po khoziaistvennym voprosam. Sbornik dokumentov. 4 vols. Moscow: Gosvderstvennoe izdatel'stvo politicheskoi literatury, 1957.

Direktivy VKP(b) po khoziaistvennykh voprosam. Edited by M. Savel'ev and A. Poskrybyshev. Moscow: Gosvdarstvennoe izdatel'stvo politicheskoi literatury, 1931.

Kolkhoznaia torgovlia. Postanovleniia, rasporiazheniia, instruktsii, tsirkuliary. Leningrad: Lenizdat', 1932.

KPSS v rezoliutsiiakh i resheniiakh s"ezdov, konferentsii i plenumov TsK. Moscow: Gosvdarstvennoe izdatek'stuo politicheskoi literatury, 1970–72.

O bor'be so spekuliatsiei. Moscow: Iuridicheskoe izdatel'stvo Narodnogo komissariata iustitsii, 1942.

Resheniia partii i pravitel'stva po khoziaistvennym voprosam (1917–1967 gg.). 5 vols. Moscow: Izdatel'stvo Politicheskoi literatury, 1968.

Sbornik ofitsial'nykh i spravochnykh materialov po voprosam rabochego snabzheniia i sovetskoi torgovli. Leningrad: Oblastnoi i gorodskoi otdel snabzheniia, 1933.

Sbornik postanovlenii o promyslovoi kooperatsii. Edited by I. A. Selitskii. Moscow: Vsesoiuznoe kooperativnoe ob"edinennoe izdatel'stvo, 1939.

Sistematicheskii sbornik dekretov i rasporiazheniia pravitel'stva po prodovol'stvennomu delu. Book 1: 1 oktiabria 1917–1 ianvaria 1919 g. Nizhnii Novgorod, 1919.

Sobranie postanovlenii pravitel'stva SSSR. Series 1. Moscow: Iuridicheskoe izdatel'stvo Narodnogo komissariata iustitsii, 1923–53.

Sobranie uzakonenii i rasporiazhenii raboche-krest'ianskogo pravitel'stva RSFSR. Series

1. Moscow: Iuridicheskoe izdatel'stvo Narodnogo komissariata iustitsii, 1917–1923.

Zakonodatel'stvo i administrativnye rasporiazheniia po vneshnei i vnutrennei torgovli. Moscow: Narkomtorg, 1928–30.

PUBLISHED STATISTICAL SOURCES

Cultural Progress in the U.S.S.R.: Statistical Returns. Moscow: TsSU, 1958.

Itogi vsesoiuznoi perepisi naseleniia 1959 goda Vol. 1: USSR. Moscow: Gosudarstvennoe statisticheskoe izdatel'stvo, 1962.

Kolkhoznaia torgovlia v 1932–34 gg. Moscow: TsUNKhU, 1935.

Narodnoe khoziaistvo SSSR v Velikoi Otechestvennoi Voine, 1941–1945 gg. Statisticheskii sbornik Moscow: Informatsionno-izdatel'skii tsentr, 1990.

The National Economy of the USSR: A Statistical Compilation. Moscow: TsSU, 1956.

Sovetskaia torgovlia. Statisticheskii sbornik. Moscow: Gosudarstvennoe statisticheskoe izdatel'stvo, 1956.

Soviet and East European Foreign Trade, 1946–1969: Statistical Compendium and Guide. Edited by Paul Marer, with Gary J. Eubanks. Bloomington: Indiana University Press, 1972.

SSSR v tsifrakh. Statisticheskii sbornik. Moscow: Gosudarstvennoe statisticheskoe izdatel'stvo, 1958.

Torgovlia Soiuza SSR. Statisticheskii ezhegodnik. Moscow: Narkomat/Ministerstvo Torgovli, 1938–53 (available in RGAE f. 7971, op. 2).

Trudy Tsentral'nogo Statisticheskogo Upravleniia, vols. 8 (nos. 1–8) (*Statisticheskii ezhegodnik*) and 30 (nos. 1–2) (*Sostoianie pitanie gorodskogo/sel'skogo naseleniia SSSR, 1919–1924 gg.*).

Vsesoiuznaia perepis' naseleniia 1926 goda. Moscow: TsSU, 1928–31.

Vsesoiuznaia torgovaia perepis' 1935 g. Vol. 1: *Kolichestvo torgovykh predpriiatii i chislennost' torgovykh rabotnikov na 15 aprelia 1935 goda.* Vol. 2: *Kadry sovetskoi torgovli.* Vol. 3: *Roznichnaia torgovaia set' SSSR.* Vol. 5: *Roznichnye i optovye organizatsii.*

PUBLISHED DOCUMENT COLLECTIONS

Golos naroda. Pis'ma i otkliki riadovykh sovetskikh grazhdan o sobytiiakh 1918–1932 gg. Edited by A. K. Sokolov et al. Moscow: Rosspen, 1998.

Intimacy and Terror. Edited by Véronique Garros, Natalia Korenevskaia, and Thomas Lahusen. Translated by Carol A. Flath. New York: New Press, 1995.

Neizvestnaia Rossiia. XX. vek. Vols. 1–4. Moscow: Istoricheskoe nasledie, 1992.

Pis'ma vo vlast', 1917–1927: Zaiavleniia, zhaloby, donosy, pis'ma v gosudarstvennye struktury i bol'shevistskim vozhdiam. Moscow: Rosspen, 1998.

Pobeda oktiabr'skoi revoliutsii v Uzbekistane. Sbornik dokumentov. Tashkent: Gosudarstvennoe izdatel'stvo UzSSR, 1972.

Potrebitel'skaia kooperatsiia v rekonstruktivnyi period. Sbornik programm i materialov dlia kooperativnykh kruzhkov. Ed. P. Gel'bras. Moscow: Moskovskii rabochii, 1931.

Protokoly prezidiuma Gosplana za 1921–1922 gody. 2 vols. Moscow: Ekonomika, 1979.

Protokoly Presidiuma Vysshego Soveta Narodnogo Khoziaistva. Vol. 1: *Dekabr' 1917–1918 g.* Vol. 2: *1919 g.* Moscow: Ekonomika, 1991–93.

Rapports secrets sovietiques, 1921–1991. Edited by Nicolas Werth and Gael Moullec. Paris: Gallimard, 1994.

Rossiiskaia derevnia posle voiny (iiun' 1945—mart 1953). Sbornik dokumentov. Moscow: Prometei, 1993.

The Russian Provisional Government, 1917: Documents. Edited by Robert Paul Browder and Alexander F. Kerensky. 3 vols. Stanford: Hoover Institution Publications, 1961.

Sovetskaia derevnia glazami VChK-OGPU-NKVD: Dokumenty i materialy. Edited by A. Berelowitch, V. P. Danilov, et al. Vols. 1–2. Moscow: Rosspen, 1998–2000.

Stalinskoe Politbiuro v 30-e gody. Edited by O. V. Khlevniuk, A. V. Kvashonkin, L. P. Kosheleva, and L. A. Rogovaia. Moscow: AIRO–XX, 1995.

Tragediia sovetskoi derevni: Kollektivizatsiia i raskulachivanie. Dokumenty i materialy. Vols. 1–2. Moscow: Rosspen, 1999–2000.

Trudy I. Vserossiiskago S"ezda Sovetov Narodnago Khoziaistva (25 maia—4 iiunia 1918 g.) Stenograficheskii otchet. Moscow: VSNKh, 1918.

Trudy II. Vserossiiskogo S"ezda Sovetov Narodnogo Khoziaistva (19 dekabria—27 dekabria 1918 g.) Stenograficheskii otchet. Moscow: VSNKh, 1919.

SELECTED BOOKS, ARTICLES, AND MANUSCRIPTS

Aleksandrov, G., and L. Mariupol'skii, *Okhrana sotsialisticheskoi sobstvennosti v sisteme sovetskoi torgovli.* Moscow: Iuridicheskoe izdatel'stvo, 1949.

Alexopoulos, Golfo. *Stalin's Outcasts: Aliens, Citizens, and the Soviet State.* Ithaca: Cornell University Press, 2003.

Andrle, Vladimir. *Workers in Stalin's Russia: Industrialization and Social Change in a Planned Economy.* New York: St. Martin's, 1988.

Argenbright, Robert. "Bolsheviks, Baggers, and Railroaders: Political Power and Social Space, 1917–1921," *Russian Review* 52 (October 1993): 506–27.

Arina, A. E., G. G. Kotov, and K. V. Loseva. *Sotsial'no-ekonomicheskie izmeneniia v derevne. Melitopol'skii raion (1885–1938 g.g.).* Moscow: Sel'khozgiz, 1939.

Arkhipov, V. A., and L. F. Morozov. *Bor'ba protiv kapitalisticheskikh elementov v promyshlennosti i torgovle. 20-e—nachalo 30-x godov.* Moscow: Mysl', 1978.

Arskii, R. *Kak borot'sia s chastnym kapitalom.* Moscow: Priboi, 1927.

Atlas, Z. V. *Sotsialisticheskaia denezhnaia sistema.* Moscow: Finansy, 1969.

Ball, Alan M. *Russia's Last Capitalists: The Nepmen, 1921–1929.* Berkeley: University of California Press, 1987.

Banerji, Arup. *Merchants and Markets in Revolutionary Russia, 1917–30*. New York: St. Martin's, 1997.

Bankov, E., and A. Kazantsov. "Problema tovarnogo defitsita v ekonomicheskikh diskussiiakh 20-x godov." *Ekonomicheskie nauki*, no. 6 (June 1989): 101–9.

Barber, John, and Mark Harrison. *The Soviet Home Front, 1989, 1941–1989, 1945*. London: Longman, 1991.

Belenko, V. "O tovarnom golode." *Bol'shevik*, no. 17 (September 15 1926): 44–61.

Bergson, Abram. *The Real National Income of Soviet Russia since 1928*. Santa Monica: Rand Corporation, 1961.

Berliner, Joseph. *Factory and Manager in the USSR*. Cambridge, Mass.: Harvard University Press, 1957.

Biudzhety rabochikh i sluzhashchikh. Vol. 1: *Biudzhety rabochei sem'i*. Moscow: TsSU, 1929.

Blank, G. Ia., A. K. Bykov, and V. G. Gukus'ian, *Potrebitel'skaia kooperatsiia SSSR*. Moscow: Ekonomika, 1965.

Bol'shakov, A. M. *Derevnia. 1917–1927*. With an introduction by M. I. Kalinin and S. F. Ol'denburg. Moscow: Rabotnik prosveshcheniia, 1927.

Borrero, Mauricio. *Hungry Moscow: Scarcity and Urban Society in the Russian Civil War*. New York: Peter Lang, 2003.

Boshyk, Yuri, ed. *Ukraine during World War II: History and Its Aftermath*. Edmonton: Canadian Institute of Ukrainian Studies, University of Alberta, 1986.

Briére, Paul. *Salaires et niveau de vie en U.R.S.S.* Paris: Les Iles d'Or, 1951.

Bukharin, Nikolai, and E. Preobrazhenskii, *The ABC of Communism*. Ann Arbor: University of Michigan Press, 1966 [1919].

Burdzhalov, E. N. *Russia's Second Revolution: The February 1917 Uprising in Petrograd*. Translated and edited Donald J. Raleigh. Bloomington: Indiana University Press, 1987.

Carr, E. H. *The Bolshevik Revolution, 1917–1923*. 3 vols. London: Macmillan, 1952.

———. *The Interregnum, 1923–1924*. New York: Macmillan, 1954.

———. *Socialism in One Country, 1924–1926*. 3 vols. New York: Macmillan, 1958–64.

Carr, E. H., and R. W. Davies, *Foundations of a Planned Economy, 1926–1929*. 2 vols. London: Macmillan, 1969.

Carstenson, Fred V. *American Enterprise in Foreign Markets: Studies of Singer and International Harvester in Imperial Russia*. Chapel Hill: University of North Carolina Press, 1984.

Castillo, Greg. "Moscow: Gorki Street and the Design of the Stalin Revolution." In Zeynap Çelik, Diane Favro, and Richard Ingersoll, eds., *Streets: Critical Perspectives on Public Space*. Berkeley: University of California Press, 1994.

Chambre, Henri, Henri Wronski, and Georges Lasserre. *Les coopératives de consommation en U.R.S.S.* Paris: Éditions Cujas, 1969.

Chapman, Janet G. *Real Wages in Soviet Russia since 1928*. Cambridge, Mass.: Harvard University Press, 1963.

Chase, William J. *Workers, Society, and the Soviet State: Labor and Life in Moscow, 1918–1929*. Urbana: University of Illinois Press, 1987.

Cherniavskii, U. G. *Voina i prodovol'stvie. Snabzhenie gorodskogo naseleniia (1941–1945)*. Moscow: Nauka, 1964.

Chmyga, A. F. "Iz istorii organizatsii tovaroobmena v Sovetskoi Rossii v 1921 g." *Nauchnye doklady Vysshei shkoly. Istoricheskie nauki* no. 1(1958): 74–84.

Christian, David, and R.E.F. Smith. *Bread and Salt: A Social and Economic History of Food and Drink in Russia*. Cambridge: Cambridge University Press, 1984.

Chumak, A. F. "K voprosu o vovlechenii kustarei i remeslennikov v sotsialisticheskoe stroitel'stvo." *Voprosy istorii KPSS* (July 1967).

Colton, Timothy J. *Moscow: Governing the Socialist Metropolis*. Cambridge, Mass.: Harvard University Press, 1995.

Dallin, Alexander. *German Rule in Russia, 1941–1945. A Study of Occupation Policies*. Revised edition. Boulder: Westview, 1981 [1957].

Dallin, David. "The Black Market in Russia." *The American Mercury* 69 (December, 1949): 676–84.

Davies, R. W. *Development of the Soviet Budgetary System*. Cambridge: Cambridge University Press, 1958.

———. *The Socialist Offensive*. Cambridge, Mass.: Harvard University Press, 1980.

———. *The Soviet Economy in Turmoil, 1929–1930*. Cambridge, Mass.: Harvard University Press, 1989.

———. *Crisis and Progress in the Soviet Economy, 1931–1933*. London: Macmillan, 1996.

Davies, R. W., Mark Harrison, and S. G. Wheatcroft, eds. *The Economic Transformation of the Soviet Union, 1913–1945*. Cambridge: Cambridge University Press, 1994.

Davies, R. W., M. J. Ilic, H. P. Jenkins, C. Merridale, and S. G. Wheatcroft. *Soviet Governmental Officials, 1922–1941: A Handlist*. Birmingham: CREES, 1989.

Davies, R. W., and Oleg Khlevniuk, "The End of Rationing in the Soviet Union, 1934–1935." *Europe-Asia Studies* 51, no. 4 (1999): 557–609.

Davies, R. W., M. B. Tauger, and S. G. Wheatcroft, "Stalin, Grain Stocks, and the Famine of 1932–1933," *Slavic Review* 54, no. 3 (fall 1995): 642–57.

Davies, Sarah. *Popular Opinion in Stalin's Russia: Terror, Propaganda, and Dissent, 1934–1941*. Cambridge: Cambridge University Press, 1997.

Davydov, A. Iu. "Meshochnichestvo i sovetskaia prodovol'stvennaia diktatura. 1918–1922." *Voprosy istorii* 3 (1994): 41–54.

Davydov, M. I. *Bor'ba za khleb: prodovol'stvennaia politika kommunisticheskoi partii i sovetskogo gosudarstva v gody grazhdanskoi voiny (1917–1920)*. Moscow: Mysl', 1971.

Derevnia pri NEP"e. Kogo schitat' kulakom, kogo—truzhenikom; chto govoriat ob etom krest'iane? With an introduction by L. S. Sosnovskii. Moscow: Krasnaia nov', 1924.

Dikhtiar, G. A. *Vnutrenniaia torgovlia v dorevoliutsionnoi Rossii*. Moscow: Izdatel'stvo Akademii Nauk, 1960.

———. *Sovetskaia torgovlia v period postroeniia sotsializma*. Moscow: Izdatel'stvo Akademii Nauk, 1961.

———. *Sovetskaia torgovlia v period sotsializma i razvernutogo stroitel'stva kommunizma*. Moscow: Izdatel'stvo Akademii Nauk, 1965.

Dmitrenko, V. P. "Bor'ba Sovetskogo gosudarstva protiv chastnoi torgovli." In S. S. Khesin, ed., *Bor'ba za pobedu i ukrepleniiu sovetskoi vlasti, 1917–1918*. Moscow: Nauka, 1966.

———. "Nekotorye itogi obobshchestvleniia tovarooborota v 1917–1920 gg." *Istoricheskie zapiski* 79 (1966): 225–42.

———. *Torgovaia politika sovetskogo gosudarstva posle perekhoda k NEPu, 1921–1924 gg*. Moscow: Nauka, 1971.

———. *Sovetskaia ekonomicheskaia politika v pervye gody proletarskoi diktatury*. Moscow: Akademiia Nauk, 1986.

Dmitrenko, V. P., L. F. Morozov, and V. I. Pogudin, *Partiia i kooperatsiia*. Moscow: Izdatel'stvo politicheskoi literatury, 1978.

Druzhin, N. K., A. D. Bok, and E. G. Diukova, *Usloviia byta rabochikh v dorevoliutsionnoi Rossii*. Moscow: Nauchno-Issledovatel'skii Institut Truda, 1958.

Dudukalov, V. I. *Razvitie sovetskoi torgovli v Sibiri v gody sotsialisticheskogo stroitel'stva (1921–1928 gg.)*. Tomsk: Izdatel'stvo Tomskogo universiteta, 1978.

Dunham, Vera S. *In Stalin's Time: Middle-class Values in Soviet Literature*. Enlarged and updated edition. Durham, N.C.: Duke University Press, 1990.

Erlich, Alexander. *The Soviet Industrialization Debate, 1924–1928*. Cambridge, Mass.: Harvard University Press, 1967.

Fabrichnyi, Andrei. *Chastnyi kapital na poroge piatiletki. Klassovaia bor'ba v gorode i gosudarstvennyi apparat*. Moscow: Kommunisticheskaia Akademiia, 1930.

Fain, L. E. *Otechestvennaia kooperatsiia: istoricheskii opyt*. Ivanovo: Ivanovskii gosudarstvennyi universitet, 1994.

Feigel'son, M. "Meshochnichestvo i bor'ba s nim proletarskogo gosudarstva." *Istorik Marksist* 85, no. 9 (September 1940): 70–84.

Figes, Orlando. *A People's Tragedy: A History of the Russian Revolution*. New York: Viking, 1996.

Filtzer, Donald. *Soviet Workers and Stalinist Industrialization*. Armonk, N.Y.: M. E. Sharpe, 1986.

———. "The Standard of Living of Soviet Industrial Workers in the Immediate Postwar Period, 1945–1948." *Europe-Asia Studies* 51, no. 6 (summer 1999): 1013–38.

Fitzpatrick, Ann Lincoln. *The Great Russian Fair: Nizhnii Novgorod, 1840–1890*. London: Macmillan, 1990.

Fitzpatrick, Sheila. "After NEP: The Fate of NEP Entrepreneurs, Small Traders, and Artisans in the 'Socialist Russia' of the 1930s." *Russian History/Histoire Russe* 13, nos. 2–3 (summer–fall, 1986): 187–234.

———. "Becoming Cultured: Socialist Realism and the Representation of Privilege and Taste." In idem, *The Cultural Front: Power and Culture in Revolutionary Russia*, 216–37. Ithaca, N.Y.: Cornell University Press, 1992.

———. *Stalin's Peasants: Resistance and Survival in the Russian Village after Collectivization*. New York: Oxford University Press, 1994.

———. *Everyday Stalinism. Ordinary Lives in Extraordinary Times: Soviet Russia in the 1930s*. New York: Oxford University Press, 1999.

———. *"Blat* in Stalin's Time." In Stephen Lovell, Alena Ledeneva, and Andrei Rogachevskii, eds., *Bribery and Blat in Russia: Negotiating Reciprocity from the Middle Ages to the 1990s*, 166–83. London: Macmillan, 2000.

Frumkin, M. *Tovaroobmen, kooperatsiia, i torgovlia*. Moscow: Gosizdat', 1921.

Gimpel'son, E. G. *Formirovanie sovetskoi politicheskoi sistemy, 1917–1923*. Moscow: Nauka, 1995.

———. *NEP i sovetskaia politicheskaia sistema. 20-e gody*. Moscow: RAN, 2000.

Ginzburg, Abram Moiseevich. *Chastnyi kapital v narodnom khoziaistve SSSR. Materialy komissii VSNKh SSSR*. Moscow: VSNKh, 1926.

Gohstand, Robert. "The Internal Geography of Trade in Moscow from the Mid-Nineteenth Century to the First World War." Ph.D. dissertation, University of California Berkeley, 1973.

Gol'bert, Ia. M. ed. *Novaia torgovaia praktika (k kharakteristike vnutrennei torgovli v pervoi poloviny 1924–25 g.). Po materialam Soveta S"ezdov birzhevoi torgovli*. Moscow: Vseros. Sovet S"ezdov birzhevoi torgovli, 1925.

———. Introduction to Ts. M. Kron, *Chastnaia torgovlia v SSSR. Po materialam Soveta S"ezdov Birzhevoi Torgovli*. Moscow: Izdatel'stvo MGSPS—Trud i kniga, 1926.

Goldman, Marshall I. "Commission Trade and the Kolkhoz Market." *Soviet Studies* 10, no. 2 (October 1958): 136–45.

———. *Soviet Marketing*. London: Collier-Macmillan, 1963.

Gorlizki, Yoram. "Rules, Incentives, and Soviet Campaign Justice after World War II." *Europe-Asia Studies* 51, no. 7 (November 1999): 1245–65.

Gregory, Paul. *Before Command: An Economic History of Russia from Emancipation to the First Five-Year Plan*. Princeton, N.J.: Princeton University Press, 1994.

Grossman, Gregory. "The 'Second Economy' of the USSR." *Problems of Communism* 26, no. 5 (September–October, 1977): 25–40.

Gregory Grossman and Vladimir Treml, eds. *Berkeley-Duke Papers on the Second Economy in the USSR*. See, especially, No. 21, ed. Gregory Grossman, "The Second Economy in the USSR and Eastern Europe: A Bibliography."

Gumilevskii, N. *Biudzhet sluzhashchikh v 1922–1926 gg.* Edited and with an introduction by E. O. Kabo. Moscow: Izdatel'stvo TsK Soiuza Sovetskikh Torgovykh Sluzhashchikh, 1928.

Hanson, Philip. *The Consumer in the Soviet Economy*. Evanstan, Ill.: Northwestern University Press, 1968.

Harrison, Mark. *Soviet Planning in Peace and War, 1938–1945*. Cambridge: Cambridge University Press, 1985.

Häusler, Eugen. *Der Kaufmann in der russischen Literatur*. Königsberg: Gräfe und Unser, 1935.

Hessler, Julie. "A Postwar Perestroika? Toward a History of Private Enterprise in the USSR." *Slavic Review* 57, no. 3 (fall 1998): 516–42.

———. "Cultured Trade: The Stalinist Turn towards Consumerism." In Sheila Fitzpatrick, ed., *Stalinism: New Directions*, 182–209. London: Routledge, 2000.

Hubbard, Leonard. *Soviet Trade and Distribution*. London: Macmillan, 1938.

Hunter, Holland, and Janusz M. Szyrmer. *Faulty Foundations: Soviet Economic Policies, 1928–1940*. Princeton, N.J.: Princeton University Press, 1992.

Iakovlev, Ia. *Derevnia kak ona est'. Ocherk Nikol'skoi volosti*. Moscow: Rabotnik prosveshcheniia, 1923.

———. *Nasha derevna. Novoe v starom i staroe v novom*. Moscow: Krasnaia nov', 1924.

Ibragimova, D. Kh. *NEP i perestroika. Massovoe soznanie sel'skogo naseleniia v usloviiakh perekhoda k rynku*. Moscow, 1997.

Iurovsky, L. N. *Currency Problems and Policy of the Soviet Union*. London: L. Parsons, 1925.

Ivanchenko, A. A., and V. N. Ge. *Sovetskaia torgovlia Leningrada i Leningradskoi oblasti, 1931–1934 gg.* Leningrad: Leningradskoe gosudarstvennoe izdatel'stvo, 1935.

Jasny, Naum. *The Socialized Agriculture of the USSR*. Stanford: Stanford University Press, 1949.

———. *The Soviet 1956 Statistical Handbook: A Commentary*. East Lansing: Michigan State University Press, 1957.

———. *Soviet Industrialization, 1928–1952*. Chicago: University of Chicago Press, 1961.

Jones, Jeffrey Wade. "'In my opinion this is all a fraud!': Concrete, Culture, and Class in the 'Reconstruction' of Rostov-on-the-Don, 1943–1948." Ph.D. dissertation, University of North Carolina at Chapel Hill, 2000.

Kabanov, V. V. *Oktiabr'skaia revoliutsiia i kooperatsiia (1917g.—mart 1919g.)*. Moscow: Nauka, 1973.

———. *Kooperatsiia, revoliutsiia, sotsializm*. Moscow: Nauka, 1996.

Kabo, E. O. *Pitanie russkogo rabochego do i posle voiny (po statisticheskim materialam 1908–1924 gg.)* Moscow: Voprosy truda, 1926.

———. *Ocherki rabochego byta. Opyt monograficheskogo issledovaniia*. Moscow: VTsSPS, 1928.

Kaktyn', A. M. *O podkhode k chastnomu kapitalu*. Moscow: Moskovskii rabochii, 1924.

Kalinin, M. I. *O sovetskoi torgovle*. Moscow: Partizdat', 1932.

Kantorovich, Ia. A. *Chastnaia torgovlia i promyshlennost' SSSR po deistvuiushchemu zakonodatel'stvu*. Leningrad: Seiatel', 1925.

Katsenelinboigen, Aron. "Coloured Markets in the Soviet Union." *Soviet Studies* 29, no. 1 (January 1977): 62–85.

Kazakov, E. D. *Gosudarstvennye prodovo'stvennye rezervy. Istoricheskie ocherki*. Moscow, 1956.

Kerblay, Basile. *Les marchés paysans en U.R.S.S.* Paris: Mouton, 1968.

Kessler, Gijs. "The Peasant and the Town: Rural-Urban Migration in the Soviet Union, 1929–40." Ph.D. dissertation, European University Institute, 2001.

Khaziev, R. A. "Rol' svobodnoi torgovli v ekonomike Bashkirii perioda 'voennogo kommunizma' (1919–1921 gg.)." *Vestnik Leningradskogo Universiteta*, series 2, no. 2 (1989): 85–87.

Kir'ianov, Iu. I. *Zhiznennyi uroven' rabochikh Rossii*. Moscow: Nauka, 1979.

Klimov, A. P. *Potrebitel'skaia kooperatsiia v sisteme razvitogo sotsializma*. Moscow: Ekonomika, 1980.

Koenker, Diane, William G. Rosenberg, and Ronald Grigor Suny, eds. *Party, State, and Society in the Russian Civil War: Explorations in Social History*. Bloomington: Indiana University Press, 1989.

Kolesnikov, L. *Litso klassovogo vraga*. With an introduction by Iu. Larin. Moscow: Molodaia gvardiia, 1928.

Kondrat'ev, N. D. *Rynok khlebov i ego regulirovanie vo vremia voiny i revoliutsii*. Moscow: Nauka, 1991 [1922].

Kondurushkin, I. S. *Chastnyi kapital pered sovetskim sudom*. Moscow: Gosudarstvennoe izdatel'stvo, 1927.

———. *Ekonomicheskie sudebnye protsessy perioda NEPa. Obvinitel'nye rechi*. Moscow: Gosudarstvennoe izdatel'stvo, 1930.

Kornai, János. *The Socialist System: The Political Economy of Communism*. Princeton, N.J.: Princeton University Press, 1992.

Kotkin, Stephen. *Magnetic Mountain: Stalinism as a Civilization*. Berkeley: University of California Press, 1995.

Kritsman, L. N. *Novaia ekonomicheskaia politika i planovoe raspredelenie*. Moscow: Gosudarstvennoe izdatel'stvo, 1922.

———. *Geroicheskii period velikoi russkoi revoliutsii*. Moscow: Gosudarstvennoe izdatel'stvo, 1924.

Kron, Ts. M. *Chastnaia torgovlia v SSSR. Po materialam Soveta S"ezdov Birzhevoi Torgovli*. Moscow: Izdatel'stvo MGSPS—Trud i kniga, 1926.

Larin, Iurii. *Chastnyi kapital v SSSR*. Moscow: Gosudarstvennoe izdatel'stvo, 1927.

———. *Gosudarstvennyi kapitalizm voennogo vremeni v Germanii*. Moscow: Gosudarstvennoe izdatel'stvo, 1928.

Lenin, V. I. *Polnoe sobranie sochinenii*. 5th ed. Moscow: Gosudarstvennoe izdatel'stvo, 1958–1965.

———. *State and Revolution*. New York: International, 1943.

Lewin, Moshe. *The Making of the Soviet System: Essays in the Social History of Interwar Russia*. New York: Pantheon, 1985.

Lih, Lars T. *Bread and Authority in Russia, 1914–1921*. Berkeley: University of California Press, 1990.

Liubimov, A. V. *Torgovlia i snabzhenie v gody Velikoi Otechestvennoi Voiny*. Moscow: Ekonomika, 1968.

Lozinskii, Z. *Ekonomicheskaia politika vremennogo pravitel'stva*. Leningrad: Priboi, 1929.

Malafeev, A. N. *Istoriia tsenoobrazovaniia v SSSR (1917–1963)*. Moscow: Mysl', 1964.

Malle, Silvana. *The Economic Organization of War Communism, 1918–1921*. Cambridge: Cambridge University Press, 1985.

Manning, Roberta T. "The Soviet Economic Crisis of 1936–1940 and the Great Purges." In J. Arch Getty and Roberta T. Manning, eds., *Stalinist Terror: New Perspectives*, 116–41. Cambridge: Cambridge University Press, 1993.

Matthews, Mervyn. *Privilege in the Soviet Union: A Study of Elite Life-Styles under Communism*. London: Allen and Unwin, 1978.

McAuley, Mary. *Bread and Justice: State and Society in Petrograd, 1917–1922*. Oxford: Oxford University Press, 1991.

Mikoian, Anastas. "Disproportsiia i tovarnyi golod." *Bol'shevik* nos. 23–24 (December 31, 1926): 23–33.

———. *Tak bylo: razmyshleniia o minuvshem*. Moscow: Vagrius, 1999.

Miliutin, V. P., ed. *Kooperatsiia v SSSR za desiat' let*. Moscow: Izdatel'stvo Kommunisticheskoi Akademii, 1928.

Miliutin, V. P., et al., eds. *Na novykh putiakh: Itogi novoi ekonomicheskoi politiki 1921–1922 g.g.*, Vol. 1. *Torgovlia*. Moscow: Sovet Truda i Oborony, 1923.

Mindlin, Z. L. "Sotsial'nyi sostav evreiskogo naseleniia SSSR." In *Evrei v SSSR: Materialy i issledovaniia*. Vol. 4. Moscow: Pravlenie Vseros. ORT, 1929.

Mingulin, I. S. *Puti razvitiia chastnogo kapitala*. With a preface by A. Z. Gol'tsman. Moscow: Moskovskii rabochii, 1927.

Morozov, L. F. *Reshaiushchii etap bor'by s nepmanskoi burzhuaziei*. Moscow: VPSh, 1960.

———. *Ot kooperatsii burzhuaznoi k kooperatsii sotsialisticheskoi*. Moscow: Nauka, 1969.

Moshkov, Iu. A. *Zernovaia problema v gody sploshnoi kollektivizatsii SSSR (1929–1932 gg.)*. Moscow: Izdatel'stvo Moskovskogo universiteta, 1966.

Moskoff, William. *The Bread of Affliction: The Food Supply in the U.S.S.R. during World War II*. Cambridge: Cambridge University Press, 1990.

Na novom etape sotsialisticheskogo stroitel'stva. Sbornik statei. Edited by G. M. Kzhizhanskii. Moscow: Gosudarstvennoe planovoe khoziaistvennoe izdatel'stvo, 1930.

Neiman, G. Ia. *Vnutrenniaia torgovlia SSSR*. Edited by E. I. Kviring. Moscow: Gosudarstvennoe sotsial'no-ekonomicheskoe izdatel'stvo, 1935.

NEP: Priobreteniia i poteri. Moscow: RAN, 1994.

Novaia ekonomicheskaia politika. Voprosy teorii i istorii. AN SSSR Institut Istorii. Moscow: Nauka, 1974.

Nove, Alec. *Economic Rationality and Soviet Politics; or, Was Stalin Really Necessary?* New York: 1964.

———. *An Economic History of the U.S.S.R.* London: Penguin, 1969.

———. "Victims of Stalinism: How Many?" In J. Arch Getty and Roberta Manning, eds., *Stalinist Terror: New Perspectives*. Cambridge: Cambridge University Press, 1993.

Novozhilov, V. V. "Nedostatok tovarov." *Vestnik finansov*, no. 2 (February 1926): 75–96. Reprinted in idem, *Voprosy razvitiia sotsialisticheskoi ekonomiki*. Moscow: Nauka, 1972.

Orlov, N. *Deviat' mesiatsev prodovol'stvennoi raboty sovetskoi vlasti*. Moscow: Komprod, 1918.

———. *Sistema prodovol'stvennoi zagotovki*. Tambov, 1920.

Osokina, Elena A. *Ierarkhiia potrebleniia. O zhizni liudei v usloviiakh stalinskogo snabzheniia*. Moscow: MGOU, 1993.

———. "Liudi i vlast' v usloviiakh krizisa snabzheniia 1939–1941 gody." *Otechestvennaia istoriia*, no. 3 (May–June 1995): 16–32.

———. "Za zerkal'noi dver'iu Torgsina." *Otechestvennaia istoriia*, no. 2 (April 1995): 86–104.

———. *Za fasadom "stalinskogo izobiliia." Raspredelenie i rynok v snabzhenii naseleniia v gody industrializatsii, 1927–1941*. Moscow: Rosspen, 1998. In English: *Our Daily Bread: Socialist Distribution and the Art of Survival in Stalin's Russia*. Translated Kate Transchel and Greta Bucher. Armonk, N.Y.: M.E. Sharpe, 2000.

Ostrovskii, V. B. *Kolkhoznoe krest'ianstvo SSSR. Politika partii v derevne i ee sotsial'no-ekonomicheskie rezul'taty*. Saratov: Izdatel'stvo Saratovskogo universiteta, 1967.

Otchet Khar'kovskogo gubernskogo ekonomicheskogo soveshchaniia za 1 ianvaria—1 oktiabria 1921 g. Khar'kov: Khar'kovskogo gubernskogo Ekoso, 1921.

Paduchev, G. P. *Chastnyi torgovets pri novoi ekonomicheskoi politike (po dannym biudzhetnogo obsledovaniia)*. Voronezh: n.p., 1926.

Pavliuchenko, S. A. *Voennyi kommunizm v Rossii: vlast' i massy*. Moscow: First Monograph, 1997.

Pethybridge, Roger. *The Spread of the Russian Revolution: Essays on 1917*. London: Macmillan, 1972.

———. *One Step Backwards, Two Steps Forward. Soviet Society and Politics in the New Economic Policy*. Oxford: Oxford University Press, 1990.

Piat'desiat' let sovetskoi potrebitel'skoi kooperatsii. Moscow: Ekonomika, 1967.

Popov, V. P. *Ekonomicheskaia politika sovetskogo gosudarstva, 1946–1953 gg*. Tambov: Izdatel'stvo TGTU, 2000.

Potrebitel'skaia kooperatsiia ot VI k VII s"ezdu sovetov Soiuza SSR. Moscow: Tsentrosoiuz, 1935.

Preobrazhenskii, E. A. *O morali i klassovykh normakh*. Moscow: Gosuderstvennoe izdatel'stvo, 1923.

Randall, Amy E. "'Revolutionary Bolshevik Work': Stakhanovism in Retail Trade." *Russian Review* 59 (July 2000): 425–41.

———. "Women Workers and the Gendering of Soviet Trade." Unpublished paper presented at the annual conference of the American Association for the Advancement of Slavic Studies in Denver, 2000.

Riauzov, N. N., and N. P. Titel'baum. *Statistika torgovli*. 5th ed. Moscow: Statistika, 1968.

Rimmel, Lesley A. "Another Kind of Fear: The Kirov Murder and the End of Bread Rationing in Leningrad." *Slavic Review* 56, no. 3 (fall 1997): 481–99.

Ruane, Christine. "Clothes Shopping in Imperial Russia: The Development of a Consumer Culture." *Journal of Social History* (summer 1995): 765–82.

Rubinshtein, G. L. *Razvitie vnutrennei torgovli v SSSR*. Leningrad: Izdatel'stvo Leningradskogo Universiteta, 1964.

Rykov, A. I. *Khoziaistvennoe polozhenie sovetskikh respublik i ocherednye zadachi ekonomicheskoi politiki*. Moscow: Biblioteka ekonomicheskoi zhizni, 1924.

———. "Voprosy snabzheniia i raspredeleniia." In *Izbrannye proizvedeniia*. Moscow: Ekonomika, 1990.

Schulte, Theo J. *The German Army and Nazi Policies in Occupied Russia*. Oxford: Berg, 1989.

Shanin, Teodor, ed. *Neformal'naia ekonomika: Rossiia i mir*. Moscow: Logovaz, 1999.

Shearer, David R. *Industry, State, and Society in Stalin's Russia, 1926–1934.* Ithaca, N.Y.: Cornell University Press, 1996.

———. "Crime and Social Disorder in Stalin's Russia: A Reassessment of the Great Retreat and the Origins of Mass Repression." *Cahiers du Monde russe* 39, nos. 1–2 (January–June 1998): 119–48.

Shishkin, V. A. *Vlast'. Politika. Ekonomika.* Saint Petersburg: RAN, 1997.

Siegelbaum, Lewis H. *Stakhanovism and the Politics of Productivity in the USSR, 1935–1941.* Cambridge: Cambridge University Press, 1988.

———. *Soviet State and Society between Revolutions, 1918–1929.* Cambridge: Cambridge University Press, 1992.

Sokol'nikov, G. Ia. *Novaia finansovaia politika na puti k tverdoi valiute.* Moscow: Nauka, 1991.

Sokolov, V., and R. Nazarov. *Sovetskaia torgovlia v poslevoennyi period.* Moscow: Gosudarstvennoe izdatel'stvo politicheskoi literatury, 1954.

Solomon, Peter H., Jr. *Soviet Criminal Justice under Stalin.* Cambridge: Cambridge University Press, 1996.

Sorok let sovetskoi torgovli. Moscow: Gostorgizdat, 1957.

Sorokin, Pitirim A. *Hunger as a Factor in Human Affairs.* Translated by Elena P. Sorokin. Gainesville: University of Florida Press, 1975 [1922].

Sotsialisticheskoe narodnoe khoziaistvo SSSR v 1933–1940 gg. Moscow: Izdatel'stvo Akademii Nauk, 1963.

Sovetskoe narodnoe khoziaistvo v 1921–1925 gg. AN SSSR Institut Ekonomiki. Moscow: Ekonomika, 1960.

Stalin, I. V. *Sochineniia.* 13 vols. Moscow: Gosudarstvennoe izdatel'stvo politicheskoi literatury, 1952–53.

———. *Voprosy leninizma.* 11th ed. Moscow: Partizdat', 1948.

———. *Sochineniia.* 3 vols. [14–16]. Stanford: Hoover Institution, 1967.

Strumilin, S. G. *Zarabotnaia plata i proizvoditel'nost' truda v russkoi promyshlennosti za 1913–1922 gg.* Moscow: Voprosy truda 1923.

———. *Rabochii byt v tsifrakh: Statistiko-ekonomicheskie etiudy.* Moscow: Izdatel'stvo Planovoe khoziaistvo, 1926.

———. *Ocherki sovetskoi ekonomiki. Resursy i perspektivy.* Moscow: Gosudarstvennoe izdatel'stvo, 1928.

———. *Statistiko-ekonomicheskie ocherki.* Moscow: Gosudarstvennoe statisticheskoe izdatel'stvo, 1958.

———. *Izbrannye proizvedeniia v piati tomakh.* Moscow: Izdatel'stvo Akademii Nauk, 1963–64.

Thurston, Robert, and Bernd Bonwetsch, eds. *The People's War: Responses to World War II in the Soviet Union.* Urbana: University of Illinois Press, 2000.

Timasheff, Nicholas S. *The Great Retreat: The Growth and Decline of Communism in Russia.* New York: E. P. Dutton, 1946.

Tri goda bor'by s golodom. Kratkii otchet o deiatel'nosti narodnogo komissariata po prodovol'stviiu za 1919–20 god. Moscow: Izdatel'stvo otdela Narodnogo komissariata po prodovol'stviiu, 1920.

Trifonov, I. Ia. *Klassy i klassovaia bor'ba v SSSR v nachale NEPa (1921–1925).* Part 2: *Podgotovka ekonomicheskogo nastupleniia na novuiu burzhuaziiu.* Leningrad: Izdatel'stvo Leningradskogo universiteta, 1969.

———. *Likvidatsiia ekspluatatorskikh klassov v SSSR*. Moscow: Izdatel'stvo Politicheskoi literatury, 1975.

Trotskii, Leon. *K sotsializmu ili k kapitalizmu? (Analiz sovetskogo khoziaistva i tendentsii ego razvitiia)*. Moscow: Planovoe khoziaistvo, 1925.

———. *The Revolution Betrayed: What Is the Soviet Union and Where Is It Going?* New York: Doubleday, Doran, 1937.

———. *The New Course*. Translated by Max Schachtman. Ann Arbor: University of Michigan Press, 1965 [1923].

Turetskii, Sh. Ia. *Ocherki planovogo tsenoobrazovaniia v SSSR*. Moscow: Gosudarstvennoe izdatel'stvo politicheskoi literatury, 1959.

Tyl sovetskikh vooruzhennykh sil v Velikoi Otechestvennoi Voine. Moscow: Institute of Military History, Ministry of Defense, 1977.

Ustinov, V. M. *Evoliutsiia vnutrennei torgovli v Rossii, 1913–1924*. Moscow: Ekonomicheskaia zhizn', 1925.

Vaisberg, R. I. *Den'gi i tseny (Podpol'nyi rynok v period "voennogo kommunizma")*. Moscow: Gosplan, 1925.

Vasil'ev, S. *Natsionalizatsiia vnutrennei torgovli*. Moscow: n.p., 1918.

Vladimirov, M. *Meshechnichestvo i ego sotsial'no-ekonomicheskie otrazheniia*. Khar'kov: Izdatel'stvo Poiugzapa i Poukrsovtrudarma, 1920.

Voznesenskii, N. A. *Voennaia ekonomika SSSR v period otechestvennoi voiny*. Moscow: Gosudarstvennoe izdatel'stvo politicheskoi literatury, 1948.

Vyltsan, M. A. *Sovetskaia derevnia nakanune Velikoi Otechestvennoi Voiny (1938–1941 gg.)* Moscow: Izdatel'stvo politicheskoi literatury, 1970.

Wädekin, Karl-Eugen. *The Private Sector in Soviet Agriculture*. Edited by George F. Karcz. Translated by Keith Bush. Berkeley: University of California Press, 1973.

Wedel, Janine, ed. *The Unplanned Society: Poland during and after Communism*. New York: Columbia University Press, 1992.

West, Sally. "The Material Promised Land: Advertising's Modern Agenda in Late Imperial Russia." *Russian Review* 57, no. 3 (July 1998): 345–63.

Wheatcroft, Steve. "Famine and Factors Affecting Mortality in the USSR: The Demographic Crises of 1914–22 and 1930–33." CREES Discussion Papers, Soviet Industrialization Project Series, nos. 20–21. Birmingham, United Kingdom, 1981–82.

Whitman, John T. "The Kolkhoz Market." *Soviet Studies* 7, no. 4 (April 1956): 384–204.

Wildt, Michael. *Der Traum vom Sattwerden. Hunger und Protest, Schwarzmarkt und Selbsthilfe:* Hamburg: VSA-Verlag, 1986.

———. *Am Beginn der "Konsumgesellschaft." Mangelerfahrung, Lebenshaltung, Wohlstandshoffnung in Westdeutschland in der fünfziger Jahren*. Forum Zeitgeschichte, Bd. 3. Hamburg: Ergebnisse-Verlag, 1994.

Zagorskii, S. O. *K sotsializmu ili k kapitalizmu?* Prague: Verlag "Svobodnoi Rossii," 1927.

Zaleski, Eugéne. *Planning for Economic Growth in the Soviet Union, 1918–1932*. Edited and translated by Marie-Christine MacAndrew and G. Warren Nutter. Chapel Hill: University of North Carolina Press, 1971.

———. *Stalinist Planning for Economic Growth, 1933–1952*. Edited and translated by Marie-Christine MacAndrew and G. Warren Nutter. Chapel Hill: University of North Carolina Press, 1971.

Zalkind, L. B., ed. *Chastnaia torgovlia v SSSR. Sbornik statei.* Moscow, 1927.

Zima, V. F. *Golod v SSSR 1946–1947 godov: proiskhozhdenie i posledstviia.* Moscow: RAN, 1996.

Zolotarev, S. A. *Chetyre smeny molodezhi (1905–1925).* Leningrad: n.p., 1926.

Zubkova, E. Iu. *Obshchestvo i reformy, 1945–1964.* Moscow: First Monograph, 1993.

———. *Russia after the War: Hopes, Illusions, and Disappointments, 1945–1957.* Edited and translated by Hugh Ragdale. Armonk, N.Y.: M.E. Sharpe, 1998.

———. *Poslevoennoe sovetskoe obshchestvo: Politika i povsednevnost', 1945–1953.* Moscow: Rosspen, 1999.

Index

Page references in italics refer to tables and illustrations.

administrators, local. *See* managers/administrators, local
advertising, of merchandise, 55, 212–14, 247
agricultural cooperatives, 60, 89
agricultural implements, 63, 289
Alexopoulos, Golfo, 107
All-Russian Congress of Economic Soviets (1918), 59
All-Russian Food-Supply Conference (1921), 60
All-Union Congress of Stakhanovites (1935), 222, 230
All-Union Leather Syndicate, 143–44
Andrle, Vladimir, 3
Anosova, M. A., 125
anti-peasant discrimination. *See* urban-rural discrimination
anti-Semitism, 27–28
anti-trade policies: Bolsheviks and, 19, 24–38, 48–49, 51–52, 103, 119; Stalin-era, 137–38, 141–42, 241
Apocalypticism, 233
Arbat market (Moscow), 254, 275
aristocracy, 45, 120
Arkangel'sk *guberniia*, 26
artels, 60, 92
artisans and artisanal trade, 9, 34; cloth/clothing trade and, 32, 101, 104, 123–24, 138; consumer goods manufacturing and, 32, 49, 101, 287–88; furniture manufacturing and, 32; repression of, 262–63; "second economy" and, 289–91; "self-provisionment" and, 32, 43; shoe/leather goods and, 142–43; sweets and, 124; unemployment and, 107; wages and, 107
Arzhilovskii, A. S., 231–32, 261
Astrakhan, 37, 70
Atlas, Z. V., 78, 306

Babine, Alexis, 39–40, 42
"bagging" *(meshochnichestvo)*, 19, 35–38, 41–43, 91, 103n.6, 252, 273–79; cloth/clothing trade and, 35, 48; grain trade and, 35–36, 48; peasants and, 41, 47–48, 70; railroad industry and, 37, 279, 282; workers and, 41. *See also* buying agents
Bakaleia (bakery chain), 201, 206
Baku, 70
Ball, Alan, 107, 110
Banerji, Arup, 116
bars. *See* drinking establishments
bartering, individual, 48–49, 268–69. *See also* contracts and barter agreements
Basavin, I. A., 272
Bashkir ASSR, 312
bazaars, 9, 19, 29–35, 49, 184, 192–93, 252–73, 284–85, 294, 334–35; artisanal manufacturing and, 32, 286–88; as collective-farm markets, 189, 192; cultured trade and, 253; decrees on, 189–91, 254–55, 263; as farmer's markets, 35; goods sold in, 31, 125, 252–53, 261–62; hours of trade and, 118; illegal activities in, 31, 35, 271–72, 312; layouts of, 29–30, 125, 259; legal status of, 30–31, 34, 170, 190–93; modernization policies and, 244; police raids on, 30–32, 187–88, 265; prices in, 186; utilization policies and, 34, 251; wholesale trade and, 35. *See also* flea markets; outdoor markets
Beatty, Bessie, 40
Belenko, V., 145
Bel'kovskii *raion*, 287
Belorussia, 21, 27–28, 34, 172
Bezprozvannyi, D. A., 122–23
Bidlack, Richard, 279
billiard halls, 12, 127, 147, 285–86, 291
Bim Bum, 45

black markets, 11, 33, 265, 277, 292, 294–95
Bolsheviks: anti-market/trade policies of, 19, 24–38, 48–49, 51–52, 103, 119; "bagging" under, 35, 37–38, 70; commodity exchange and, 69–73; consumer cooperatives and, 53–61, 92, 167; Marxism and, 60; pricing/price controls and, 8, 25, 75–79; rationing and, 53, 63–69; repression by, 114; *smychka* and, 333; speculation and, 19, 25, 191; standardization and, 58; stockpiling and, 158
Bone, Jonathan, 181n.122
bonuses-in-kind, 43, 69, 103
book industry, 47, 229
Borushek, I. A., 122–23
bourgeoisie: *kulaks* and, 28, 52, 57, 92–93, 109, 160, 172, 188, 220; rationing and, 63; as trade specialists, 25, 28, 34, 52, 55, 68, 102, 120
Bragin, E. G., 283–84
bread trade, 33, 38–39, 165–66, 201, 207–8, 305–6
Brezhnev, L. I., 131
Briansk *oblast'*, 74
bribery, 85–87, 283, 311
Brower, Daniel, 45
Bukharin, N. I., 116
bureaucratism, 82, 86–87, 99, 170; cultured trade and, 215–22, 245; defined, 53, 80; trade unions and, 183
bureaucratization policies: consumer cooperatives and, 53–61; crisis socialism and, 11; post-revolutionary, 25, 79–80, 84, 98–99; rationing and, 62–69; shortages and, 10; Stalin-era, 136, 156, 169–70, 245; wartime, 296
buying agents, 7; cloth/clothing trade and, 138–40; for cooperatives and state agencies, 82–85, 91; for factories, 83, 180–83; "queuing specialists" as, 138–40, 236; for socialist-sector trade, 244; for trade organizations, 216; travel permits and, 282; in wartime, 282–84. *See also* "bagging" (*meshochnichestvo*)
buying-up points, 266

cafeterias and canteens, 5, 63–65, 125, 177–79, 208, 286, 301
capital mobilization, 57–58, 110–13, 119, 292

Carr, E. H., 32
Central Agricultural Region, 21, 156
Central Committee (Communist Party), 170, 242, 317
centralization policies, 56–58, 80, 98, 136, 167–68, 241, 273. *See also* decentralization policies
Central Statistical Administration (TsSU, TsUNKhU), 9, 226–27
Central Union of Consumer Societies (*Tsentrosoiuz*), 55, 57, 73, 91, 93, 94, 167–68, 208, 212
Chernigov *guberniia*, 26
children, 40, 42–43, 284
cigarette trade. *See* tobacco and cigarette trade
Civil Code (1923), 113–14, 120
class rationing, 5; Bolsheviks and, 63, 65–67; NEP and, 137, 155, 161, 167–69; popular communism and, 223–24; Stalin-era, 14, 167–69, 171, 174–76, 241–42; urban residents and, 168; war communism and, 161, 175; wartime, 298–99, 301–2
class warfare, 49; anti-trade policies and, 28, 34, 51–52, 142; destruction of wealth and, 11; kulaks and, 52; rationing and, 171–72; utilization policies and, 101; in wartime, 296
clerical employees. *See* salesclerks/assistants
Clinton, Bill, 158n.56
"closed distributors" (*zakrytye raspredeliteli*), 178–80, 208, 225, 242–43
cloth and clothing trade, 121–23, 201, 331; anti-trade policies and, 138–42; artisans and, 32, 101, 123–24, 138; "bagging" and, 35, 48; household budgets and, 46, 123, 227–28, 259, *309*; in Kiev, 121; labor strikes in, 183; licensing and, 123; in Moscow, 35, 138; in Petrograd/Leningrad, 35, 121–23; pricing/price controls in, 81; rationing and, 63, 69–70, 140, 165; repression and, 145–46, 159; in Rostov, 139; shortages in, 138, 145; textile workers and, 45–46; wholesalers and, 115
collective-farm markets, 189–90, 192, 244
collective farms, 191, 257, 289
collectivization, 131, 161–62, 173, 182, 194, 230, 251

Colton, T., 161
commercial class. *See* bourgeoisie
Commissariat of Agriculture, 94
Commissariat of Domestic Trade, 212–13,
  216–17, 221, 263, 265, 330
Commissariat of Education, 94
Commissariat of Finance, 81, 146–48, 185,
  265
Commissariat of Food Supplies (*Komprod*),
  26, 37, 55–57, 69, 73–74, 94
Commissariat of Foreign and Domestic
  Trade (*Narkomtorg*), 137
Commissariat of Health, 94
Commissariat of Internal Affairs, 42,
  185
Commissariat of Justice, 264, 271–72
Commissariat of Light Industry, 213
Commissariat of Provisionment
  (*Narkomsnab*), 137, 168, 216
Commissariat of Trade, 82, 147, 167–68,
  242, 257
Commission for Transfers to Red Army
  Rations, 67
Commission for Worker Supplies, 67
commission stores, 266
Committee on Reserves, 159
Committees of Market Traders, 118–19
Committees of Poor Peasants (*kombedy*),
  59, 71
commodity exchange (*tovaroobmen*), 53,
  70–75, 136–37, 161–63, 268
Conolly, Violet, 204–5
Constantinople, 35
consumer behaviors, 5, 120–21; dependency syndrome and, 41–43; hoarding
  and, 11, 39, 65–66, 126, 155, 157, 184,
  231, 267; panic buying and, 11, 22, 184;
  social class status and, 11–12; theft/
  pilfering and, 11, 31–32, 43, 45, 280–81,
  311–12, 315; travel from home and, 11,
  22–23, 43, 49, 191, 231, 235–37, 239,
  273–81, 284. *See also* queues and
  queuing
consumer cooperatives, 19–20, 54–61, 87–
  94; administration of, 52, 55–57, 93,
  137, 167, 170, 220; bourgeoisie trade
  specialists and, 55; buying agents for,
  82–85, 91; capital mobilization in, 57–
  58, 90–91; commodity exchange and,
  73–74; corruption in, 160, 311–13;

credit and, 90, 116; cultured trade and,
  198–99, 208, 220; decrees on, 55–56,
  61, 94, 199; hours of trade and, 58; moralism of, 55; number of, 87–88; panic in
  face of German invasion and, 281; peasants and, 88–90, 145, 167; pricing and,
  55, 74, 153, 306–7; private trade in,
  256–57, 285–86, 289, 293, 312–13; rural
  trade and, 167, 209; shortages and, 153–
  54; tax dodgers, repression of, and, 147;
  urban residents and, 22, 208, 222; ZRKs
  and, 178
consumerism, 11–12, 212–13, 245–46
consumption rights, 14, 170, 174. *See also*
  class rationing
contracts and barter agreements, 7, 73, 83,
  181, 244, 256–57, 312–13
cooperatives. See *specific type (e.g., con-*
  sumer cooperatives)
corporatism, 173–84, 196
Council of Labor and Defense. *See* STO
  (Council of Labor and Defense)
credit, 90, 102, 108, 110, 116, 292
criminal activities, 10; black markets and,
  11, 33, 265, 277, 292, 294–95; bribery
  and, 85–87, 283, 311; money laundering
  and, 314; queuism and, 140; shoplifting
  and, 205; show trials and, 85–86, 93,
  160, 219–20, 311; theft/pilfering and,
  11, 31–32, 43, 45, 280–81, 311–12, 315;
  trapping, waterfowl/fur and, 45; travel
  permit counterfeiting and, 282–83. *See
  also* repression, government
Criminal Code, 117–18
crises, cyclical patterns of, 3, 5, 8, 11, 49–
  50, 137
crisis socialism, 5–8, 11, 19
cultural expenditures, 47, 229
cultured Soviet trade, 14, 198–215, 244,
  297, 310, 316–25, 328, 330; bureaucratism and, 215–22; consumer cooperatives
  and, 198–99, 208, 220; flea markets and,
  270; peasants and, 230–43; popular communism and, 224; urban residents and,
  222–30
currency policies: commodity exchange
  and, 73–74; demonetization as, 46, 63,
  74–75, 78–79, 98, 161–62, 296; labor
  units of value and, 52; new rubles and,
  288–89, 306, 314; stabilization and, 6

customer service, 199, 205–6, 208, 218–19, 310, 317
Czechoslovakia, 319

dacha cooperatives, 183
Dalin, David, 80
Danilov, V. P., 130
Davies, R. W., 3, 170–71, 186
Davies, Sarah, 224
Davydov, A. Iu., 41
"dead souls," 66, 175–76, 300
decentralization policies, 6, 80, 217–18, 330; procurement (detszagotovki) and, 181–82
decrees. See regulatory controls and decrees
demonetization, 46, 63, 74–75, 78–79, 98, 161–62, 296
department stores, 8, 202, 204–7, 217, 235–37, 247, 285; in Leningrad, 202, 206–8, 235; in Moscow, 21, 204–5, 208, 221, 235–37, 285, 318–24; in United States, 205–7, 210; in Western Europe, 205
dependency, psychology of: consumers and, 41–43; shopkeepers/managers and, 218
deportations, 237–38, 241–42, 265, 273, 317
D'iakov, D. A., 28, 111
Dikhtiar, G. A., 13–14, 72, 209, 240–41
dining halls, public, 63–65
displays, of merchandise, 55, 201, 205, 213
Dmitrenko, V. P., 15, 74, 89
Dnepropetrovsk, 139, 166, 261, 265
Donbass, 163
drinking establishments, 12, 101, 124–25, 127–28, 147. See also vodka trade
Dunham, Vera, 328

Eastern Siberia, 172–73
East Germany, 319
economic soviets (sovnarkhozy), 55, 96
Eismont, N. B., 144
Eliseev delicatessens, 21, 202, 203
employee rights, 118
Engels, Friedrich, 329
entertainment trade, 101; billiard halls and, 12, 127, 147, 285–86, 291; movie industry and, 94, 229; in NEP years, 124,

127–28; outdoor markets/bazaars and, 12, 261, 271, 294; taxation and, 128
"entitlement" mentality, 41–42
"expediters" (tolkachi), 181–83
expositions, commodity, 213–14, 247

Fabrichnyi, Andrei, 84
factories: buying agents for, 83, 180–83; dining halls/cafeterias in, 64–65, 178; productivity in, 67–68, 177, 183; worker provisionment and, 65–66, 177–84, 195–96, 215, 299
factory farms, 182–83, 258, 299
fairs, 7, 20, 192
Fal'kner, S. A., 76–78
famines, 5–6, 49, 78, 88, 296–97, 326; (1891), 158; (1921–22), 5, 37, 155–56, 158; (1932–33), 5, 163, 172–74, 200, 255–56; (1946–47), 5, 286, 304–5, 311; in Ukraine, 161, 172, 185
farmers' markets, 35, 190, 270
farms: collective, 191, 257, 289; factory, 182–83, 258, 299
fast-food stands, 30, 125, 286, 291
February Revolution, 24, 157
fees, commercial. See licenses and fees, commercial
Feigel'son, M., 41
feminization of retail work, 13, 211, 222, 315–16
Filtzer, Donald, 305
Finland, 267
five-year plans, 14, 136, 178, 187, 241, 262
flea markets, 20, 31, 35, 189, 192, 251, 258–70, 288
food: household budgets for, 33, 46–47, 151, 228–30; militarized procurement campaigns and, 5, 23, 72; rationing of, 5, 14, 31, 62–69, 158, 165–71; sales indicators for, 304; shortages of, 11, 24, 35–36, 38–39, 154–61, 183, 194–95, 241, 277, 307, 323. See also famines
food committees, local (prodkomy), 26, 55, 68, 72
"food dictatorship," 23, 25, 67
food services industry, 101, 124–26; cafeterias and, 63–65, 177–79, 286, 301; canteens and, 5, 64, 125, 177, 179, 208; fast-food stands and, 30, 125, 286, 291;

public dining halls and, 63–65; restaurants/cafés and, 63, 254, 285, 301

foraging, 49, 65–66, 177, 280, 282. *See also* travel for trade

France, 118, 294

free trade, 26, 216, 231, 234, 237

fuel crises, 22, 43–45, 63

furniture manufacturing, 32

Gamerman, V. I., 112–13

gardens, 182–83, 299–300

garment trades. *See* cloth and clothing trade

Gartenschläger, Uwe, 279

Gastronom (delicatessen chain), 201–2, 206, 302

Georgia, 286

Germany: black markets in, 295; department stores in, 205; employee rights in, 118; private trade attitudes and, 282; Russian invasion/occupation by, 251, 267, 279–82, 298; wartime economy of, 51, 169

Glavosobtorg shops, 199, 201–2

GOKO, 278

Goldenveizer, A. A., 45

Gol'tsman, A. Z., 99–100, 330

Gomel' *oblast'*, 74

"goods famine," 116, 137–38, 142, 149, 154–55, 297

Gor'kii. *See* Nizhnii Novgorod

Gorlizki, Yoram, 327

Gosbank, 94, 110

Got'e, Iu. V., 29, 33–34, 42, 44

grain trade: "bagging" and, 35–36, 48; in bazaars/outdoor markets, 31, 33; commodity exchange and, 72, 90, 162; decrees on, 23, 160, 163, 190; Khleboprodukt and, 94; price controls and, 23, 76; repression of, 159–61, 163; stockpiling and, 158–59

"Great Break," 4, 7, 10

Great Britain, 3, 51, 205, 334

Greenwall, Harry, 184–85

"greeting trade" *(vstrechnaia torgovilia)*, 255–56, 268

Harrison, Marguerite, 28, 34, 44–45, 51

Harvard University, 3

hawkers and hawking, 9, 20, 49, 137, 259, 334; decrees on, 267; famines and, 103; goods sold by, 261–62, 270; hours of trade and, 118; household budgets and, 105; repression of, 187–88; wartime, 269

Hayek, Friedrich von, 1

historiography, economic, 2–4, 10, 13–15, 53, 102, 304

hoarding, 11, 65–66, 126, 155, 157, 184, 231; in Moscow, 39; in Riazan' *oblast'*, 267

hours of trade, 58, 118, 208

household budgets: archival sources of, 9, 226–27; cloth/clothing trade and, 46, 123, 227–28, 259; cultural expenditures and, 47, 229; in cultured trade period, 226–30, 259; food and, 33, 46–47, 151, 228–30; in-kind wages and, 104–5; of ITR (engineering-technical) employees, 227, 230; in Moscow, 46, 151; in post-war years, 120–21, 308–9; in restructuring period, 186–87; in revolutionary period, 46–47; in 1920s, 150–51; shoes and, 26, 123, 259; of urban residents, 33, 46–47, 150–52, 186, 192, 259, 308–9; in wartime years, 269–70; of workers, 33, 45–47, 88–89, 104–5, 125–26, 151, 186, 227, 229–30, 269–70

housewives, 118, 240, 277

Hubbard, Leonard, 186

Iagoda, G. G., 159–60

Iakovlev, Ia., 92

Iakovleva, V. N., 140–41, 148–49, 151

Iaroslavskii Market (Moscow), 259, 262

Ibragimova, D. Kh., 42

imported goods, 126–27, 319, 321

incomes. *See* household budgets; wages and salaries

income taxes, 113, 117

industrialization policies, 135, 141, 173–75, 194

inflation, 22, 84, 186; hyper-, 110; "managed," 76, 81

Isaevna, Liliana, 290–92

issue prices *(otpusknye)*, 115

Italy, 304

ITR (engineering-technical) households, 227, 230

Ivanovo, 146, 183, 287, 300

Japan, 1
Jews, 27–28, 34, 107–10, 124, 172, 330
Jones, Jeffrey, 279, 284

Kabo, Elena, 103
Kaliadin, A. N., 121–22
Kalinin, Mikhail, 106–7, 284–85
Kaluga *guberniia*, 35
Karelia, 156
Kasimov, 274
Kazakhstan, 172, 300
Kazan' *oblast'*, 35, 37
Kemerovo *oblast'*, 300
Kerblay, Basile, 253
kerb-merchants, 29–30, 186, 259
Khabarovsk, 208
Khar'kov, 43, 45–46, 139, 142, 151, 208, 235, 264
Kherson, 166
Khleboprodukt (quasi-state corporation), 94, 99
Khlevniuk, O. V., 186
Khrushchev, Nikita, 308, 310
Kiev, 45–46, 121, 166, 235, 265
Kirov, Sergei, 225
Komprod. See Commissariat of Food Supplies *(Komprod)*
Komsomol, 220
Komvnutorg, 82, 84, 159
Kondrat'ev, N. D., 19, 38
Kondurushkin, I. S., 85
Konorev, N. I., 290
Kopaigorod, 108
Kornai, János, 4
Kostroma *oblast'*, 35–36, 48, 156
Kotkin, Stephen, 219–20, 276
Kozyrev (Moscow chief of police), 236
Kredit-biuro, 102, 110
Kritsman, Lev, 30–31, 33, 38, 62, 170, 252
Kuibyshev *oblast'*, 300
kulaks: class warfare and, 52, 109, 160, 172, 188; consumer cooperatives and, 57, 92–93, 167, 220; as trade specialists, 28
Kursk, 255, 288, 290, 324–25
Kursk *oblast'*, 28, 35, 74, 83, 96–97
Kurtorg (Kursk, state corporation), 83, 96–97

labor unrest, 183
Larek (Ukraine, state corporation), 95–96, 99, 128

Larin, Iurii, 79–80, 92, 127, 154, 169
lavki (small shops), 20–21
leather goods trade, 142–45, 159–60, 228
Lenin, V. I.: "bagging" and, 41; commodity exchange and, 72, 74; cooperatives, "consumer communes" and, 55–56, 59, 92–94, 98; cultured trade and, 244; government repression and, 5; impersonators of, 261–62; *mnogoukladnost'* and, 130–31; modernization and, 6; monetized trade and, 215; NEP and, 7, 101; outdoor markets and, 192, 252; petty/private trade and, 46, 49, 101, 106, 139, 191; *State and Revolution* and, 329; utilization and, 25; war communism and, 169, 177
Leningrad: department stores in, 202, 206–8, 235; deportations from, 238, 265; food services industry in, 125; leather trade in, 143; luxury goods trade in, 126–27, 201; outdoor markets/bazaars in, 264, 270; popular communism in, 224–25; queues/queuing in, 237, 240; rationing in, 302; retail trade in, 151; Torgsin shops in, 200; travel for trade to, 235, 238; urban-rural discrimination and, 163, 309; ZRK shops in, 179, 182
Lentorg, 128–29
Levenson (deputy, Commissariat of Domestic Trade), 247
Lewin, Moshe, 3, 326
Lezhava, A. M., 85–86, 220
licenses and fees, commercial, 113; cloth/clothing trade and, 123; government corporations and, 94, 98; luxury goods and, 117, 121; petty trade and, 105–8, 117–18, 262, 284–85; rural trade and, 89
Lih, Lars T., 41
liquor monopoly, state, 20. *See also* vodka trade
Liubimov, A. V., 243, 268, 277
livestock, slaughter of, 228, 230, 258
luxury goods trade, 11–12, 120–22, 243, 246; in Leningrad, 126–27, 201; licensing and, 117, 121; in Moscow, 121, 147, 201; popular communism and, 223, 226; in St. Petersburg, 122. *See also* cultured Soviet trade

Macy's Department Store, 207, 210
magaziny (large, metropolitan shops), 20–21
Magnitogorsk, 219–20, 261, 276
Maiakovskii, V., 111–12
mail-order firms, 138
Makhachkala, 146
Malafeev, A. N., 81, 115–16, 164, 307
managers/administrators, local: Bolshevik anti-trade policies and, 24–26; decentralization and, 316–17; price controls and, 268; proprietary psychology and, 66, 81, 84, 99, 174, 184, 242–43, 283, 300–301; rationing and, 173–76, 183, 242, 268; taxation and, 73
manufacturing cooperatives, 60, 288–90
Mariupol, 166
Martin, Terry, 317, 325
Marx, Karl, 169
Marxism, 3, 60
McAuley, Mary, 41
Mensheviks, 93
Mercantile Exchange Committees, 118
mercantile exchanges, 7, 83, 216
Mikoian, Anastas, 145, 160, 167, 217n.63, 226
military provisionment, 67, 69, 168, 241–42, 299
Miliutin, V. P., 59, 76–77, 78
Mingulin, I. S., 114
Ministry of Trade, 330
Minsk, 235, 264–65, 281
Mizelle, Christopher, 69
mnogoukladnost', 130–31, 253, 262, 335
modernization, 6, 8, 14, 117, 214, 244, 251
Moldavia, 261
Molotov, Viacheslav, 160, 313
money. *See* currency policies
money laundering, 314
Moscow: black market trade in, 292; cloth/clothing trade in, 35, 138; commodity expositions in, 213–14; consumer cooperatives in, 54; cultured trade in, 317–18; department stores in, 21, 204–5, 208, 221, 235–37, 285, 318–24; deportations from, 237, 265; disabled veterans in, 284; food shortages in, 156–58, 160–61; fuel shortages in, 45; gardening in, 300; hoarding in, 39; household budgets in, 46, 151; luxury goods trade in, 121,

147, 201; nutritional intake and diets in, 126; outdoor markets/bazaars in, 20, 29–31, 34, 151n.41, 184–86, 189–90, 251, 254, 258–59, 262, 264, 267, 270, 275, 284, 319; panic in face of German invasion in, 281; queues/queuing in, 154, 231, 235–40, 273; rationing in, 63, 65, 70, 166, 176, 302; shoe trade in, 142; shopping districts of, 21, 204–5; tax dodgers, repression of, in, 147–48; travel for trade to, 35, 235–37, 273–75, 277, 331; urban-rural discrimination and, 163, 194–95, 238–39, 309; worker provisionment in, 181
Moscow *oblast'*, 26, 185, 300
Moskoff, William, 269
movie industry, 94, 229
Muggeridge, Malcolm, 200
Muir and Merilees (Moscow department store), 21
municipalization policies, 26–27, 47, 61
MVD, 313

Narkomfin, 117
Narkomvnutorg, 117
nationalization policies, 26–27, 43, 45, 49, 60–61
Nazarov, V., 287
Neiman, G. Ia., 177
Nepmen, 111–12, 120, 141, 167, 169, 171
New Economic Policy (NEP), 4–5, 7, 14, 53, 98, 335–36; bureaucratization and, 80–81, 86–87, 92, 99; buying agents and, 82–85, 181; currency policies of, 63; *mnogoukladnost'* and, 130–31, 253, 335; peasants and, 72; pricing/price controls in, 7–8, 81–82; private trade/traders and, 9–10, 291–93; rationing and, 137, 155, 161; utilization and, 101, 114, 137
newspapers, 47, 160, 223
Nikolaev, 45, 174
Nizhnii Novgorod, 24–25, 31, 37, 271
NKVD, 234, 237, 265, 279
normalization policies, 5–6, 12, 304–5, 310, 325–26
Nove, Alec, 78n.79, 243, 333
Novorossiisk, 153–54
Novozhilov, V. V., 139, 154
nutritional intake and diets, 126–27, 227, 299

Odessa, 90, 95, 166, 181, 219, 254–55, 282
officials, local. *See* managers/
    administrators, local
OGPU, 114, 143–44, 146, 159–60, 163,
    192
Omsk, 36, 166
Orel *oblast'*, 42, 47, 74, 156
Orlov, N., 70
orsy (worker provisionment departments),
    179–83, 215, 299
Osokina, Elena, 14, 193, 200, 212, 241,
    285
outdoor markets, 20, 28–32, 52, 106, 184–
    93; entertainment value of, 12, 261, 271,
    294; goods sold in, 31, 45, 123; in
    Leningrad, 264, 270; in Moscow, 20,
    29–31, 34, 151n.41, 184–86, 189–90,
    251, 254, 258–59, 262, 264, 267, 270,
    275, 284, 319; in Odessa, 254–55; sani-
    tary conditions and, 253–54, 257–58,
    270–71; travel for trade and, 239; in
    Ukraine, 32. *See also* bazaars; flea
    markets

panic buying, 11, 22, 184
Party Congresses, 60, 95
Passazh Department Store (Leningrad),
    202, 206–7, 235
peasants: anti-Semitism and, 27; Apocalyp-
    ticism of, 233; attitudes toward, 72, 172–
    73, 193; "bagging" and, 41, 47–48, 70;
    commodity exchange and, 69–75, 136–
    37, 161–63, 268; consumer cooperatives
    and, 88–90, 145, 167; cultured trade
    and, 230–43; "entitlement" mentality
    and, 42; fuel crises and, 45; "greeting
    trade" and, 255–56; petty trade and, 9,
    109, 170, 252–54; popular communism
    and, 233; private land plots of, 241; pur-
    chasing power of, 21–22; shoe industry
    and, 143; *smychka* and, 72, 74, 181, 189,
    333; stimulation campaigns and, 163–64,
    255; taxation of, 191; travel for trade by,
    145, 185, 231; war communism and, 72.
    See also urban-rural discrimination
Penza *guberniia*, 26
perfume industry, 226
Petrograd: cloth/clothing trade in, 35,
    121–23; February Revolution in, 24,
    157; food shortages/famine in, 24, 38–

39, 157; fuel shortages in, 45; gardening
    in, 182; Petrokommuna of, 53–54, 61;
    queues/queuing in, 38–40; rationing in,
    63–64, 66; retail trade in, 25–26; travel
    for trade to, 35; urban-rural discrimina-
    tion and, 70. *See also* Leningrad
Petrokommuna, 53–54, 61
petty trade and traders, 20, 102, 251–52;
    decrees on, 25–26; disabled veterans
    and, 284–85; hawkers/hawking and, 9,
    20, 49, 103, 105, 118, 137, 187–88, 259,
    261–62, 267, 269, 334; kerb-merchants
    and, 29–30, 186, 259; licensing and,
    105–8, 117–18, 262, 284–85; market
    share of, 149–53; peasants' attitude to-
    ward, 109; poverty and, 102–13; unem-
    ployment and, 103; urban residents and,
    9, 187–88, 265–66, 280; wages and, 107.
    See also "bagging" *(meshochnichestvo)*; ba-
    zaars; black markets; flea markets; out-
    door markets
Piatakov, G. L., 82
Pliatskii, Semen, 85, 111
Poland, 294
Ponafidine, Emma, 40–41
popular communism, 223–26, 233, 279
Portnov, A. S., 121–22
poverty, 10, 103, 105–10, 225–26, 273,
    277, 334
Price Committee, 77, 81
pricing and price controls: in bazaars, 186;
    Bolsheviks and, 8, 25, 75–79; cloth/
    clothing trade and, 81; commodity ex-
    change and, 70, 74; in consumer cooper-
    atives, 55, 74, 153, 306–7; grain trade
    and, 23, 76; modernization and, 215;
    NEP and, 7–8, 81–82; postwar, 305–6,
    310, 326–27; rural trade and, 164, 268;
    scissors crisis and, 82, 90, 109, 114–16,
    131, 136–37; Stalin-era, 221; stockpiling
    and, 158–59, 161; war communism and,
    53, 161–62, 193; wartime, 22, 302–3
priests, 57, 63, 92, 161
private trade and traders: in consumer co-
    operatives, 256–57, 285–86, 289, 293,
    312–13; in department stores, 285; Ger-
    man occupation and, 282; in Odessa,
    282; repression of, 6, 114, 119, 185,
    193, 262, 310. *See also* petty trade and
    traders

procurement campaigns, militarized, 5–6,
23, 72, 186, 192
productivity, worker, 67–68, 177, 183
Prokof'ev, G. E., 159–60
property rights, 113, 180
"proprietary psychology" behaviors, 180,
196; decentralized procurement and,
181; local authorities and, 66, 81, 84, 99,
174, 184, 242–43, 283, 300–301; worker
cooperatives and, 178
Provisional Government, 23, 35, 75
provisionment: decrees on, 25–26, 61, 63;
preferential (udarniki), 180; worker, 65–
66, 177–84, 195–96, 215, 299
public opinion, 41, 157, 161, 222–23, 232
"pushers" (tolkachi), 181

queues and queuing, 22, 38–41, 184, 191,
231–41, 246–47; decrees on, 236–37, 267,
273, 317; goods famine and, 154–55; in
Moscow, 154, 231, 235–40, 273; nighttime,
ban on, 236–37, 267; in Petrograd/
Leningrad, 38–40, 237, 240; as public
opinion information source, 41, 157, 232;
"specialists" in, 40, 138–40, 236; violence/
rebellion in, 40, 154, 231, 233–34, 236
queuism (ocherednichestvo), 139–40

Rabkrin, 92, 139–40, 146, 148, 219, 264
Radzinskii, M. M., 223
railroad industry, 21; "bagging" and, 37,
279, 282; buying agents and, 283; food
shortages and, 24; petty trade of workers
in, 45–46; rationing for employees of,
66; travel restrictions and, 237, 277–78
Randall, Amy, 211
RAND Corporation, 2n.2, 3
Rathenau, W., 169
rationing: Bolsheviks and, 53, 63–69; class,
5, 14, 63, 65–67, 137, 155, 161, 167–69,
171, 174–76, 223–24, 298–99, 301–2; of
cloth/clothing, 63, 69–70, 140, 165;
"dead souls" and, 66, 175–76, 300; end
of, 201; of food, 5, 31, 62–69, 158, 165–
71; of fuel, 63; illegal coupon trade and,
31, 271–72, 312; local authorities and,
173–76, 183, 242, 268; in Moscow, 63,
65, 70, 166, 176, 302; in Petrograd/
Leningrad, 63–64, 66, 302; philosophy
of, 216, 311–12; popular communist attitudes toward, 223–24; Stalin-era, 14,
158; war communism and, 161–62, 175–
76; wartime, 62, 298–302, 304. See also
urban-rural discrimination
regulatory controls and decrees, 82, 113–
19; on bazaars, 189–91, 254–55, 263; on
"commercial" trade, 303; on commodity
exchange, 73, 162–63; on consumer
cooperatives/communes, 55–56, 61, 94,
199; on decentralization, 80; on grain
trade, 23, 160, 163, 190; on hawking,
267; on livestock procurement/meat
trade, 190; on petty/private trade, 25–
26; on provisionment, 25–26, 61, 63; on
queues, 236–37, 267, 273, 317; on speculation, 190–91, 237, 263, 278; on trade
organization/sales tax reduction on agricultural products, 190–91, 263; on travel
for trade, 237–39, 273, 277–79; on urban gardening, 300
repression, government, 4–5, 11, 99, 252,
330; of agitation in queues, 234; of artisanal manufacturing, 262–63; bazaars/flea
markets and, 265; of cloth/clothing trade,
145–46, 159; consumption rights and, 14;
grain trade and, 159–61, 163; leather
trade and, 143–45, 159–60, 228; livestock
trade and, 258; mass operations and, 144–
45, 159–60, 163, 265, 331; of newspapers,
160; of private trade/traders, 6, 114, 119,
185, 193, 262, 310; show trials and, 85–
86, 93, 160, 219–20, 311; of speculation,
159, 263–65, 272–73; of tax dodgers,
146–48. See also criminal activities
restaurants and cafés, 63, 254, 285, 301
retail trade: density of, 21–22, 89, 195,
273, 303; feminization of, 13, 211, 222,
315–16; reprofessionalization of, 102–
13; state-run, 95–97, 99–100; Westernization of, 244, 334. See also shops and
shopkeepers
Riazan' oblast': black markets in, 292; consumer cooperatives in, 90; corruption in,
314; food services industry in, 301;
goods assortment in, 324; hoarding in,
267; hours of trade in, 118; municipalization in, 26; outdoor markets/bazaars
in, 187; shortages in, 156, 307–8; tobacco trade in, 36; travel for trade in,
283–84; wholesale trade in, 94–95

Rimmel, Lesley, 224
Robbins, R., 158
Rokhovich, G., 79
Rostov, 139, 264, 284, 286
Rozhevskii, I. I., 128–29
Rubinshtein, G. L., 13
Rumiantsev, V. N., 125
Rumiantsev & Co., 122
Rumiantsev Museum, 44
rural trade, 12, 89–92, 101, 162; commercial licenses and, 89; cooperatives and, 167, 209; food purchases and, 33; number of shops and, 105–6; pricing and, 164, 268. *See also* peasants
Rykov, Aleksei I., 7, 26, 65–66, 81, 84, 105–6, 131, 144–45, 174

saboteurs, 257–58
St. Petersburg, 21, 122
salaries. *See* wages and salaries
salesclerks/assistants, 12–13; cooperatives of, 56; education/training and, 206, 209–12, 310, 315–16, 317; feminization of, 13, 211, 222, 315–16; misconduct by, 281, 310–15; wages of, 218
sales taxes, 117, 129, 190–91
salt trade, 36–37, 81, 111
Samara, 255
sanitary conditions, 253–55, 257–58, 270–71
Saratov *oblast'*, 35, 39–40, 139
Schumpeter, Joseph, 1
scissors crisis (1923), 82, 90, 109, 114–16, 131, 136, 137
"second economy" trade, 289–93, 314, 327
"self-provisionment" *(samosnabzhenie)*, 45; artisanal production and, 32, 43; foraging and, 49, 65–66, 177, 280, 282; gardens and, 182–83, 299–300; home production and, 43; theft and, 11, 43. *See also* factory farms
Selivanov, T. A., 302
Sen, Amartya, 11
services trade, 34, 49
Shearer, David, 7, 265n.53
shoes and shoe industry, 26, 123, 142–43, 228, 259, *309*
shoplifting, 205
shops and shopkeepers, 87–97, 119–31; closings of, 11–12, 22–23, 25, 48, 63,

136, 146, 185, 191, 243; cooperative, 20; dependency syndrome and, 218; number of, 21, 32n.45, 87–88, 105, 195, 303, 324; service, 34; types of, 20–21. *See also* salesclerks/assistants
shortages, 10–11, 136; of cloth, 138, 145; of consumer goods, 22, 35, 76, 116, 137–38, 149, 154–55, 194–95, 240–41, 307–8; of food, 24, 35–36, 38–39, 154–61, 183, 194–95, 241, 277, 307, 323; of fuel, 22, 43–45. *See also* famines
show trials, 85–86, 93, 160, 219–20, 311
Siberia, 33, 172–73, 300
Simbirsk *oblast'*, 26, 35–36
Simkin, D. G., 283, 292
Singer Company, 21
Slavkin, I. A., 261–62
Smit-Fal'kner, M. N., 78
social class: consumption rights and, 14, 170, 174; rationing and, 5, 14, 63, 65–67, 137, 155, 161, 167–69, 171, 174–76, 223–24, 241–42, 298–99, 301–2; status/individuality and, 11–12
Socialist Revolutionaries (SRs), 93
Sokolov, V., 287
soldiers, 40, 45, 67, 113
Solomon, Peter H., 192, 315
Sorokin, Pitirim, 11
Soviet Industrialization Project (University of Birmingham), 3
Sovnarkom, 56, 117, 144, 159, 164, 170, 201, 236, 242, 265
speculation, 38, 189–92; attitudes toward, 19, 25, 188, 191, 239; decrees on, 118, 190–91, 237, 263, 278; deportation and, 237–38, 265; pre-revolutionary, 22; repression of, 159, 263–65, 272–73
Stakhanovism, 214, 333
Stalin, Joseph: commercial prestige and, 211; cultured trade and, 14, 215; government repression and, 5, 114, 330; industrialization policies and, 135–36; "Life has become better" speech, 222, 225, 230; modernization and, 6, 14; NEP and, 7, 135; outdoor markets/bazaars and, 170, 192, 252; provisionment and, 175, 180; rationing and, 193, 304; urban-rural discrimination and, 326, 333; vodka policies and, 165; war communism model and, 170

"Stalin Constitution" (1936), 169, 331
Stalinism, 4–5, 14, 135–36, 222–30, 245
standardization, 58–59
State Defense Committee, 277–78
State Trade Inspectorate, 313
stimulation campaigns (stimulirovanie), 163–64, 199, 255
stockpiles, 158–59, 161
STO (Council of Labor and Defense), 79, 117, 169, 170; Committee on Reserves of, 159; Komvnutorg and, 82, 84, 159; trade commission of, 82
street vending. See petty trade and traders
strikes, labor, 183
Strumilin, S. G., 47, 106
sugar trade, 81, 115, 201
Sukharevka bazaar (Moscow), 29–31, 34, 190, 251
Sumy, 29
Supreme Economic Council. See VSNKh (Supreme Economic Council)
Supreme Soviet, 277
Sverdlovsk, 139, 235, 255
Swianiewicz, Stanislaw, 4
syndicates (glavki), 61, 111, 216

Tambov oblast', 35–36, 156
Tarasenko, E. N., 125
taxation: black markets and, 265; of businesses and owners, 24–25, 113, 117, 141, 185; of entertainment trade, 128; of income, 113, 117; in-kind, 73; of peasants, 191; of sales, 117, 129, 190–91; of savings, 314; superprofits surcharge and, 146; tax dodgers and, 146–48
Taylorism, 62, 296
teachers' cooperatives, 56
Temkina, Leia Aizikovna, 122
textile trade. See cloth and clothing trade
TEZhE (Moscow cosmetics store), 205, 225–26
theft and pilfering, 11, 31–32, 43, 45, 280–81, 311–12, 315
Tiflis, 35, 139
Timasheff, Nicholas, 244
Tishinskii Market (Moscow), 251, 267, 319
tobacco and cigarette trade, 26, 36, 81, 201
Torgsin shops, 199–201, 221, 224–25
trade commissions, 84

trade organizations, 83, 91, 212–13, 216, 255, 313
trade unions, 89, 182–83, 196, 299
travel for trade, 22–23, 273–79, 281, 284; decrees on, 237–39, 273, 277–79; food shortages and, 11; to Moscow, 35, 235–37, 273–75, 277, 331; peasants and, 145, 185, 231; to Petrograd/Leningrad, 35, 235, 238; urban residents and, 43, 191, 280. See also "bagging" (meshochnichestvo); buying agents; foraging
travel permits, 237, 277, 282–83
treasury shops, 20
Trofimov, F. E., 276
Trotsky, Leon, 101, 225–26, 230, 242
Tsaritsyn, 37
Tsiurupa, A. D., 75, 144–45
TsSU/TsUNKhU. See Central Statistical Administration (TsSU, TsUNKhU)
TsUM (Moscow department store), 204, 221, 235–36, 285, 318–24
Tula oblast', 26, 42
Turkestan, 24
Tver' guberniia, 41

Ukraine: bazaars/outdoor markets in, 32; buying agents in, 182; drink retailing in, 128; famine in, 161, 172, 185; food services industry in, 125; as food supply source, 33; gardening in, 300; merchants in, 110–11; state retail corporations in, 95–96
unemployment, 103, 106–7, 277
United States, 2, 13, 129, 205–7, 210, 213, 215, 334
University of Birmingham, 3
Urals, 126, 176, 300
urban cooperatives, 208, 222
urban residents: cafeterias and, 65; class ration and, 168; cooperatives and, 22; gardening and, 299–300; household budgets of, 33, 46–47, 150–52, 186, 192, 259, 308–9; nutritional intake and diets of, 126–27; petty trade and, 9, 187–88, 259, 265–66, 280; travel for trade and, 43, 191, 280; unemployment and, 106–7
urban-rural discrimination, 4–5, 12, 145, 153, 241, 331, 333; commodity exchange and, 74; "food dictatorship" and, 67; food shortages and, 69, 172–73; Moscow

urban-rural discrimination (*cont.*)
and, 163, 194–95, 238–39, 309; profit
motive and, 89
USSR Procuracy, 236–37, 264, 271
Ustinov, V. M., 27, 37–38, 82, 86
utilization policies, 25, 34, 131; class warfare and, 101; cooperatives and, 208–9;
"goods famine" and, 142, 149; NEP and,
101, 113–19, 137, 141

vacation homes, 183
Vanni, Ettore, 271
Vasil'ev, S., 46
Veitser, I. Ia., 209–10, 216–19, 229, 246
vendors. *See* petty trade and traders
veterans, disabled, 106, 284–85
Viatka *oblast'*, 35–36
village cooperatives, 209, 251
Vladimir *oblast'*, 287, 312
vodka trade, 22, 47, 127, 164–65, 201, 301,
303–6, 323
Voroshilov, K., 156–59
Voznesenskii, N. A., 302
VSNKh (Supreme Economic Council), 26,
57, 77, 111, 144–45
VTsIK, 79

wages and salaries, 180, 210–11; bonuses
in kind and, 43, 69, 103; demonetization
of, 46, 104; in-kind payment and, 32,
104–5. *See also* household budgets
war communism, 5, 14, 19, 98–99, 197,
296; bureaucratization and, 62, 86; buying agents and, 83; distribution policies

of, 52–53, 161; peasants and, 72;
pricing/price controls and, 53, 161–62,
193; psychology of dependency and, 42;
rationing and, 161–62, 175–76
Western and European economies, 1, 8,
13, 294
Western *oblast'*, 172
Wheatcroft, Stephen, 241
wholesale trade, 7, 35, 83, 94–95, 115. *See
also* "bagging" *(meshochnichestvo)*
worker cooperatives, 57, 94, 153; bureaucratization and, 91; closed (ZRKs),
178–80, 208, 225, 242–43; household
budgets and, 88–89; "proprietary psychology" and, 178
workers: "bagging" and, 41; household
budgets of, 33, 45–47, 88–89, 104–5,
125–26, 151, 186, 227, 229–30, 269–70;
productivity and, 67–68, 177, 183;
smychka and, 72, 74, 181, 189, 333. *See
also* wages and salaries
Workers and Peasants Inspection. *See*
Rabkrin
workplace shops, 5
World War I, 22–23, 51, 62
World War II, 251, 267, 279–82,
298

Zhdanov, Andrei, 193–94
Zhemchuzhina, Polina, 205, 225–26
Zima, V. F., 305
ZRKs (closed worker cooperatives), 178–
79, 181. *See also* "closed distributors",
orsy
Zubkova, Elena, 288